SCOTTISH HISTORY SOCIETY

SIXTH SERIES

VOLUME 7

The Highland Destitution of 1837

The Highland Destitution of 1837

Government Aid and Public Subscription

Edited by
John MacAskill

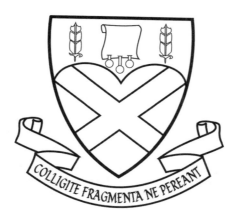

COLLIGITE FRAGMENTA NE PEREANT

SCOTTISH HISTORY SOCIETY
2012

THE BOYDELL PRESS

First published 2013

A Scottish History Society publication
in association with The Boydell Press
an imprint of Boydell & Brewer Ltd
PO Box 9, Woodbridge, Suffolk IP12 3DF, UK

and of Boydell & Brewer Inc.
668 Mt Hope Avenue, Rochester, NY 14620-2731, USA

website: www.boydellandbrewer.com

ISBN 978-0-906245-37-8

A CIP catalogue record for this book is available
from the British Library

The publisher has no responsibility for the continued existence or accuracy of URLs for external
or third-party internet websites referred to in this book, and does not guarantee that any content
on such websites is, or will remain, accurate or appropriate.

Papers used by Boydell & Brewer Ltd are natural, recyclable products
made from wood grown in sustainable forests

Typeset by Word and Page, Chester, UK

Printed and bound in Great Britain by
CPI Group (UK) Ltd, Croydon, CR0 4YY

CONTENTS

List of Illustrations   vi
Preface and Acknowledgements   vii
Abbreviations   xi
Biographical Notes   xiii
Introduction   xxiii
Editorial Conventions   lxix
The Sources   lxx

Part 1. The Letters of Robert Graham of Redgorton   1
Part 2. The Journal and Letters of Captain Sir John Hill, RN   111
Part 3. Petition, Memorials, Resolutions and Reports   199
Part 4. Government Correspondence and Other Documents   251
Part 5. Treasury Minutes   275

Bibliography   287
Index   301

ILLUSTRATIONS

Portrait of Robert Graham of Redgorton

Maps

1.   Robert Graham's tour of the Highlands and Islands
2.   Sir John Hill's tour of the Highlands and Islands

Tables

1.   Quantity of kelp, price, expense and net proceeds
2.   Sir John Hill's accounts

PREFACE AND ACKNOWLEDGEMENTS

My research into the destitution that struck the Highlands and Islands of Scotland in 1837 was prompted by previous research I had undertaken in relation to the effective destruction of the kelp industry of the region caused by the changes in the salt and barilla taxes from around 1822, research that led me to the letters of Robert Graham of Redgorton that are published in this book, and a determination to explore the events they describe. There were two moments during my research that are particularly memorable. Both concerned the two protagonists whose manuscripts are at the heart of this book. The first was when I found the definitive documentary proof that the author of the Graham letters was not, as had previously been assumed, Dr Robert Graham, the professor of botany at Edinburgh University, but was the Whig advocate, Robert Graham of Redgorton. The second was a piece of pure serendipity; I had, I thought, finished my research into the life of Sir John Hill, but sitting one late afternoon in the manuscripts reading room at the National Library of Scotland, something prompted me to have one last look in the card index system for accession documents. I knew there was nothing more to find – after all, I had been through the card index on a number of previous occasions. But I was wrong. There it was, a brand new card saying that the library held Hill's personal journal of his time in Scotland in 1837. I discovered that the library had only recently acquired the journal from a private source, and with the help of the manuscripts' library staff and the sales agent, I was put in touch with Hill's distant relatives, who were more than happy to speak to me about the sea-trunk containing Hill's papers that they had inherited, including the personal log of his experiences at the Battle of the Nile, his personal journals recording his time in Ireland and Scotland, and a large selection of his correspondence with the duke of Wellington. It was one of those precious moments that make the long hours of digging in dusty archives so worthwhile.

There are many people who have helped me in my research, but the person I am especially glad to acknowledge is Professor Ewen A. Cameron, the Sir William Fraser Professor of Scottish History and Palaeography at the University of Edinburgh, who, since he examined my doctoral thesis in 2003, has helped, advised, encouraged and inspired me in equal measure in my research activities; he has always found the time to read and comment on my drafts and he has my deepest gratitude and respect.

I gratefully acknowledge the contributions and help of my friends Dr Annie Tindley and Dr Neil MacGillivray, who have always been happy to answer my questions, read my drafts and share information gleaned from their own research. Annie Tindley read the whole of the text and I am especially indebted to her for her invaluable comments. I have benefited hugely from the facilities afforded me through being an honorary postdoctoral fellow in Scottish history at the University of Edinburgh. I am, of course, particularly grateful to the Scottish History Society for agreeing to let me edit this book, and specifically to those who have held office during the genesis of the book: Dr Sharon Adams, Dr Ulrike Hogg and Dr John McCallum.

I would like to thank the staff and curators of the many libraries and repositories in which I have undertaken research for this book: the National Library of Scotland; the National Records of Scotland; the National Register of Archives for Scotland; the National Library of Ireland; the British Library (including the Newspaper Library at Colindale and the nineteenth-century British Library Newspaper Database); the National Archives, London; the libraries of the universities of Edinburgh, Cambridge and Nottingham; New College Library, Edinburgh; the Clan Donald Centre, Isle of Skye; and Dunvegan Castle, Isle of Skye. Mr and Mrs Alexander Stewart of Ardvorlich made me very welcome at Ardvorlich, Lochearnhead, where the Stewart family of Ardvorlich papers are kept, as did Mr and Mrs Robert Maxtone Graham at their home in Sandwich, Kent, where they gave me access to private papers concerning Robert Graham, and a delicious lunch. Mr Maxtone Graham's nephew Robert Oliphant Maxtone Graham was also very helpful, making available papers of Robert Graham in his possession at his home in Perthshire. Mr and Mrs Michael Slinger welcomed me into their home at Withersfield in Suffolk and gave me much information about the papers of Sir John Hill.

I am indebted to the owners of muniments for their permission to publish transcripts in this book: Alexander Stewart of Ardvorlich; the Trustees of the National Library of Scotland; the National Records of Scotland; the Keeper of Collections of the National Library of Ireland; and the National Archives, London. I am also indebted to his grace the duke of Buccleuch for his permission to quote from material in the papers of the Montague-Douglas-Scott family, dukes of Buccleuch collection at the National Records of Scotland; to his grace, the duke of Hamilton, for his permission to quote from the papers in the Douglas-Hamilton family collection; to the earl of Dalhousie for his permission to quote from the papers in the Maule family, earls of Dalhousie collection at the National Records of Scotland; and to Robert Maxtone Graham for his permission to quote from the papers of Robert Graham in his possession and to reproduce the portrait of Robert Graham by Sir John Gordon-Watson.

Whilst I have received much assistance from those mentioned above, any errors of fact or interpretation remain mine alone.

Finally, and most especially, I would like to thank my wife Gwyneth for all her love and support through the years of research; at times she must have felt that she was living her life not just with her husband but also with two men from the nineteenth century!

ABBREVIATIONS

BL	British Library, London
CDC	Clan Donald Centre, Isle of Skye
CUL	Cambridge University Library
FES	H. Scott (ed.), *Fasti Ecclesiae Scoticanae: The Succession of Ministers in the Parish Churches of Scotland, from the Reformation, 1560, to the Present Time*, 7 vols. (Edinburgh, 1915–28)
Lumsden	*Lumsden & Sons Steam-Boat Companion or Stranger's Guide to the Western Isles and Highlands of Scotland* (Glasgow, 1839)
NCL	New College Library, Edinburgh
NLI	National Library of Ireland, Dublin
NLS	National Library of Scotland, Edinburgh
NRA	National Register of Archives, London
NRAS	National Register of Archives for Scotland, Edinburgh
NRS	National Records of Scotland, Edinburgh
NSAc	*The New Statistical Account of Scotland*, 15 vols. (Edinburgh, 1845)
ODNB	*Oxford Dictionary of National Biography* (Oxford University Press online edition) (http://www.oxforddnb.com)
OGazS	F. H. Groome, *Ordnance Gazetteer of Scotland, A Survey of Scottish Topography, Statistical, Bibliographical and Historical*, 6 vols. (London, 1893–5)
OSG	*Ordnance Survey Gazetteer of Great Britain* (London, 1999)
[Parl. Debs]	Parliamentary Debates
Pigot	*Pigot & Co.'s National Commercial Directory of the Whole of Scotland* (London, 1837)

[PP]	Parliamentary Papers (the year, volume and sessional number is given)
SHR	*Scottish Historical Review*
SSC	C. Johnson, 'Scottish secular clergy, 1830–1878: the western district', *The Innes Review* 40.1 (Spring 1989), 106–52
TNA:PRO	The National Archives, London
1839 Poor Law Report	[PP] 1839 XX (177), *Report by a Committee of the General Assembly on the Management of the Poor in Scotland*
1841 SC (*or* 1841 select committee)	[PP] 1841 VI (182) and (333), *First and Second Reports from the Select Committee on Emigration, Scotland*
1844 Poor Law Inquiry	[PP] 1844 XXI (564), *Poor Law Inquiry (Scotland), Appendix, Part II*

BIOGRAPHICAL NOTES

John Cunninghame, Lord Cunninghame (1782–1854)

Cunninghame was born in Port-Glasgow in 1782, the son of John Cunninghame, a banker in Greenock. He served an apprenticeship as a writer to the signet but passed advocate in March 1807. He enjoyed a considerable practice at the bar and in 1830 was appointed deputy to Lord Jeffrey, then lord advocate. In 1831 Cunninghame was appointed sheriff of Elgin and Moray, and in 1835 he was appointed solicitor-general for Scotland in Lord Melbourne's administration, from which position he resigned in 1837 on the death of Lord Balgray to take his position as a judge of the court of session. Cunninghame resigned his seat on the bench in 1853 and died the following year.[1]

Fox Maule, second baron Panmure and eleventh earl of Dalhousie (1801–74)

Fox Maule was born at Brechin castle in 1801, the eldest son of William Ramsay Maule, first baron Panmure of Brechin and Nevar, Perthshire. He joined the seventy-ninth regiment (the Cameron Highlanders) as ensign in 1819 and left as regimental captain in 1831. In 1835 Maule entered politics as liberal MP for Perthshire, where he was the member until he lost his seat at the general election in August 1837 (for which Robert Graham was his campaign manager). He was liberal MP for Elgin Burghs from 1838 until 1841, when he became liberal MP for Perth, where he remained until he succeeded to his father's peerage in 1852. Maule was under-secretary of state at the Home Office in Lord Melbourne's administration from 1835 to 1841, as the minister chiefly responsible for Scottish affairs. He was vice-president of the Board of Trade between June and September 1841. In 1846 Maule was appointed to the War Office as secretary at war in Lord John Russell's administration, entering the cabinet in the post in October 1851, and in 1852 he became president of

---

[1] See J. Kay, *A Series of Original Portraits and Caricature Etchings*, 2 vols. (Edinburgh, 1838), ii, 466.

the Board of Trade, but a month later the government fell and Maule was out of office until Palmerston succeeded Lord Aberdeen in February 1855 and he was appointed secretary of state for war, in which role he had ministerial responsibility for the Crimean campaign. He did not serve in the government after 1858. His hot temper and unhappy knack of offending too many people did not help his cause. He died without issue in 1874.[2]

Robert Graham of Redgorton (1784–1859)

Robert Graham was born in 1784 in Perthshire, the second eldest son of John Graeme of Eskbank, a member of the Graeme family of Balgowan. He was educated at the High School, Edinburgh, and at Edinburgh University. He had entertained, as a young man, the idea that he should go to India 'to make his fortune'; he was, however, dissuaded[3] and instead he followed the more predictable route for a man of his background and upbringing, and he was called to the Scottish bar in 1805. The enlightenment had left Edinburgh with a legacy of clubs which both preserved and promoted culture and history, and Graham was one of the original thirty-one members of the Bannatyne Club, which became the template for the historical clubs which followed.[4] He was also a member of the Speculative Society, a literary and debating society of high standards, where he was introduced to a circle of Whig lawyers, including Francis Jeffrey and Henry Cockburn, who became his intimate friends; Graham was president of the Society in 1807–8. Graham also organised an exclusive club named the Crichton Club, whose members in 1821 were a roll-call of men who would become distinguished lawyers – Francis Jeffrey, Henry Cockburn, J. A. Murray, G. J. Bell, James Moncrieff and Andrew Rutherfurd.[5] But Graham's interests were not, by any means, limited to matters of the intellect. Although Graham was admitted as an advocate, his practice was restricted as his time was mainly occupied assisting his father and a relative, Robert Graham of Fintry, in the management of the Perthshire estates and political interests of his second cousin, Lord Lynedoch (who as General Sir Thomas Graham had been a distinguished soldier of the Napoleonic wars), to whose estates Graham was to succeed and at whose request Graham changed the spelling of his name from Graeme.[6] Graham had a keen and lively interest in country pursuits, especially coursing – he was a

[2]   See J. Sweetman, 'Maule, Fox [later Fox Maule-Ramsay], second Baron Panmure and eleventh earl of Dalhousie (1801–1874)', *ODNB*.
[3]   NLS, Lynedoch papers, MS 16023, fos. 69–74, Henry Home Drummond to Graham, 16 and 18 Dec. 1801.
[4]   M. Lynch (ed.), *The Oxford Companion to Scottish History* (Oxford, 2001), 310.
[5]   NLS, Lynedoch papers, MS 16037, fos. 74 and 95–6, Members and expenses of the Crichton Club 1821–2.
[6]   *The Scotsman*, 24 Mar. 1859.

member of the Midlothian Coursing Club – and he was particularly interested in the improvement of agriculture. He was an ordinary director of the Highland and Agricultural Society of Scotland and wrote detailed memoranda on the rural economy.[7] He also played his part in the second regiment of the Mid-Lothian local militia as the captain of a company of grenadiers.[8]

Graham's interest in politics for the Whigs came to the fore when he was chairman of the earl of Ormelie's general election committee in 1832 for the county seat of Perthshire, and when Ormelie succeeded his father as marquis of Breadalbane in 1834, Graham stood as the Whig candidate against Sir George Murray, but was defeated in a contest that was marred by allegations that his opponent had secured votes through the intimidation of the tenantry.[9] Henry Cockburn had thought that Graham's standing for the seat was a noble act 'and considering the effect of keeping up the cause of independence in Scotland, it is one for which he ought to be gazetted instantly. The Tories say Sir George is to walk the course. Backwards, I trust.' And when defeat came he described Graham's reaction as being 'hearty and manly' in the face of a 'victory of the owners of the soil achieved by the forced services of their helots and serfs. Their conduct has been atrocious.'[10] Between April and July 1834, Graham was the Scottish lord of the treasury in the Grey and Melbourne governments, an occupation he told his mother would be useful and agreeable, and one in which 'I have a better chance of being of some good to Scotland than I had before'; but there was, he said, a downside: it would take him away for a long time every year from Scotland and would give him far less command of his own time. His tenure of the position was, however, short-lived: he had to relinquish the position when he failed to be elected as MP for Perthshire.[11] In 1835 he was one of the Commissioners appointed to inquire into the state of the municipal corporations in Scotland.[12]

As the next male heir to his second cousin, Lord Lynedoch, Graham found that a considerable amount of his time and energies were taken up with accompanying Lynedoch on his frequent and extensive continental journeys; between 1817 and 1820 they visited Belgium and the Rhineland, Copenhagen, Stockholm, St Petersburg, Moscow, Vienna, Venice, Milan, Verona, Nice, Marseilles, Narbonne, Toulouse and Bordeaux. Graham was also much travelled on his own account on the continent and in Ireland, England and Scotland, and he kept detailed notes and

---

[7]   Private papers of Robert Maxtone Graham, Memorandums on rural economy.
[8]   NLS, Lynedoch papers, MS 16037, fos. 26–7, Regimental orders, 25 Mar. 1813.
[9]   *The Scotsman*, 24 May 1834; NLS, Lynedoch papers, MS 16142, fos. 13–15, Stewart of Ardvorlich to Graham, 24 May 1834.
[10] H. Cockburn, *Letters Chiefly Connected with the Affairs of Scotland from Henry Cockburn to Thomas Francis Kennedy, MP* (London, 1874), 502, 507.
[11] NLS, Lynedoch papers, MS 16009, fo. 49, Graham to Mrs Graham, 6 Apr. 1834.
[12] [PP] 1835 XXIX (30), *General Report of the Commissioners Appointed to Inquire into the State of Municipal Corporations in Scotland.*

diaries about his travels in Ireland in 1835, 1836 and 1838,[13] and his travels in the
Highlands and Islands in 1805, 1811, 1826 and 1833.[14] After a visit in the company
of friends to the Rhine and the northern part of Switzerland in 1840, Graham
wrote a short document entitled 'Hints to Tourists', which gave an account of his
tour to satisfy, as he put it, the demands from his many friends.[15] He was a man
'with an insatiable appetite for information, willing to journey long distances
by coach in successive days . . . and striding vigorously through each locality he
visited, to examine its scenery, antiquities and estates'.[16]

    Graham never married, but, trusted and admired, he became the kindly and
wise autocrat of family councils, in particular the family of his sister Alexina,
who was married to Anthony Maxtone of Cultoquhey. While 'there was yet
something alarming in his personality, and everyone was afraid of him' it was also
said that he showed 'deep, sincere, unfailing kindness and generosity' to his family
and friends.[17] Graham's mother and unmarried sisters lived at 18 Heriot Row in
Edinburgh and moved in the appropriate social circles. But, despite inheriting
Lord Lynedoch's estates in 1843, Graham never settled in any country house, a
fact which rather vexed his sisters, who did not like his insistence on living, as
one of them described it, in the 'Butt and Ben style to the surprise and regret
of your oldest, best and most intimate gentlemen friends'. Graham's sister Eliza
urged him to 'settle yourself on the hill of Redgorton without delay, live in it,
work your estate like any other gentleman, and do not waste the best part of
your life by shifting about from one unseemly establishment to another, having
no companionship with men of your own standing'.[18] Graham did not take his
sister's advice. What he really enjoyed was doing up a few rooms at a farm, or
adding something in the way of a library to a small roadside house, and using it
as a *pied-à-terre* whenever he came north. He died suddenly of a heart attack, aged
75, on 16 March 1859,[19] leaving as his heir his sister Alexina's eldest son Anthony,
who, on succeeding his uncle, added Graham to the family name.

[13] H. Heaney, *A Scottish Whig in Ireland, 1835–1838 – The Irish Journals of Robert Graham of
      Redgorton* (Dublin, 1999). NLS, Lynedoch papers, MS 16049, Notes, observations, letters
      1835–6 by Graham during his tour of Ireland. There are limited references to Graham's
      Irish journals in W. H. A. Williams, *Tourism, Landscape and the Irish Character – British Travel
      Writers in Pre-Famine Ireland* (Madison, 2008), 119, 133, 152, 186–7.
[14] Private papers of R. Maxtone Graham, Robert Graham, A Tour thro' Part of Scotland in
      Autumn 1805; NLS, Lynedoch Papers, MS 16005, fos. 24–33, Letters from Graham to his
      father Sept. and Oct. 1811; NRS, Papers of the Maxtone Graham family of Cultoquhey,
      Perthshire GD 155/1182 Notes of a trip to the Highlands Sept. 1826 and GD 155/995 Graham
      to Alexina Maxtone, 16 June 1833.
[15] NLS, Lynedoch papers, MS 16057, fo. 368, Hints to Tourists, July 1840.
[16] J. F. McCaffery, 'A Scottish Whig in Ireland, 1835–1838: the Irish journals of Robert Graham
      of Redgorton', *SHR* 80.1, no. 209 (Apr. 2001), 144.
[17] E. Maxtone Graham, *The Maxtones of Cultoquhey* (Edinburgh, 1935), 155.
[18] Maxtone Graham, *The Maxtones*, 189.
[19] NLS, Lynedoch papers, MS 16107, Mary Graham's journal.

Captain Sir John Hill, RN (1774–1855)

Sir John Hill was born in 1774 at Portsea, Hampshire. Aged 7 he entered the navy as captain's steward on the bomb vessel *Infernal* under his uncle Captain James Alms, and he then served, variously, as able seaman, master's mate and midshipman, on other ships. He was appointed lieutenant in July 1794, experienced the Spithead mutiny in the spring of 1797 and was appointed first-lieutenant of the seventy-four-gun *Minotaur* under Captain Sir Thomas Louis and took part in the Battle of the Nile, during which the *Minotaur* relieved the severe pressure that Nelson's flagship the *Vanguard* had come under from the French ships *Le Spartiate* and *Aquilon*. After a two-hour duel, the *Minotaur* received the surrender of the seventy-four-gun *Aquilon* and Nelson directed Hill to take command of the *Aquilon* and sail her to Lisbon. Hill's written recollection of the battle contains a unique account of the meeting between Captain Louis and Nelson, which took place after Nelson, who had been wounded during the duel with *Le Spartiate* and *Aquilon*, asked Louis to come to the *Vanguard* so that he could express his thanks. The meeting, Hill's recollection recorded, was 'affecting in the extreme'.[20]

Hill's career then turned to troop transport. He spent a number of years in various transport ships in the North Sea and off the Dutch and French coasts and in the Baltic, also serving with the army ashore in Egypt. In 1815 he was the resident agent of transports and was responsible for the disembarkation of the duke of Wellington's army and materials prior to the Battle of Waterloo; that this was achieved, in Hill's own words, 'without a single accident to a soldier and with the loss only of two horses'[21] is something of a surprise given General Alexander Mercer's dramatic account of the landing at Ostend of the men, horses and equipment of G troop, the Royal Horse Artillery:

> Our keel had scarcely touched the sand ere we were abruptly boarded by a naval officer (Captain Hill) with a gang of sailors, who, *sans cérémonie*, instantly commenced hoisting our horses out, and throwing them, as well as our saddlery, etc., overboard, without ever giving time for making any disposition to receive or secure the one or the other. To my remonstrance his answer was, 'I can't help it, sir; the Duke's *orders are positive that no delay is to take place in landing the troops as they arrive, and the ships sent back again; so you must be out of her before dark.*' It was then about 3 p.m.; and I thought this a most uncomfortable arrangement.[22]

[20] J. Sugden, *Nelson – The Sword of Albion* (London, 2012), 94–6.
[21] TNA:PRO, Admiralty ADM 9/3/1868, memorandum of the services of Captain Sir John Hill.
[22] General A. C. Mercer, *Journal of the Waterloo Campaign* (London, 1870), 2012 edition, ed. A. Uffindell, 54.

After the battle he took on board the wounded British soldiers and a large number of French wounded and prisoners. On Wellington's recommendation Hill was promoted to post captain in October 1815 and, at Wellington's request, was sent to Calais with the army of occupation, where for three years all sea-borne troop movements were under Hill's direction. In February 1820 Hill was appointed agent victualler at Deptford, one of the navy's three yards with responsibility for feeding the navy.

When famine struck the west coast of Ireland in June 1831 Hill was chosen by Sir James Graham, the first lord of the Admiralty, to be the agent of the government to administer relief. Hill was in Ireland from the middle of June until August 1831. On his return he was knighted for his services.

Hill was appointed captain superintendent of the victualling and dock yards at Deptford in 1832. When famine again struck Ireland in 1836 Hill was sent by the Chancellor of the Exchequer, Thomas Spring Rice, to Donegal in July. After only six months back at Deptford came Hill's appointment to the Highlands and Islands in March 1837 to take charge of government relief. Only four months after Hill's return from Scotland, his appointment at Deptford was terminated in somewhat unhappy circumstances. Hill had believed his tenure of the post was, on the recommendation of the duke of Wellington, permanent. To Lord Minto, the first lord of the Admiralty, however, the position of superintendent was simply one of those that, following the reforms instituted by Sir James Graham in 1832, fell to be dealt with in the same way as other naval appointments. Hill secured the support of Sir James Graham and the second viscount Melville, two former first lords of the Admiralty, John Wilson Croker, a former first secretary to the Admiralty, and Lord Lynedoch, who wrote letters on his behalf to Lord Minto. The duke of Wellington, however, declined to assist on the grounds that 'my interference with the Admiralty would do you more harm than good'. Minto was not moved by letters from these men, which had included pointed references to Hill's service in Ireland and Scotland. Indeed, Minto suggested that Hill's actions in soliciting such support was indiscreet and that the letters might be seen as the ill-advised intervention of over-zealous friends.[23] In the event, however, he secured for Hill a berth as captain superintendent of the dockyard at Sheerness.[24] Hill returned to Deptford in 1842 but in 1846 his tenure was again threatened. On this occasion Hill secured

[23] NLS, Minto papers, MS 12048E, Minto to Hill, 4 Jan. 1838; MS 12058, fos. 80–1, Hill to Lynedoch, 8 Jan. 1838; MS 12058, fos. 75–9, Lynedoch to Lord John Russell, 11 Jan. 1838; MS 12058, fos. 65–6, Melville to Hill, 11 Jan. 1838; MS 12058, fos. 69–70, Graham to Hill, 11 Jan. 1838; MS 12058, fos. 63–4 Hill to Minto, 12 Jan. 1838; MS 12058, fos. 67–8, Hill to Minto, 16 Jan. 1838; MS 12058, fos. 73–4, Minto to Lynedoch, 19 Jan. 1838; MS 12058, fos. 71–2, Minto to Hill, 19 Jan. 1838; NRA 44729, Hill papers and correspondence, fo. 79, Wellington to Hill, 16 Jan. 1838; and fos. 80–1, Croker to Hill, 21 Jan. 1838.
[24] NLS, Minto papers, MS 12048E, Minto to Hill, 5 Mar. 1838.

the support of Lord FitzRoy Somerset, the then military secretary at the Horse Guards,[25] Spring Rice[26] and the duke of Wellington, who felt able to write in glowing terms of Hill's service.[27] This time, however, the first lord of the Admiralty, Lord Auckland, decided that 'there is no danger of my disturbing you in the office which you fit so well'.[28]

On his retirement from Deptford in 1851 Hill acquired Walmer Lodge on the Kent coast. The duke of Wellington promised to do all that was in his power to make his residence there agreeable, and appointed Hill to be captain of one of the Cinque Ports, Sandown Castle. He was promoted rear admiral of the blue in April 1851 and of the white two years later. He died aged 81 on 20 January 1855.

Hill's naval career was marked not by heroic exploits in ships of the line; he was not a 'hero of the quarter deck' as Thomas Mulock scathingly described the half-pay naval officers appointed in 1847 as government inspectors during the great famine.[29] Rather, he had a reputation for intelligence, reliability, solidity and integrity earned in the less colourful, but nonetheless vital, area of transport and supply, attributes which had recommended him to successive governments for his missions in Ireland and Scotland.[30] Above all, he earned the esteem and friendship of the duke of Wellington, something that is reflected on the memorial tablet dedicated to him on the north wall of the knave in the church of the Blessed Mary of Walmer, where he was buried.

Andrew Rutherfurd, Lord Rutherfurd (1791–1854)

Rutherfurd was born Andrew Greenfield in 1791, the son of William Greenfield. His mother, Janet Bervie, was descended from the old Scottish family of Rutherfurd, which name he adopted some time before the commencement of his public career. He passed as advocate in June 1812 and was said by Henry Cockburn to be one of the most eminent men in his

[25] NRA 44729, Hill papers and correspondence, fo. 110, FitzRoy Somerset to Hill, 15 Sept. 1846. E. M. Lloyd, rev. John Sweetman, 'Somerset, FitzRoy James Henry, first Baron Raglan (1788–1855)', *ODNB*.

[26] Who was now Lord Monteagle – he suggested Hill should send to the Admiralty a copy of his letter of 11 Aug. 1837 (see p. 266 below) as testimony of Hill's service in Scotland (NRA 44729, Hill papers and correspondence, fos. 114–16, Monteagle to Hill, 16 Sept. 1846).

[27] NRA 44729, Hill papers and correspondence, fos. 111–12, Wellington to Hill, 16 Sept. 1846.

[28] NRA 44729, Hill papers and correspondence, fo. 119, Auckland to Hill, 30 Sept. 1846. At the Admiralty, Auckland had the reputation of being an 'administrator of the highest calibre': see P. J. Marshall, 'Eden, George, earl of Auckland (1784–1849)', *ODNB*. See J. MacAskill, 'Hill, Sir John (1774–1855)', *ODNB*.

[29] T. M. Devine, *The Great Highland Famine – Hunger, Emigration and the Scottish Highlands in the Nineteenth Century* (Edinburgh, 1988), 132.

[30] Spring Rice wrote to Sir Robert Peel that 'in his good sense and discretion I had every reason to place the most entire reliance'. BL, Peel papers, vol. cccxcvi, Add. MS 40576, fos. 322–6, Monteagle to Peel, 24 Oct. 1845.

profession. He succeeded John Cunninghame as solicitor-general for Scotland in Lord Melbourne's administration in 1837, became lord advocate and was elected liberal MP for Leith Burghs in April 1839. When Sir Robert Peel came to power in 1841, Rutherfurd resigned his office as lord advocate but returned to the office in 1846 with Lord John Russell's first administration. In 1851 he was appointed a judge of the court of session. He died in 1854. He was remembered as a profound lawyer, a successful law-reformer and an accomplished scholar; a delightful companion in private life, as a public man he suffered from an unconciliatory and haughty demeanour.[31]

Sir Alexander Young Spearman, first baronet (1793–1874)

Spearman was born in 1793, the eldest son of Alexander Young Spearman, a major in the Royal Artillery. He entered public service in 1808 as deputy assistant commissary-general, progressing to become controller of the Stationery Office in 1823. He was transferred to the Treasury in 1824 as assistant clerk, rising next to chief clerk, then auditor and finally, in January 1836, assistant secretary – the most senior permanent official at the Treasury. Ill-health forced his early retirement in 1840, when he was replaced by Sir Charles Trevelyan. He was created a baronet in 1840 in recognition of his public service. By 1850 his health had recovered sufficiently for him to be appointed secretary and comptroller of the National Debt Office. He finally retired in 1873 and died the next year. He was a public servant of exceptional ability; he was 'one of the old school and always wore a jabot or frilled shirt front'.[32]

Thomas Spring Rice, first baron Monteagle of Brandon (1790–1866)

Spring Rice was born in Limerick in 1790 into a well-connected Irish gentry family. He became MP for Limerick in 1820, where he sat until 1832, when he became MP for Cambridge, remaining as such for the rest of his Commons career. He was appointed under-secretary at the Home department in 1827 in Canning's coalition administration and in 1830 he became secretary to the Treasury in Earl Grey's ministry, colonial secretary in 1834 and then Chancellor of the Exchequer in Lord Melbourne's administration in 1835. He was deeply unhappy with his time as chancellor, a position from which

[31]   See G. F. R. Barker, rev. H. J. Spencer, 'Rutherfurd [formerly Greenfield], Andrew, Lord Rutherfurd (1791–1854)', *ODNB*.
[32]   See J. C. Sainty, 'Spearman, Sir Alexander Young, first baronet (1793–1874)', *ODNB*.

he always hoped to be free. He believed himself inadequate in the office and said that more than once he had shrunk from the weight of responsibility of the office; indeed, he was widely regarded by his contemporaries as not being up to the job. He had long been interested in being speaker of the Commons, a position he sought on a number of occasions, one of which was on the death of the king in June 1837, when he asked Lord Melbourne for his name to be put forward for the position. He continued reluctantly in office until 1839, when he was appointed to the House of Lords as first baron Monteagle of Brandon. Spring Rice died in Limerick in 1866.[33]

Robert Stewart of Ardvorlich (1799–1854)

Stewart was born in 1799, the eldest son of William Stewart and Helen Maxtone, the eldest daughter of James Maxtone of Cultoquhey and the sister of Anthony Maxtone of Cultoquhey, who married his second cousin, Robert Graham's sister Alexina. He was apprenticed to James Dundas, WS, of Ochtertyre and became a writer to the signet, practising in Edinburgh. Stewart succeeded to the Ardvorlich estate in February 1838. Ardvorlich House on Loch Earn in Perthshire had been built by Robert Ferguson in 1790, probably incorporating fabric from an earlier castle, round which Sir Walter Scott wrote *The Legend of Montrose*, renaming Ardvorlich as 'Darnlinvarach'. Stewart's letter of January 1830 to Scott, on what Stewart believed was the correct family history about which Scott had written, is contained in Scott's Introduction to his book. Stewart, an amiable man, seems to have been dominated by his elderly mother and was described by his sister Marjory as being rather idly disposed with little to employ him and nothing in which he took much interest.[34] However, this was probably too harsh a judgement. Stewart was actively involved on behalf of the Whig cause in Perthshire and the election of Fox Maule to the county seat. As a Gaelic speaker he was thought to be the ideal companion for Robert Graham on his tour of the distressed districts of the Highlands and Islands; he was also Graham's second cousin. Stewart died unmarried in July 1854.

---

[33] See E. A. Wasson, 'Rice, Thomas Spring, first Baron Monteagle of Brandon (1790–1866), *ODNB*; C. M. Murphy, 'The Life and Politics of Thomas Spring Rice, 1st Baron Monteagle of Brandon, 1790–1866' (University College Cork, MA thesis, 1991).

[34] Private information.

INTRODUCTION

The Highlands and Islands of Scotland, with their climatic variability and low crop yields, were no strangers to recurrent subsistence crises and famines during the seventeenth, eighteenth and nineteenth centuries. 'The frequency and scale of these crises were such as to ensure that most Highlanders and Hebrideans living before the mid-nineteenth century would have experienced the realities of famine more than once in their lives.'[1] The most notable of these crises were the famine of the so-called 'ill years' of 1695–1702, the last national famine to occur in Scotland; a harvest crisis between 1738 and 1741; an extended famine in 1782, when the government was first asked to supply food for relief of the Highlands and which was serious enough to be referred to parliament;[2] a year of scarcity in 1817, which followed an unfavourable season in 1816, when the government was called on to provide a large supply of oats to the Western Isles, which it agreed, reluctantly, to do; the serious destitution in the Highlands and Islands in 1837, which is the subject of this book; and the great Highland potato famine of 1846–7. Apart from the famine of the 1690s, the harvest crisis between 1738 and 1741 and the famine of 1846–7, which have all received detailed scholarly attention,[3] the other famines and food scarcities have not been the subject of detailed published research and little is known of them.[4]

There is no doubt that the conditions in 1837 were not so extreme as those in 1695–1702 or, indeed, in 1846–7, but were they nonetheless such that they may properly be described as a famine? While there should be little or no argument that the conditions in the Highlands and Islands in 1837 satisfy the *Oxford English Dictionary* definition of the term 'famine' – extreme and general scarcity of food – there is a considerable literature on famine and hunger that takes the definition further and seeks to analyse, discuss and, indeed, to define it by reference to a number of indicators, including mortality and sickness

[1]   R. A. Dodgshon, 'Coping with risk: subsistence crises in the Scottish Highlands and Islands, 1600–1800', *Rural History* 15 (2004), 1–25, at 1.
[2]   [PP] 1846 XXXVII (281), *Distress (Scotland): Documents Relative to the Distress and Famine in Scotland in the Year 1783, in Consequence of the Late Harvest and Loss of the Potato Crop.*
[3]   K. J. Cullen, *Famine in Scotland: The 'Ill Years of the 1690s'* (Edinburgh, 2010); P. R. Rossner, 'The 1738–1741 Harvest Crisis in Scotland', *SHR* 90.1, no. 229 (Apr. 2011), 27–63; and Devine, *Highland Famine.*
[4]   Dodgshon, 'Coping with risk', 1.

levels, signs of social breakdown, availability of markets, levels of eviction and emigration, availability of relief mechanisms.[5] As it is not the intention of this book to examine or categorise the conditions in 1837 in this way, and as the term 'famine' raises serious humanitarian and emotive issues and needs to be used with caution,[6] the more neutral, but no less significant, term 'destitution' has been preferred: this, after all, was the predominant contemporary description, often with an adjectival emphasis such as 'utter', 'fearful', 'lamentable', or 'total'.[7]

The destitution of 1837 had its immediate genesis in the cold and wet spring weather of 1835 that meant the planting and sowing of the potato and corn crop for the year had been carried out in very unfavourable circumstances; this was followed by a late and wet harvest and the potato crop was attacked by disease. At the end of 1835, therefore, the quality and quantity of food available was limited. Snow from early February until March in 1836 and intermittent rain and sleet delayed the planting and sowing of the crop for that year, and the potatoes that were planted suffered from the disease of the previous year. Heavy rain from the end of May through the whole summer and autumn, and then severe frosts and gales during October, meant that the harvest for 1836 was yet again diminished in both quality and quantity.[8] These two successive years of much-reduced harvest meant that the people of the Highlands and Islands began 1837 with an almost total lack of food for the present and of the seed needed to provide for the future.

This book has two objectives. The first is to put flesh on the bones of what is known, and to provide a record of the destitution of 1837 through four sources.[9] The first is the eyes and ears of Robert Graham of Redgorton, who was appointed by the Home Office to undertake an investigation into the distressed districts and the state of the Highlands and Islands, and of Captain Sir John Hill, who

[5] See, by way of example, C. O'Grada, *Famine – A Short History* (Oxford, 2012); J. Vernon, *Hunger – A Modern History* (London, 2007); P. Howe and S. Devereux, 'Famine intensity and magnitude scales: a proposal for an instrumental definition of famine', *Disasters* 28.4 (2004), 353–72, and the works therein cited.

[6] O'Grada, *Famine*, 6.

[7] See, for example, NRS, Papers of the Mackenzie family, earls of Seaforth GD 46/13/199/8, Extracts from letters transmitted by clergymen, magistrates and others relative to the present destitution in the Highlands and Islands of Scotland. We should note, however, that contemporaries did also refer to the conditions in 1837 as being a famine (see, for example, *Caledonian Mercury*, 2 Feb. 1837) although less frequently than describing them as destitution. Eric Richards describes the events of 1837 as famine (E. Richards and M. Clough, *Cromartie: Highland Life 1650–1914* (Aberdeen, 1989), 200).

[8] Subscriptions were raised in 1836 in Edinburgh, Glasgow, Paisley and Greenock (NRS, Papers of the Maxtone Graham family of Cultoquhey, Perthshire, GD 155/1347 Island of Lewis – Deplorable scarcity of food, 19 May 1836; *Inverness Courier*, 23 May 1836; and *The Scotsman*, 18 June 1836).

[9] A detailed analysis of a fifth source, the contemporary press reporting on the reactions to the destitution, and the appeals of the various committees for public subscriptions, is to be found in J. MacAskill, '"It is truly, in the expressive language of Burke, a nation crying for bread": the public response to the highland famine of 1836–1837', *The Innes Review* 61.2 (Autumn 2010), 169–206.

was appointed by the Treasury to administer financial aid to be provided by
the government, as recorded in their letters to the government and, in the case
of Hill, also through the pages of his private daily journal. The second source
is the words of memorials, petitions and resolutions seeking government aid
and subscriptions from the public, and the reports of the committees formed
in Edinburgh, Glasgow and London to solicit these public subscriptions. The
third source is the words of official and private government letters. The fourth
source is Treasury minutes. The other objective is to give an appreciation of the
significance of Robert Graham's letters in the context of attempts to understand,
and find a solution to, the problem facing the Highlands and Islands and its
'redundant population';[10] and to place the response of the government in the
wider context of famine relief policy in Ireland and Scotland between 1817 and
1845.

The major part of the book is comprised of Robert Graham's letters and Sir
John Hill's letters and journal. Part 1 contains the official letters which Robert
Graham wrote to the honourable Fox Maule, MP, the under-secretary of state
at the Home Office, but also included are letters (or extracts) from Graham to his
mother and one to his married sister Alexina Maxtone, at the family home, 18
Heriot Row, Edinburgh, while on his tour of the distressed districts because these
more personal letters provide a further insight into his tour. Graham's evidence
to the 1841 select committee was based on his 1837 letters to the government,
and on occasions he read *verbatim* extracts to the committee; the corresponding
sections of 1841 select committee are drawn attention to in footnotes to the
transcripts of the letters. Graham was accompanied on his tour by Robert Stewart
of Ardvorlich who was Graham's second cousin once removed, and there are
also included three letters from Graham to Stewart which reflect on Graham's
appointment by the government (pp. 5, 6 and 110). Stewart wrote a number
of letters to his sister, Marjory, during the tour; while these letters are not
included in the text, they are referred to, where relevant, in the footnotes
to the transcripts of Graham's letters. This Introduction describes briefly
Graham's tour of the distressed districts and then considers the issues he
raised in his letters to the government and the significance of those letters.
Historiography has not been kind to Graham: not only has the value of his
letters been under-appreciated by historians[11] but the authorship of the letters
has been wrongly attributed by historians to Graham's namesake, the professor

---

[10] [PP] 1826–7 V (550), *Third Report from the Select Committee on Emigration from the United Kingdom:
1827*, 14; 1841 SC, Q 38; J. Hunter, *The Making of the Crofting Community* (Edinburgh, 1976),
39.
[11] A notable exception is Margaret Adam, who suggested that Graham's report, which stressed
that the real problem was want of occupation for too many people, bore out the view she
was propounding that the destitution in the Highlands and Islands was not due to any special
oppression by the proprietors (M.I. Adam, 'Eighteenth century Highland landlords and
the poverty problem', *SHR* 19.75 (Apr. 1922), 161–79, at 179).

of botany at Edinburgh University, Dr Robert Graham, a mistake which it seems was first made in 1967 and perpetuated ever since.[12]

Part 2 contains the daily journal kept by Sir John Hill during the four and a half months he spent in Scotland as the agent of the government charged with the administration of the aid provided by the government, and the official and private letters he wrote to the assistant secretary at the Treasury, Alexander Spearman and to Thomas Spring Rice, the Chancellor of the Exchequer. Spearman's letter to Hill instructing him to proceed to Scotland and his letter informing him that he was, at the end of his duties, at liberty to return to London are also included (pp. 113 and 188), as is Hill's letter to Lord Lynedoch informing him of his appointment (p. 114). This Introduction describes briefly Hill's activities in Scotland and then reflects on his role as the administrator of funds provided from the public purse.

The papers included in Part 3 have been selected to show the representations made to the government and to the public seeking aid, and the formation and workings of the destitution committees in Edinburgh, Glasgow, Aberdeen and London to solicit such aid (pp. 201–11, 211–20 and 220–43); and those in Parts 4 and 5 to show the inner workings of the government relating to the decision of the Home Office to appoint Graham to undertake his investigation and the Treasury to provide financial aid and to appoint Hill to administer this aid. This Introduction looks at the activities of the committees in Edinburgh and Glasgow, and considers government policy over the destitution, showing how it largely followed the policies of successive governments, both Tory and Whig, over famine relief in both Ireland and Scotland between 1817 and 1837; it also looks at the role of the Home Office and parliament.

★

The disastrous situation in the Highlands and Islands at the beginning of 1837 was made public through letters and reports from ministers and others[13] and through petitions and memorials sent to the government. Public meetings were held in February and March in Edinburgh, Leith, Glasgow, Aberdeen, Inverness, London and many other towns and cities throughout England, and destitution committees were formed to seek subscriptions from the public to provide funds for food, clothing and seed to distribute in the effected parishes.[14] The Edinburgh committee resolved to send a deputation to London and to tour the English towns

---

[12] D. S. Macmillan, *Scotland and Australia 1788–1850* (Oxford, 1967), 278; Devine, *Highland Famine*, 27. The authorship has also been attributed to the secretary of state for the Home Department (in E. M. MacArthur, *Iona: The Living Memory of a Crofting Community 1751–1914* (Edinburgh, 1990), 63).

[13] See, for example, NRS, Papers of the Mackenzie family, earls of Seaforth, GD 46/13/199/8, Extracts from letters transmitted by clergymen, magistrates and others, relative to the present destitution in the Highlands and Islands of Scotland, 1837.

[14] A detailed analysis of the appeals of the various committees for public subscriptions is to be found in MacAskill, 'Public response', 169–206.

and cities, seeking funds. The deputation consisted of the Rev. Dr Norman Macleod, moderator of the general assembly and a Gaelic scholar with a great interest in schemes for the welfare of the Highlands,[15] John Bowie, an Edinburgh writer to the signet and agent of a number of Highland proprietors, and Charles Baird, the secretary to the Glasgow committee. The resolutions of the Edinburgh, Glasgow and London public meetings (pp. 211–20) explained the situation in the Highlands and Islands[16] – that out of a population of 167,000, some 86,000 people were destitute and in immediate need of food, clothing and seed, and appealed for subscriptions from the public.[17]

The Edinburgh and Glasgow committees divided their responsibilities. The Edinburgh committee took responsibility for the provision of seed; the committee was dominated by landed proprietors and there was controversy over the motivation of the proprietors in seeking funds from the public to provide for the supply of seed that would ensure the payment of rent on their properties.[18] The committee published the terms on which they would supply seed with the funds subscribed (p. 245) and these terms were, as is noted below, also adopted by the government (p. 278), and they are, therefore, of some importance. The critical point was that seed was not, in general, to be supplied free of charge. The original resolutions of the Edinburgh committee as to the supply of seed were published and distributed on 2 March 1837, but Macleod and Bowie, who were on their fund-raising tour in England, had not seen them until they were forwarded to them in London with instructions to submit a copy to the government, and they had a number of comments on them which led to their writing a note on the 14 April 1837 (p. 246) to rectify misunderstandings which they said had arisen. Following this important note there were four classes of beneficiary for the seed distribution, each with a different obligation to pay, and one guarantor. The first class comprised tenants paying yearly rent of between £10 and £20; here the obligation was

[15] But described in Hill's journal as appearing to be 'a troublesome character' (p. 128). See H. C. G. Matthew, 'Macleod, Norman (1783–1862)', *ODNB*.
[16] Including Orkney and Shetland.
[17] Graham's estimate of the destitute population (excluding Sutherland, Caithness, Orkney and Shetland) was 70,000 (p. 71). On the basis of the estimates of meal which Graham said was required to last the season – ½ boll per head – discussed below, and the abstract of the total supplies of meal provided by the destitution committees (p. 226), the total number of people supplied by the destitution committees with meal on the west coast and islands was 37,202, in Orkney 4,256 and in Shetland 10,914.
[18] See MacAskill, 'Public response', 176, 189–95. In 1847 the Central Board of Management determined that none of the public subscriptions should be spent on the purchase of seed. Funds spent this way would, the board resolved, be a diversion from the express purpose of the fund, which was to meet destitution and, the board said, the provision of seed was, in any event, more properly the duty of either individual proprietors or the government (NLS, Highland destitution reports (1846–51), Resolutions of the Central Board, 23 Feb. 1847). It seems possible, indeed likely, that the concerns raised over the use of public subscriptions in 1837 to purchase seed influenced the determination of the Central Board in 1847.

to pay for the seed at prime cost by Candlemas 1838. The second comprised tenants paying yearly rent of between £5 and £10; here the obligation was to pay for the seed at prime cost or three quarters of prime cost according to the circumstances of the tenants, as determined by the local committee. The third class of beneficiary comprised crofters and others paying yearly rent of less than £5, who were obliged to make a return for the seed in money or labour in proportion and to the extent determined by the local committee. The fourth class of beneficiary, which had not been included in the original resolutions, comprised cottars and possessors of small patches of land whether they paid a rent of £5 or no rent at all. They were, as for the third class, obliged to make a return for the seed in money or labour in proportion and to the extent determined by the local committee, but there was no real expectation of payment in money. The vast majority of the tenants, crofters and cottars fell into the £10 or less classes and it seems that with few exceptions the seed was supplied to crofters in the third class and a great proportion to cottars and others in the fourth class.[19] The resolutions provided that the relevant estate proprietor, or someone authorised by him, should guarantee the repayment in money to the Edinburgh committee of at least one-half of the cost of the supply of seed to individuals on his estate. The requirement for a guarantee was strictly enforced by the committee,[20] but the requirement for a guarantee as to a half seems to have caused some confusion as to what, exactly, was to be paid for the seed and by whom. For example, Robert Graham, in his letter of 15 March 1837 to Fox Maule (p. 22), and the Rev. Alexander Ross of Ullapool[21] both said that the terms of the resolutions were that those receiving the seed should pay for one-half of it when in fact the resolutions provided for payments of the whole, three-quarters or a discretionary amount while the obligation as to one-half was that of the guarantee by the proprietors. As to the requirement for the guarantee, it is clear that the proprietors, with John Bowie as an influential adviser, were sensitive to any charge that a call for public money was a call made on behalf, and for the benefit, of the proprietors. This applied, in particular, to calls for aid for seed corn and potatoes because it was from these crops that tenants were enabled to pay their rents. And this sensitivity was not limited to the call for public subscriptions; the proprietors must also have been aware of government attitudes to the landed proprietors and views on the role that proprietors had played in the creation of the circumstances that now existed and on the role they should play in the relief of destitution amongst the people on their estates, as

---

[19]   See Devine, *Highland Famine*, 5. NLS, Lynedoch papers, MS 16147, fos. 235–6, Report of the Edinburgh committee, 21 Dec. 1837 (see p. 221).

[20]   As is shown by minutes of meetings of the trustee and commissioners upon the sequestrated estate of Col. Roderick MacNeill of Barra, and of the agents for the heritable creditors (NRS, Court of session: productions in process CS 96/4274/131–2, Minutes of meeting, 21 Apr. 1837, and CS 96/4274/131/102–6, Minutes of meeting, 27 Apr. 1837).

[21]   [PP] 1844 XXI (564), *Poor Law Inquiry (Scotland)*, Appendix, part II, 424.

discussed below. Certainly, James Stewart Mackenzie of Seaforth, the Whig MP for Ross and Cromarty, was alive to the issue: in a letter to Lord John Russell of 2 March 1837 he said that if public money was to be provided by the government for the supply of seed.

> I feel bound to suggest, that the supply of seed ought only to be given as an advance, and that for the amount of its cost the proprietors and their local agents should, in each case, grant their bills, payable in two moieties, at 18 and 24 months after delivery of the seed, with a moderate addition of interest. They can best recover payment in money or in kind, and ought not to hesitate to take that risk themselves; nor can I doubt their readiness to do so: to all applicants who sent to me their statements I have pointed this out invariably.[22]

It seems likely, then, that the requirement for the proprietors to give the guarantee was conditioned by an understanding that a call for public and government aid had to make clear that the proprietors were playing their part. It is interesting to note, however, that there was no mention made in the publicity for the Edinburgh subscriptions of the concentration of that committee on the supply of seed or of the proprietors' guarantee.[23] Nor, perhaps more significantly, was there a reference to the fact that the tenants and crofters were required to pay for the supply of seed in varying proportions. The public who subscribed to the funds might not then, perhaps, have appreciated that the cost of the supply of seed financed by their subscriptions was to be repaid, in varying proportions, by the tenants and crofters and that, therefore, at least a part of the funds which they had subscribed were, in effect, only to be lent by the committee to the destitute poor, which might have had an effect on fund-raising if the full facts had been clear.

The Glasgow committee concentrated on the supply of food and clothing, which it determined to supply without any stipulation for repayment or return.[24] It objected to the Edinburgh resolutions concerning the supply of seed and the suggestion that both committees should be bound by them, particularly as aid provided by the government was linked to the resolutions. The Glasgow committee refused to comply with the government's requirement that it could only access state aid provided it spent, on a pound for pound basis, its own funds on seed (and on the conditions for repayment set out in the Edinburgh resolutions), and Hill, who was in the middle of this dispute, told the Treasury that, in the

---

[22] NRS, Papers of the Mackenzie Family, earls of Seaforth, GD 46/13/199/1, Stewart Mackenzie to Russell, 2 Mar. 1837.

[23] A point that is emphasised by the criticism in May 1838 by *Tait's Edinburgh Magazine*, which noted that of the total cost of £7,639 for the supplies sent by the committee to the west coast, only £49 was spent on food, the rest being for seed.

[24] See p. 210, memorial of 25 Mar. in Part 3.

circumstances, he would confine his assistance to the Edinburgh committee.[25] Hill suspected jobbery by the Glasgow committee, but in his evidence to the 1841 select committee on emigration, Charles Baird defended the position of the Glasgow committee: 'We had raised our fund for the support of the poor people, and I have no doubt the chief reason was, that we did not wish to give anything that might be ultimately a benefit to the landlords.'[26]

The Aberdeen committee was mainly responsible for the supplies sent to Orkney and Shetland. The total of all subscriptions received as a result of the public subscriptions amounted to not less than £67,000.[27] By comparison, in 1847 the Central Board had at its disposal £209,376 available for famine relief raised voluntarily.[28] The total expenditure on seed, food and clothing by the Edinburgh and Glasgow committees was around £415,000, which left a surplus of the subscribed funds of around £20,000, and there was considerable and heated debate and controversy over the purposes to which this surplus should be put[29] and ex post facto justification by the committees of the fact that there was a surplus at all.[30] Some 16 per cent of the expenditure of the total subscriptions received from the public was on the supply of seed and the balance of 84 per cent on food and clothing.

The government in London had been made aware of the situation in the Highlands and Islands through petitions and memorials (pp. 201–11) and also through the reports from the solicitor-general for Scotland, John Cunninghame, to the Home Office (pp. 253–8); there was also a deputation to the Chancellor of the Exchequer, which included a number of Scottish MPs.[31] The Treasury was, it seems, convinced that there was a problem that required

[25] Hill's journal entries for 25 Mar. (p. 118), 12, 13 and 14 Apr. (p. 128); TNA:PRO, Treasury T 1/4201, Hill to Spearman, 25 Mar. 1837 (p. 118); NRS, Commissary General and Treasury HD 7/9, Memorial of Glasgow committee, 25 Mar. 1837 (p. 210); and HD 7/10, Hill to Spearman, 16 Apr. 1837 (p. 129).

[26] 1841 SC, Q 1183.

[27] NLS, Lynedoch papers, MS 16147, fos. 235–6, Report of Edinburgh committee, 21 Dec. 1837 (p. 220); 1841 SC, 109; Morning Chronicle, 27 Oct. 1837. The sum of £67,000 is equivalent to around £5 million in 2010. Contemporary estimates of the total of subscriptions varied – see MacAskill, 'Public response', 186.

[28] Devine, Highland Famine, 115.

[29] See MacAskill, 'Public response', 184–8 and below as to the proposal that the surplus be used for emigration.

[30] See pp. 220, 232 and 241, Edinburgh, Glasgow and London committee reports.

[31] The deputation which had an interview with the chancellor of the exchequer on 13 Mar. 1837 was composed of the duke of Argyle; the Rev. Dr Norman Macleod; John Bowie; Charles Baird; Mr J. A. Stewart Mackenzie, the Whig MP for Ross and Cromarty; the Hon. Colonel F. W. Grant, the Tory MP for Elgin and Nairn counties; Mr W. F. Campbell of Islay, the Whig MP for Argyllshire; Mr Alexander Bannerman, the Whig MP for Aberdeen; Mr Roderick Macleod, the Whig MP for Sutherland county; Mr T. Balfour, the Tory MP for Orkney; Major Cumming Bruce, the Tory MP for Inverness district; Mr J. Hope Johnston, the Tory MP for Dumfriesshire; Norman Macleod of Macleod; and Major John Campbell of Melford (The Scotsman, 18 Mar. 1837).

government intervention, as is discussed below, and resolved to provide £10,000 to acquire seed on the same terms as seed supplied by the Edinburgh committee, and sent Captain Hill to administer the funds. As to funding the supply of food, the Treasury resolved that a decision on this should await the reports of Robert Graham; in the event, the Treasury left this decision to the discretion of Captain Hill (p. 282). The position of the Home Office was equivocal. Cunninghame's letters to the Home Office had shown that there was a problem, but there was some scepticism within the department as to its extent and, indeed, on the role of the proprietors in seeking public aid. The decision was taken, on Cunninghame's recommendation, to send Robert Graham to make a report for the Home Office on the distressed districts, although this decision seems to have been as much motivated by suspicions of, and to counter, Tory jobbery as it was by a genuine concern to investigate the situation; Cunninghame's letters to Fox Maule (pp. 253–8) are full of suspicion and criticism of the role of the proprietors. Graham himself had set off with the firm view that the Home Office 'rather supposed the case had been exaggerated' (p. 5). The despatch of Graham was noted by *The Times* newspaper, no friend of the Whig government, with a sarcastic leader:

> Oh! A certain Mr R. Graham, formerly a Whig Lord of the Treasury, and formerly a defeated candidate for Perthshire, happens to be out of place just now. Mr Robert Graham is, therefore, invested with a Government *commission*, and despatched in an Admiralty cutter to visit the highlands and islands of Scotland, for the purpose of ascertaining and reporting the extent of the famine alleged to exist! The testimony of every newspaper in the north of Scotland – the recorded minutes of public Courts connected with the church – the pledged characters of the deputation who represented the prevalent distress – the powerful corroboration and zealous support of several senators of the highest respectability, – all this would not do for our circumspect and suspicious Ministry. So Mr. Robert Graham must needs weigh anchor, steer to the nor'ard, take notes, arrange schedules, frame his report, and finger his pay; while the wretched islanders are left to wait and weather it as best they can, till Mr Robert (please God) shall return.[32]

★

Robert Graham's appointment by the Home Office was, in terms, to visit the distressed districts and to report to Fox Maule on his 'observations and

---

[32] *The Times*, 10 Mar. 1837. The *Caledonian Mercury* objected to this criticism and wrote a long comment in response, including: 'The cold blooded misrepresentations, the daring mendacity, and the scurrilous personal abuse which on political topics so famously distinguish *The Times* newspaper, become singularly conspicuous, we have frequently observed, wherever the statements of that journal happen to relate to Scotland' (*Caledonian Mercury*, 16 Mar. 1837). For further contemporary newspaper comment on the famine, see MacAskill, 'Public response', 169–206.

[his] knowledge gathered on the spot and what local proprietors have done and that, with any other information you can afford in to decide government in forming a judgement as to its future course' (p. 259). On receipt of these instructions, Graham wrote to a number of proprietors south of Oban to establish if he needed to visit that district. He also wrote to Robert Brown, the duke of Hamilton's factor, explaining his plans and seeking guidance on them, in particular on the state of Islay and Arran; he told Brown that 'The object is to narrow the circle within which we are absolutely obliged to report upon as much as with propriety can be done'.[33] Graham also met immediately with the Edinburgh and Glasgow committees, which brought a rebuke from Fox Maule who told him his mission was supposed to be confidential to the government and not one to be conducted in conjunction with the committees (p. 259). Graham very soon determined that he would not be able to fit in a visit to Orkney and Shetland. Graham's understanding was that Orkney would not require assistance but that the situation in Shetland was serious (p. 8).[34] He also decided it was not necessary to include Caithness in his tour and that the county of Sutherland could be left to the ducal family who owned it. Although the destitution in Sutherland was serious[35] Graham was correct in his assumption that the family would look after its own Sutherland estate of roughly 1.1 million acres without recourse to external aid; in a letter to James Loch, the Commissioner, the second duke asked Loch to make it clear that 'we don't intend to request any assistance from the subscription for the western Highlands as far as Sutherland is concerned, tho' also a poor district . . . I think you will have an arduous task this year as Sutherland to such a great extent being left to be provided for. I shall be ready to do all I can.'[36] This message from the duke was duly noted in the contemporary newspapers, coupled with statements about the countess-duchess ordering 5,000 bolls of meal and making an advance of £3,000,[37] culminating with a letter describing the countess-duchess as 'cherishing in her bosom from her earliest of days, the ardent attachment to her people which glowed in the breasts of her noble ancestors', and her munificence as being 'worthy of her name, her family and fortune'.[38] This must have been music to the

---

[33] NRAS, Douglas-Hamilton family, MS 2177, bundle 6254/2, Graham to Brown, 5 Mar. 1837.

[34] Shetland, in fact received around 26 per cent of all the meal supplies sent by the Aberdeen committee and Orkney received around 10 per cent (NLS, Lynedoch papers, MS 16147, fos. 235–6, Report of Edinburgh committee, 21 Dec. 1837 – see p. 220 below). It is unclear how it was that the government considered it was to understand the accurate position of the problem in Shetland given Graham's exclusion of the island from his tour (but see p. 260 below); as to Orkney, the Treasury received detailed information from the collector of customs at Kirkwall (p. 131), and see [PP] 1844 XXI (564), 246..

[35] E. Richards, *The Leviathan of Wealth* (London, 1973), 245–9.

[36] NRS, Papers of the Loch family of Drylaw, GD 268/236/17, duke to Loch, 10 Mar. 1837.

[37] *Caledonian Mercury*, 30 Mar. 1837, *The Scotsman*, 1 Apr. 1837.

[38] *Inverness Courier*, 10 May 1837.

ears of the ducal family, whose image and reputation had been badly damaged by the clearances on the estate from 1801 to 1821 and whose decision not to tap public money during the 1837 destitution was an example of the influence on estate policy of a desire to avoid further accusations and criticisms.[39]

Graham also determined, on the basis of the advice he received from Robert Brown and a number of proprietors, that he did not need to visit the southern part of Argyll or the islands of Islay and Arran, which, Brown had told Graham, would be looked after by their respective proprietors – Walter Frederick Campbell of Islay and the duke of Hamilton.[40] And so, in the company of his second cousin, Robert Stewart of Ardvorlich, who was to act as his Gaelic interpreter, Graham set off on 9 March by steamer for Oban where he arrived at 2 pm the following day. They left Oban on 12 March and travelled to Fort William and thence to Arisaig and Loch Moidart via Corpach, Loch Eil, Loch Sheil and the Glenfinnan monument, by land as the revenue cutter that Graham had been told to expect had not arrived, and crossed the mouths of Loch Ailort and Loch nan Uamh in a large boat provided by Macdonald of Glenaladale. Graham and Stewart then went south to Loch Sunart, Ardnamurchan and from there by 'country boat' to Tobermory on Mull, arriving on the evening of 19 March, where Graham made his headquarters for some days as the revenue cutter had still not arrived and he considered it an excellent place to enquire into Mull, Ardnamurchan and Morvern. They left Tobermory in the revenue cutter *Swift* on 23 March en route to Barra, but as the wind was not favourable they went to Loch na Lathaich in the Ross of Mull, and to Iona. On 25 March they sailed to Loch Tuath on Mull, where they were detained for five days by heavy gales from the north and thick showers of snow, and so took the opportunity of visiting the island of Ulva on 27 March and receiving a deputation of the people on board the cutter. They eventually managed to leave Loch Tuath in the morning of 30 March, but the wind was still not fair for Barra, so they sailed to the Sound of Sleat, Skye, pausing briefly at Sleat, and anchored in Loch Alsh on the evening of 30 March. Leaving Loch Alsh, they anchored in Loch Kishorn just north of Plockton, from where Graham wrote on 3 April. From here they visited Broadford and Portree, and received information on Skye. Leaving Skye on 7 April, Graham and Stewart sailed to Poolewe en route to Loch Broom and Ullapool, from where Graham wrote to Fox Maule on 11 April that they had reached the most northerly point on the mainland to which they considered it necessary to go. Graham's next letter was from Stornoway on 14 April, where they obtained their information on the island of Lewis. They then sailed to Loch Tarbet on Harris and thence to Lochmaddy on North Uist, from where

---

[39] A.M. Tindley, *The Sutherland Estate, 1850–1920* (Edinburgh, 2010), 167–70.
[40] NRAS, Douglas-Hamilton family, MS 2177, bundle 6254/2, Brown to Graham, 7 Mar. 1837. Hill also received information from Brown about the distressed districts (p. 11).

Graham and Stewart visited Benbecula and South Uist. Having concluded their investigation of the Long Island, they sailed from Lochboisdale to Oban (via Barra), where they arrived on 30 April, nearly two months after setting off from Glasgow. They had been unable to visit the islands of Tiree, Colonsay, Jura, Rum, Eigg or Muck but sent in reports from information they had been able to glean. They returned home overland via Inveraray and then by sea to Glasgow and then to Edinburgh, from where Graham wrote his final letter to Fox Maule on 6 May.

John Cunninghame's recommendation that Graham, an Edinburgh advocate totally unconnected with the Highlands (p. 257) and a man who was said to lack 'the skills to interpret the minds of the common people perceptively',[41] should be appointed to make the investigation was, at first sight, perhaps an odd one.[42] It was, however, probably driven by the fact that Graham was well known to, and trusted by, the Whig legal establishment in Edinburgh and he would be a safe choice in the context of the suspicions of Tory jobbery. He might have been expected to do only what was necessary to defuse the demands for action from the government. However, this would have been to underestimate the man. It is true that the journals Graham wrote while touring Ireland in 1835, 1836 and 1838 show little interest in life beyond the nobility, gentry, grand estates, scenery and antiquities, but one of Graham's letters of introduction for one of his Irish journeys said that he was making the tour 'to see the state of agriculture and the condition of the people',[43] and Graham did have an 'interest in social conditions in Scotland [which] fuelled his investigation of life beyond the nobility and gentry'.[44] In the copious unpublished notes he made of his Irish journeys there are a number of references to the condition of the poor people and their living conditions.[45] Rather than accept invitations of accommodation from the gentry during his tour of the distressed districts, Graham was determined to avoid all 'good society': he told his mother that this should be the 'rule when employed in such a duty' (p. 13). Graham made his tour during the early months of the destitution, and he was clearly affected by the sorry state of the people. When he had initially discussed his proposed visit to the distressed districts with Robert Stewart he had, as we have seen, told Stewart that the government had rather supposed that the case had been exaggerated. What Graham saw later did not bear this out. His letters to Fox Maule display a real attempt to get

[41] Heaney, *A Scottish Whig*, 14.
[42] Indeed, Devine's attribution of the authorship of Graham's letters to Professor Robert Graham may have been influenced by the fact that Professor Graham was 'an early enthusiast of social medicine and a close associate of the social reformer, William Alison' (Devine, *Highland Famine*, 27), and as such a more likely candidate for the role.
[43] NLS, Lynedoch papers, MS 16057, fo. 333, Letter of introduction, 11 May 1835.
[44] Heaney, *A Scottish Whig*, 14.
[45] NLS, Lynedoch papers, MS 16049, Notes, observations, letters 1835–6 made by Graham during his tour of Ireland.

to grips with, and to understand, the position of the distressed Highlanders. There is genuine sympathy to be found in his letters.

Graham had been told by Robert Brown that getting correct information would not be easy, and so Graham spoke to as many people as he thought would be able to provide him with the information he needed; these included estate proprietors, tacksmen, agents, doctors,[46] lawyers, bankers, businessmen, schoolmasters and, principally, factors and ministers. The factor in the Highlands and Islands had immense social, political and economic influence and 'was the symbolic figure of estate authority in place of often absentee or disinterested owners'.[47] As we saw, before he left on his tour, Graham had consulted Robert Brown, who had been Clanranald's factor for the Uists from 1796 to 1811 and then factor to the duke of Hamilton, and during his tour Graham spoke with factors in all of the distressed districts he visited, including John Maxwell and Edward Gibbon in Skye, Donald and Charles Shaw in the Uists and Thomas Knox in Lewis. The frequent references in Graham's letters to the views and opinions of ministers and their position in relation to the administration of the relief funds, in particular Graham's suggestions that the government could rely on the assurances of ministers that crofters provided with credit would repay it, indeed would provide a guarantee of payment (pp. 22 and 52) provide us with examples of the leadership role which ministers played and of their position in the community as 'a distinctive elite [who] were normally respected by outsiders as fairly objective observers of social condition'.[48] The ministers were closest to the people and had a real knowledge and experience of their lives that had no equal in other members of the community with education and status, such as the factors and the proprietors. The fact that Graham sought the views of ministers as to the condition of the people and the importance he attributed to their views is confirmation of their social function as 'intermediaries or interpreters between an English-speaking state and a Gaelic-speaking community which remained largely outside the state'.[49] But Graham was aware of the dangers of ministers being too close to the people; he noted that ministers would be inclined to give as much of the food to their people as they could without, perhaps, regard to what might be a more prudential supply (p. 56). And Graham's letters also

---

[46] Medical men in the Highlands were few and far between – Hill recorded in his journal that there was 'not a medical man living within 50 miles of Loch Ewe or Ullapool' (p. 163) – as there were many difficulties associated with their recruitment (N. MacGillivray, 'Medical practice in the Highlands and Islands at the time of the potato famine: 1845–1855', *Transactions of the Gaelic Society of Inverness* 64 (2004–6), 282).

[47] A. Tindley, '"They sow the wind, they reap the whirlwind': estate management in the post-clearance Highlands, c. 1815 – c. 1900', *Northern Scotland* 3 (2012), 66–85, at 66.

[48] A. W. MacColl, *Land, Faith and the Crofting Community – Christianity and Social Criticism in the Highlands and Islands of Scotland, 1843–1893* (Edinburgh, 2006), 9.

[49] D. Paton, 'The Church in the Northern Highlands 1790–1850: Spiritual Witness and Social Crisis' (Open University, Ph.D. thesis, 2000), 53–4.

provide a good example of the conflict of interest of the minister as an
intermediary, of how the ministers 'occupied a position between landlords
and tenants which required something of a balancing act in attempting to
serve two masters';[50] his letters contain a number of references to the fact that
ministers had not made special applications to the heritors or asked for legal
assessments under the poor laws, perhaps demonstrating a reluctance to commit
the proprietors financially.

Estimates of the amount of meal that would be required to prevent starvation
and the organisation of the committees that had the responsibility for distribution
of aid, were matters that Graham raised frequently in his letters. He gave lists of
the men he considered could be trusted to serve on these committees and who
would deal efficiently and fairly with the distribution of supplies. As emphasis
of the significance of the role of ministers mentioned above, of the 30 committee
members recommended by Graham for Mull and the neighbouring islands, 17
were ministers; of the 19 recommended for Skye, 10 were ministers; of the 27
recommended for Arisaig, Glenelg, Lochalsh, Kintail, Glenshiel, Lochcarron,
Applecross, Gairloch and Lochbroom, 14 were ministers; and of the 10 committee
members recommended for Lewis, 6 were ministers. As to the quantities of meal
that might be required, he estimated the number of bolls per head which would
be needed to last until the next harvest – a period of around 5 months. He said
that the estimate was 2½ bolls (or 350 lbs) per family of 5 (2 adults and 3 children),
which gave a daily allowance of around 2½ lbs per family, or ½ lb per person
per day (p. 56).[51] Graham had been surprised at the size of this allowance that
he said had been accepted by all the committees in the areas he had visited. He
contrasted it with the ordinary allowance in the low country for one working
ploughman of 1 stone of meal per week (or 2 lbs per day). But he pointed out that
the working ploughman had other means of support and also that 'Unhappily
too, it is a moral lesson which it is necessary to teach to the poor themselves,
even in the midst of their affliction, that it is not full meals or plentiful supplies
that ought to be served out to them' (p. 71). Graham confirmed his estimate
by reference to the calculations of Thomas Knox, the Lewis factor (p. 77).
Knox wrote that the minister of Cross parish had told him that his people
needed 1 lb of meal per day for each individual – an amount which *The Times*
described as 'in point of coarseness and stint such as an Englishman would

[50]   S. M. Kidd, '"Caraid nan Gaidheal" and friend of emigration', *SHR* 80.1, no. 21 (Apr. 2002),
       69.
[51]   The Act of Union introduced English measures into Scotland but Scottish weights and
       measures gradually disappeared only after the weights and measures act of 1824 (5 Geo. IV
       c 74), which standardised the imperial measures throughout Britain, and local variations
       were still in use in some areas some years later (see I. Levitt and C. Smout, 'Some weights
       and measures in Scotland, 1843', *SHR* 56.2, no. 162 (Oct. 1977), 146–52). Graham noted the
       difficulties that were caused by the different views as to the sizes of barrels, bolls etc. (p. 53)
       and the point should be borne in mind if making comparisons with, for example, the daily
       allowances of food in the famine in 1846–7.

be ashamed to offer to his horse or dog'.[52] Knox did not believe that even this much was appropriate: it was: 'more than some families could make away with . . . can anybody believe that they ever consumed as much of their own meal. I am sure they would be compelled to give part of their allowance to others, or their cattle.'[53] Knox believed the correct estimate for a family of 5 would be 2½ bolls of meal. This might be compared with the daily allowance from the Central Board during the famine of 1847 of 1½ lbs per adult male, ¾ lb per adult female and ½ lb for each child under the age of 12, and the 'destitution test' from early 1848 of 1 lb per day for a day's labour, thought at the time to be enough to prevent starvation and, indeed, to be 'parsimonious even by the standards of other schemes established in Scotland to relieve distress';[54] or, as the radical journalist Thomas Mulock described it, to be 'systematised starvation'.[55]

Graham was clear in his letters that over-population was the key to the problem in the Highlands and Islands that had led to the destitution he witnessed. It was, he thought, caused by a variety of circumstances – the consequences of peace after the Napoleonic wars; the failure of the kelp manufacture (and on this Graham, while recognising that the proprietors had been 'thoughtless' as to the consequences of their profiting from the industry during the good times, did not hesitate to criticise the Tory government's legislative changes to the salt and barilla taxes, which, he said, were 'too hastily applied, perhaps, to be quite consistent with the truest policy' (p. 97));[56] the failure of the fisheries; the cessation of public works (but Graham also noted that public works might not always be a positive benefit – the Caledonian canal, he thought, provided an important lesson on this (p. 20)); the want of regulations by landlords; and the non-enforcement of the poor laws. He also said that the increase in the number of sheep farms had contributed to the problem – a reference, if a rather elliptical one, to the fact that the clearances, by causing congestion of poor people in marginal areas, had been a critical element in the problem.[57] Graham frequently returned in his

[52] *The Times*, 24 Apr. 1837.
[53] NRS, Papers of the Mackenzie family, earls of Seaforth, GD 46/13/199/4, Knox to Stewart Mackenzie, 7 Feb. 1837.
[54] Devine, *Highland Famine*, 128, 131 and 133.
[55] T. Mulock, *The Western Highlands and Islands of Scotland Socially Considered* (Edinburgh, 1850), 81.
[56] J. MacAskill, 'The Highland kelp proprietors and their struggle over the salt and barilla duties, 1817–1831', *Journal of Scottish Historical Studies* 26.1+2 (2006), 60–82.
[57] E. Richards, *The Highland Clearances – People, Landlords and Rural Turmoil* (Edinburgh, 2008), 416. A point which was made rather more bluntly – 'dispossessing a large number of small tenants' – by the two reporters for the Glasgow destitution committee (p. 233) and also by the anonymous author of *Observations on the Causes and Remedies of Destitution in the Highlands and Islands of Scotland* (Glasgow, 1837), 4 – 'Another cause of an excess population, not generally, but in certain quarters, is, no doubt, the introduction of sheep, to make way for whom wide tracts of land have been depopulated, and the inhabitants who did not, or could not, emigrate to America, crowded into other localities'. Sir John Hill, in his letter of

letters to two in particular of these causes: the failure of estate management
and the non-enforcement of the poor laws. He was critical of the proprietors
in their management of their estates. There had, he believed, been a lack of
regulation that had resulted in a proliferation of sub-divisions of properties that
had encouraged an unsustainable increase in the population, particularly of an
impoverished population. It was, he said 'the want of sharp active management
which is at the bottom of a great deal of this evil' (p. 27). He was also critical
of the determination of proprietors to abolish joint holdings, to enlarge
possessions and to change the systems of management of cultivation. He
gave as an example of sound estate management the island of Canna, but
this depended for its success on a much-reduced population and rigorous
application of sound principles of management: indeed, the two should go
hand in hand.[58] As to the poor laws, Graham made a number of interesting,
important and surprising comments on the effectiveness of the Scottish poor
laws in his letters to Fox Maule, and in his evidence to the 1841 select committee.
The two most prominent issues on the poor laws concerned legal assessments on
heritors for funds to be provided for the poor, and whether the able-bodied poor
were entitled to relief. It was the accepted position that the funds for the poor
should be raised voluntarily, principally through collections at the church door
and other voluntary contributions, and that if, and only if, these funds were not
sufficient should the heritors be required, as a matter of law, compulsorily to
contribute to the funds required through a legal assessment. In his *Remarks on the
Poor Laws* published in 1834, David Monypenny of Pitmilly, a former senator of
the College of Justice, had been crystal clear:

> it has been held and acknowledged as law, that an assessment need not,
> and ought not, to be introduced in any parish in which the poor can be
> maintained without it . . . the characteristic, in short, of the Scottish system
> is, and always has been . . . to shun [legal] assessment as a great and regularly
> increasing evil.[59]

Reports of the general assembly of the Church of Scotland on the poor
laws in 1817, 1818 and 1820[60] had all made the same point – the 1818 report being

---

[58] 16 June 1837 to the Treasury, observed that the conversion in Skye of farms and 'vast ranges
of' grazing lands was a 'great cause of the want of employment for the people' (p. 171).

[58] The system of management on Canna did not, however, prevent subsequent emigration and
clearance from the island (J. L. Campbell, *Canna – The Story of a Hebridean Island* (Edinburgh,
1994), 157–71).

[59] D. Monypenny, *Remarks on the Poor Laws and on the Method of Providing for the Poor in Scotland*
(Edinburgh, 1834), 21–3.

[60] [PP] 1817 VI (462), *Report from the Select Committee on the Poor Laws with the Minutes of Evidence
Taken before the Committee and an Appendix*, 145–153; [PP] 1818 V (358), *Third Report from the
Select Committee on the Poor Laws (1818) with an Appendix Containing Returns from the General
Assembly of the Church of Scotland*, 22–85; [PP] 1820 XX (195), *Supplementary Report of the
Committee of the General Assembly on the Management of the Poor in Scotland*.

especially clear about the evils of the 'pernicious tendency in general . . . of compulsory taxation'. 'It was', the committee who produced the report said,

> Their decided conviction, not only that the practice of legal and compulsory assessments for the support of the poor is radically unwise and dangerous, but also that the crisis has already arrived, when Scotland should in every quarter take the alarm and form precautions against the farther spread in our country of so baneful a national calamity.[61]

Of course, it would be wrong to suggest that this seemingly decisive interpretation of the poor laws was unchallenged, or that it really reflected what the evidence that had been collected for the purposes of the report actually said. Rosalind Mitchison has shown that compulsory assessment had featured prominently in the founding statutes of the Scottish poor laws but that it had been interpreted out of existence by the early years of the nineteenth century, and that the distinguished group of 'new Whig' lawyers, which included such men as Henry Cockburn, J. A. Murray, James Moncrieff, Francis Jeffrey, T. F. Kennedy, G. J. Bell, Alexander Dunlop and David Monypenny, made sure that this interpretation remained the dominant one.[62] It was also the accepted position that the able-bodied poor were not entitled to poor relief, notwithstanding a Court of Session decision that suggested the opposite.[63] It was, again, the powerful clique of new Whig lawyers that had achieved this interpretation.[64]

Robert Graham as a Whig advocate and the intimate friend and colleague of many of these new Whig lawyers,[65] men who, as Rosalind Mitchison entertainingly put it, had nobbled the umpire, would have been expected to take the same position on these two issues of the Scottish poor laws, particularly as he had played an influential part as a member of the committee of the general assembly that produced the reports of 1818 and 1820 that had so forcefully warned of the dangers of legal assessments.[66] On the issue of the able-bodied poor, Graham did toe the party line. The awkward

---

[61] [PP] 1818 V (358), 31. Graham was a member of this committee.

[62] R. Mitchison, *The Old Poor Law in Scotland – The Experience of Poverty, 1574–1845* (Edinburgh, 2000), 31, 149.

[63] Pollock v. Darling (1804), Morr. 10,591, a decision that was only finally over-ruled in 1852 in McWilliam v. Adams (1852), MacQueen's Appeals, vol. i, 220–34.

[64] R. Mitchison, 'The creation of the disablement rule in the Scottish poor law', in T. C. Smout (ed.), *The Search for Wealth and Security* (London, 1979), 199–217, which describes how the Scottish poor laws were subverted by a battery of Whig legal opinion.

[65] See the Biographical Notes on p. xiv.

[66] NRS, Register of general assembly at Edinburgh, CH 1/2/78; NLS, Lynedoch papers, MS 16028, fos. 53–4, Graham to Lord Chancellor, 19 June 1820, Graham to Sec. of State for the Home Dept., 20 June 1820 (fos. 55–6); [PP] 1820 XX (195), 130. Graham had been appointed to the general assembly in April 1811 as the ruling elder for the burgh of Perth (NLS, Lynedoch papers, MS 16025, fo. 14, Peddie to Graham, 3 Apr. 1811).

case of Pollock v. Darling was, he thought, a bad decision and 'I believe I am safe in stating that, in the opinion of the bar, it could not be supported'.[67] But on the issue of legal assessments, he was distinctly off-message. In his letters to Fox Maule, Graham had frequently noted that no legal assessment had been made in the parish he was examining, but he also said that he was no advocate of compulsory assessments (p. 17) and that he thought they were a 'baneful remedy' (p. 26). However, he had also said that the government should not be asked to contribute until the provisions of the poor laws had been fully enforced. And by the time he came to write his final letter of 6 May 1837, he was very clear in his criticism of what he described as the 'non-enforcement of the poor laws by the kirk session' (p. 102); he wrote that under, as he put it, the modified poor law, assessments need not necessarily be compulsory if the voluntary contributions were sufficient to maintain the poor who were entitled to relief. But – and this is where he parted company from his colleagues – he was in favour of an element of compulsion. He said, albeit reluctantly, that the underlying obligations for legal assessments *should* be enforced (p. 17) and, furthermore, that he had a preference for legal assessments over voluntary contributions; more was gained, Graham said, by forcing all parties to pay.[68] He also said (and, again, in this he parted company with the mainstream view that relief for the poor, and especially relief that was compulsorily provided, was bad for the recipient) that he did not believe there was any difference between legal and voluntary assessment in their effect on the moral character of the people.[69] As if to emphasise the gap that had opened up between Graham's views on enforcement of the poor laws and the mainstream views, a committee of the general assembly under the chairmanship of Alexander Dunlop reported in 1839 that the characteristic distinction of the Scottish poor law system was that 'it never imposes a compulsory assessment so long as hopes can be reasonably entertained of procuring without it the needful assistance'.[70] But the 1839 Poor Law Report revealed that in the years 1835, 1836 and 1837 there had been no legal assessments in any of the parishes that had been affected by the destitution, and that the availability of voluntary funds there fell woefully short of what was required. Graham's own letters to Fox Maule had, time after time, recorded the pitifully small amounts available for the poor which were raised through church collections and the fact that there had been no legal assessments; and the 1839 Poor Law Report noted that the parish of Kilmuir in Skye forcibly illustrated the point: in March 1836 the sum of £6–3–6 collected at the church door had been divided among sixty-eight paupers but, the minister said, if the available 'funds had been of greater amount it would

---

[67] 1841 SC, Q 366.
[68] 1841 SC, Q 357.
[69] 1841 SC, Q 337.
[70] 1839 Poor Law Report, 4 (this part of the report was written by David Monypenny of Pitmilly). Graham did not serve on this committee.

be necessary to admit no fewer than 200 paupers on the roll'.[71] If ever there had been a case for the enforcement of legal assessments under the poor laws, the position of the Highlands and Islands in 1837 was surely it. And yet the 1839 Poor Law Report made no encouraging noises in this direction. Nor, indeed, did the report in 1844 of the royal commission on the Scottish poor law. The commissioners were opposed to a compulsory assessment; in their view 'the desired result will be best obtained, not so much by authoritative interference with the managers as by the influence of reason and good feeling, aided by public opinion, in gradually leading them to a right exercise of the powers with which they are invested'. If the 'voluntary method' failed, the commissioners said, 'recourse can always be had to an assessment according to the provisions of the existing law'.[72] But it was precisely because the voluntary method had so obviously failed in the Highlands and Islands in 1837 and yet there had been no recourse to legal assessments in any of the parishes that Graham had visited, that Graham had felt there was no alternative but to call for the compulsory enforcement of legal assessments. It was not enough to rely on reason, good feeling or public opinion. Graham's words had, however, fallen on deaf ears.[73] The poor laws in the Highlands and Islands were, indeed, 'little more than a dead letter',[74] a 'do nothing'[75] system.

But Graham was also clear that the Scottish poor laws, even if properly enforced, 'would do little to meet the present difficulties' (p. 103) in the Highlands and Islands; while the lame and the maim of course needed help, the great body of those who needed help were the able-bodied poor for whom there was a want of occupation: the poor laws, he said, did not provide for them. Nor did the 1844 royal commission conclude that they should; the commissioners accepted 'the Whig story that [the able-bodied poor] had never been entitled to aid' – adding the 'mythical historical dimension' which had arisen through the misrepresentation of the past by clergy and lawyers, that this was the 'distinguishing excellence' of the old Scottish poor laws.[76] It is interesting to note that six months before Graham was writing, George Nicholls had concluded that a general famine was 'a contingency altogether above the powers of a poor law to provide for'; this was in the context of his recommendation for an Irish

[71] 1839 Poor Law Report, 13.
[72] [PP] 1844 XX (557), *Report from Her Majesty's Commissioners for Inquiring into the Administration and Practical Operation of the Poor Laws in Scotland*, xviii–xix.
[73] It does not appear that Graham gave any evidence to the royal commission or that his 1837 report was considered by it. Indeed, the events of 1837 were very sparsely mentioned in the evidence that was given.
[74] A. Fullarton and C. R. Baird, *Remarks on the Evils at Present Affecting the Highlands and Islands of Scotland; with Some Suggestions as to their Remedies* (Glasgow, 1838), 64. In his evidence to the 1841 select committee, Baird had said that it was 'absolutely necessary to have a compulsory provision for the poor in the Highlands and Islands' (1841 SC, 111).
[75] *Morning Chronicle*, 31 May 1838.
[76] Mitchison, *Poor Law*, 210.

poor law that did make compulsory provision for the able-bodied through the workhouse system.[77]

Over-population was, for Graham, the key to the problem. It was a matter, he said, that the government had to attend to. The 'over-population' theory was later promoted by a number of people during the 1847 famine, but Devine argues that the proponents of the theory began from a false premise: the problem was not that there were too many people, but too few secure economic opportunities for those who lived in the Highlands.[78] This is not a criticism that can be levelled at Graham. He said very clearly that 'the evil consists in the want of occupation for the great mass of the population in any way which will pay in any quarter' (p. 103). But Graham was also convinced that even with all the employment that could be provided from all the obvious sources (and he suggested the improvement of roads and the fisheries) it was hardly to be expected that in future years the existing population could, as he put it, 'be carried through without adventitious supplies'. This was a pre-industrial Malthusian world. As Eric Richards has said, 'the vulnerability of the Highlands to famine in the 1840s was a consequence of the perpetuation of pre-industrial conditions; in essence the dangerously increasing population was caught in an economy in which the demand for labour was declining'.[79] Graham believed, therefore, that 'to whatever extent in other ways employment can be found, emigration in one shape or another must continue to take place' (p. 107). He gave a prophetic warning: 'Within a given time, famine and disease would give bounds to the evil, if other means are permanently withheld' (p. 103). What was required was government-aided emigration on a great scale. For Graham, a state of equilibrium in the Highlands as regards the level of population and the means of subsistence could only be achieved by reducing the population through emigration, provided this was also linked to a rational and properly policed system of estate management. The two had to go hand-in-glove.[80] Emigration on its own was not a cure-all for long-term poverty.

It is notable that this reflected what the Rev. Robert Malthus had said on the subject in 1827. In his earlier writings, Malthus had been clear that emigration could never be an adequate solution to the problem of over-population because of the strong tendency for the vacuum created by emigration to be filled by a re-growth in the population – the 'vacuum effect'.[81] However, in his evidence

[77] [PP] 1837 LI (69), *Report of Geo. Nicholls, Esq., to His Majesty's Principal Secretary of State for the Home Department, on Poor Laws, Ireland*, 7 and 21.
[78] Devine, *Highland Famine*, 296.
[79] Richards, *The Highland Clearances*, 416. See also E. Richards, 'Highland emigration in the age of Malthus: Scourie, 1841–55', *Northern Scotland* 2, new series (2011), 60–82; and E. Richards, 'Malthus and the uses of British emigration', in K. Fedorowich and A. S. Thompson (eds.), *Empire, Identity and Migration in the British World* (Manchester, 2013).
[80] A point that was also made by the Edinburgh committee (see p. 223 below).
[81] See Richards, 'Malthus and the uses of British emigration'.

to the 1826–7 select committee on emigration, Malthus had been a little more positive. Asked what measures he suggested should be adopted to render a system of emigration in Ireland effective, and what would contribute to avoiding the vacuum effect, Malthus told the committee that the prevention of sub-letting without landlord consent would be a useful measure but that what would be most beneficial would be 'a determination on the part of the landlords to manage their lands in a different way'; he did not see a way for this to be enforced by the government and so 'a great deal must depend on the landlords themselves'.[82] In his letter of 6 May 1837, Graham was more sanguine than Malthus had been. He said that while the government might recoil at the economic sense of the necessary degree of emigration, he believed that if 'the landlords, as well as tenants, shall be thus compelled to adopt a more rational system of managing their lands' this would be followed by a return to sound principle. It was vital, Graham said, for 'the proprietors [to be] participators in this scheme . . . and if they bend their minds to the subject . . . there can be no great difficulty in keeping the population within the proper bounds' (p. 108). If necessary, the government should provide some rigid method of enforcing this participation[83] and in one of his earlier letters to Fox Maule, Graham had made clear that he believed the government should be prepared to step in to regulate matters as between landlord and tenant (p. 92).[84] Both Malthus and Graham advocated the pulling down of houses vacated by the emigrants and that landlords should be prevented from building afresh, as a security against 'recurrence of the abuses'.[85]

The government had been conducting assisted emigration to New South Wales and Van Diemen's Land; Dr David Boyter, RN, a naval surgeon, had been appointed in 1836 by Sir Richard Burke, the governor of New South Wales, as 'colonial emigration agent' in Scotland with a roving commission to find – and these are the two crucial words – suitable candidates for emigration, and to liaise with T. F. Elliot, the British government's agent-general for bounty emigration.[86] Boyter had been told in April 1837 by Lord Glenelg, the secretary of state for the colonies, that in consequence of applications to the government from parties on the west coast of Scotland for assistance for emigration,[87] Glenelg considered it would 'be expedient to dispatch one or two

---

[82] [PP] 1826–7 V (550), Q 3326.
[83] 1841 SC, Q 398.
[84] This was in relation to arrangements between proprietors and fishermen, but the language used by Graham suggests that he would also countenance government interference in estate management.
[85] [PP] 1826–7 V (550), Q 3391; 1841 SC, Q 448.
[86] M. Ray, 'Elliot, Sir Thomas Frederick (1808–1880)', *ODNB*.
[87] Bowie and the Rev. Dr Macleod had had meetings with Glenelg when they came to London as part of the deputation to the Treasury referred to above, and Bowie later recorded that 'the great question of Emigration was speedily taken up by Lord Glenelg . . . with a degree of ardor and kindly feeling which does honor to his Lordship's head and heart' and that the government had agreed to bear the whole expense of the passage of

ships from the Clyde to New South Wales in the course of the present spring
with emigrants of a suitable class for that colony' and that Boyter should liaise
with the Edinburgh and Glasgow committees to see if a 'sufficient number
of married persons of good character and of an age not exceeding thirty
five' could be found in the Highlands.[88] The official criteria – the suitable
candidates – for government-assisted emigrants to New South Wales and Van
Diemen's Land had been clearly spelled out by Elliot, and they went further
than insisting on married people under the age of 35. The people selected had
to be 'deemed likely to prove eligible settlers. They must belong to the class
either of mechanics or if persons capable of being useful farm servants, must
be married men with their wives living and be accompanied by their wives
and children to the colony, the age of neither the husband or wife to exceed
thirty, or at utmost thirty five years.'[89] But the need, Graham was told again
and again, was for emigration to be conducted on the basis of whole families
and not on this selective basis. Graham wrote to Fox Maule that 'no advantage
can come to this country by inducing the best and most useful parts of the
population to go while the feeble and the least enterprising are left behind.'
(p. 62). The Edinburgh committee made the same point; in the Highlands,
the committee said, 'there had always been a deficiency of skilful labourers,
such as intelligent shepherds, farm servants and mechanics', and such
people had had to be brought in from 'the more cultivated districts; in
making their selection, the emigration agents have in many, if not in most
instances, chosen those parties whom it would be for the interest of the
district to retain'.[90] While it was, of course, in the financial interest of the
proprietors to retain the more useful members of the community, there was a
more fundamental point at stake (albeit not one which may have been evident
to those who criticised the selection policy), a point that has been explained by
Cormac O'Grada in relation to the Irish famine in 1847: selective emigration
was an inefficient form of disaster relief because it did not target those who
were at greatest risk of dying. Those who emigrated from Ireland were more
likely to have been from the artisanal or small-farm background – precisely
the category that Elliot's selection criteria required – than from the proletarian
populace who suffered most from famine conditions.[91]

emigrants to Australia (J. Bowie, *Notes on Australia for the Information of Intending Emigrants* (Edinburgh, 1837), 5–6).

[88] TNA:PRO, War and Colonial Department and Colonial Office: Emigration original correspondence, CO 384/42, Grey to Boyter, 11 Apr. 1837; Macmillan, *Scotland and Australia*, 272–6 and 279; and M. Harper, *Adventurers and Exiles – The Great Scottish Exodus* (London, 2003), 133.

[89] TNA:PRO, War and Colonial Department and Colonial Office: Emigration original correspondence, CO 384/42/89, Elliot to a new surgeon, 3 July 1837.

[90] TNA:PRO, War and Colonial Department and Colonial Office: Emigration original correspondence, CO 384/50, Minute of Edinburgh destitution committee, 25 July 1838.

[91] C. O'Grada, *Black '47 and Beyond – The Great Irish Famine* (Princeton, 1999), 107.

The period from 1815 to the end of the 1840s marked a considerable change in the attitude of Highland landlords towards emigration. It has been said that it was not until the end of this period that a majority of landowners who were against emigration had turned into a majority which accepted the necessity of it.[92] However, the kelp proprietors, who were faced with the problems caused by the removal in the 1820s of the fiscal support for the industry, had, during those years, not just accepted the necessity of emigration but actively canvassed it,[93] and during the recurrent subsistence crises of the early nineteenth century, aid for the tenantry provided by landowners and distributed by the factors had become the norm. The factors, who were faced with the social consequences of these crises, in particular those from the kelp estates, felt that the only solution to the Highland problem was massive emigration of the poor population.[94] It is no surprise, therefore, to find that on Graham's tour of the distressed districts the issue of the need for emigration was raised frequently by many of the people he spoke to, in particular estate proprietors, ministers and factors. Indeed it is no exaggeration to say that Graham was assailed on all sides by those who saw no option but for extensive emigration. So far as the ministers were concerned, many of them genuinely believed that emigration would help alleviate the suffering of their parishioners,[95] and strongly supported it – in his evidence to the 1841 select committee on emigration, Charles Baird declared that 'I can show from reports and letters now before me that in 44 cases out of 49 the clergymen of the Highland parishes, to whom the question was specially put, recommended an extensive emigration'.[96] It is no surprise, therefore, that Graham should have been faced with repeated requests from factors and ministers for government-aided emigration; and although it is not possible to judge the extent to which his letters to the government on the subject of emigration were influenced or flavoured by such frequently and often forcefully expressed opinions we should bear such a possibility in mind; in this context we might take note of Graham's views on emigration as a young man. In an account of a journey he had made to the Highlands in the autumn of 1805 he commented that

[92] J. M. Cameron, 'A Study of the Factors that Assisted and Directed Scottish Emigration to Upper Canada, 1815–1855' (University of Glasgow, Ph.D. thesis, 1970), 295.

[93] See the correspondence between James Stewart Mackenzie of Seaforth and the then Chancellor of the Exchequer, Nicholas Vansittart, in 1822 and the arguments in the 1827 memorial and report of the kelp proprietors as described in MacAskill, 'The Highland kelp proprietors', 60–82; and the reports of Clanranald's factor, Duncan Shaw at NRS, Papers of the MacDonald family of Clanranald, GD 201/5/1217/46, 29 Jan. 1827, and GD 201/1/354, 8 May 1827, and also GD 201/4/97, Shaw to Hunter, 25 Feb. 1827.

[94] Tindley, 'Estate management', 72.

[95] S. M. Kidd, 'The Prose Writings of Rev. Alexander MacGregor, 1806–1881' (University of Edinburgh, Ph.D. thesis, 1999), 77.

[96] 1841 SC, 111.

Much has of late been said and written as to the propriety of emigration. The necessity of de-populating the Highlands for the improvement of the country in general has been gravely insisted on.[97] The impossibility of preventing emigration has been roundly averred. But there is still a very wide field between enforcing a measure and allowing it, and an important distinction ought to be observed betwixt encouraging emigration and tacitly permitting it. If it is necessary for our welfare and for the support of the Highlanders that they should leave their native hills, we can only submit to the necessity. But do not let us force our men away; do not let us hold out temptations to them in another land. Throughout the whole of Scotland there are vast tracts of unimproved land which may find employment for thousands.[98]

In his early letters to Fox Maule, Graham was reluctant to pass on the views on emigration and the role the government should have; he was concerned that in doing so he might be 'considered as out stepping the bounds of duty required of me', but he resolved this dilemma by telling Fox Maule (p. 28) that

> to report exclusively upon the failure of the last crop as creating destitution would be to report on a small portion of the causes of the present affliction, and would reduce my duty simply to a question of degree, a mere affair of how many weeks or months of additional sufficiency are likely to occur this year in the same districts, where from an excess of population, every year there is a portion, and in many of them a great portion of necessary misery.

This passage and the strength of the argument for extensive government-aided emigration presented by Graham in his final letter of 6 May 1837 and the way it was presented – in particular that emigration was only part of his suggested remedy: it had to be linked to a proper system of estate management for which the proprietors would be principally responsible – suggest that he was not just mouthing the opinions of others, but that he had reached his own independent conclusions on the subject.

Graham's recommendations for government-aided emigration on a great scale without the imposition of strict selection criteria were passed by the Home Office to the Treasury and by the Treasury to Lord Glenelg at the Colonial Office, who asked Thomas Elliot to give them his consideration.[99]

---

[97] Graham's account of his tour was written around the time of the publication of the earl of Selkirk's book *Observations on the Present State of the Highlands of Scotland with a View of the Possible Causes and Probable Consequences of Emigration* (London, 1805).

[98] Private papers of R. Maxtone Graham, Robert Graham, 'A Tour thro' part of Scotland in Autumn 1805', 43.

[99] Requests to Hill from the Edinburgh and Glasgow committees that he should bring to the attention of the Treasury their views that extensive emigration was needed (pp. 191, 192 and 285) were also passed by the Treasury to the Colonial Office.

Although Elliot did concede that 'few cases could arise to which the remedy of emigration on a great scale would appear to be more appropriate than to this of the distress in the Hebrides' and that 'to make a deep impression on the case' emigration should include the aged, the weak and the sick and not just the active and enterprising, he proceeded to give a long list of reasons why he could not recommend such a government-assisted emigration, albeit making it clear that the reasons he gave were not insurmountable – 'that being a question involving general principles of policy' which he had not been asked to advise on (p. 269). Lord Glenelg suggested, following Elliot's conclusions, that, while such emigration to New South Wales and Van Diemen's Land was not possible, the Treasury might perhaps consider the alternative of British North America; but, as he pointed out that the funds available to the government for emigration to Australia could not be used for this, any such scheme would have to be at the public expense (p. 273) – not an observation that would have appealed to the Treasury. The thorny problem of cost and availability of public funds raised its head again when, at the beginning of 1838, Bowie and the Edinburgh committee returned to the subject, this time linking it with a proposal that the surplus funds available to the destitution committees should be added to government funds, for the purpose of emigration to Canada.[100] Again, Thomas Elliot was asked to consider the proposal and, again, he quashed it, and this time squarely on the basis of the propriety of public funds being used for the purpose. It would, he said, create a dangerous precedent (he referred to a probable future request from Ireland) and the point of principle involved – should emigration be made an object of national encouragement, fostered by national funds – had never, he said, been resolved. The main difficulty, Elliot said, was that there were no funds available 'and to ask them on this particular occasion would be to sanction a highly important and extensive principle which has not been discussed and adopted on its own merits.'[101] But, while Graham's recommendation and the destitution committees' requests for government-funded emigration fell on stony ground, they were not buried without trace. In June 1840, William Smith O'Brien, the Irish nationalist and MP for Limerick County urged large-scale state assisted emigration to a poorly attended House of Commons, and although this was rejected by the government,[102] (and, again, the appropriateness of providing public funds for such an exercise was an issue), a short debate was held in February 1841 on the proposal of Henry Baillie, the Tory MP for Inverness-shire,[103] for the establishment of a select committee to

[100] NLS, Lynedoch papers, MS 16147, Report of the Edinburgh committee, 21 Dec. 1837 (see p. 220); TNA:PRO, War and Colonial Department and Colonial Office: Emigration original correspondence, CO 384/50, Bowie to Grey, 5 Jan. 1838.
[101] TNA:PRO, War and Colonial Department and Colonial Office: Emigration original correspondence, CO 384/46, Elliot to Stephen, 2 Feb. 1838.
[102] [Parl. Debs] third series, vol. liv, cols. 832–94, 2 June 1840.
[103] Baillie, the grandson of Evan Baillie of Dochfour, was a close associate of Disraeli and a

inquire into the condition of the population of the western Highlands of Scotland with a view to affording the people relief by means of emigration.[104] Baillie told the house that he was not an enthusiast in the cause of large-scale government-assisted emigration 'unless a very urgent, special, and peculiar case could be made out'. He believed such a case existed in the Highlands and Islands, caused by the collapse of the kelp-manufacturing industry. The industry, he said, had 'long been fostered and encouraged, perhaps unsuitably, by protecting duties' and the removal of that protection[105] had left the Highlanders with

> no hope or expectation that their condition could ever be improved, – no influx of capital, no ingenuity of man could devise any means by which those barren rocks and mountains which they inhabited could be made capable of affording food for the population which at present existed. For them there was but the choice of one or two alternatives – either to remain where they were and perish by diseases engendered by the unwholesome, improper, and insufficient food, or to remove to some distant country, where by industry they might hope to obtain the means of existence.

It was, Baillie said, the 'famine which it must be remembered by the House took place in the year 1837' that was 'the natural consequence of the state of things which he had described'. The prompt assistance of the government and the philanthropy and generosity of the British public in 1837 had, Baillie said, averted the evil in its course but

> the disease was not cured, it still existed, and so certainly and so surely as that failures of their crops must, in the nature of things, again take place, so certainly would that famine again return, so surely would Government be called upon to interfere, and the British public be again appealed to.

This was not, Baillie thought, something that ought to exist in a civilised country and he urged that the House should ask itself 'whether the Legislature was not bound to take some steps to remove an evil which it had itself in a great measure been the means of creating. . . . All he asked was for a committee.'

Lord John Russell, the then secretary of state for the Colonies, repeating what he had said during the 1840 debate on emigration,[106] declared that he did not believe the situation in the Highlands and Islands presented a special case for the grant of public money for emigration, and he was also concerned that such a grant, if made, would create a difficult precedent leading to claims from

---

member of the Young England group. He was the MP for Inverness-shire between 1840 and 1868 and served as joint secretary of the Board of Control in 1852 and as under-secretary of state for India between 1858 and 1859.

[104] [Parl. Debs] third series, vol. lvi, cols 514–28, 11 Feb. 1841.
[105] See MacAskill, 'The Highland kelp proprietors', 60–82.
[106] [Parl. Debs] third series, vol. liv, cols 885–91, 2 June 1840.

others who were equally distressed from the 'depression of particular species of industry' – he had in mind the hand-loom weavers. However, although Russell thought that 'there are many reasons for differing from the conclusions to which [Mr Baillie] has come', he 'would not take the harsh steps of objecting to a committee of inquiry'. Support for an inquiry, but not for the principle of state-funded emigration, also came from Sir Robert Peel and Francis Baring, the then Chancellor of the Exchequer. Baring, however, had particular concerns over the wording of Baillie's proposal – he

> Objected, above all, to raising expectations which it would be impossible to realise, and as the wording of the motion might lead to misconstruction, he advised that 'with a view to affording relief' should be erased, and 'on the practicability of affording relief' be substituted.[107]

Joseph Hume, the radical MP for Middlesex, objected to both an inquiry and the principle of public money being used for emigration. It is strange that neither Baillie nor any of the other contributors to the debate made any mention of Robert Graham's appointment in 1837 to inquire into the state of the Highlands and Islands or, indeed, of his principal recommendation – published as a parliamentary paper – for large-scale state-assisted emigration. A select committee was, however, set up under the chairmanship of Henry Baillie.

The 1837 destitution featured prominently in the evidence given to the select committee.[108] One of the principal witnesses was Robert Graham. He could be forgiven if he had felt frustrated that he considered it necessary to repeat *verbatim* large chunks of his letters to the Home Office in 1837. The two reports of the select committee published in March and May 1841 reached conclusions that were strikingly similar to those reached by Graham in his final letter of May 1837: in its second report, the select committee warned the government that 'the country is not only liable to a return of such a visitation as that which occurred in the years 1836 and 1837, but that in the nature of things, it must recur'.[109] Graham's message to the Home Office in his May 1837 letter had been that 'it is hardly to be expected, under the present circumstances of the Highlands, that in future years the present population can possibly be carried through without adventitious

---

[107] The motion that was agreed to was 'to inquire into the condition of the population of the Islands and Highlands of Scotland, and into the practicability of affording the people relief by means of emigration'. Baring also raised concerns over the extent to which the government should interfere in such matters, as is mentioned below.
[108] 1841 select committee. See, in particular, the evidence of Robert Graham, Charles Baird (whose evidence was largely a restatement of his and Allan Fullarton's book *Remarks*), John Bowie, the Rev. Dr Norman Macleod, Evander McIver, Andrew Scott, Alexander Mackinnon, Alexander Macdonald and Thomas Knox. McIver's evidence is discussed in E. Richards and A. M. Tindley, 'After the clearances: Evander McIver and the "Highland Question", 1835–73', *Rural History* 23.1 (2012), 41–57.
[109] 1841 SC, 24 May 1841, iv.

supplies'. It was, he said, 'very likely' that there would be 'a recurrence of distress experienced, not much less in degree than now' (p. 107).

No action was taken by the government on the findings and reports of the select committee, and, indeed, it would seem that Graham's letters and the reports of the 1841 select committee were forgotten about, because in the aftermath of the major famine in 1846–7 'several proposals came from a number of quarters in Scotland that government should undertake an inquiry into the social and economic conditions of the Highlands in order to probe the reasons for the disaster which had overwhelmed its society. After due consideration, all these suggestions were rejected.'[110] It was not until 1851 that the next inquiry, by Sir John McNeill, was set up, which, finally, resulted in action being taken by the government over a significant level of assisted emigration. McNeill expressly acknowledged the prophetic warning in Graham's final letter and said of it and of the same warning by the 1841 select committee: 'on both occasions, the necessity of emigration with a view to avert greater evils than had then been endured, was strongly expressed. The predictions of that time have been verified. The evil has increased.'[111]

★

Captain Sir John Hill was the obvious man for the Chancellor of the Exchequer to turn to, to take charge of the administration of the fund of £10,000 that the government was to provide for the purchase of seed. He had just returned in October 1836 from the north-west coast of Donegal in Ireland, where he had been conducting a similar operation for the Treasury,[112] and he had spent three months on the west coast of Ireland in the summer of 1831 engaged in administering government aid.[113] Hill was summoned to the Treasury, where he met Alexander Spearman, the assistant secretary, and the Chancellor of the Exchequer on 15 March 1837, and together with George Waller, who was to

110 Devine, *Highland Famine*, 121.
111 [PP] 1851 XXVI (1397), *Report to the Board of Supervision by Sir John McNeill, GCB on the Western Highlands and Islands*, xxxvi. It should, of course, be acknowledged that voices were raised against the need for emigration – e.g. William Pulteny Alison (*Letter to Sir John McNeill, GCB on Highland Destitution and the Adequacy or Inadequacy of Emigration as a Remedy* (Edinburgh, 1851)) and Dr John Mackenzie (*Letter to Lord John Russell on Sir John McNeill's Report of the State of the Highlands and Islands of Scotland* (Edinburgh, 1851)); and N. MacGillivray, 'Dr John Mackenzie (1803–1886): proponent of scientific agriculture and opponent of Highland emigration' (*Journal of Scottish Historical Studies* 33.1 (2013), 81–100); and there was much contemporary debate over the extent to which the emigration that did take place in the aftermath of the 1847 famine did, in fact, benefit those who remained behind (Devine, *Highland Famine*, 294–6).
112 NLI, Monteagle papers, MS 13383, bundle 1, Spring Rice to Hill, 15 July 1836; [PP] 1846 XXXVII (734), *Correspondence and Accounts Relating to the Different Occasions on which Measures were Taken for the Relief of the People Suffering from Scarcity in Ireland between the Years 1822 and 1839*, 17–20.
113 His letters to Sir James Graham relating to this operation are at BL, Graham papers, Add. MS 79659, fos. 1–139, and his personal journal is at NLI, Journal MS 41,705/1–8.

act as his secretary,[114] he left for Edinburgh by the mail coach the next evening, arriving in Edinburgh on the afternoon of 17 March. Hill and Waller then spent the next 10 weeks shuttling between Edinburgh, Glasgow and Aberdeen liaising with the destitution committees and negotiating for the purchase and distribution of seed corn and potatoes. By the end of May he had secured the necessary supplies, and the Treasury instructed him to make a tour of all the food depots in the distressed districts, to establish if there was a need for government aid in the supply of food (p. 282). Hill and Waller left Glasgow on this tour on 29 May and returned to Glasgow on the 23 June 1837. Their journey took them by steamer from Greenock to the head of Loch Long and then overland to Oban and Fort William, from where they took the steamer to the islands of Mull and Skye. They joined the revenue cutter, *Prince of Wales* at Portree and from there they sailed to South Uist, Benbecula, North Uist, Harris and Lewis. On their return from Stornoway they sailed to Ullapool and then Poolewe on the mainland and then to Oban, where they left the *Prince of Wales* and retraced their outward journey overland to Glasgow. After a brief holiday with his wife and one of his daughters, who had joined him – he describes the places they visited in his journal – Hill returned to the dockyard at Deptford at the beginning of August.

Hill's letters to the Treasury concerning his work in Edinburgh, Glasgow and Aberdeen are formal and to the point, but informative as to his work in securing and shipping supplies of seed and his experiences with the committees in Edinburgh and Glasgow and the tensions between these committees mentioned above. Hill's letters telling Spearman of his visits to the Highland depots were written principally so that the Treasury could decide if government relief for food supplies was required, but while they are more descriptive of what he saw and heard, they are, again, formal and to the point. All his letters were written, as one would expect, in the somewhat stilted, economical style of the report of a naval officer to his superiors and give the information required but without embellishment. Hill's journal entries remind us of his profession: each day starts with a weather report as if Hill is making an entry in a ship's log. They do, however, provide more private insight into his time in Scotland, giving a more personal flavour, and so are a more interesting reflection on the man. Much of his journal is taken up with recording the great and the good whom he met, dined with and had musical evenings with; it is difficult to escape the conclusion that he was a bit of a social climber. He had an eye for the ladies and his journal contains a number of references to those he met on social occasions: some

---

[114] George Waller, of Portsea. George was Alfred Waller's brother who was a junior clerk at the Treasury and also acted as Lord Lynedoch's secretary, and who had been Hill's secretary on his mission to Ireland in 1836 but who, on this occasion, did not receive permission to go with Hill on the ground that 'he could not be spared' (NLS, Lynedoch papers, MS 16035, fos. 1–2, Alfred Waller to Graham, 28 Mar. 1837).

flattering, others less so. He was particularly taken by Lady Bruce, the wife of Sir Michael Bruce of Stenhouse: 'a very handsome woman . . . dressed in a green velvet and velvet head dress with fur tippet and gold ornaments' (p. 125). But Lady Strathmore, the wife of the earl of Strathmore, he dismissed as being 'very short and fat' (p. 144).

Hill, who visited the distressed districts after most of the relief of seed and food had been distributed, did not see any requirement for government-aided food supplies. He did, however, make a number of critical comments on how some of the local committees had dealt with the supplies of meal from the destitution committees – at Oban, for example, Hill found the oats being badly stored and eaten by rats, and he described the committee as being comprised of dealers and jobbers (p. 150). There are a number of, perhaps self-satisfied, references in his letters and journal to how well the crops sown with his seed supplies were coming on (pp. 158, 160 and 169) and Hill saw, by and large, a people who, he said, were well fed and clothed. He had some scathing comments on what he perceived as laziness, indolence and lack of personal discipline of the Highlanders. It is, perhaps, no surprise that a man whose naval career had been spent in a life that was, for the ordinary seaman, 'positively Hobbesian in its nastiness, brutality and brevity'[115] should have been hardened to scenes of destitution and poverty, but Hill, it seems, also believed that at least some of the Highlanders he came across in his travels through the destitute districts were not helping themselves. He referred to the fact that 'the men are more or less indolent and lazy and fond of hanging about with their hands in their pockets, instead of being industrious and keeping their potato grounds clear of weeds' (p. 160); and, 'the men [in Skye] are as indolent as those in the Long Island' (p. 169). His journal contains more references to indolence and comparisons with the Irish poor and their living conditions (pp. 151, 153, 154, 155 and 166). Hill had reported in similar terms about Ireland in 1836 when he said: 'The people are naturally indolent, *improvident*, and un-enterprising, the men appearing to spend half the time in attending the fairs, which are extremely numerous, and these encourage the illicit distiller, much to the detriment of their moral character'.[116]

Hill regarded himself as the guardian of the public purse. On his mission to Ireland in 1831 he had been told to resist every attempt by proprietors and local interests to extract as much aid as possible,[117] and at the finish of his duties there he received a knighthood as a reward for resisting the imprecations of the proprietors by whom he had 'been so much abused [and] whose hands he kept with difficulty out of the public purse'.[118] Similarly, on his return from Ireland

---

[115] N. Jones, 'Life on the ocean wave', *Literary Review* (Oct. 2008), 42.
[116] [PP] 1846 XXXVII (734), 17.
[117] BL, Graham papers, Add. MS 79659, fos. 75–6, Graham to Hill, 8 July 1831.
[118] CUL, Graham papers, MS 26, bundle 6, Graham to Earl Grey, 25 Aug. 1831.

in 1836 Hill wrote to the Chancellor of the Exchequer of the saving he had
made: 'having executed this service to the best of my judgment and endeavor in
economizing the public money and [I] have been the means I firmly believe of
saving to the Crown a considerable sum'.[119] In 1837, Hill wrote of a disposition on
the part of the committees to improvident expenditure and jobbing with money
handed to them (p. 143). Hill's final accounts to the Treasury for his activities
in 1837 (p. 196), show that he spent only £7,065 of the £10,000 that had been
made available to him. He told Spearman (p. 194) that the Treasury would be

> agreeably surprised to find so small a sum expended when you consider
> how hard the Treasury was pressed by the Scotch Deputations who
> calculated upon getting at least £20,000 out of you; and the saving shows
> the advantage of having a person on the spot on such occasions.

At the end of Hill's tour of duty in Scotland, the committees in Edinburgh,
Glasgow and Aberdeen all passed resolutions recording their thanks to Hill
for the work he had done. Hill's 'cordial, zealous and energetic co-operation',
his 'zeal, energy and ability' and his 'zealous and efficient manner' were how,
respectively, the Edinburgh, Glasgow and Aberdeen committees described
him and he was diligent in ensuring that copies of these encomiums were seen
by his masters at the Treasury. Guardian of the public purse Hill may have
been but this did not stop him from suggesting to the Treasury that he should
receive a special payment for his services as he had 'been put to considerable
and unexpected expense by my removal from [Deptford]', reminding the
Treasury that he had received £200 for his work in Ireland in 1831 (p. 194);
the Treasury responded by authorising Hill to retain £200 of the balance
in his hands 'as a special remuneration to you for your services upon the
occasion in question'.[120]

★

In the last part of this Introduction we consider government policy over the
destitution and also look at the role of the Home Office and parliament.

Government policy over relief in Scotland in 1837 as conducted by the
Treasury largely followed the policies of successive governments, both Tory
and Whig, over famine relief in Ireland and Scotland between 1817 and 1845.[121]

---

[119] NLI, Monteagle papers, MS 13383/4, Hill to Spring Rice, 3 Oct. 1836; these words are
omitted from the printed copy of Hill's letter in [PP] 1846 XXXVII (734).
[120] NLS, Sir John Hill 1837: diary and papers Acc 12738 Spearman to Hill, 16 July 1838. Hill had
also been awarded a civil list pension of £150 per annum for his services in Ireland in 1831
and 1836 (NRA 44729, Hill papers and correspondence 1792–1855, fo. 72, King's warrant,
27 Apr. 1837).
[121] As to famine relief in Ireland for these years, see R. D. Collison Black, *Economic Thought
and the Irish Question 1817–1870* (Cambridge 1960); P. Gray, *Famine, Land and Politics – British
Government and Irish Society 1843–50* (Dublin, 1999), 126–8; T. P. O'Neill, 'State, Poverty
and Distress in Ireland, 1815–1845' (National University of Ireland, Dublin, Ph.D. thesis,

Certain general principles, although they may have differed in the details, were recognised consistently by governments over the period. The guiding principle was driven by the leitmotif of the age: the belief in *laissez-faire*. It was not for the government to intervene to provide gratuitous assistance,[122] especially where to do so might affect prices or markets.[123] Relief, if it was necessary, should primarily come from landowners[124] and the public through charitable giving[125] – government interference would tend to relieve landowners of their primary responsibility and might lessen charitable effort; aid from the government should be in support of, not in substitution for, charitable giving.[126] Government aid must not discourage charitable efforts and there must be no undue expectations encouraged by government action.[127] It was for this reason that undue publicity should not be given to action by the government or, if and to the extent that it was given, it should be stressed that in all cases the principal providers of aid should be private benevolence and the proprietors, and that anything the government did was strictly to be limited to the support of these agencies.[128]

However, while the principle of *laissez-faire* 'was all-pervasive . . . the claims of the non-interference principle could never be wholly excluded from ministerial calculations, [and] decisions on policy often took an interventionist course. Even where the desirability of non-interference was conceded in principle, expediency demanded and secured policies which breached both the letter and the spirit of *laissez-faire*.'[129] If actual starvation was possible, the government accepted a departure from principle might be required

1971–2); and M. A. Trant, 'Government Policy and Irish Distress 1816–19' (University College, Dublin, MA thesis, 1965).

[122] TNA:PRO, Treasury Board: Minute books T 29/149 Treasury minute, 23 May 1817.

[123] [Parl. Debs] first series, vol. xxxv, col. 891, 5 Mar. 1817; NLI, Monteagle papers, MS 551, fo. 51, Spring Rice to Morpeth, 4 July 1835.

[124] BL, Peel papers, vol. cxlviii, Add. MS 40328, fos. 45–6, Goulburn to Wellesley, 2 Apr. 1822; BL, Graham papers, Add. MS 79659, fos. 75–6, Graham to Hill, 8 July 1831; NLI, Monteagle papers, MS 542, fo. 39 Spring Rice to Mulgrave, 7 June 1836.

[125] BL, Peel papers, vol. cxiv, Add. MS 40294, fo. 89, Peel to Colthurst, 28 Nov. 1817; BL, Graham papers, Add. MS 79659, fos. 75–6, Graham to Hill, 8 July 1831; and [PP] 1837 LI (69).

[126] BL, Peel papers, vol. cxiv, Add. MS 40294, fo. 89, Peel to Colthurst, 28 Nov. 1817; BL, Peel papers, vol. cxiv, Add. MS 40294, fos. 102–3, Peel to Bishop of Down, 16 Dec. 1817; BL, Graham papers, Add. MS 79659, fos. 75–6, Graham to Hill, 8 July 1831.

[127] BL, Graham papers, Add. MS 79659, fos. 75–6, Graham to Hill, 8 July 1831.

[128] CUL, Graham papers, MS 26, bundle 5, Stanley to Graham, 8 June 1831; BL, Graham papers, Add. MS 79659, fo. 55, Graham to Hill, 29 June 1831; [Parl. Debs.] third series, vol. iv, cols. 801–2, 5 July 1831.

[129] A. J. Taylor, *Laissez-faire and State Intervention in Nineteenth-Century Britain* (London, 1972), 48. Christine Kinealy expresses a hard-headed view of the doctrine of *laissez-faire*: overall, the doctrine and adherence to it provided a useful shield with which to deflect any untoward demands being made on the resources of government; and that although *laissez-faire* could be 'raised to the status of dogma, on the other hand . . . it could be disregarded when convenient'. C. Kinealy, *This Great Calamity – The Irish Famine 1845–52* (Dublin, 1994, 2006), 8 and 9, and also 355–6.

and that state aid might be necessary – people could not be allowed to starve,[130] but, in these circumstances, the government would only contribute if a detailed inquiry into the real state of distress as represented to the government was made by a person who could be trusted, and government aid would then be limited strictly to what was necessary to preserve human life, and be administered by a person appointed by the government.[131]

The Treasury minute of 14 March 1837 (p. 277) and the letters of Spring Rice of 18 and 19 March 1837 (pp. 264 and 265) and 11 August 1837 (p. 266) reflect all of these general principles. The words used in the Treasury minute as to the dangers of government interference with the food supply, preventing the 'abundance of one district being brought in aid of the deficiency of another' (p. 277) are very similar to those used by the Chancellor of the Exchequer, Nicholas Vansittart, in March 1817 at the time of the scarcity in the Western Isles of Scotland, when the initial position of the government was that a moderate supply was all that was required and that the most effectual means of securing this was for the government to preserve the free circulation of grain so that 'the surplus of one district might supply the deficiency of others'.[132] But the severity of the situation required this basic principle to be broken and by May 1817, the Treasury had decided that conditions required the government to supply grain to the proprietors. But as the government 'felt the strongest objection to affording gratuitous relief', it should be on the basis of a loan for the payment of the cost of supply secured by heritable bonds from the proprietors.[133] The grain supplied by the government on this occasion was distributed by the proprietors to the tenants on terms that it was to be paid for at

---

[130] BL, Peel papers, vol. cxiv, Add. MS 40294, fos. 174–8, Peel to Whitworth, 8 Mar. 1817; CUL, Graham papers, MS 26, bundle 5, Graham to Stanley, 6 June 1831; [Parl. Debs] third series, vol. iv, cols. 801–2, 5 July 1831; NLI, Monteagle papers, MS 13383/1, Spring Rice to Hill, 15 July 1836.

[131] BL, Peel papers, vol. cxiv, Add. MS 40294, fos. 174–8, Peel to Whitworth, 8 Mar. 1817; BL, Wellesley papers (Series II), vol. xxvi, Add. MS 37299, fos. 206–7, Goulburn to Wellesley, 11 June 1822; BL, Graham papers, Add. MS 79659, fos. 8–13, Graham to Hill, 6 Jun, 1831; NLI, Monteagle papers, MS 13383/1, Spring Rice to Hill, 15 July 1836.

[132] [Parl. Debs] first series, vol. xxxv, col. 891, 5 Mar. 1817.

[133] TNA:PRO, Treasury papers, T 29/149, Treasury minute, 23 May 1817; CDC, GD 221/221, Heritable Bond and Security 1817; and NRS, Papers of the MacDonald family of Clanranald, GD 201/6/47/11, Memorial, 26 Mar. 1817. A paper produced for Spring Rice as part of his deliberations over the aid to be provided to the Highlands and Islands in 1837 showed that in 1817 the Treasury had expended a net £29,587 on the supply of 3,000 quarters of oats, 1,000 bolls of oatmeal, 147 bolls of barley and 192 tons of potatoes to Lord Reay, Lady Hood Mackenzie, Lord Macdonald, Lt Col Macdonald, Mr Grant, Macdonald of Clanranald, Macdonald of Boisdale, Macdonald of Borinish and Macdonald of Barra. The paper explained the terms of security for the supply and said that in the long term, the proprietors who had sought the aid were excused one-half of the cost of the supply and that the remaining sums were only recovered some years afterwards (NLI, Monteagle papers, MS 13384/8, undated paper).

prime cost, but some years later large sums were still outstanding.[134] The supply of grain to Lewis was mired in confusion as to what Lady Hood Mackenzie had actually asked the Treasury for and the amount she was liable to pay, and James Stewart Mackenzie described the whole issue as a 'disagreeable, ill-conducted, hazardous, though perhaps well-intentioned measure'. It was the view of Stewart Mackenzie, who had married Lady Hood Mackenzie after the event and who took it upon himself to go through her extensive correspondence, that Lewis had received an over-supply of grain, and not the meal that had been asked for – the particular problem faced by Lewis was that there was only one mill in which to grind oats into meal – as a result of the unauthorised actions of his wife's agents, who, it appears, had mistakenly thought that the government had made a gratuitous offer of aid.[135] In 1837 the Treasury expressly stated that the principles laid down in the resolutions of the Edinburgh committee of 2 March 1837 (p. 245) discussed above should apply to 'the delivery of the seed' to be supplied with the £10,000 of government aid (p. 278). It is not clear if this meant that the requirements both for the payment for seed and the guarantee by the proprietors should apply to the government aid, but a minute of the Edinburgh committee in December 1838 suggests that it was, indeed, the intention of the government that, in a manner similar to the supply in 1817, the terms as to payment and guarantee should apply equally to the supply of seed by the government as it did to the supplies provided from the public subscriptions raised by the Edinburgh committee.[136]

In 1837, Spring Rice believed strongly in the principle of encouraging self-reliance; he said that 'if any large portion of the subjects of Her Majesty were to be impressed with a belief that they had a right to rely upon the interposition of the State . . . the strongest motives to foresight, industry and frugality would be withdrawn and a principle would be laid down inconsistent with the well-being of Society' (p. 266). However, the 'calamity . . . was so overwhelming that it appeared that without assistance from other sources, suffering and loss of life must have ensued . . . and so the application of [the] general principles [of encouraging self-reliance and non-interference with the food supply] should be subject to certain modifications' (p. 266). Responsibility still lay primarily with the proprietors and then with public benevolence. It was only if these two sources proved inadequate that 'the funds of the State could have been with justice and propriety applied for such a purpose' (p. 266).

---

[134] 1841 SC, Q 2813; NRS, Papers of the Macdonald family of Clanranald, GD 201/1/352, Report by Mr Shaw, 21 Apr. 1823.

[135] NRS, Papers of the Mackenzie Family, earls of Seaforth, GD 46/13/170/1–4, undated note by James Stewart Mackenzie; and GD 46/13/178/3–6, Mary Stewart Mackenzie to Atholl, 27 Aug. 1817.

[136] TNA:PRO, War and Colonial Department and Colonial Office: Emigration original correspondence, CO 384/50, Extract from the minutes of meeting of Edinburgh committee on Highland and Island Destitution, 14 Dec. 1838.

It was important, however, that expectations of relief to be provided by the government should not be encouraged lest they should discourage the charitable efforts of the public and, indeed, the sympathy of the proprietors (pp. 264 and 267). Spring Rice was reported in the *Caledonian Mercury* as having told the deputation he received from the Edinburgh and Glasgow committees and MPs on 13 March 1837 that 'frankly, we are disposed to do something for you – but don't tell the public that – say that we are a cruel, reckless, hard-hearted government' and that if the deputation was to make it known that the 'government was about to assist them it would ruin their Mansion House meeting [to set up a London public subscription]'.[137] Great caution, prudence and well-directed benevolence (p. 267) were vital and, as on previous occasions, this meant that a government-appointed agent should be sent – except that this time there were two: Sir John Hill appointed by the Treasury, and Robert Graham by the Home Office. Spring Rice's letter to Hill of 11 August 1837 (p. 266) is a key document. Written some five months after the event it was, it seems, an *ex post facto* explanation or record of the Treasury's position and of its decision to act – indeed it may be seen as a justification of the modification of the general principles which Spring Rice considered should otherwise direct the actions of the government.

A further example of Spring Rice's adherence to these general principles is contained in a letter he wrote to the Home Secretary, Lord John Russell, over Russell's proposals to help famine relief in Ireland in 1837; Russell did not have the same doctrinal objections to intervention as did Spring Rice and Spring Rice was keen to emphasise the importance of the general principles.[138]

> I fear your letter will create great alarm difficulty and embarrassment. It is a pledge that the Government will do something without stating the amount or of the relief intended. It will therefore stop all prudence and economy – it will discourage private subscriptions and efforts – it will prevent speculation that would enable the abundance of one district to supply the deficiency of another. No merchant will venture to ship grain to the distressed districts. Whatever is done should be done as quietly as possible and with the least disturbance of prices and markets.[139]

If, however, the report from the *Caledonian Mercury* referred to above of the meeting held between the Scottish deputation and Spring Rice is accurate, it was not just these general principles which directed Spring Rice. It was said that he 'showed every disposition to relieve the wants of the Highlanders'; and all that held him back was that he felt constrained by the fear of creating

---

[137] *Caledonian Mercury*, 29 May 1837.
[138] P. Mandler, *Aristocratic Government in the Age of Reform – Whigs and Liberals 1830–1852* (Oxford, 1990), 173.
[139] NLI, Monteagle papers, MS 542, Spring Rice to Lord John Russell, 6 Feb. 1837.

a precedent: that in providing aid he would give 'the English and Irish a right to establish the same claims'. And when told that 'government ought to do something for the Highlands because, owing to the measures of former governments, the people had been deprived of their means of subsistence' – a reference to the loss of fiscal protection for the kelp manufacture – it was said that 'Mr Rice was delighted to find that there was a principle on which he could assist the Highlanders, without the English or Irish having reason to complain'.[140] We noted above, in relation to the proposals for government-funded emigration, the sensitivities within the government that help for the Highlands would be taken as a precedent for being obliged to take similar steps for Ireland.

In February 1841, when the House of Commons debated the motion of Hugh Baillie MP for a select committee on the condition of the population of the western Highlands and Islands of Scotland and emigration, Francis Baring, the then Chancellor of the Exchequer, re-affirmed the principles which had informed government action on famine relief since 1817 and which had been the policy in 1837 when he was financial secretary at the Treasury. He said:

> The interference of Government in cases of the kind was in general much to be deprecated, but, when it could not be avoided, instead of voting a sum of money, it had been found that the most expedient course was to send down an officer, in whom full confidence could be reposed, and to enable him at his discretion to administer relief. . . . It was his firm opinion that by far the wisest and safest course was to interfere as little as possible with the exercise of private benevolence.[141]

When famine conditions in Ireland were discussed within the Tory government in the autumn of 1845 these principles were re-examined, in particular the instructions given to Hill on his missions to Ireland in 1831 and 1836, and Scotland in 1837. Lord Monteagle[142] wrote to the prime minister, Sir Robert Peel, that he had found the services of Hill on these occasions of great value[143] and on the basis of Monteagle's recommendation, Peel met with Hill, who gave Peel 'a curious account of the attempts made to impose on him [by the Irish proprietors]'.[144] On 31 October 1845, Hill delivered to Sir James Graham, the Home Secretary, a dossier which comprised Graham's own orders to Hill in 1831 and the orders given to Hill by Spring Rice governing Hill's mission in Ireland in 1836 and in Scotland in 1837.[145] It is likely that these documents were considered

140 *Caledonian Mercury*, 29 May 1837.
141 [Parl. Debs] third series, vol. lvi, col. 526, 11 Feb. 1841. But Baring seemed to have forgotten that the Treasury had, in fact, voted a sum of £10,000 in 1837.
142 Thomas Spring Rice had been created first Baron Monteagle of Brandon in September 1839.
143 BL, Peel papers, vol. cccxcvi, Add. MS 40576, fos. 322–6, Monteagle to Peel, 24 Oct. 1845.
144 BL, Peel papers, vol. ccxcvi, Add. MS 40576, fos. 499–501, Peel to Freemantle, 31 Oct. 1845. Peel told Freemantle that copies of Hill's instructions were being sent to him.
145 NLS, Sir John Hill 1837: diary and papers Acc 12738 Note by Hill, 31 Oct. 1845.

by the cabinet at their meeting that day or at the next day's meeting, when Peel
read to them a memorandum on the measures which government should take in
Ireland. Amongst Peel's recommendations was the suggestion that Hill should be
sent to Ireland 'to aid the Lord-Lieutenant and the Commission [which should be
appointed to consider how relief should be provided] with his local knowledge
and experience. The instructions under which he acted at former periods should
be sent to the Lord-Lieutenant [of Ireland].'[146] In a letter which was read out to
the cabinet, Graham wrote to the lord lieutenant of Ireland, Lord Heytesbury,
in November 1845, sending him the instructions given to Hill in 1831, 1836 and
1837, and told Heytesbury that the letter containing Hill's instructions in July 1831
'contains a statement of the Principles and caution to be observed, which on full
consideration I still think sound and necessary to be regarded'.[147] When Andrew
Rutherfurd, the lord advocate of Scotland, wrote to the Home Secretary, Sir
George Grey, in September 1846 on the failure of the potato crop in the Highlands
and Islands of Scotland he suggested that Grey should speak to Hill, 'who had
discharged his duty admirably' as 'he might give you useful information' as to
the administration of government aid.[148]

Spring Rice was a moderate liberal who held orthodox economic opinions.[149]
Behind his adherence to these long-standing principles for government
involvement in famine relief we see the influence of the writings of two
individuals: the Rev. Dr Thomas Chalmers and Edmund Burke. Boyd Hilton
considers that Chalmers's views had enormous influence over the conventional
wisdom of the day;[150] Spring Rice had considerable respect and admiration
for Chalmers,[151] especially in relation to his views on how the poor should be
supported. He had asked Chalmers to contribute to his committee hearings into
the state of the Irish poor in 1830 because 'most particularly with respect to your
exposure to North Britain, your evidence would be of the most extreme value
and importance'.[152] But it was not just in relation to the poor laws that Spring
Rice found himself agreeing with Chalmers: as he wrote to the editor of the
Edinburgh Review, his opinions were 'in all respects those of Dr Chalmers'.[153]
Chalmers believed that if people became systematically trained to expect relief
as a right this would destroy the connection between economy and independence

[146] R. Peel, *Memoirs by the Rt. Hon. Sir Robert Peel*, 2 vols. (London, 1856–7), ii, 142.
[147] CUL, Graham papers, MS 40, bundle 95A, Graham to Heytesbury, 3 Nov. 1845; and Graham
to Peel, 12 Nov. 1845.
[148] [PP] 1847 LIII (788), *Correspondence Relating to the Measures Adopted for the Relief of Distress in
Scotland*, 10.
[149] Gray, *Famine, Land and Politics*, 16.
[150] B. Hilton, *The Age of Atonement – The Influence of Evangelicalism on Social and Economic Thought
1785–1865* (Oxford 1986), 55.
[151] NCL, Special collections, CHA4.188.64, Spring Rice to Chalmers, 21 Feb. 1832.
[152] NCL, Special collections, CHA4.147.2.819, Spring Rice to Chalmers, 26 Mar. 1830.
[153] BL, Macvey Napier papers, Add. MS 34614, fo. 431, Spring Rice to Napier, 15 Nov. 1830.

and between improvidence and want;[154] self-reliance should be encouraged in the people and the relief of genuine destitution should be left to private charity:[155] all principles that were affirmed by Spring Rice in his letter of 11 August 1837 (p. 266). Edmund Burke, an ideological heir to Adam Smith, did not believe the government should interfere in the market to supply the poor in times of famine – the opening and closing sentences of *Thoughts and Details on Scarcity* leave no room for doubt: 'Of all things, an indiscreet tampering with the trade of provisions is the most dangerous, and it is always worst in the time when men are most disposed to it: that is, in the time of scarcity' and 'My opinion is against an over-doing of any sort of administration, and more especially against this most momentous of all meddling on the part of authority; the meddling with the subsistence of the people'.[156] This was sound Enlightenment economics as expressed by Adam Smith: while a dearth in food supply was almost always a fault of the seasons, famine had never arisen from any other cause but by the government interfering and attempting to remedy the inconveniences of the dearth.[157] For Burke, aid for the impoverished was 'a matter of charity and a Christian duty, but it [was] beyond the right or obligation of government to perform'.[158]

Spring Rice made explicit reference to *Thoughts and Details on Scarcity* in the letter to Lord John Russell in 1837 about Russell's open-ended offer of assistance in Ireland referred to above. Spring Rice had ended the letter with the words 'Pray think on Burke's unanswerable observations in the Thoughts on Scarcity'.[159] As to expediency and intervention, although Burke had expressed firm principles, these did admit of exceptions and his 'faith in laissez-faire, it would seem, was less than fanatical, and recognised that there were situations in which government interference was not only permissible but necessary'.[160] These were sentiments with which Spring Rice agreed. Although a dedicated believer in *laissez-faire* economics during his years in government, it seems that he lost his belief in the face of the great Irish potato famine, when he urged the 'abandonment of economic theories he had upheld for a lifetime in face of the immediate need

---

[154] O. Checkland, 'Chalmers and William Pulteney Alison: a conflict of views on Scottish social policy', in A. C. Cheyne (ed.), *The Practical and the Pious: Essays on Thomas Chalmers (1780–1847)* (Edinburgh, 1985), 131.

[155] Collison Black, *Economic Thought and the Irish Question*, 93–4. D. Paton, *The Clergy and the Clearances – The Church and the Highland Crises 1790–1850* (Edinburgh, 2006), 133.

[156] E. Burke, *Thoughts and Details on Scarcity Originally Presented to the Right Hon. William Pitt, in the Month of November, 1795* (London, 1800), 1 and 48.

[157] A. Smith, *An Inquiry into the Nature and Causes of the Wealth of Nations*, 2 vols. (Oxford, 1979), i, 526–7.

[158] F. Canavan, *The Political Economy of Edmund Burke – The Role of Property in his Thought* (New York, 1995), 135.

[159] NLI, Monteagle papers, MS 542, Spring Rice to Lord John Russell, 6 Feb. 1837.

[160] Canavan, *Edmund Burke*, 140. Also A. Bourke, *'The Visitation of God'? The Potato and the Great Irish Famine* (Dublin, 1993), 172.

"to keep society together"'.[161] In a letter to Sir Robert Peel in October 1845 he wrote: 'if we have to deal with a famishing people then adherence to ordinary rule becomes impossible and human life must be saved even though the principles of ordinary Economical Science are set aside for the time'.[162]

As we have seen, successive governments, both Tory and Whig, since 1817 had been very clear in their beliefs that it was the landed proprietors, not the state, who should take the principal responsibility for famine relief on their lands. Criticism of the Irish landed proprietors, in the context, particularly, of famine in Ireland is, of course, well recorded as, indeed, it is in the context of the famine of 1847 in the Highlands and Islands of Scotland, although not all proprietors should be tarnished with the brush of failing in their traditional responsibilities to their tenants.[163] But the landed proprietors were, at least in Ireland, the hate-figures for zealous Whigs.[164] In 1837 in Scotland it is clear that the government saw the prime responsibility for relief as lying with the landed proprietors, many of whom were Tory and a number absentee, and that it also disapproved generally of their relief efforts and of their estate management. This critical attitude is well laid out in the letters of John Cunninghame and Andrew Rutherfurd to Fox Maule (pp. 257 and 261), which state clearly that it was the responsibility of the proprietors to support the people on their lands. They show the suspicion that the proprietors wished to use the appeals for financial and other help to advance their own economic interests – the references to Tory jobbery in Rutherfurd's letters would have appealed to Lord John Russell – and also disclose the belief that the system of estate management had contributed to the distress, and that this should, in due course, be revealed to the public. This critical attitude was not limited to the government. As we have noted, Graham himself was critical of the attitudes of proprietors to legal assessments under the poor laws, and of the lax system of estate management that had been a significant contributory factor in the increase of population. It is also shown by the reportage in the contemporary press as to the motives and role of the proprietors in seeking public subscriptions to alleviate the destitution;[165] as mentioned above, the proprietors were themselves sensitive that they were perceived not to have done enough to help their tenants, and that the public would consider their appeals for public subscriptions to be self-serving.

---

[161] Wasson, 'Spring Rice'.

[162] Quoted in Murphy, 'Spring Rice', 187.

[163] As to Scotland, see Devine, *Highland Famine*, 83–105. As to Ireland, Alvin Jackson suggests that no clear picture of landlord efforts has emerged (A. Jackson, *Ireland 1798–1998 – War, Peace and Beyond* (Oxford, 2010), 75–6); and Christine Kinealy warns of the dangers of making generalisations as to the role of landlords in the context of the Great Famine (Kinealy, *Great Famine*, 348). See also J. S. Donnelly, Jr, '"Irish property must pay for Irish poverty" – British public opinion and the Great Irish Famine', in C. Morash and R. Hayes (eds.), *'Fearful Realities' – New Perspectives on the Famine* (Dublin, 1996), 60–76.

[164] Jackson, *Ireland*, 76.

[165] As to which, see MacAskill, 'Public response', 189–95.

We have seen the importance of a, perhaps, dogmatic belief in *laissez-faire* which dictated the limits of state intervention. Alvin Jackson attributes the limitations of British relief policy during the Great Irish Famine to the severities of liberal economic thought and observes that the work in particular of Boyd Hilton[166] has 'tended to underline the providentialist outlook of those senior British officials who were characterized by a narrow form of evangelical religious outlook'.[167] Writing of the Great Irish Famine, Peter Gray follows this thesis, arguing that British famine relief policy was greatly constrained by evangelical fears about the demoralising effects of state intervention,[168] noting that government policy, in particular as carried out by officials at the Treasury, was 'the fruit of a powerful social ideology that combined a providentialist theodicy of "natural laws" with a radicalized and "optimistic" version of liberal political economy' and that 'an attitude of mind . . . suffused the British political public, and set the parameters of state activity. The belief that the blight was a providential visitation . . . shaped contemporary attitudes and subsequent apologetics.'[169] The letters of Spring Rice in 1837 (pp. 264 and 266) do not contain the providential language of Sir Charles Trevelyan in 1847 that 'the Irish famine was the judgement of God on an indolent and unselfreliant people, and as God had sent the calamity to teach the Irish a lesson, that calamity must not be too much mitigated'.[170] And although Spring Rice had made clear his belief that the state should not, in twenty-first-century language, encourage a welfare-state dependency culture as this would lessen people's desire and ability to look after themselves, this belief did not constrain him from providing relief for the Highlands and Islands. So far as the attitude of the public was concerned, there was no deep moralising over the causes of the destitution, no rigid or deterministic interpretations of providence in response to the destitution, no equivocation as to the need for aid and compassion.[171] While there was recognition of the hand of God in the onset of the destitution in 1837, this was a recognition of a 'benign' providence: there was no suggestion that it was 'a retributive act of Divine vengeance against the Highlanders' which would have prevented steps being taken to 'alleviate the effects of what was intended to inflict maximum suffering'.[172] Indeed, the contemporary reportage of the distress in the Highlands and Islands frequently expressed the

---

[166] Hilton, *The Age of Atonement*.
[167] A. Jackson, *The Two Unions — Ireland, Scotland, and the Survival of the United Kingdom* (Oxford, 2012), 192.
[168] MacColl, *Land, Faith*, 20.
[169] Gray, *Famine, Land and Politics*, 331 and 337.
[170] J. Hart, 'Sir Charles Trevelyan at the Treasury', *English Historical Review* 75, no. 295 (Jan. 1960), 99.
[171] MacAskill, 'Public response', 195–200; and see MacColl, *Land, Faith*, 19–57, for MacColl's demolition of the view that Scottish Presbyterian ministers were constrained in their reaction to the great famine of 1847 in Scotland by a 'rigid, deterministic' interpretation of providence.
[172] MacColl, *Land, Faith*, 34.

Christian duty of those blessed by providence to provide for the needs of the suffering. Acceptance of the fact that the destitution was the visitation of divine providence did not mean that nothing should be done.[173] Even those who did believe that the destitution was a visitation of God's wrathful providence did not extend this belief by a resolution that nothing should therefore be done to help.[174]

The role of the Home Office and, in particular, its under-secretary with responsibility for Scottish affairs, the honourable Fox Maule, is of interest. It was only in 1828 that the Home Office was placed in charge of Scottish affairs. This had followed the long period during the eighteenth century and then the half-century that straddled 1800, when the administration of Scottish affairs was effectively handled by a 'manager' in Scotland – the second and third dukes of Argyll and Lord Milton: the 'People Above',[175] followed by Henry Dundas and his son, Robert: the 'Dundas despotism'.[176] Hopes by the Whigs that, after the change made in 1828, the Home Secretary would have real and not just nominal control over Scottish affairs[177] were not realised: Scottish affairs did not become the exclusive preserve of the Home Office. As an executive matter, responsibility was divided between the Home Office and the lord advocate with the Home Secretary delegating practically all his responsibilities to the lord advocate.[178] The upshot was the perpetuation of the system of semi-independence from Westminster.[179] Henry Cockburn had explained in his journals why it was inappropriate for responsibility for Scottish affairs to rest with the lord advocate; he had suggested that a Scottish secretary should be appointed, something that only happened in 1885.[180] Although the appointment of Fox Maule as under-secretary in April 1835 with part of his brief to include Scottish affairs was a step forward, the role of the lord advocate remained. But the lord advocate, John Murray, was largely ineffective in his political role[181] and so it is not surprising that the initiative for action over the destitution in 1837 came, not from the lord advocate, but from the solicitor-general for Scotland, John Cunninghame, with his successor Andrew Rutherfurd maintaining the interest.[182] Cunninghame reflected the concerns expressed by Henry Cockburn and was anxious that the appointment and running of the necessary inquiry should be made by Fox Maule at the Home Office as he did not believe 'lawyers sitting in Edinburgh' would do any real good (p. 257).

[173] *The Times*, 24 Mar. 1837.
[174] *Caledonian Mercury*, 1 May 1837.
[175] A. Murdoch, *'The People Above' – Politics and Administration in Mid-Eighteenth Century Scotland* (Edinburgh, 1980).
[176] M. Fry, *The Dundas Despotism* (Edinburgh, 1992), xiii.
[177] M. Fry, *Patronage and Principal – A Political History of Modern Scotland* (Aberdeen, 1987), 70.
[178] H. J. Hanham, 'The creation of the Scottish Office', *Juridical Review*, 1965, 205–6.
[179] P. Jupp, *The Governing of Britain 1688–1848* (London, 2006), 148.
[180] H. Cockburn, *Journal of Henry Cockburn 1831–1854*, 2 vols. (Edinburgh, 1874), i, 125–7; ii, 309–11.
[181] Fry, *Patronage and Principal*, 32.
[182] Hill's journal records that he had frequent meetings with both Rutherfurd and Cunninghame.

The appointment of Robert Graham to undertake the inquiry was the first time that the Home Office, in its new role since 1828, had taken such a step in Scotland but it was probably something of a burden to Fox Maule, who was already very bound up in his own departmental work without having this extra responsibility.[183] The very fact that the Home Office contrived to lose a number of Graham's letters to Fox Maule (p. 110) and had, it appears, failed to send to the Treasury copies of Graham's letters until after he had completed his visit to the Highlands and Islands (p. 281), suggests a lack of grip and commitment, as does the want of any obvious action by the Home Office on the conclusions, recommendations and warnings in Graham's letters as to the inevitable repeat of the events of 1837 unless action was taken. Graham's main suggestion for government-assisted emigration on a great scale was, it is true, passed for consideration to the Treasury and then to the Colonial Office but, as we have seen, the report from the agent-general for emigration to the colonial secretary meant that nothing was done; and the Treasury did ask the commissioners of Highland roads and bridges to take Graham's suggestions for road works forward, the commissioners responding by recommencing the Dingwall to Ullapool and Poolewe to Achnasheen lines, as well as a road from Barvas to Ness in Lewis, and roads in Mull. But the dissolution of the government on the death of the king in June 1837 weakened the political impetus to act.[184] This apart, there is no sense that the Home Office really took on board the implications of what Graham had written in his letters. This should not, perhaps surprise us. As J. P. Day has said 'though the State was largely responsible for the condition of affairs in the Highlands and Islands, it had done little or nothing to rescue the people from the hopeless position into which they had been allowed to drift'[185] and the 'loose rather uncoordinated style of government'[186] relating to Scottish affairs, and the *laissez-faire*, light-touch approach of the government, which was slow to identify itself with improvement and to look for long-term palliatives,[187] did not help the position. A pattern of demand for large-scale inquiry as to the conditions in Ireland, but a lack of action on the recommendations made, had become a concern by the 1830s;[188] the lack of action taken by the Home Office over Graham's letters may be said to have followed this pattern. Nor should we lose sight of the fact that the appointment of Graham was not exclusively a result of concern for the state of the Highlands

[183] I. G. C. Hutchison, *A Political History of Scotland, 1832–1924* (Edinburgh, 1986), 34.
[184] J. A. R. Smith, 'From Isolation to Integration: The Development of Roads in the Northern Highlands of Scotland 1800–1850' (University of Aberdeen, Ph.D. thesis, 2001), 161.
[185] J. P. Day, *Public Administration in the Highlands and Islands of Scotland* (London, 1918), 88.
[186] Lynch, *The Oxford Companion to Scottish History*, 277.
[187] Jupp, *Governing of Britain*, 180.
[188] J. Innes, 'Legislating for three kingdoms: how the Westminster parliament legislated for England, Scotland and Ireland, 1707–1830', in J. Hoppit (ed.), *Parliaments, Nations and Identities in Britain and Ireland, 1660–1850* (Manchester, 2003), 34.

and Islands: the countering of Tory jobbery was as much on John Cunninghame's mind when he put forward the suggestion to Fox Maule as was the condition of the Highlands.

The distress was barely discussed within parliament, but to the extent that it was, ministerial reluctance to be open about aid provided by the government was marked, as, indeed, it had been when Hill had been sent by the government to administer aid in Mayo and Galway in Ireland in 1831: the then chief secretary for Ireland, Edward Stanley, was told that since unguarded speeches had been made in the House of Commons as to the involvement of the government, private subscriptions had much decreased and in many cases ceased. When Stanley was asked to provide information of the extent of relief being provided, he gave a very guarded reply (albeit an attempt to lock the stable door after the horse had bolted): 'It might do harm, and could do no good, for him to declare how much or little Ministers intended to do'.[189] Major Cumming Bruce, the Tory MP for Inverness district, asked Fox Maule on 20 February 1837 whether the Home Office had received any communications from Scotland about the distress in the Highlands and Islands and 'whether the government was willing, as it was certainly able, to afford relief'. Fox Maule replied that 'the attention of government had been directed to this subject and as it was understood that distress really existed, they would be prepared to meet the question when it came before them'.[190] On 10 April, by which time it was public knowledge that Graham and Hill had been sent off on their missions,[191] Joseph Hume, the radical MP for Middlesex and a man who had made his name through his unremitting scrutiny of the government's finances, asked the Chancellor of the Exchequer if reports that the government had agreed to contribute for relief in the Highlands and Islands, were true. Spring Rice's response was very guarded. He told Hume that the subject needed to be treated with discretion, but that as he had been asked the question, he would answer it. The government had, indeed, the Chancellor of the Exchequer told Hume, been made aware of the fact that great distress existed and that committees had been formed in Edinburgh and Glasgow to raise subscriptions from the public, but that 'pressure was still so great that public assistance was absolutely necessary. Under the circumstances His Majesty's Government had thought it their duty to instruct a full inquiry into the circumstances on the spot and to send to Scotland for that purpose some responsible individual.' That person, he told Hume, was Sir John Hill who was authorised 'to afford aid in extreme cases, dependant, however entirely upon the amount of subscriptions, and upon local benevolence and assistance. He could go into no further explanation at

---

[189] [Parl. Debs] third series, vol. iv, cols. 801–2, 5 July 1831.
[190] Although this exchange is reported in the Imperial Parliament, House of Commons section of the *Inverness Courier*, 1 Mar. 1837, there is no reference to it in [Parl. Debs].
[191] On Graham's appointment, see *Caledonian Mercury*, 9 Mar. 1837; on Hill's appointment and the £10,000 of government aid for seed, see *The Scotsman*, 25 Mar. 1837.

present; and he hoped no further discussion would at present be provoked, as it might lead to the most injurious consequences.' Hume told Spring Rice that the government should have given notice to the House of Commons of the aid provided, before public money was appropriated to such a purpose but Spring Rice denied that the government had 'acted in any way contrary to usage'. The course that had been pursued by the government was, he said, neither unsound nor objectionable: 'It was exactly the course which had been pursued in all other cases – in the case of distress in the Hebrides,[192] in the case of distress in Ireland, and in fact in all cases of a similar description'.[193] This exchange reveals the intense sensitivity felt by the government about the fact of providing aid and the amount of that aid, even when it was public knowledge that government aid was being given to the extent of £10,000. It reflected the concern that has been described above in the discussion of Treasury practice on the provision of aid and, indeed, is reflected in a number of letters set out in Part 4: undue publicity about government involvement tended to exaggerate expectations of aid and lessen the contributions from private benevolence and the contributions of proprietors.

★

The contemporary press that had so sarcastically dismissed the appointment of Graham to make his investigation, was distinctly underwhelmed at the publication of his conclusions:

> Mr Robert Graham, who was appointed by the Government to make a personal inspection of the destitute districts in the Highlands, has published a summary of the information obtained during his tour. The cost of this tour is not stated, but, however small it may be, it is money all but thrown away – for the said abstract does not make the public acquainted with a single fact of which they were previously ignorant.[194]

This, however, is far too harsh a judgment. Graham's letters have been said to provide an authoritative guide to West Highland society in the 1830s,[195]

---

[192] A reference to the aid provided in 1817 by means of secured government loans.

[193] [Parl. Debs] third series, vol. xxxvii, cols. 924–6, 10 Apr. 1837 (Hume misquoted this response in the debate on the setting up of the select committee in 1841 – see [Parl. Debs] third series, vol. lvi, cols. 525–6, 11 Feb. 1841). This exchange between Hume and Spring Rice brought the withering comment from *The Times* that 'whether from terror of Joseph Hume's declared hostility to the relief of his countrymen out of the national Exchequer, or from desire to encourage voluntary contributions, to which the said Joseph has not given a single farthing, or from some other cause which "avoids publicity", no assistance of any kind is to be expected from government.... All that Ministers contemplate is the conditional advance of a sum of money to supply the tenantry with seed – a piece of liberality which may be very useful in propitiating the political support of highland landlords, but which will not provide a single potato for the existing necessities of the population' *The Times*, 24 Apr. 1837.

[194] *Inverness Courier*, 26 July 1837.

[195] Devine, *Highland Famine*, 27.

but their significance goes much further than just being a guide. In his two-
month investigation of the distressed districts, Graham seems to have been able
to distil from what he saw and heard a remarkable grasp of the fundamental
issues that had given rise to the conditions in which the people of the Highlands
and Islands found themselves. The message Graham gave in his final letter was
unequivocal: the fact that destitution had occurred from the failure of two seasons
indicated not merely great poverty but 'some great and radical errors as to their
condition and management' (p. 96) which had to be addressed if the recurrence
of the distress was to be prevented. Graham had shown clearly that there
was, indeed, a problem and not just an immediate one, but one which had
serious structural implications for the future sustainability of the people of
the Highlands and Islands. Graham's analysis in his final letter of 6 May was,
of course, not unique. The same or substantially similar conclusions were
reached by an anonymous author in 1837,[196] and also in the Glasgow committee
memorial to the Treasury (p. 207); by Fullarton and Baird[197] in 1838 and by the
Rev. Alexander Macgregor in two articles in 1839 and 1840 in the *Quarterly Journal
of Agriculture*.[198] But Graham's analysis was the first publicly stated warning as to
the need for extensive emigration directed to the government that was published
as a parliamentary paper,[199] and the fact that it been achieved without all the
panoply of a government-appointed select committee of the great and the good,
the submission of answers to long questionnaires and weeks of formal witness
hearings and, notably, was repeated in the findings of two such select committees
on the condition of the Highlands and Islands in 1841 and 1851,[200] is surely a
testament to his insight. Eric Richards has said that the 1841 select committee
on emigration 'exposed the roots of the Highland problem to public scrutiny. It
revealed fully the subsistence vulnerability of the west coast: indeed to a degree
it was a harbinger of the great famine which descended on the west Highlands
in 1846/7'.[201] Robert Graham had already done just this in 1837: Richard's words
describe precisely what Graham's letters had already exposed and revealed some
4 years before the select committee sat. As to the destitution of 1837, Richards
has said that, apart from the evidence given to the 1841 select committee, it 'is

[196] Anon., *Observations*.
[197] Fullarton and Baird, *Remarks*.
[198] 'On the causes of the destitution of food in the Highlands and Islands of Scotland in the
years 1836 and 1837', *Quarterly Journal of Agriculture* 9, no. xlii (1839), 159–99; and 'On the
advantages of a government grant for emigration from the Highlands and Islands of Scotland',
Quarterly Journal of Agriculture 11, no. li (1840–1), 277–97.
[199] The report in 1827 from the select committee on Emigration from the United Kingdom
([PP] 1826–7 V (550), 14) had concluded that a case for emigration from the islands and
western coast of Scotland to deal with the redundant population there existed only 'in
some degree'.
[200] The 1841 SC and [PP] 1851 XXVI (1397).
[201] Richards and Clough, *Cromartie*, 201.

otherwise virtually unrecorded'.[202] But, of course, the destitution of 1837 *was* otherwise recorded: the record is set out in this book through Graham's and Hill's letters, through the words of the memorials, petitions and resolutions seeking government aid and subscriptions from the public, through the reports of the destitution committees and through the words of official and private government letters and minutes.

[202] Richards and Clough, *Cromartie*, 202.

EDITORIAL CONVENTIONS

1. Punctuation, capitalisation, paragraphing and spelling are modernised.

2. Except in the case of Hill's journal, scribal abbreviations are extended.

3. Place names in the Highlands and Islands have undergone frequent changes of spelling over the years; in order to reduce confusion, place names are given the spellings found in the *OSG* or the *OGazS*, and parish names are given in accordance with the *FES*.

4. The spelling for names of people has generally been standardised to provide some consistency. The names of ministers are given in accordance with the *FES* and the names of Roman Catholic priests are given in accordance with the lists given in SSC. Graham's and Hill's letters and Hill's journal contain many personal names but in almost all cases they give just the title of the person and the surname. Where it has been possible positively to identify a person (by the use, largely of the contemporary post office directories *Pigot* and J. Findlay, *Directory to Gentlemen's Seats, Villages etc. in Scotland* (Edinburgh, 1843), and *The Edinburgh Almanac or Universal Scots and Imperial Register for 1837*), the Christian name or initial is added in square brackets and, if it is thought of particular interest, further information is given by way of a footnote.

5. Interpolations (i.e. the insertion of new matter, or for omissions in, or expansions of, the original text) are placed in square brackets.

6. Editorial omissions are denoted by three points thus . . . or by four to include a full stop. If the omission is in the original this is explained in a footnote. Blanks, damage or alterations in the manuscript, resulting in the omission (represented by points) of words, are explained in footnotes. Where a word is illegible this is denoted by three or four (as the case may be) points within square brackets thus [. . .].

7. Where the equivalent of the value of the £ is given in 2010 money, this is based on the retail price index using L. H. Officer and S. H. Williamson, 'Purchasing Power of British Pounds from 1245 to Present', MeasuringWorth, 2011 (URL http://www.measuringworth.com/ppoweruk/)

THE SOURCES

1. In Part 1, unless indicated otherwise, Robert Graham's letters to the Hon. Fox Maule, MP, at the Home Office and the note titled 'Distress in the Highlands' are taken from the copy letters at TNA:PRO, Treasury, T 1/4201. There are also copies of the letters at NRS, Commissary General and Treasury, HD 7/9. The letter dated 6 March 1837, in Graham's own hand, is taken from the copy at NLI, Monteagle papers MSS 13384/8, rather than from the copy at TNA:PRO, Treasury, T 1/4201, except where indicated by footnote. The final letter dated 6 May 1837 is reproduced as a parliamentary paper, [PP] 1837 LI (501), *Distress in the Highlands (Scotland)*, and is also printed in the 1841 select committee report. The original autograph letters from Graham to Fox Maule have not been traced; it is likely they were at TNA:PRO, Home Office: Scotland: letters and papers, HO 102/43, but large parts of this file are missing, believed destroyed.

The three letters from Graham to Robert Stewart of Ardvorlich are all at NRAS, Stewart family of Ardvorlich papers, 2654/1 Box 6/Bundle 18.

The letters from Graham to his mother are all at NLS, Lynedoch papers MSS 16011, and the letter from Graham to his sister Alexina is at NRS, Papers of the Maxtone Graham family of Cultoquhey, Perthshire, GD 155/995/7.

2. In Part 2, Hill's journal is taken from his manuscript journal at NLS, Sir John Hill, 1837: diary and papers Acc 12738, where can also be found a bound and typed version of the manuscript journal. The typed version was probably prepared by Hill's grandson Major-General John Edwin Dickson Hill, the eldest son of General John Thomas Hill, who was Hill's only son. The typed version contains a number of minor alterations from the manuscript journal but the manuscript journal is followed in this book.

All the letters are taken from TNA:PRO, Treasury, T 1/4201, apart from Hill's letter to Lord Lynedoch, which is taken from NLS, Lynedoch papers MSS 3621 fo. 202; Hill's letter to Spearman dated 7 July 1837, which is taken from TNA:PRO, War and Colonial Department and Colonial Office: Emigration Original Correspondence, CO 384/43; and the two letters from Spearman to Hill which are taken from NLS, Acc 12738.

3. In Section 1 of Part 3, the Petition to the Treasury from the Parochial Synod of Shetland is taken from NRS, Commissary General and Treasury,

HD 7/9; the Memorial to the Treasury of the committee appointed by the public meeting in Edinburgh is taken from NRS, Commissary General and Treasury, HD 7/9; the Memorial to the Treasury of the committee appointed by the public meeting in Glasgow is taken from NRS, Maclaine of Lochbuie papers, GD 174/1975/6; and the Memorial to the Treasury of the committee in Glasgow for the relief of the destitution in the Highlands and Islands of Scotland is taken from NRS, Commissary General and Treasury, HD 7/9.

In Section 2 of Part 3, the Edinburgh resolutions are taken from *The Scotsman*, 1 February 1837; the Glasgow resolutions are taken from the *Glasgow Herald*, 10 February 1837; the Aberdeen resolutions are taken from the *Aberdeen Journal*, 22 February 1837; and the London resolutions are taken from *The Times*, 20 March 1837.

In Section 3 of Part 3, the report by the Edinburgh committee is taken from NLS, Lynedoch papers MSS 16147; the two reports by the Glasgow committee are taken from TNA:PRO, Treasury, T 1/4201; the abstract of the Treasurer's account of the Glasgow committee is taken from the 1841 select committee report, 109; the statement on the closing of the London committee appeal is taken from the *Morning Chronicle*, 18 July 1837; and the report by the London committee is taken from the *Morning Chronicle*, 27 October 1837.

In Section 4 of Part 3, the resolutions of the Edinburgh committee which regulated the terms for the supply of aid for seed and which were adopted by the government to regulate the use of the funds made available to Hill, and the covering letter from the Edinburgh committee dated 2 March 1837, are taken from TNA:PRO, Treasury, T 1/4201. The note by Macleod and Bowie dated 14 April 1837 and the extract from minutes of a meeting of the Edinburgh committee dated 20 April 1837, are taken from NRS, Commissary General and Treasury, HD 7/9.

4. In Section 1 of Part 4, the source of each letter is given as a footnote. In Section 2 of Part 4, the report of T. F. Elliot, the agent-general for emigration, is taken from NRS, Commissary General and Treasury, HD 7/9, but printed copies of his report are also to be found at [PP] 1837–8 XL (388) *Copy of a Report to the Secretary of State for the Colonies from the Agent-General for Emigration from the United Kingdom*, Appendix 1, 11–13; and [PP] 1841 XXVII (60) *Report from the Agent-General for Emigration on the Applicability of Emigration to Relieve Distress in the Highlands*. The formal response of Lord Glenelg, the secretary of state for the Colonies, to the Treasury's request that he consider Graham's suggestion for an extensive emigration, is taken from TNA:PRO, Treasury, T 1/4201.

5. In Part 5, the Treasury minutes are, unless otherwise indicated, taken from TNA:PRO, Treasury Board: Minute Books, T 29/387, 388, 390, 391, 392 and 393.

PART 1

THE LETTERS OF ROBERT GRAHAM OF REDGORTON

Portrait of Robert Graham of Redgorton by Sir John Watson Gordon
© Robert Maxtone Graham, Sandwich, Kent

Robert Graham of Redgorton's Tour

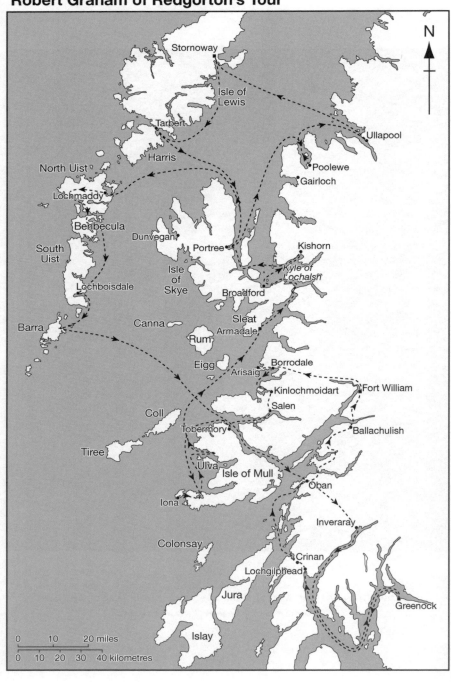

Edinburgh 22 February 1837

Private

My dear Stewart, You are probably aware that deputations have gone up from Edinburgh and Glasgow about the alleged destitution of the Highland districts. In the hurried information about them Government people have been able to collect, with the view of giving advice at Headquarters, it is rather supposed that the case has been exaggerated, but at all events they have recommended that somebody should be sent to the country to make enquiry and report. I have been strongly required to undertake this duty, and I suppose my name has been transmitted to the Government, in case they should think this the line to be followed, as recommended here.[1] I urged very strongly upon them, if possible, to get Sir John Hill (of the victualling department at Deptford), who was employed in the north of Ireland on a similar mission last year, employed on this occasion, as being likely from his experience, to do the work more easily and better than one quite unused to it. My second request was that, if I was to go, you should be added as my associate. Independent of your general knowledge on the subject and your capabilities for the enquiry, your being able to handle the language of the country would be an essential advantage to any person undertaking such a duty.[2] It struck both to them and me, that the only objection to this was withdrawing you from the point where you may be so much required in the event of a dissolution; but that did not appear to me to be sufficiently strong to induce me to give up my request for your assistance at all events in the context; though I have my own misgivings as to the chance of Maule (who may be concerned in the determination) consenting to your absence.[3]

I write this, however, to let you know what has happened. I have no definite views as to the chance of my going or not. I shall be very happy to avoid it although it is impossible for me to refuse if it is thought right to select me. I trust you will be guided by the same feeling if it is resolved that you should be added to the mission.

[1] That is, in Edinburgh by John Cunninghame, the outgoing solicitor-general for Scotland (p. 257 below).

[2] Stewart's ability to speak Gaelic may, in fact, have been of limited practical use given the fact that almost every district in the Highlands had a separate dialect (see, for example, the difficulties experienced by the ministers of the Church described in Paton, 'The Church in the Northern Highlands', 56–9).

[3] The ill-health of the king raised the possibility of a general election having to be called (it would be the last time this would be constitutionally required) and the Whig party in Perthshire, where Fox Maule was the county member, was anxious about retaining the seat; Graham himself had failed to be elected to the seat in 1834 and Fox Maule had only just recaptured it from the Tories at the last election in 1835. Robert Stewart was an important member of the Whig party machine in the county. In the event this did not prove an issue: the king died in June and the election took place in August, when Graham was Fox Maule's campaign manager and Fox Maule lost the seat (NLS, Lynedoch papers, MS 16144).

The communication to London only went off this morning, so the 27th is the earliest time that we can know any result. If we are to go, not an hour should be lost in proceeding to the ground that can be saved. I wish you would make your plans armed with this. As you proposed to be in Edinburgh about this time, probably the best way would be to make your arrangements in the country to come here as soon as possible and in such way as to allow of an absence of a few weeks, if affairs should take that long. Yours very truly.

Edinburgh 4 March 1837

My dear Stewart, I have just got an official document from Maule desiring me to start on the mission I referred to, and to take you with me. It is very general; but we shall find a revenue cutter at Fort William to facilitate our passage from one island to another. I think of going to Glasgow on my way to put myself in correspondence with the committee there; and as I am desired to go instanter in a private note, I must not be long of collecting information here and starting from this. I think your best plan (but you will judge according as this reaches you) is to meet me at Glasgow, where you can send a note at the post office and enquire for one from me. Failing that, Fort William would probably be the next point of position. I shall have people to see there, so you will have time to make up with me, if you are not at the ground first.[4] Adieu. Ever yours.

Edinburgh 6 March 1837

Sir, I had the honour of receiving your letter of the 2[nd][5] on the evening of the 4th and I have devoted my time since to the object of collecting information regarding the important duty on which I have been employed.

It appeared, in the first instance, highly advisable that I should put myself in communication with both the committees of the Edinburgh and Glasgow associations for ameliorating the condition of the distressed highlanders;[6]

[4]   In the event Stewart met up with Graham in Glasgow.
[5]   Fox Maule sent a copy of his letter to Graham, to Rutherfurd (p. 258). Fox Maule also wrote to the first secretary to the Admiralty, 'for the information of the Lords Commissioners of the Treasury', of Graham's appointment by the Home Office and asked for a letter to be provided to Graham giving instructions to the commanders of the revenue cruisers and the coast guard stations to afford Graham the means of transfer to and from, and among, the islands (TNA:PRO, Treasury T 1/4201, Fox Maule to Wood, 2 Mar. 1837).
[6]   This drew a sharp response from Fox Maule that the matter was confidential and that Graham was not to involve himself with either of the committees (p. 259). However, by 15 March, Fox Maule appears to have changed his mind and suggests that Graham should be the 'openly accredited agent of Government' (p. 263).

and I have attended a meeting of the former committee this day. I should have abstained from making the present communication until I had had an opportunity of being also present at a meeting of the Glasgow association; more especially as most of the documents belonging to the former body have been transmitted to the association at Glasgow, as being nearer the scene of distress, and better situated for promoting the means of relieving it. But I am induced now to write from having taken a prospective view of the immense district which may be included in the words of my instructions; and I venture to suggest that, with great advantage to the interest of the public and probably to such unhappy sufferers as may exist in that district, I might to be relieved from the anxiety and responsibility of reporting on the state of the Shetland Islands.[7]

The situation of these islands form a special case for themselves. They are isolated and widely apart from any other more favoured district on which they can throw themselves for assistance; and their locality is actually more within the reach of the metropolis, than any point on the west coast, or among the isles where to all appearances my humble questions must be directed in the first instance.

I subjoin, as an appendix, the substance of what was stated at the meeting today in regard to this district.[8] The exertions made in its favour by the Society of Friends, at the same time that they afford an evidence of the humanity of that fraternity, equally afford in my mind a proof that they are convinced that destitution exists to a certain amount; for it is not to be presumed that sensible men, as the leaders in this work of humanity are considered to be, would be so

---

[7] Graham had been told by Henry Cheyne, WS, of Tangwick, that it was vital to send a separate commissioner to the Shetlands, as to await Graham's report before granting assistance would be too late, that Shetland had a claim on the government because it had supplied more men in the Napoleonic wars than other regions and had never had a grant for roads or bridges (see NRS, Lord Advocate's Department, Miscellaneous papers, AD 58/87, Cheyne to Graham, 6 Mar. 1837, which contained a copy of the petition of the synod of Shetland to the Treasury; see p. 201 below). Graham told the solicitor-general for Scotland, Andrew Rutherfurd, that he felt compelled to write to Fox Maule asking that he be relieved of going to the Shetland islands. He told Rutherfurd that Shetland's cry for seed was increased and, referring to the terms on which aid was being given (see p. 245 below), he said that the landlords may not have the power to provide their required half of the assistance and asked 'Would government advance this half on the security of the landlords?' (see NRS, Lord Advocate's Department, Miscellaneous papers, AD 58/87, Graham to Rutherfurd, 6 Mar. 1837). Rutherfurd wrote to Fox Maule on 14 Mar. 1837 about the situation in the Shetland islands and, in particular, about the position of the landlords there (p. 260).

[8] It might have been expected that the subjoined appendix would have been a copy of Henry Cheyne's letter of 6 Mar. 1837 to Graham, but in fact it is a rather less informative note from John Wigham who had already written to Rutherfurd about the position in the Shetlands and the role of the landlords there (see NLI, Monteagle papers, MS 13384/8, Wigham to Rutherfurd, 3 Mar. 1837). John Wigham was a noted member of the Society of Friends, an ardent politician and social reformer. His home at 10 Salisbury Road in Edinburgh was a centre of the social, political and philanthropic movements of Edinburgh; Sir John Hill met Wigham and thought him a 'very intelligent man' (p. 132).

far led away by feeling alone, if they were not satisfied in their own minds, that serious distress did exist. The point, which was urged today, was in regard to <u>seed corn</u> which there is reason to believe exists in very small quantity in these islands; and which, to be useful in that district at all, must be supplied <u>immediately.</u>

Mr [Thomas] Balfour, the member for the district, as I understand, is the only other authority who has reported on Shetland. He gives a similar account of the state of that county.

Having stated this much I am afraid I must conclude anything I shall have an opportunity of saying from any respectable authority for a long time, regarding this district. When I make some progress in the western isles it will be nearly impossible for me to have information as to Shetland on which any reliance can be placed.[9]

Mr Balfour and others report that Orkney will not require assistance; and the committee seem to have been informed that instances of exportation are actually taking place from these islands.

There seems to be very good authority that it would be inexpedient, at the present time, to interfere with Caithnessshire; and the whole district of Sutherland ought naturally to be left in charge of the benevolent and patriotic family to whom almost the whole county belongs.[10]

If you can devise some other plan of watching the interest of the Shetland islands such an arrangement would relieve me from every anxiety about the whole of the districts immediately in the north; and might probably enable me to devote my exertions exclusively to the western coasts of Argyllshire, Invernessshire and Rossshire with their respective islands where I am in some degree prepared to meet with scenes which may employ my whole attention, without extending the district beyond it.

In obedience to the permission granted me I have applied for the services of Mr Stewart of Ardvorlich to accompany me in my tour. He is, in my opinion, eminently qualified to take a large share in this business with zeal, fidelity and judgement; and he possesses an additional qualification, of which I cannot boast, in a competent knowledge of the Gaelic language.

I go to Glasgow tomorrow and have made arrangements for meeting the committee there on Wednesday; and the following day I propose to go by steam to Fort William, where I presume the revenue cutter by this time awaits me. I have the honour to be, sir, Your most obedient servant.

Appendix No 1 Mr Wigham's statement relative to the Shetland islands at the committee meeting 6 March 1837[11]

[9] This sentence is present in the copy letter at TNA:PRO, HM Treasury, T 1/4201, but not in the letter in Graham's own hand at NLI, Monteagle papers, MS 13384/8.
[10] The ducal family was 'among the top rank of British patrician landowners . . . their position based on a seemingly unshakeable bastion of wealth' (Tindley, *The Sutherland Estate*, 1).
[11] This appendix is not with the copy letter at TNA:PRO, Treasury T 1/4201, but is with

Edinburgh 6th of March 1837

Esteemed Friend R. Graham, David Priestman of York and some others of the Society of Friends paid a religious visit to the Shetland islands in the summer of 1835 when they became acquainted with many persons of all classes on these islands and from several of whom the following information has been received, but chiefly from John Turnbull, minister of the parish of Tingwall, James Ingram, minister of Unst, Hay & Ogilvy[12] and Laurence Tail, minister in Lerwick;[13] these persons state that the fisheries had been unprofitable both in 1835 and 1836. That their crops in 1835 were very deficient both in straw and grain and the late spring in 1836 compelled the farmers to divide their own food with their cattle in order to keep them alive and after all hundreds of them died of want.

The cold summer of 1836 made their crops very late and the snow storm with severe frost came on before the corn was generally cut down, or the potatoes taken up which rendered both these (then only crops) of little value for the use of man and both it is said are generally unfit for seed.

A great part of the inhabitants are represented as subsisting on potatoes injured by the frost with such occasional supplies of fish as they can procure.

Funds to the extent of about £550 have been collected principally through the exertion of D. Priestman and R. A. Barclay of Daytonstone. £160 was sent in money and distributed we believe by the different kirk sessions.

Glasgow 8 March 1837[14]

Sir, I have met several of the influential gentlemen of the Glasgow association for the relief of the destitute highlanders this day, and have received some information from them. Most of their documents have been carried to London by their secretary, but I have got a copy of an abstracted table of the population and proportion of the poor in the districts reported to them, and I expect before leaving this to be furnished with a statement of the measures of relief which they have as yet adopted.

I have finally determined that it would be a waste of my time to devote much of it at present to minute investigation of the state of the county on the mainland and in the southern portions of Argyllshire. I have therefore resolved to push on to the north west, and to leave the inspection of the district to the south of Oban, till my return from the north as by

---

Graham's letter in his own hand at NLI, Monteagle papers, MS 13384/8. Further information is set out on p. 260, 14 March letter in Part 4.
12 Fish curers and merchants in Lerwick.
13 FES has the minister of Lerwick as being the Rev. Thomas Barclay.
14 See 1841 SC, Q 305–16.

all accounts I have received that district, if it does require any extraneous supplies at all will not need it before May or June.[15] I am happy to find that this determination is fortified by any information which has reached the sheriff of the county,[16] who considers the destitution to be confined entirely to the islands and to the northern part of the county comprehending Morvern, Ardnamurchan etc. and I have received such information in private communion with Mr [Robert] Brown of Hamilton factor to the duke of Hamilton, Mr [Alexander] Lamont of Knockdow, Sir Donald Campbell of Dunstaffnage, Mr [Richard] Campbell of Achnabreck [and Carradale] and several other Argyllshire gentlemen as satisfied my mind that I should not be justified in remaining long in that quarter of the country, when I have reason to believe that so great a portion of country much more seriously affected lies before me. In the meantime I content myself with saying generally as the result of the information collected by me that in the districts of Appin, Lorn, Argyll, Conal and Kintyre the proprietors will be found able and willing to support the poor on their lands without any aid from the Government.

It was stated, indeed, to me that some of the poorer people in Arran and Islay would require to be supported; and I believe both the islands of Jura and Colonsay have been brought under the notice of the committee of the association of Glasgow and Edinburgh. But, as far as my information goes, unless it was an object to devise a general means of relief for all the poorer classes in Scotland, in comparison with the districts where distress is felt in its full extent, these localities do not present cases which should in the first instance occupy much of the attention of the Government.

I have reason to believe that with respect to the poor of the isle of Arran they are "ill enough situated" as the poorer classes unhappily are this season in many other districts even in the mainland which are generally considered good parts of the country, but the duke of Hamilton has ordered a sum of money to be advanced to give them immediate support; and there is reason to hope that they will not make further application before the beginning of next summer. Islay may be designated as comparatively a fertile island and it is believed to be in fully as good a state as to provisions as Arran, and the great proprietor there[17] has the character of being at all times disposed to act up to the best of his powers in attending to the peoples' wants in the meantime. From what I can learn I consider myself safe in reporting that in this island (the population of which is 17,000)

---

[15] This was the conclusion of Robert Brown, the duke of Hamilton's factor, who Graham had written to for his advice. Graham had told Brown that 'It is evident that the Home Office are impressed with the idea that the distress exists chiefly in the western islands and all evidence which has come through my hands seems to confirm this' (NRAS, Douglas-Hamilton family, MS 2177, bundle 6245/2, Graham to Brown, 5 Mar. 1837, and Brown to Graham, 8 Mar. 1837). In fact, Graham did not visit the area on his return from the north.

[16] Robert Bruce.

[17] Walter Frederick Campbell of Islay, MP.

owing to the liberality of the proprietor and the exertion of his principal tenants in affording employment, no public assistance will be required.[18]

Since these few lines were written a statement has been made to me that some complainings of hardship in Jura have been reported to the associations, but no evidence has come within my reach as to this part of the country; and that island, which is generally reported in good circumstances, has one advantage if overtaken by present difficulties viz. that its greatest if not its sole proprietor (who is likewise proprietor of some of the minor isles in the neighbourhood)[19] is more amply provided with the means of affording assistance to his people than most of the highland proprietors (and I believe is equally ready to employ them).

The case of Colonsay has been reported to the Edinburgh association, and this island is one which has the advantage of a good resident protecting head, to whom I believe the whole island belongs.[20] I have Mr McNeill's report before me; and certainly it does not appear to me to afford evidence of sufficient destitution to call for the interference of Government. The number of families is stated at 145. No less than 50 of these are stated under the head of "destitute at present" − an infinitely greater proportion than the average of the ordinary pauper population of Scotland, but perhaps not very much out of proportion to what might be expected and probably exists in other parishes where so much reliance is placed on potatoes for food, and where that crop has very commonly failed this year to the extent of one half. The failure of potatoes in this island is stated at 2/3rds of the usual quantity. Mr McNeill does not expect that many additional families will become destitute before harvest. At present in a population of 870 there are only 12 able-bodied men considered destitute, to whom however the proprietor gives occasional employment; and these 12 men with 70 more have the prospect of being employed at kelp making from May to August. I should have forwarded the report which contains a good many other details, that you might judge for yourself, but I wish to retain it, in case I should visit that island afterwards; and as some answers would require to be brought out more sufficiently than is now done before I could make up my mind to recommend it as a special case for extraneous interference.

I have dwelt longer on these cases than I otherwise should have done, because I think I have already traced symptoms of relaxation upon the part of the natural assistants of the poor, in the expectation that some great measure of the

---

[18]   Graham's information about Arran and Islay was derived from a letter from Robert Brown, who Graham had written to asking for 'a candid and impartial report as to the state of Arran and Islay' (NRAS, Douglas-Hamilton family, MS 2177, bundle 6245/2, Graham to Brown, 5 Mar. 1837, and Brown to Graham, 8 Mar. 1837). Graham's comment confirmed what John Cunninghame had thought about W. F. Campbell of Islay − a man who would 'not take [the government's] shilling' (p. 257 below). See also Hill's journal entry for 25 Apr. 1837 (p. 134 below). But the Glasgow committee second report at p. 236 below suggests that public assistance was required for the parish of Bowmore.

[19]   Colin Campbell of Jura.

[20]   John McNeill of Colonsay.

Government will relieve them from the unusual pressure which a succession of bad seasons has increased, though they cannot be said wholly to have induced it. I take every opportunity of impressing on those I communicate with, that enquiry is the only point to which Government is yet committed; and I think it might be a wholesome measure for you to take some means of informing such of the highland proprietors as are in London of the districts which are from time to time reported to you as belonging to the class with which it is not necessary for the Government to concern themselves at present. If I should have come to any conclusions too hastily such an indication might lead to expiscate[21] the truth, and you might be enabled to judge whether it be right for me to reconsider these cases, or to visit some of the districts on my return which I am disposed to pass by at present. But in the meantime I have reason to think that such a step would release various denominations of people from a state of suspense arising from vague expectations as to what Government will do, and a confused belief that there is less necessity for personal and individual exertion in order to overcome present difficulties, because the Government has given a patient attention to the statements which have been laid before them.

The same authorities which have enabled me to give so far a favourable report of those parts of Argyllshire I have spoken to, lead me to expect that in the town of Oban the case is somewhat different. I propose therefore to stop there on my way to Fort William tomorrow.

I do not expect to be detained very long at Fort William, but I shall probably remain longer at Tobermory as I conceive it to be a good centre for receiving information, not merely with regard to Mull, but from the adjoining islands of Tiree, Coll, Canna, Rum, Eigg, and the opposite coast of Ardnamurchan, and it may require some time to ensure the presence of parties from these various points. If the officer of the cutter will agree to take me from Tobermory to Barra, I shall prepare to traverse the chain of islands. And from Stornoway in Lewis, I can conveniently come back upon Skye and the western coast of Rossshire and Invernessshire.

Mr Stewart has just joined me and we proceed tomorrow in the Fort William steamer at 12. I have the honour to be, sir, Your most obedient servant.

Glasgow 9 March 1837 11 o' clock

My dear Mother, We have finished our business here, and are preparing to start in the Fort William steamer at 12 o' clock. Robert Stewart joined me last night.

We may stop at Oban; but Fort William is the best address until I write again. Tobermory will probably be our next point. Yours ever.

---

[21]   To fish out; to find out by scrutiny.

Oban 11 March 1837

My dear Mother, We had a very good passage from Glasgow here. The swelling in my face is much diminished. We go by land to Fort William tomorrow – and, in the course of the week, go, by land, through a part of Argyllshire, which will lead us [to] Tobermory, where I shall expect to hear from you. We shall probably remain there 2 or 3 days.

Let me know whether Maine got into, or was blackballed, at the Club.[22] I would not have given him much money for his chance the week before I left Edinburgh. I had a kind note from Ardgour,[23] wanting us to make our headquarters there; but I wrote him that we were obliged to avoid all "good society" in our responsible tour; and it is necessary to make this rule when employed in such a duty.

The hills of Mull are as white as Mont Blanc. The weather looked dirty as we came down the Clyde; but it improved much on our trajet[24] through the Crinan Canal, and at Easdale and Oban, the sea looked like a mirror. Adieu kindest love to all. Yours ever.

Fort William 13 March 1837[25]

Sir, Mr Stewart and I reached Oban about 2 o' clock on the 10th. As we passed Easdale we sent notices on shore to several individuals connected with that populous neighbourhood to attend us on the following day at Oban; and the result of our enquiries as to that place was so far satisfactory as to lead us to the expectation that though there is a great shortcoming of the ordinary supplies in consequence of the partial failure of the last two seasons, the difficulties experienced in consequence are not of such a nature as to require any very extraordinary remedy. Mr [Duncan] Maclean, minister of Kilbrandon and Kilchattan spoke for a population of 2,750 inhabiting 5 small islands and part of the mainland. These people derive subsistence partly from the slate quarries and partly from the produce of the land. The list of poor cases on the roll at present is 82, and at the last distribution it was made up to this number by an increase of 13. Since that time the minister and elders instituted an enquiry as to the amount of destitution in the parish, by means of the

[22] The New Club, Edinburgh. Graham was a prominent member of the Club, serving on the committee which decided on the Club's move to its new premises on Princes Street (H. A. Cockburn, *A History of the New Club, Edinburgh 1787–1937* (Edinburgh, 1938), 56; see also Hill's journal entry for 11 May 1837, p. 141).

[23] Colonel Alexander Maclean of Ardgour's estate was on the west side of Loch Linnhe and along the side of Loch Eil; he was a 'spirited, active little man' (J. Mitchell, *Reminiscences of My Life in the Highlands*, 2 vols. (Newton Abbot, 1971), i, 180).

[24] A crossing, passage.

[25] See 1841 SC, Q 334, 336, 363, 364 and 402.

elders of each district furnishing district reports upon each case. The number of cases reported amounted to 90, comprising 350 individuals. A statement of this was submitted first to the parish and there was collected from the resident inhabitants £40, which there is the prospect of increasing to about £60. The statement was afterwards forwarded to the large proprietors, but there has not been time yet to receive their determination. As a proof of the falling off of supplies in the present and preceding year, Mr Maclean stated that the manager of the slate quarries at Easdale[26] is always in the habit of purchasing the surplus produce of the grain in the parish and its vicinity – that in 1834, the amount lodged in the store of Easdale amounted to 900 bolls – in 1835 it only amounted to 350, and [of the] crop of 1836 up to this time, only 200 bolls have been deposited there, and there is no prospect of more. Mr Maclean stated that there never has been a legal assessment for the poor in this parish; and his own opinion is decidedly opposed to an assessment; he would rather forfeit Government assistance than have an assessment in the parish.[27] Mr Maclean stated that similar steps were about to be taken to relieve the temporary wants in the adjoining parish of Kilninver, and that the minister[28] did not intend to make any external application for the poor till he had laid the case before the heritors.

Mr [James] Robertson, factor for the marquess of Breadalbane the most extensive proprietor in this parish and neighbourhood was one of those whom we summoned to attend us at Oban. He was unable to attend on account of his health; but he stated in writing that the "destitution of the parish was great, and such as will certainly entitle us to relief should we find it necessary to apply; but I am in hopes that we may ourselves with the assistance of the marquess of Breadalbane be able to carry through the poor, for the most wealthy parishioners, besides contributing to a fund for the purpose, are most liberal in bestowing private charity, with the wish that we may not be obliged to ask aid from the south."[29]

Mr [John] Campbell of Glenmore, himself a proprietor and a well known country gentleman in Argyllshire, and factor for General Campbell of Lochnell[30] the 4th or 5th proprietor in extent and value in Argyllshire, stated that he was well acquainted with the parishes of Kilburlford, Kilenan[31] and Craignish, and

26 The quarries were owned by the marquess of Breadalbane and operated by the Nether Lorn Slate Company.
27 Graham's letters, and particularly this one, and his evidence to the 1841 select committee (Q 334–98) contain a number of references to the workings of the poor law and the making of assessments – or rather the lack of them; the issues raised are explored in the Introduction.
28 The Rev. Donald Campbell, the minister of the parishes of Kilninver and Kilmelford.
29 Confirming what Cunninghame had predicted to Fox Maule – that 'Lord Breadalbane will not take our shilling' (p. 257).
30 General Duncan Campbell of Lochnell and Barbreck, who died on 9 Apr. 1837 – a man who, according to Joseph Mitchell, had lived in some style: 'the General appeared in the drawing-room in silk stockings, and in undress scarlet coat' (Mitchell, *Reminiscences*, i, 177).
31 Neither of these parishes appears in *FES* or *NSAc*.

that he could also speak as to General Campbell's property in the parishes of Ardchattan, Lismore, Kilmore and Kilbride. The inhabitants of these parishes were much worse off than in former years in consequence of the failure both of grain and potato crop, both of which he considered had failed to the extent of one half. Many persons able to work cannot find employment. Many heritors are non-resident and contribute nothing to the poor. There never has been an assessment in any of these parishes. Mr Campbell stated that on one estate, the estate of Melfort, there were 25 able-bodied men who could find no employment. These men fish herring during autumn, but the fishing failed last year. There is a great want of sound grain for seed. General Campbell of Lochnell has ordered 100 bolls for his own tenants, and he has no doubt the other proprietors will do the same. All will in some way or other procure seed oats. There is much greater difficulty in getting seed potatoes as there are very few sound potatoes in the county. Mr Campbell of Glenmore stated that for his own part he would rather support all the poor on his own property rather than submit to a parochial assessment even although that was coupled with the fact that it was difficult for the Government to interfere, till subsequent to the present law for the poor being carried into effect and having been found to have failed. [He] thinks it would be very advantageous to the highlands were Government to adopt some general plan for emigration and considers that that would be better than employing the surplus population at home. He is of opinion that the proprietors in general have had a lesson in the management of their property which would induce them to interpose some checks against the quick renewal of the population, if they could get rid of the present excess.

Mr [Alexander] Kelly, manager of the Lorne Furnace Company,[32] spoke as to the parish of Muckairn and the neighbouring parish of Kilchrenan and Inishail, all portions of the general district to which the whole of the present report relates. He said that many of the inhabitants were in great destitution in consequence of the failure both of the grain and potato crop – the former of which he considered to have failed nearly to the extent of $2/3^{rd}$ and the latter to the extent of $1/3^{rd}$ at least. Many able-bodied men are in want and cannot get enough to support their families. There is no difficulty in getting grain and meal, but the people are so poor they cannot afford to buy them. The only funds in these parishes for the poor are the collections at the church doors, and other voluntary contributions. No assessment has ever been made.

The town of Oban is in the united parishes of Kilmore and Kilbride. It has lately been formed into a separate parish by the church courts for ecclesiastical purposes; but in as far as regards the management of the poor, the control and regulation of them remains in the hands of the conjoined board of kirk session and heritors of the whole parish as it stood before the disjunction *quoad sacra*.[33] I state

---

[32]   The company made pig iron at Bonawe.
[33]   A *quoad sacra* parish was a parish constituted for ecclesiastical purposes only, and without civil

this because it does not seem to have been perfectly understood by the parties. The magistrates of the town, and those who have formed themselves into an association for the suffering poor, complain of a disposition manifested by the heritors of the original parish to relieve themselves of the burden of the poor in the town of Oban; while the kirk session of Kilmore and Kilbride state that the town of Oban has never applied to the parish, as a parish, for relief from the burden of the poor unable to work which you are aware is the only portion of the poor which by the law of Scotland has a legal claim for relief. The population of the whole parish is about 2,000, of which nearly 1,500 are included in the town and that part of the landward part of the parish which has been allocated to the new parish *quoad sacra*.

The absence of the minister of Kilmore and Kilbride[34] prevented us from having his views of the state of the poor. But we were attended by Mr Campbell the session clerk, and by Mr [Dugald] McDougall of Gallanach an heritor and a member of the kirk session and well acquainted with the affairs of the parish. The poor roll of the united parishes is at present 87 of which about 2/3rds belong to the village of Oban. The sum annually collected and distributed is about £36. No part of this sum is collected by assessment. Mr McDougall attended a meeting of the parish a few days ago in consequence of the circular from the Edinburgh committee.[35] Several of the heritors were present, and the meeting were of the opinion, in so far as regarded the landward part of the parish, that they had no occasion for seed or meal, and a report was sent to the committee accordingly. Potatoes are on sale within the bounds of the united parishes, but will all be required at home. [He] states that there is no doubt great distress in the village of Oban this year aggravated by the failure of the potato crops in the small patches of land held by the villagers, but that in ordinary years there is a considerable list of paupers who flock to Oban as a last resource who are forced to give up their small possessions in the country, and that this influx is rather upon the increase. [He] does not think an assessment would cure this evil.

The Rev. Mr [Alexander] Mackenzie minister of the new parish including the town of Oban, and Mr [Thomas] Stevenson the chief magistrate there, differ from Mr McDougall in their views and state that they consider such an assessment

responsibilities, jurisdiction or significance (see N. M. de S. Cameron *et al*. (eds.), *Dictionary of Scottish Church History and Theology* (Edinburgh, 1993), 688). The *quoad sacra* parish of Oban was created in 1834 under the Declaration Enactment as to Chapels of Ease passed by the General Assembly on 31 May 1834 (*NSAc*, vii, 530). By this declaration presbyteries were permitted to create the district in which there was a chapel of ease as a separate territorial district to be a separate parish *quoad sacra*. The declaration gave these chapels of ease spiritual jurisdiction over the separate district, and the ministers of the *quoad sacra* parish were deemed to be constituent members of the relevant presbytery; but the civil laws respecting poor relief and the provision of parish schools did not apply to the new parish (*Acts of the General Assembly of the Church of Scotland 1638–1842* (1843), 1028–42, online at British History Online, http://www.british-history.ac.uk/report.aspx?compid=60236, accessed 22 March 2013).
34   The Rev. Dugald Neil Campbell.
35   This refers to the resolutions of the Edinburgh committee and covering letter dated 2 Mar. 1837 on the supply of seed corn and potatoes (p. 245).

to be absolutely indispensable, unless heritors come forward voluntarily to relieve the present distress.

It is unnecessary for me to state to you that by the Scots law, the minister and kirk session, and the heritors of the parish, have authority on two fixed days in the year to assess the parish to the amount of what is necessary for the support of the indigent and infirm of the parish; but it has hitherto been the boast of the management of the poor in Scotland that a compulsory assessment has comparatively been little resorted to, the heritors for their own interest being inclined to make voluntary contributions to avoid an assessment, and the people being influenced by a certain pride of character which made them strongly disinclined to come upon the parish roll. The clergymen have considered it a duty to do everything in their power to maintain this elevation of character, and in many parishes voluntary assessments take place, which are not attended with the formality of a legal one, nor with the compulsory power of forcing every party in the parish to bear a share in the expense. If however the exigencies of the case require it, this is the legal remedy to be resorted to, and we cannot consider a complete case to be brought of a reasonable claim for external aid unless a separation has formally been made between the indigent and the industrious poor and unless the heritors have taken upon themselves the burden of that portion of the poor which by law have a right to be maintained by them. We are no advocates for assessments; on the contrary we think the longer they are deferred the better, and we think the Scottish clergy have great merit in having staved them off so long. In this respect, and with the object of sustaining the character for independence of the Scottish peasantry, they have more in their power than the legislature and we are grateful for the way they have used this power, and wish earnestly that they may long continue to do so. But cases may arise when these wishes cannot be fulfilled, and we think the Government must find some difficulty in extending even temporary relief where the provisions of the law have not been enforced, which if carried into effect would at all events lessen the amount of the evil though it did not entirely remove the necessity of further aid. The case of Oban seems to be one in point and unless the heritors set themselves fairly to the work it seems difficult to suppose that an assessment can be long postponed. This village has grown up rapidly within a few years, very much from a change which is gradually operating in the management of highland properties, by which the system of croft holders is in progress of being diminished and of being converted into a system of holdings upon larger possessions. These small crofts were originally of dimensions barely sufficient for the support of a family. They were frequently split down, by the connivance of landlords and without any increase of rent into multiplied holdings for the increasing population. Portions of these are by degrees pushed out of the possession of any part of their holdings from the absolute impossibility of being maintained upon them or from some system of improvement in the general management, and before being entirely thrown upon the world, or taking to a wandering life, they get a temporary settlement by hiring a room in the town of Oban, and similar places to the great inconvenience of those who have to look after the general interests of the neighbourhood. There seems to be no ultimate remedy for this, but to enforce the law as it stands. The burden of the necessitous poor is imposed upon the parish, through the medium of the board of heritors and kirk session. If an assessment were introduced, it would assuredly induce some system of rural police to prevent the augmentation of this evil, and even the threat of an assessment might lead the heritors to take such measures as might correct or at least diminish this evil, [and] without the necessity of resorting to so unpopular and so undesirable a mode of relief, a step of some kind must probably be taken soon. The local association has been at work [for] 10 weeks in the course of which time it has exhausted more than one half of the funds collected by subscription, the balance will be exhausted within a shorter period as the roll has mounted up to 60 from being 30 or 40 at the beginning. The first Tuesday of August is the legal day on which the heritors and kirk session can impose an assessment for the maintenance of the indigent poor for the next 6 months, and the chief magistrate can at the present time foresee no other mode of maintaining the indigent of the town than by having recourse to that remedy – partial as that must be in comparison with the amount of the present burdens on the local committee.[36]

We were led to form disagreeable opinions as to the state of destitution on the island of Lismore from statements which had been made in which it was conveyed to us that the inhabitants of that island were likely to suffer more severely than others from some of the landlords living upon the island, and from their neglect of it, although they were attending to their properties on the mainland. But on the information drawn from the gentlemen we saw at Oban we are authorised to state that 3 at least out of the 5 proprietors of the island[37] are taking active steps for the interests of their people generally and that this island will not be neglected in the allotment of assistance afforded by them.

Mr [John] Stewart of Fasnacloich spoke more particularly as to the district of Appin, with which he was more particularly acquainted. Though the destitution this year was greater than in ordinary years yet he did not consider any interference of Government was necessary here to prevent starvation. The only thing the people stood in need of was seed oats of which there are none in the parish, potatoes are to be had, only the price is high. He had guaranteed to the committee of Edinburgh half the price of all the oats required by the parish.[38] He knew that Mr [Robert] Downie of Appin had taken steps to remove all the difficulties among his poorer people by the distribution of seed oats, meal and potatoes gratis or at a deduction of 30 per cent.

---

[36]   No such assessment was made (1839 Poor Law Report, 73).
[37]   The five proprietors were: Sir Duncan Campbell of Barcaldine; Donald Campbell of Bailereolan; Campbell of Lochnell; Cheyne of Kilmaran in Fife; and Coll Levingstone of Bachil.
[38]   As required by the Edinburgh resolutions of 2 Mar. 1837 (p. 245).

Mr Stewart stated in answer to a query supposing a given sum to be laid out in improvements at home or emigration, which would be most beneficial to the country, that in his opinion works of improvement at home would be of most advantage and he is ready to suggest works in the neighbourhood which might employ all the spare population to great advantage to the country. Mr McDougall of Gallanach concurred in this view and did not think that emigration would materially benefit the immediate locality as in his view the best labourers go away, and the worst are left behind.

On our progress from Oban to this place, we had an opportunity of seeing Mr H. Stewart of Ballachulish who spoke even favourably of the state of the crops in his neighbourhood and consequent good state of the people. He said it was with a feeling of surprise that he learned from the newspaper accounts that any part of the mainland on the western coast of Argyllshire was in a state to call for foreign aid.

This day we examined several individuals on the subject of the destitution more immediately connected with Fort William and its neighbourhood.

Mr [Hugh] Macdougall (Mr Maclean of Ardgour's factor) had prepared some statistical tables for the use of the Edinburgh committee of the state of the population on the Ardgour estate, distinguishing the rents payable by each, and those of the tenants who could pay in full upon getting credit, those who could pay a part and those who were unable to pay anything, also distinguishing those as well and those who were unable to work. Seed is all which is required here. There was no want of food as the crop last year was abundant enough, but it was much damaged by the wet weather and not fit for sowing. The result of his statement implied that nothing was expected from the Government.

Mr Henderson, factor to Sir [James] Riddell had been similarly employed in making up views of that extensive estate. He thinks that the parish in general will be able to get on this year, were a little credit afforded to them for purchasing seed and meal, and is in correspondence on this subject with the Edinburgh committee.

The Rev. Mr [John] Swanson[39] and Mr [Robert] Flyter the sheriff substitute gave an account of the local association formed for the behoof of the poor which has existed here since the beginning of December. Upwards of £100 had been collected with this object and about one fourth of which was now expended. The persons drawing relief from this fund are at present 197 out of a population of 1,800 (being the population of the new mission as separated from the old parish which comprises a population of 6,000). Double the number will probably be in want before the end of next month. The association were anxious to establish a soup kitchen for the poor, but their funds did not warrant them in attempting to do so. They do not consider that giving money to the poor is the best way of relieving them, but by distributing to them coals and meal and other articles of food. It would [be] of great advantage to get employment for the population,

[39]   The Rev. John Swanson, minister of Duncansburgh.

or to get rid of the excess by emigration. Mr Flyter considers that permanent employment in public works would be preferable to emigration. A good deal might be done in improving the people in the art of fishing and giving them supplies of tackle. I have the honour to be, sir, Your most obedient servant.

Borrodale near Arisaig 15 March 1837[40]

Sir, Mr Maclean of Ardgour waited upon us at Fort William, and had previously sent a note by his factor respecting the state of the people in his district in which he says: "I am happy to think with very few exceptions the people in Ardgour will have food enough to carry them thro' until the next crop is ready." Statistical tables of this district made up for the use of the Edinburgh committee have been already referred to in the information afforded by Mr Maclean's factor.

Being in the neighbourhood of the Caledonian Canal, it may be proper here to take notice in reference to the disputed point whether it is better to employ the surplus population on works at home, or to encourage their emigration abroad. That the Caledonian Canal was undertaken at a great expense principally to afford work to the natives of the county, the ultimate utility was much disputed at the time.[41] The temptation of an uninterrupted valley running diagonally across the breadth of Scotland and containing a succession of extended lakes connected by water communications of easy fall suggested the idea originally that employment might be given to the people, by making a canal from sea to sea, which would be of benefit to the country. The work however was considerably advanced before it was discovered that the navigation of these lochs was so precarious as to defy the certainty of safe and easy transport; and if steam communication had not come into use, the Caledonian Canal must have been a failure. As it was it failed in the object of giving employment in the country. The engineers and contractors were all Englishmen, the labourers were chiefly Irish and what was worse still the result of that experiment for giving employment to the people of the district is felt at this day in the number[42] of exotic crofters, who stationed themselves on small patches of land, in the huts and temporary habitations which were run up for the labourers as the work went on and which are still kept up and tenanted in

---

[40] See 1841 SC, Q 406–27.

[41] Graham had taken an interest in road-building in the Highlands and in the Caledonian Canal and had taken steps with James Hope, WS, the agent for the Commissioners of Highland Roads and Bridges, to procure a full set of the commissioners' reports (NRS, Papers of the Maxtone Graham family of Cultoquhey, Perthshire, GD 155/995/1016, Hope to Graham, 8 Sept. 1836).

[42] The word 'number' is taken from the 1841 SC, Q 406; in the copy at TNA:PRO, HM Treasury, T 1/4201, the word appears to be 'cup'.

the neighbourhood of Corpach, and other stations of the Canal, in form and comfort not of a higher character than the cabins in the most over peopled and most complained of districts in Ireland.[43] Thus, the great national improvement which was stigmatised as a job for the advancement of this particular district has been the active means of entailing upon it a certain weight of this crofting evil which is universally admitted to be an immediate cause of permanent distress in the country, and affords a lesson that the statesman may do well to consider with how much caution it is necessary to proceed in attempting to provide for a surplus population unless the means adopted are of a permanent and enduring nature.

At Fort William we had an opportunity of receiving information from the clergyman of Kilmonivaig[44] as to the state of the parish; and in our progress towards Arisaig, we stopped at the manse belonging to the minister of Kilmallie which is the parish to which Fort William belongs, though the last now divided from it for religious purposes in a separate mission.

Kilmonivaig is probably the largest parish in Scotland being in one direction 60 miles long. The minister had been engaged in making up statistical tables in support of a call on the Edinburgh committee for seed oats and potatoes for the smaller tenants and cottars. The demand for the portion he had yet gone over was 140 bolls of oats and about 200 bolls of potatoes. The failure of potatoes last year was to the amount of half the crop. Mr [John] Macintyre, [minister of Kilmonivaig] stated that almost all, at all events the great majority of those he had taken upon his list as wanting seed, would be able to repay the price if it were advanced to them on a little credit, and is confident that at least 3/4ths of the money would be recovered.

Mr [Thomas] Davidson, minister of Kilmallie, stated that the population of his whole parish amounted to 5,514, but that a portion had been disjoined, and now form the parliamentary parish of Ballachulish, and the population of Fort William as I have already stated is taken off his hands *quoad sacra* under a lately appointed mission there. He has been lately occupied in taking lists of the poorer classes at Corpach where he lives, and in other portions of the parish amounting to a population of 1,905. He finds that of that number there are 200 cases in want of seed oats and seed potatoes. These cases scarcely average a boll of grain each, and he estimated the quantity required in this portion of the parish at 200 bolls of oats and 800 barrels of potatoes. He has taken the lists in three classes, and he considers that, of the 200, about a half are able to pay at prime cost, and about 20, 3/4ths and the remainder some portion at all events among them. All however will require a little credit. He thinks that at present the 3rd class only are ill off for food. Besides these there are 73 paupers on the poor roll and who receive aid from the parish funds, but the collections are very trifling.

---

[43] Which, of course, Graham had recently seen for himself (see the Biographical Notes above).
[44] The Rev. John Macintyre.

The cases of the parishes of Kilmonivaig and Kilmallie seem to me to be good illustrations of the mistaken policy, if by general neglect these unfortunate classes of poorer tenants should not be put into a position to sow their ground. There is not much seed to be had of the growth of the respective [. . .] but it may be had in the neighbourhood for a little credit, and there is good reason to believe, always under the exception of another bad crop following the present one, that advances made for this purpose would be in great measure repaid. The terms of the Edinburgh committee are to condition for a repayment of one half[45] and I should hope in both these parishes the heritors or others will come forward, as they ought to do, to enable this portion of ground to be sown. The funds of the association are totally inadequate however to carry this object into execution generally where assistance may be required; and the sowing of the ground is so important in a national view, that it might be worth the attention of Government where it could be done with little risk to afford some facilities for aiding individual exertions, or even assisting heritors or others who may be unable to advance the money themselves. £5,000 placed in the hands of the Crown agent[46] and advanced in loan under such securities as received the sanction of the Crown Council might in this way go a great way to relieve distress and probably all be returned by Martinmas 1838. Suppose an amount at once be lent by Government equivalent to what would discharge the conditions imposed by the charitable associations, the whole amount so advanced would be a new fund for these associations of which they are willing to risk one half and if the application of this accommodation was limited only to cases where every ordinary means had failed, and only as a last resource, it might be guarded by proper attention against abuse. With regard to the securities required, the Government might be rendered safe in many cases by engagements from the heritors, trustees, factors etc., but even in cases where the country people are neglected or where the best securities are not to be had in time, rather than allow the ground to remain unsown, Government might think it right perhaps to make a little sacrifice and run a little risk. I believe it is a good practical rule in regard to the lower classes in Scotland not to stickle so much about the amount of a security, as to get a respectable person to say that he will become security of all, and for a moderate advance and with few exceptions I should consider the assurance of the clergyman who take up the lists of the proportions in which the advances can be repaid by the smaller tenants as a sufficient test of the faith to be reposed in these people, that they would relieve him of the guarantee he makes for them, always excepting the chance of providence choosing to revisit the country with another calamitous season, when, of course, a beneficent

<hr/>

45 The 2 Mar. 1837 Edinburgh resolutions (p. 245). But see p. xxviii above.
46 Captain Sir John Hill, RN, was to be appointed as such an agent on 14 Mar. 1837 but at the time Graham's letter was written, the Treasury had not yet appointed him. However, Graham had already recommended to the government that Hill should be so appointed (see p. 5).

Government would be ready to relieve the clergyman from his obligation.[47]

I should hope, in the two cases I have quoted, there will not be the necessity of Government interference; but they are good cases to illustrate the view I take; and that cases exist where the judicious and timely interposition of the Government may prevent the ground from remaining unsown, I think is very possible.

Mr McGregor, factor on the estates of the marquess of Huntly in this neighbourhood, stated that on the estate of Glengarry, out of a population of 315, 35 families or 122 individuals are quite destitute. They inhabit, as he termed it, black_huts, meaning thereby that they have no land; and none of them pay any rent. On the Lochaber estate it is not so bad, though there are there 10 families of 21 souls destitute. Mr McGregor thinks it would be of great advantage to get rid of this population, and he holds the most obvious way would be by emigration. He considers the people would be very well disposed themselves to emigrate, if facilities were held out to them. He stated that many of these people were induced to locate themselves at the time when abundance of work was to be had, when the Caledonian Canal was forming; and now, that that resource has failed, they have no means of supporting themselves, but by poaching, and other demoralising occupations. I have the honour to be, sir, Your most obedient servant.

Tobermory 18 March 1837

My dear Mother, I wrote you from Oban, but had not time to do so from Fort William. We went across from that, by the side of Loch Eil, by the side of Loch Shiel and by Loch Eilt, and the head of Loch Ailort, to Borrodale, near Arisaig. This was the country where Charles Stewart planted his standard in 1745, and we passed a monument to celebrate the spot where the clans were first assembled at the head of Loch Shiel. Borrodale stands on the opposite side of the bay from the point at which he landed, and it was the last house he was in before leaving the mainland for the isles. It belongs to a family of the name of Macdonald the head of which is lately married to a Miss Watson from Edinburgh, (all Catholics) and we were as hospitably entertained by the present house, though it is Lent, as the Prince could have been by the former proprietor.[48]

After inspecting the neighbourhood of Arisaig, we embarked probably from very near the spot where Charlie took his boat, and were rowed in a capital barge with 6 oars across the Lochs nan Uamh, and Ailort, and came in by the north sound to Kinlochmoidart. It is shallow and of difficult entrance

---

[47] In fact, as is seen from the Treasury minute of 14 Mar. 1837 (p. 277) the government had already decided to provide £10,000 for the purchase of seed on the terms of the Edinburgh resolutions.

[48] Joseph Mitchell gives a vivid description of dining with Macdonald of Borrodale at Borrodale House on the day he had become engaged to be married (Mitchell, *Reminiscences*, i, 197–9).

when the tide is not full, and we were considerably impeded by ice in going up the sound. The family of Kinlochmoidart were not at home, but we found the way had been found for our reception there, if we had been inclined to stay at the house; however, after seeing some of the people, we proposed going on to a place called Dalelia on the side of Loch Shiel where we were taken in and hospitably entertained by another family of Macdonalds. From this we went per cart and foot about 10 miles to Salen where we had bespoke a boat to be in attendance, and we arrived here last night.

I avail myself of the post going off to send this. I found no letters here yet, but the post which is only 3 times a week comes in tonight. Our cutter has not appeared, but at any event from our arrangements we cannot leave this before the 22nd. Adieu kindest love to all. Yours ever.

P.S. The only thing curious, except the wildness and ruggedness of the district, in our trajet from Fort William, was at Lochailort, when we stopped to refresh the horses. We found in the house there 8 or 10 girls at the occupation of fulling a woollen web, to the tune of a Gaelic song, in which they all joined in [. . ..] You will see a description of this in Pennant.[49] The only difference is that they did it on boards with their hands, while he represents it as done with the feet: but I am assured that the last process is done by the feet to this day, so that I suppose this country in this respect is exactly in the situation it was in at his time.

Tobermory 20 March 1837[50]

Sir, After passing Corpach, and the banks of Lochiel, we came into a very wide and comparatively desert looking country along the side of Loch Eilt in the direction of Arisaig. This was the country where Charles Edward Stewart planted his standard in 1745. A stranger might pass this without supposing the possibility of it being over-peopled, but when brought out of their fortresses and gathered together from the sea shores where indeed the bulk of the population is to be found (settled under a mixed crofting and fishing system) the population at present is much more considerable, particularly in the western part of the district, than the natural means of the country coupled with its humid and late climate can ever sustain.

This district forms a portion of the very large parish of Ardnamurchan, which was formerly under the pastoral charge of one minister. By late arrangements, two parliamentary parishes besides have been erected out of it, and latterly, 2 other portions have been deducted from the original bounds, and are placed for ecclesiastical purposes under the charge of the

---

49   See T. Pennant, *A Tour in Scotland and Voyage to the Hebrides 1772* (Chester, 1774), 327–8.
50   See 1841 SC, Q 428–54.

two missionaries. There are besides 2 catholic priests within the old bounds of the parish.

It is in regard to one of these missions that I now propose to limit my observations – the mission of Arisaig[51] which is under the charge of the Rev. Mr McCallum missionary at this place and assistant clergyman in the old parish. The population of the mission is 1,500 but it is believed there are not more than 50 protestants in its bounds, and all the rest belong to the flock of the catholic priest,[52] whose chapel and residence is a little more inland but close to the neighbourhood of Arisaig.

The proprietors within the bounds of this mission are 5 in number. Lord Cranstoun and Mr [Alexander] Macdonald of Glenaladale are proprietors about equal in amount as to rental and comprising together 2/3rd of the value of the mission. The other 3 smaller proprietors divide the other 3rd nearly in equal portions among them. The great bulk of the population however is on Lord Cranstoun's property. The other heritors have chiefly an inland and sheep farming population. The united number of souls on the 4 properties do not exceed 200, so that 1,300 of the whole 1,500 are scattered over Lord Cranstoun's estate which, in point of rental and produce, does not exceed one third of the whole.

It is plain to the observation of any one accustomed to such a country that a very moderate proportion of population only can be maintained upon it, and that this promontory is over-peopled is manifest from the accounts given by the people themselves. In ordinary years the country does not produce anything like the amount of its consumption, and native highlanders who can trace connection with the territory for 600 years back are gradually abandoning the feeling of local affection which have always stood so much in their way, both as to internal improvement and for the success of the highlanders abroad, and a very general disposition is growing among the people of this district to emigrate, if the means of doing so were more within their reach. Last year 8 families were induced to leave this mission, on terms offered by the agent of the New Brunswick [Land] Company, and several more are only looking for the return of the same individual this season to join those who are already gone.

There is a considerable complaint of want of provisions now, and of course that must be increased as the season advances. The report made to us by the medical man of this district amounts to this, that 60 families are in extreme want and are real objects of charity and would require 4 months' provisions, that 60

[51]   The parish of Arisaig was, at the time, a mission station of the Royal Bounty Committee, established to 'strengthen the Presbyterian presence in the "popish parts" of the Highlands' and which later helped to provide a more adequate ministry in overlarge Highland parishes (de S. Cameron, *Dictionary of Scottish Church History and Theology*, 733). Robert Stewart wrote to his sister of the visit to Arisaig: '[we] were given to understand the people were very ill off . . . and certainly a poorer or more wretched set I never saw' (NRAS, Stewart family of Ardvorlich papers, 2654/1, box 16, bundle 3, Stewart to Marjory Stewart, 22 Mar. 1837).

[52]   Angus MacDonald.

families require 2 to 3 months' provisions, but would be able to pay in part. There are nearly the same proportion who are able to pay at prime cost for what they want. We ascertained that some families are without potatoes now, and that others are consuming their stock so fast that there is danger of their being without the means from their own stock of planting their patches of ground. But the result of our general enquiry was that there are as many potatoes in the district provided they are not exported, as may serve all the inhabitants for seed; but, of course, security must be given to the holders of these that the price will be paid, provided they sell them to the people of the district. We are sorry to observe that no arrangements have been made in any district for stopping the consumption of potatoes, and substituting meal which [can] more easily be had, and can be imported at less expense. There is not much apprehension either that the ground will not be filled with seed or that any part of the population will starve for want of food. What between the kindness of the poor to one another, the care of the resident interests, appeals to the absent ones, and expectations formed of assistance and support from the charitable associations, no hope seems to be entertained by themselves that this mission affords a case where any direct interference of the Government can be expected this year. Even if these sources of supply were drained to the last, still, as a resort to the legal remedy[53] as far as it will go has not been made, it is impossible to hold that any case for Government support can be made in favour of this mission at present. It would be hard upon that portion of the mission which is not over peopled to have to bear an equal share with the property which contains all the excess; but that is the law at present, and assessments, and poor laws, must of necessity come, if the landed proprietors (where they have it in their power) do not conduct their affairs under a better management, and so preclude the necessity of adopting so unpopular and so baneful a remedy for the evil which has been allowed to grow up.

I am happy in being able to select Lord Cranstoun's case in illustration of this part of my report. He is a new proprietor in this district, and a young man who has lately come into possession and it is no disgrace to him, that he should not be able at once to possess himself of the most matured views of managing the difficulties of a highland estate. We have some reason to think that his own views are very judicious on the subject.[54] He is moreover in a situation where if he is

---

53   That is, a legal assessment under the poor law.
54   Lord Cranstoun was one of Professor Devine's 'new elite', men who acquired highland estates in the half century after 1800, who represented a change from hereditary ownership, and 'who could afford to indulge themselves because they were amongst the wealthiest in Britain' (T. Devine, 'The emergence of the new elite in the Western Highlands and Islands, 1800–60', in T. Devine (ed.), *Improvement and Enlightenment* (Edinburgh, 1989), 108–42). Cranstoun inherited the Arisaig estate from his relative Lady Ashburton who had purchased it from the creditors of her then husband, Reginald George Clanranald (Mitchell, *Reminiscences*, i, 205). Graham's assessment of Cranstoun was not borne out: during the 1847 famine, it was said that his estate had been negligently managed and that the population on it was excessive; and he was criticised for the fact that he did not give work to crofters ([PP] 1847 LIII (788), 69, 233, 325–8).

willing he has the power to apply the necessary remedy. If in addition to that he can be satisfied that it is in his interest to do so, it is he as a landholder who should apply the remedy, and before Government in such a case is called on to encourage emigration or location on some other territory at home (one or other of which seems decidedly for this district the only remedy) the landlords should be required at their own expense to purge their properties of the unnatural excess, and to improve their own situation at the same time that they ward off an impending evil on the country. I am aware that there are unfortunately many cases where the landlords would find it a difficult task to undertake the expense of reducing the population of their estates to a wholesome amount, by transporting the excess to foreign settlements; but it is probable that in this way much may be done which is now not at all attempted; and landed proprietors, trustees of estates, and even creditors should be made aware of the encroachment which will be made in the respective subjects under their management, if the poor law, even as it exists at present, should come generally into operation in the form of assessments.

In such a case as Lord Cranstoun's, there is little difficulty for the landlord, and no ground for the interference of Government, unless some general system was adopted for relieving the whole country from an excess of population. His lordship paid £50 last year as a subscription to the poor. The circumstances of the present year are a good ground for expecting that he must increase the donation, and there seems to be no great reason to hope that under any circumstances he can be relieved of a renewal of his charity on a similar scale every year. If his lordship was to make a judicious selection of the people on his property, and pay at once the expense of settling the surplus abroad, it is believed he might place the population of his property in a wholesome state, probably at a sacrifice of less than half a year's rental, which would not be a sacrifice of capital at all equivalent to the tax he must in all probability continue to pay to keep his present population alive. Good regulation and careful surveillance is all that would be necessary to keep them at a fitting number, if they were once cleared off to the proper scale. I know no reason why a low country estate might not be very easily covered with an excess of population, if the proprietor made no rules of management, or if he permitted his farms and fields to be split down *ad infinitum* and huts and cottages to be erected at the pleasure of any one who had a fancy to settle on his ground. Really, it is the abuse of old habits, and the want of sharp active management which is at the bottom of a great deal of this evil after all.[55]

I cannot refrain, even at the risk of going into too much detail from illustrating this view by a case which presented itself accidentally to our notice at Arisaig. A person of the name of Galbraith, a farmer on Lord Lovat's estate in the parish of Glenelg and paying a rent of about £100 a year told us that on entering

[55]   In his evidence to the 1841 select committee Graham qualified this by saying that the want of such management had not taken place in Lord Cranstoun's time but rather was 'from the habits of the country' (Q 430).

into possession the ground he occupies was covered with small possessors. He happened to have facilities in aiding and encouraging them to emigrate; and what between their own means and the goodwill of the emigrant agent, he last year had 34 individuals carried to a foreign settlement, when their situation was improved, at an expense which he hopes to redeem within 3 years by the improved condition of his farm, in consequence of their absence. If this remedy is adopted by a tenant on a lease of ordinary currency how much more is it an object for the landlord even for his own interest to look to this mode of bringing his property into proper shape; and he ought to avail himself of favourable times for doing it, as in a year of scarcity they are much more easily induced to emigrate, than when food is plenty at home.

There is a great disposition in Arisaig to emigrate at the present time: and the feeling of dislike to this way of bettering the conditions of the lower classes is chiefly to be traced to their want of confidence in agents and others who have formerly transplanted part of the population on very unfavourable terms, and with very unfortunate results; and, therefore, a benevolent landlord will take some care in smoothing the arrangements for relieving his estates in this way. The New Brunswick [Land] Company last year offered terms so tempting that though it was late in the season many families emigrated immediately from Arisaig, Moidart and Skye. The accounts which have been received from these people since their arrival have determined many others to go when the agent again appears; and it is only to be feared that the complement for the wants of this Company may be filled up before all the voluntary emigrants of this very season can be taken upon their lists. Landlords, however, should look out for similar sources of relief; and it may be a question for the Government whether it might not be worth while to afford some facilities to landlords in doing so, to remove more quickly and thereby more effectually a grievance which has imperceptibly grown to a scale which it may baffle their unassisted means to effect.

I am aware that in suggesting these views I may be considered as out stepping the bounds of the duty required of me; but to report exclusively upon the failure of the last crop as creating destitution would be to report on a small portion of the causes of the present affliction, and would reduce my duty simply to a question of degree, a mere affair of how many weeks or months of additional sufficiency are likely to occur this year in the same districts, where from an excess of population, every year there is a portion, and in many of them a great portion of necessary misery.

It is alleged against the Arisaig population that they are apathetic in their disposition and idle in their habits, and that attempts to increase their means of living by teaching them to fish, and affording them boats and tackle have been made without effect.

By the attention of Mr [Alexander] Macdonald of Glenaladale we were enabled to cross Loch nan Uamh and Loch Ailort on the 11th March and we entered Loch Moidart by the northern sound. On the passage we saw many boats employed in fishing for cod and ling and we were afterwards informed that single boats that day had caught as many as a 100 head, for which a ready market is open at 4d each for cod and 6d for ling. All these boats belonged to the Moidart side.

Under the name of Moidart I speak of a population of about 1,300 being the part of the parliamentary parish of Acharacal[56] which lies to the north of Loch Shiel. The other portion of that parish amounting to about 700 will fall to be spoken of more properly along with the rest of the population of Ardnamurchan. The chief proprietors in this district are the family of Kinlochmoidart, who are generally resident though unluckily now from home, and another family of the name of Macdonald, who live at a place called Dalelia on Loch Shiel.[57] Both these families are doing a good deal at present in giving work to portions of the inhabitants; and as long as this disposition continues, the district has physically the means of chalking out employment for the people which the immediate neighbourhood of Arisaig does not possess. The last mentioned proprietor is improving land at a cost of £20 per acre, which affords a rent when so brought in of about £1 per acre. In doing so, however, his land is portioned out in small possessions; and as far as we could judge, his scheme of improving about 700 acres of moorland, even if it should answer as a speculation on his own estate, must lead to an over-increase of people in time. One part of his property, the island of Shona, a piece of high and rugged land which occupies the space between the northern and southern entrance of Loch Moidart, is peopled in its full amount already. There are 16 families on the island and the boast is (which must surprise a stranger) that in ordinary years they can maintain themselves. This year the failure is so great that they lean for support entirely to a lady, a relation of the family, who has the best house upon the island, and they will be maintained by her. We understand the speculation is to move a part of this population to the other land before referred to, and in this way emigration may be for a time be postponed. It is a problem not very easy of solution, and dependent in some measure upon the chances of future proprietors having the same taste and means for improving at this rate, whether this system is to contribute to the future advantage of this district, or whether it may not indirectly contribute to establish and augment the very evils of overpopulation which other districts complain of.[58]

---

[56] The church at Acharacal was one of the forty-three parliamentary churches built under the authority of the 1823 act for building additional places of worship in the Highlands and Islands of Scotland, 4 Geo. IV c.79 (see [PP] 1831 IX (330), *Sixth Report of the Commissioners for Building Churches in the Highlands and Islands of Scotland*, 4, 15 and 38; and, generally, A. Maclean, *Telford's Highland Churches* (Coll, 1989)).

[57] Alexander Macdonald of Glenaladale, who acquired the estate from Ranald George Macdonald in 1813 (J. Barron, *The Northern Highlands in the Nineteenth Century*, 3 vols. (Inverness, 1907), ii, 330).

[58] In repeating this in his evidence to the 1841 select committee, Graham added a last sentence to emphasise the problem: 'He expended £20 for what he got a return of £1 for' and he added that even this return was unquestionably subject to considerable uncertainty (Q451 and 452).

With regard to immediate wants, the failure of the potato crop which is in fact the staple of this neighbourhood is estimated at 1/3rd. Colonel [David] Robertson of Kinlochmoidart's overseer stated that many of the poor had no potatoes. He does not think there are potatoes in the district enough to serve all the people, but if they had meal for present supply, by which they could have their potatoes for planting, they might perhaps do. This district is likely to suffer from want of resident intelligence, as regards the estate of Kinlochmoidart or the power of those in charge to meet immediate emergencies. No preparations are [being made] to save potatoes for seed by a substitution of meal for food. The clergyman has just been removed to another parish;[59] and in the absence of Colonel Robertson's family, the servants and farmers are more guided by vague expectations of relief from abroad than by a decided determination to make the most of what is at home.

The overseer had made up a list of the seed oats and seed potatoes wanted in the district, which had been forwarded to Edinburgh, and which included Dr Martin of Muir and Alexander Chisholm of Lochawe's people as well as the Kinlochmoidart and Dalelia people. The list contains 146 families; [he] thinks that of these 56 can pay prime cost, 64 a reduced price, both having credit afforded them, and 26 can pay nothing.

It may be stated here that generally in all the computations we have yet met with a family [which is not] calculated to average 5 individuals.

Mr Alexander Stewart [of Kinlochmoidart], a sheep farmer on a large scale in the district, stated his knowledge that a great many families were very poor this year, and that many had no potatoes. [He] considers it to be very much over-peopled. A good many are very anxious to go to America if they had the means; [he] considers it would be of great advantage to the country if a good many were to go as there is no work for them; in every year they are in want. Almost every year their potatoes are done by the beginning of summer; and they have no resources after that, but what they can get from their neighbours. Four or five families last year went from Moidart, they have sent home good accounts to their friends; and many are now anxious to follow them.

The vacancy at Acharacal deprived us of the benefit of the information the clergyman had prepared for the charitable associations relative to the state of this parish; but the schoolmaster stated generally that the people, particularly the poorer of them, are very much worse off this year than usual. The crop last year was 1/3rd less than the average, and in some places not above one half. Many of the people are inclined to emigrate, but they have not the means. There is a great want of seed but particularly of oats, Mr Macgregor the minister had reported the amount required to the Edinburgh committee. Most of the people have enough of potatoes to plant the ground with. Were meal

---

59   The Rev. Alexander Murray Macgregor, who was transferred to Balquhidder on 23 Mar. 1837.

or seed corn or potatoes imported, he thinks the whole, except perhaps 1/10th part, would be able to pay if they got credit. This information relates to the 700 inhabitants of the parish lying on the south side of the loch of the river of Shiel, and which is part of Sir James Riddell's estate of Ardnamurchan. Mr Henderson, factor to Sir James Riddell, stated to us at Fort William, that upon Sir James' property of Ardnamurchan there were 68 individuals, mostly old men and women, who are perfectly destitute. On the Sunart parts of his estate, they are not so ill off as in consequence of the lead mines at Strontian having recommenced operations, they can find employment. He had transmitted to the committee at Edinburgh a list of them on the estate who are in want of seed corn and potatoes; and he thinks that, with few exceptions, all of them will be able to repay any advance, provided a certain time is allowed them to do so. The above 68 are in receipt of parish relief, less or more, but the funds are very limited, consisting only of the collections at the church doors and other parish dues; [he] does not think they average 5/- in the year to each of them. There is no assessment for the poor in the parish, but Sir James Riddell generally distributes a small quantity of oatmeal to them every year; [Mr Henderson] thinks all the rest of the estate will be able to get over this year, were a little credit afforded to them for purchasing seed, and such meal as they may require till the next crop becomes available. Mr Henderson thinks the recommencement of the working of the lead mines of Strontian will be of great advantage to the district. There are at present about 80 men employed, but it is expected from 200 to 300 will be employed in the course of the summer.[60]

Mr [Donald] Macdonald of Drumnatorran[61] near Strontian, was requested to attend us at Fort William. He was unable to come there as he was labouring under the effects of influenza, but he stated in a letter that he was "happy to say that in this parish (the parish of Strontian, being part of the parish of Ardnamurchan), there would not be much trouble. I sincerely hope, when proper enquiry is made, there is not the cause of alarm that is generally felt; happy will it be for all of us if there is not."

Mr Stewart and I crossed in a country boat from Salen in Loch Sunart to Tobermory and arrived there last night. I have the honour to be, sir, Your most obedient servant.

---

[60] In the event, however, the recommencement of the mines failed (*NSAc*, vii, 154).
[61] A grazier and sheep merchant.

Tobermory 22 March 1837[62]

Sir, The account given in my last letter of the state of Ardnamurchan, was confirmed by the Reverend Mr [Angus] McLaine, minister of Ardnamurchan proper who met us on the 20th at Tobermory. He had made a minute enquiry into the situation of his parishioners through the medium of his elders and others; and he considers the poor classes of the parish greatly more destitute than in former years. He considers it to be very much owing to the failure of the crops for two succeeding years; and, even if the last crop had been a good one, it would have been as much as they could do to have got over the difficulties of the partial failure of the year preceding. To the best of his judgment it will require from 140 to 150 bolls of meal to be supplied to carry the poor through to the month of August, when the potato crop begins to come in. For the last five years there has been no occasion for extra supply, beyond the ordinary parish funds and donations from the proprietor. The session funds were not augmented last year, yet he had access to know that there was greater distress among the people than usual, and greater demand upon those who could either lend or give them credit. These, he is aware, have been taxed to the uttermost and it would require several years of good seasons to restore the people to their former credit. Although this was not much of a kelp country, the failure of that manufacture had a considerable effect on the state of the people. It was before the period of his incumbency, but every year a few tons are continued to be made by the proprietor to afford employment to the people. He has not made any application to the heritors this year but intends to lay a statement before Sir James Riddell the sole heritor of the district, and also to send a requisition to the benevolent societies. The number of regular paupers on the roll of his part of the old parish is about 33. The collection at the church doors does not amount to more than £4 per annum. Hitherto the collections and other parish funds, amounting in all to about £10 per annum have sufficed for the support of the poor. There has never been any assessment and the minister is very loath to resort to that mode of supplying the poor. Upon extraordinary cases he has applied to the heritors generally; as for instance on one occasion in the case of three

---

[62] See 1841 SC, Q 455–504. Robert Stewart wrote to his sister of Mull, Morvern and Ardnamurchan that 'although no doubt there is much distress prevailing yet it is from the poverty of the people and their indolent habits a nature of yearly occurrence and from the badness of the last harvest it has come upon them a month or two earlier than usual. If I am to judge by what I have seen and heard yet, I should certainly say that the newspaper accounts are somewhat exaggerated, but I suspect we have not yet seen anything like the worst yet' (NRAS, Stewart family of Ardvorlich papers, 2654/1, box 16, bundle 3, Stewart to Marjory Stewart, 22 Mar. 1837). Graham said, in his evidence to the 1841 select committee, that he 'did not think there was serious distress till [he] came to the Islands of Mull and Skye' (Q 453).

insane paupers who were removed for a time at an expense of about £37 to asylums, and have recovered so as to be able to do for themselves.

Mr McLaine stated another permanent cause of distress to be the too minute subdivision of land. He thinks that emigration would be necessary to remedy this; but the evil would certainly recur again unless proprietors prevent this minute subdivision. Holding farms in common is another source of the evil of over-population. If the arable lands were so divided that each had his own portion to labour, he thinks it would be a great stimulus to industry, and to the improvement of lands at present nearly unproductive. [He] thinks it would be an advantage if allotments of land were made as large as £20 of rent, as such a size would enable the elder branches of the family to make the rent out of the farm, and to leave the younger members free to accumulate from their own earnings sufficient capital to set up with when they began the world for themselves. At present, in the small allotments, it requires the whole earnings of the different members of the family to support them. These are observations applicable to the district to which he belongs, but in many parts of the Highlands emigration is absolutely necessary in the first instance, to cure the evil.

The population of Morvern is 2,137. Mr Macleod the minister[63] stated that there was a great aggravation of distress in his parish this year owing to the low prices of black cattle last year, the prevalence of sickness and lastly the failure of the crops, which as to potatoes (the staple of the district) amounted to fully one third, and as to the grain (taking into view that a great part of what was saved was in an unwholesome state) he estimated the failure at two thirds. In many families the potatoes are expended already and several had expended them some time ago. [He] does not think there are as many potatoes in the district as it would require to fill the ground with seed and no attempts have been made to save potatoes for seed by substituting other food. He had sent a report to the [Edinburgh] association of the number of families wanting assistance, which was rather hurriedly made up and partly from that cause and partly from the backwardness of the people in making known the amount of their distress, he thinks his account was understated and he is now disposed to add 10 more families to the 50 which he reported as wanting immediate assistance. In making out the statement he drew a line between the ordinary poor and the general mass, as he considered that the former had another resource to apply to, which the other had not, having in law a right to be maintained from the funds allotted to them. There never has been any assessment in this parish. The heritors have always been very liberal in support of the poor, and also the tacksmen and tenantry. The aid usually given is in the most available way – food, wool and clothing – seldom in money. The collections at the church doors are very inconsiderable. They were

---

[63] The Rev. John Macleod, who gave his own evidence to the 1841 select committee on Morvern (see Q 1019–1148 and Q 2106–55).

reported to the Church Commissioners [and] he thinks the highest year did not amount to more than £20 [and] the ordinary poor is from 40 to 45.[64] He had previously transmitted to the association the amount of assistance which would be necessary in the shape of seed, grain and potatoes.

In assigning the causes above mentioned, Mr Macleod considers them only as aggravating the evils of the present year, not exclusively occasioning them. Like other districts, Morvern has suffered much from the failure in the manufacture of kelp. The great advantages of this manufacture were first that the price of this labour being generally retained by the landlords to the amount of rent secured their comfortable condition, and their power of assisting the poorer people when occasion required. Secondly the balance was generally paid in meal which secured food for the people and their families. Both these facilities were at once withdrawn, and both rent and food have to be drawn from more precarious sources. Another cause of distress, though not so applicable to Morvern, was the change of management in throwing small possessions into large farms by which the people have been crowded into villages, and were deprived of the immediate and natural support of the landlords, and forced to look for sustenance to daily labours, which it is difficult to find.

The isle of Mull, with the adjoining islands of Iona and Ulva and other smaller islands, is now divided into eight ecclesiastical charges, viz. the parish of Kilninian and Kilmore, containing a population of 1,920; the parish of Kilfinichen and Kilvicheoan, 3,090; Torosay, 900; the Government Church at Tobermory,[65] 1,520; at Kinlochspelvie, 519; at Salen, 933; at Ulva, 1,000; and at Iona, 1,144; [totalling] 11,026. The control and regulation of the management of the poor, if the Scots statutes were enforced, for the whole district would be in the hands of the ministers and kirk sessions of the three first parishes (which formerly included the whole district) conjoined respectively with the heritors of each parish.

We have made it a point to examine specially and separately into the state and condition of the poor in each of these ecclesiastical divisions, but as the circumstances in general are very similar except as to the Government parish which includes the town of Tobermory, and which will require a special notice for itself, I propose to state this part of my report generally as regarding the island of Mull, noticing of course, as occasion may require, circumstances of detail in which the individual parishes may differ from each other. It was uniformly reported to us that the poorer classes of this district are in much worse condition this year than in former years. In addition to the causes assigned for Morvern by Mr Macleod, and

---

[64] In his evidence to the 1844 poor law inquiry, Macleod said he had always thought it important to have a law which authorised assessment, but thought it advisable to abstain from enforcing this law as long as the poor could be maintained by voluntary charity but when that failed it would be 'a dereliction of duty not to enforce the law' (1844 Poor Law Inquiry, 178–81).

[65] The church at Tobermory was one of the forty-three parliamentary churches built under the authority of the 1823 act for building additional places of worship in the Highlands and Islands of Scotland, 4 Geo. IV c.79 (see [PP] 1831 IX (330), 4, 13 and 35).

which are equally applicable to Mull, Mr Gregorson of Ardtornish,[66] the sheriff-substitute of the district, dwelt considerably upon the effect of the low prices of black cattle which have been falling regularly since 1819, with the exception of one year 1825, and stated that though the redundant population, in addition to the failure of last year's crop, is an immediate cause of the destitution prevailing this year, it is not the only cause, nor does he expect that a succession of good seasons would entirely remove the recurrence of the evil. This examination was conducted in the presence of many individuals from the different parishes, whose testimonies concurred with his. The remedies suggested were employment for the people in some public work, road making for example, which is much wanted in Mull and totally unpractised in Morvern; and the improvement of quays with a view of encouraging the fisheries as a great assistance to internal improvement; and these remedies were recommended for adoption as a medium for avoiding the bad effects resulting from indiscriminate gratuitous charities; and before resorting to any means for facilitating emigration from the country.

The farther we advanced from the mainland, the more does the failure of the kelp manufacture come into play as a cause of distress in the Highlands. In Mull this has been considerably spoken to. The minister of Torosay (Mr [Duncan] Clark) stated that the former employment of the able-bodied who now cannot procure work was the making of kelp, of which a good deal used to be manufactured on the island, and now they are entirely deprived of this resource. Mr [John] Stewart of Achadashenaig, a gentleman of good landed estate in Mull, says that the distress in the island has been gradually increasing for the last 7 or 8 years since the failure of the kelp manufacture and in addition to that general cause, there was a great failure of harvest work in the low country last year, in consequence of which those who speculated on that source of gain were detained there for a long period, and were only afforded work for one or two days in the week. Colonel [Donald] Campbell of Knock[67] stated that the cause of the great increase of the poor population in the villages is the failure of the kelp manufacture which has forced a population on the towns, where they can rent a room for 8/- or 10/- a year. There are no assessments for the poor on this island, nor have any special applications yet been made to the heritors in consequence of the extraordinary season. The reason assigned was that they were understood to have subscribed to the general fund of the [Edinburgh and Glasgow] associations, and that they are in general liberal in their donations of private charity.[68] Mr [Donald] Stewart, the minister of Kinlochspelvie, said that

---

[66] John Gregorson, whose father Angus had been tacksman at Ardtornish, had acquired the estate from the duke of Argyll in 1819 for £9,000 (P. Gaskell, *Morvern Transformed – A Highland Parish in the Nineteenth Century* (Cambridge, 1968), 28).

[67] A proprietor and also manager of the duke of Argyll's property (1841 SC, Q 459).

[68] In his evidence to the 1841 select committee Graham said that he thought the clergymen had been 'rather lax. They seemed to think they should not succeed in consequence of the heritors having subscribed to the associations in Edinburgh and Glasgow' (Q 462).

his heritors have always been exemplary in this way, and he believed made as much exertion to support the poor as in their power. The amount of collections at the church doors in his parish is from £9 to £10 per annum and the number of the ordinary poor on the roll is from 9 to 10. In Salen there are 22 on the ordinary poor's roll; and the average annual collection for the poor cannot be estimated at more than from £15 to £18. In Kilmore and Kilninian the ordinary paupers on the roll are 40 and the whole sum distributed to them from the parish funds last year was under £7.

I would request your attention particularly to the state of this last parish which in as far as regards the poor under the authority of the Scots Acts[69] comprehends the whole interests of Tobermory, besides a portion of the old parish which is attached to Salen. The clergyman[70] for 18 months has been in a state of health which totally unfits him for the duty of the parish and his place is filled in the meantime by a preacher appointed merely by his friends. Not being ordained he cannot convene a kirk session nor take any effective step for the benefit of the poor. There is scarcely a resident heritor in the parish; and so situated the parish is very likely to suffer from neglect. The failure of the last crop is generally stated on this island as at least 1/3rd of the potato crop, and the grain in the proportion of one half, according to some and 1/3rd in the returns of others. The failure was chiefly in the oats; the barley was in general a good crop. It is of great consequence to the welfare of future seasons that good seed oats should be supplied this year, as well as that some importation of meal should take place, to secure the maintenance of the poorer classes till the crop comes in. The seed necessary has been reported or is in progress of being reported by most of the parishes to the associations. The numbers of the destitute reported to us vary in the proportions, according to different parishes, of 9, 12 and 18 per cent of the population; in the parish of Tobermory as high as 25 per cent. The number of able-bodied men who are destitute, though willing to work, varies in parishes in the proportion of from 3 to 6 per cent of the whole parish population. Besides cultivating their lands, their usual occupation consists in wood cutting, going to the low country in harvest time, and formerly kelp making; they would prefer relief by employment to getting it gratuitously. I should have been glad if it had been possible to have been more minute; but without a much larger period of detailed examination than it is possible for us to give one place, we find it difficult to come to a nearer approximation. The utility of a more strict accounting at the present time is indeed very questionable because this inconvenience is not yet felt to its fullest extent; and in the lowest of the computations above stated it is said that this is a present estimate, and that by the 1st of June it may be nearly doubled.

---

[69] A summary of the statutes and proclamations which provided for the Scottish poor law is given in A. Dunlop, *Parochial Law* (Edinburgh, 1835), 309–33.

[70] The Rev. Donald McArthur.

The most practical way of coming to a true measure or estimate of the degree of destitution would be by watching the workings of the machinery employed by the charitable associations. In the view of ultimately being obliged to do something themselves, I should strongly recommend to the Government to adopt some mode of possessing themselves of the information conveyed in tabular views and otherwise by the clergymen to these different bodies; and even to take into consideration, if their machinery proves to work well, whether it may not be the most economical and most efficient way to afford assistance in the form of food, by withholding it as much as possible till the funds of the charitable associations fail, and then adopting their machinery, by which time the imperfections in the management may be ascertained and cured, and something like the full extent of misery may be brought into view. From such information as I could hastily procure in passing through Glasgow, I have reason to think that for some of the districts we have visited, the allowance of meal destined for individual parishes will last well, with other church sources, till the 1st of June – that in other parishes the portions allowed ought, at the same rate, to last longer; whilst some parishes have been overlooked altogether which require a supply as much as others. The principal upon which the associations have started seems good; but everything of the kind must require some time and modification to bring it into shape. I cannot help thinking that it would be extremely useful for the Government, so far to put themselves in connection with these associations, as to have the means of commanding the information and knowledge of detail acquired by them in the process of organising their scheme of relief in case they should afterwards be obliged to interfere more directly and more extensively on their own account. In the course of another month, when the demand for potato seed must be ascertained, it will be more possible to come to a knowledge of what is likely to be required to carry through the poorer classes till the commencement of the next crop. The rate of supply in this district which seems to be necessary, in addition to other casual supplies, to prevent starvation, is generally computed at the rate of one boll of meal for each family (5) from the present time up to the first of June, and 1 ½ bolls for each family from 1st June till the next crop becomes available.

It is highly desirable that depots should be made in convenient stations; the fewer in number the more easy of course will be the checking of details. Even the depots should not be filled at once; but should be paid from time to time, say at the rate of a month's provisions at a time – an agent acquainted with detail should accompany the cargoes from the mainland and instruct himself at the depots of such modifications of the scheme or alterations of allowances as the experience of the local committees at the depot in the last month would enable them to recommend. As far as my information goes there need be no depot nearer the mainland than Tobermory. An allowance may be dropped in passing at Oban, if it should be ultimately necessary for

Government to do anything for that town; and supplies may be left there to be drawn up to Fort William, if Kilmonivaig and Kilmartin parishes should unfortunately not be otherwise freed from destitution.

I annex a list of the points which could easily be supplied from the general point of Tobermory, each destitute district of course finding the means of sending there for its own supplies. A very considerable district has at present been formed (according to report) by the association with Tobermory as a place of depot. The clergyman there is reported as the consignee, but he has got no official authority for this arrangement and as yet no supplies have actually arrived. In the event of Government thinking it necessary to do anything eventually in regard to this district, the following are the places (with the amount of population) which could easily be supplied from Tobermory; and I suggest the names of such of the gentlemen of the district (most of whom I have personally seen) as I should consider best qualified to regulate the proceedings as a general committee at Tobermory, and to branch themselves off for organising local committees in each respective district. I may have missed important names, but efficiency more than numbers is what is wanted in the members, and I have included no person except those whose residence and other circumstances entitle us to expect them to be efficient in the duty.

I recommend Colonel Campbell of Knock as chairman and convener, being an old officer accustomed to discipline and arrangement. He is a proprietor in the island, for 30 years has been a resident in the county, and for the last 14 years, factor to the duke of Argyll for Tiree and his estate on this island. Mr Gregorson, the sheriff-substitute of Mull and Morvern would probably prove an efficient coadjutor in the work.

District of Mull and adjoining islands.
Parish of Tobermory – population – 1,520
Salen – 933
Torosay – 900
Kinlochspelvie – 519
Kilfinichen and Kilvicheoan – 3,090
Iona – 1,144
Ulva – 1,000
Kilninian and Kilmore – 1,920
Tiree and Coll – 6,500
Small isles comprehending Rum, Eigg, Canna and Muck – 1,020
Ardnamurchan – 1,500
Acharacal including Knoydart – 2,038
Strontian – 1,200
Morvern – 2,137
*

[Total] – 25,421

Proposed committee for Mull and the neighbouring islands:–
Colonel [Donald] Campbell of Knock, chairman and convener.
John Gregorson, Esq. of Ardtornish, depute.
The eight ministers of the ecclesiastical divisions of Mull.
Mr [John] Stewart of Achadashenaig.
Colonel [Robert] Macdonald of Inchkenneth.
Mr [Henry] Nisbet, Tobermory, [agent] for the British [Fishery] Society,
and Mr [Hugh] Maclean of Coll.
Mr Middleton, factor for Colonel [Alexander] Campbell of Possil.

For Morvern:–
Reverend Mr [John] Macleod, minister of Morvern.
Mr [John] Sinclair of Lochaline.
Mr [Peter] Macnab, Achranich.
The Roman Catholic clergymen of Morvern.[71]
For Knoydart, Ardnamurchan and Sunart:–
The three ministers of Ardnamurchan, Acharacal and Strontian.
Dr [Coll] Macdonald, Lochshiel.
Reverend Alexander Macdonald, Roman Catholic clergyman, Knoydart.[72]
Mr Henderson, factor of Sir James Riddell.
Mr [Donald] Macdonald, Drumnatorran.
Mr Alexander Stewart, Kinlochmoidart.

For small isles:–
The minister of small isles.
Reverend Donald MacKay, Roman Catholic clergyman at Eigg.[73]

For Tiree and Coll:–
The minister of Tiree.[74]
Mr [Donald] Campbell, Breachacha.[75]

In the village of Tobermory, which is the chief part of the Government
parish of Tobermory, the crofters and settlers have undoubtedly suffered
much, and at present stand in need of assistance both in the shape of oats
and potatoes for seed, as well as meal for consumption. The settlers and
crofters however are not the most needy of the inhabitants of the village,
for there are many families (in number nearly as great as the feuars) who
have emigrated from different parts of the district, after being turned out of

---

[71] The only district in Morvern which is shown by SSC to have a Roman Catholic mission is
      Drimnin but no priests are given as being present until 1838.
[72] SSC gives the name of the priest as Neil MacDonald.
[73] SSC has MacKay as being an assistant priest for the Small Isles.
[74] The Rev. Neil Maclean.
[75] A tacksman and factor to Maclean of Coll.

their possessions and lodge in huts and black-houses. These people have no land, and earning a subsistence must be very precarious. The British Fishery Society, the proprietors, can have no interest in assisting such individuals, but, on the contrary, they are considered intruders upon the settlement.[76] Mr [Henry] Nisbet, the agent for the British [Fishery] Society stated that he would not consider the settlers holding of the British [Fishery] Society in need of aid, for their crofts, though small, are moderately rented and the feu duty very low. His opinion is that by industry in fishing and labouring, they should make a livelihood and render assistance in name of charity unnecessary. Colonel Campbell of Knock, who is proprietor of part of the village, as a specimen of the kind of people who have been forced upon the population of Tobermory gave in a list amounting to 123 individuals, of which 10 families consisting of 42 individuals have houses from him and a little potato ground, and nine families have houses and perhaps one ridge of land for potatoes. None of these pay any rent at all. This list, besides, includes 4 families who ought to pay rent, but they are so oppressed with numerous families and are in such distress that it is impossible to exact it. This list he produced to show the kind of destitution existing on his property in Tobermory. The 10 families were turned off the ground when the British [Fishery] Society feued from time to time their land; the others are poor people who came upon his land when they were driven off their possessions elsewhere either from too minute a subdivision of possessions, or the counter-evil from carrying the remedy too far by throwing suddenly a great many small possessions into one farm. There seems to be no remedy for such an influx, but assessments or emigration. The clergyman of the parish reported the number of ordinary poor at 40 and that the average collections at the church doors is not more than £20. The inhabitants of the place and the proprietors of the district are said to be very liberal in supplying the wants of the poor, particularly two of them – Colonel Campbell and Mr Maclean of Coll. The other heritor, the British Fishery Society, contributed in consequence of an application to them last year 20 bolls of meal, but at the time said they would not give anything in future. No assessment for the poor has ever existed in the parish. No special application has been made to the British Fishery Society this year. In answer to a question whether under all circumstances, it would not better the condition of the 40 ordinary poor of this parish, if a legal assessment was enforced, the minister said he is of opinion that it decidedly would, and that since the question had been asked of him, it was his intention to make an application to Mr James Loch MP, chairman of the Society[77] upon the subject. The minister stated generally that he had reported the state of destitution of his parish to the Edinburgh association. He thinks it

---

[76] By 1839 these intruders numbered several hundred (J. Dunlop, *The British Fisheries Society 1786–1893* (Edinburgh, 1978), 183).

[77] Loch, who had been the duke of Sutherland's commissioner was, in fact, the deputy governor (Dunlop, *British Fisheries*, 169). No record of such legal assessment is given in the 1839 Poor Law Report or in *NSAc*.

considerably on the increase since that time. Out of a population of 1,520, he had reported 50 families destitute; and he now thinks there are at least 70 families totally without supplies. The general idea on this island is that if facilities were afforded for emigration, the people would willingly avail themselves of them. I have the honour to be, sir, Your most obedient servant.

His Majesty's Revenue Cutter, *Swift*, Loch Tuath, Isle of Mull, 25 March 1837

Sir, Mr Stewart[78] and I left Tobermory in Captain Beatson's[79] cutter on the 23rd. Our intention was to go direct to Barra, but the wind proving unfavourable for that direction, we availed ourselves of Captain Beatson's offer to convey us into Loch na Lathaich in the Ross of Mull, from whence we had an opportunity of landing upon that promontory and of making some enquiry into the state of the united parishes of Kilfinichen and Kilvicheoan and the Government parish of Iona.[80]

The clergyman of the former parish[81] averages its present destitution at 6 per cent of the population, but that by the month of June it may amount to 17 per cent. Fully a third of them he considers could pay prime cost for food, on getting credit, and 2/3rd could return 15/- in the pound if work was found for them in the parish, and 10/- per pound in situations where they could not return at night to their homes. There are 60 on the ordinary poor roll not included in the above and the collections are about £20 a year. He has made no special application to the heritors in consideration of the extraordinary year but means to lay a statement before them; several of them he knows have been very liberal to the poor. 328 families want seed; the quantity, 200 bolls of oats – 110 can pay prime cost on getting credit, 123 [can pay] one half if employed in the parish. The kinds of oats best suited (which are four fifths of the quantity of seed wanted) are the Blanisley and the Hopetown;[82] the other one fifth should be half potatoes

---

[78]   Robert Stewart wrote to his sister from Loch Tuath that: 'The people on the island are [a] miserable looking set of people and many of them are very ill off at present; but really from all we could learn they are nearly as ill off every year having little else to depend upon than the little they can gather by begging from the strangers who visit this island in the summer' (NRAS, Stewart family of Ardvorlich papers, 2654/1, box 16, bundle 3, Stewart to Marjory Stewart, 26 Mar. 1837).

[79]   Mr H. D. Beatson, commander of the Customs cruiser *Swift*.

[80]   The church at Iona, built among the ruins of the ancient cathedral, was one of the forty-three parliamentary churches built under the authority of the 1823 act for building additional places of worship in the Highlands and Islands of Scotland, 4 Geo. IV c.79 (see [PP] 1831 IX (330), 4, 14 and 36).

[81]   The Rev. Donald Campbell.

[82]   Graham would have paid particular attention to these details of seed types as this was a subject in which he had a special interest on his own and Lord Lynedoch's estate (see, for example, the five large scrapbooks that he collected of largely printed material on agriculture entitled Memorandums on Rural Economy (private collection of Robert Oliphant Maxtone Graham, Perthshire).

and half bear. The failure of potatoes in the district is reckoned fully one third; of grain one half. The quantity of meal suggested as necessary for the destitution of this parish to prevent starvation before the harvest is 302 bolls.

Mr Maclean, a tacksman in the vicinity of Bunessan and Mr John Macdonald, schoolmaster concurred with the clergyman in his general views. One [of] the great causes of distress is the general failure of the herring fishery, and the population is so poor that they cannot provide themselves with proper materials. If boats, nets, salt and barrels were furnished for them they might yet prosecute the herring fishery. If roads or manufactures were set a going it would be a great temporary advantage; but eventually emigration must be resorted to. There is a great want of medical aid in the district and it has been more than usually felt this year. There is only one doctor in a range of population amounting to 8,000. Several have set up practise, but have been obliged to leave off for want of encouragement.

We had an opportunity of seeing at Bunessan, Colonel [Robert] Macdonald of Inchkenneth who spoke particularly as to his own property and the adjoining island of Gometra. His observations do not extend to a population of more than 400, but they are all in arrears, and this population has in a measure been supported by him for the last 4 years. He considers that one bad season is not the origin of the present distress. The crop of 1835 was a bad one also. The failure of the kelp manufacture, however, is the great cause, though the destitution of course is brought to its highest point in bad years. Emigration is the only cure and he is willing to go hand in hand with the Government in any scheme for drawing off part of the surplus population. He and the proprietor of Gometra have continued to make kelp for years in order to employ the people, at the prices of £3 per ton, and after paying the expense of taking it to market, the crop has amounted to about £2 a ton. Making roads, which are much wanted in Mull would be the best mode of finding temporary employment for the people.

Captain Beatson carried us up in his boat to the top of Loch na Keal and, landing us at Ardfenaig, accompanied us across a neck of land on this promontory which led us to the ferry opposite Iona. In this trajet, I had ocular demonstration of the distress among the poorer classes and had various opportunities of minute and individual investigation of cases picked out casually as we went along. I have no hesitation in reporting that there is serious distress in this vicinity. The first part of the country we passed through, in the direction of Iona, is upon the duke of Argyll's estate where the people are comparatively better off than on properties not so extensive. There are five large tacksmen who have very extensive population on their possessions, but though their crofters are more numerous than the services of the farms require, they are by no means in a distressed situation and are comparatively in comfortable circumstances. On one of these farms, I entered several of the cottages; the first contained a man and his wife and 11 children. Others had generally from five to six children, but they all had potatoes and in general some grain, and a few of them even had some value in livestock. There are 16 families of this kind upon this one farm. They have comfortable though humble dwellings; they are allowed to cultivate as much land as they choose to improve and crop with potatoes and grain; and even to have a cow and bring up young cattle, and to feed a few sheep along with those which are kept for the use of the family; they pay no rent but all the services of their families are at the disposal of the tacksman whenever he requires them. It is a kindly connection which keeps this population together and they regulate their interests not by written agreements or on any fixed or certain tenure, without the formalities of any contract; those affinities are naturally formed among them, which it is the pride of human policy in districts nominally more civilised, to confirm by written documents and signed covenants.

There is, however, a smaller class of inhabitants in this neighbourhood who are very differently situated. There are cottages without any land at all or very little, and others in very small crofts which are insufficient without some other means of livelihood (which do not exist in the country) to support a family. One or two instances of present destitution of this kind I shall state in illustration of the general class I now refer to. There are two brothers in one very small holding who support a family of six brothers and sisters, the parents being dead; one girl was in the cottage, all the rest were occupied in collecting seaware for the intended potato crop. Their stock of potatoes are almost exhausted. They are not of quality to plant; they have no grain or meal, no food except heath pulled up by the roots as demand requires. There is no work of any kind to be had and they have nothing to look to but the kindness of neighbours and the public charities, after their resources for a few days are at an end. Another case is a man and his wife and two children; they are utterly without a potato or anything else. The man was absent trying to remove part of an old wreck for fuel. The woman was cutting sea ware for the blacksmith's wife and would probably procure a day's food for the family for this service. Both this pair were young and capable of working. Another case, nearly as bad, was immediately adjoining. A young man of respectable character but who had imprudently married too soon, and who now has two or three children, is settled upon an acre and a quarter of moorish ground which has been allotted to him in a corner of a farm where the tenant himself pays only £3 or £4. He is bound to work 12 days in the year for his holding and the remainder of his time he industriously spends in labouring in his little possession. He is not strong and he has a defect in one eye but he still could spare many days for work, if work could be found. He is willing to take any wages which the gentlemen of the country think it right to award, but would work for merely half the rate if it was in his own parish or so that he could return home at night. (There is no such thing as a fixed rate of day labour in the island.) His crop has failed; he has some potatoes but not enough to serve his family and to plant. He would save the best for seed if he had a certain prospect of getting meal. He has no grain and has no money to purchase seed with. One other case I will state: the case of an Ayrshire weaver who was driven from want of work at his own trade there, and wandered into this country because his father had been born in Iona. He has married a young girl and already they have two infants. His cottage is of turf. Four short ridges allotted off an adjoining small possession is his allowance of potato ground. His return from it this year was nearly an utter failure. He has not more than half a barrel of potatoes left, and these are not fit to plant. His rent for the holding is the service of all the weaving which the tenant he holds off may require; he gets weaving work elsewhere, but this year he cannot get any payment for it. He would work at roads or otherwise if any such were to be found. One man I met on the road, who has a cottage in the neighbourhood but no land; there are six in [the] family besides himself. He stated, and with a formal affirmation − equivalent with a highlander to an oath − that he had not tasted food that day; he and his family had had a kind of meal the preceding evening, but had not at this moment a potato in his house, nor a grain of meal, and had nothing to look to but the charity of his neighbours. The afflicting thing in this case, which is far from being a solitary one, is that a bad season visits him only as far as it cripples his neighbours in their power of assisting him, for the return of harvest brings nothing to him, as a matter of right, having no land, and unless work can be provided he has no prospect but to spend his life as a beggar till his family are strong enough to make a pilgrimage in search of occupation and means of general sustenance. He is able-bodied and willing to work. [He] makes no stipulation as to wages but would work more willingly and at smaller wages if work could be afforded him near home. These are a few of the cases selected at hazard, and of these I have no doubt very numerous instances are to be found in every parish of the island. All these above enumerated are in the Mull part of the parish of Iona, which includes population of about 600.

The island of Iona itself comprises a population (and it may almost be generally be termed a pauper population) of about 500. This island is about 3 square miles in extent, one mile is covered with rock and a sprinkling of heath, so that between the two remaining square miles there is a population of 500. The population has nearly doubled within 47 years when the first census was taken up by the present schoolmaster and sessions clerk.[83] The minister[84] and elders, whom we saw, estimate the destitute families at present at 87 over the whole parish, and within a month there will be many more. 57 able-bodied men cannot find any kind of work. If they had boats and fishing implements many could support themselves. The authorities here seemed to consider that (the object being to prevent starvation) ½ a boll of meal overhead would serve the destitute population till next crop and for shorter periods in proportion. 59 bolls of seed oats are required for the parish. We are not disposed to alter our opinion as to the general amount of destitution on the island of Mull by any thing we have learned in regard to these two parishes; we think they will not materially affect the average of the other parishes.

83 Allan Maclean.
84 The Rev. Donald McVean.

I beg to add one or two general views which have occurred to us since the last letter, and which will close everything we are able to communicate at present in regard to the island of Mull. It has been impressed upon us in a variety of quarters, and particularly by the clergyman of Iona, that it would be very injudicious to bestow anything on the people gratuitously, wherever it can be avoided. Last year they got meal supplied to them and they are now looking for supplies this year also; were this system to be continued it would have the worst possible effects and would prevent them from trusting in any degree to their own resources, being themselves naturally indolent. His parishioners here are all on the duke of Argyll's property and their rents are fully 30 per cent lower than on any other property in the island of Mull; yet notwithstanding, they are in as abject a state of poverty as their neighbours. The influx of strangers to the island of Iona has had a very bad effect, the children being often in the habit of receiving money, their parents encourage them in begging and the minister has known people who were not at all in want, clothe their children in rags for the purpose of creating compassion.

In regards to works which might be invented for them that the charity may not be entirely gratuitous, if the benevolence of Government should be exerted in behalf of this miserable portion of the population, it appears to us that decidedly the improving of the roads in the island, as being of a general nature, and very much wanted, is the occupation best adapted for the people, and in every view most to be recommended. To prevent any allegation of local influence or jobbing, and to put the work in the best form for the accommodation of the people, I should recommend that the present lines from the ferry of Auchnacraig to Tobermory and from Auchnacraig by Bunessan to Iona, the line from Tobermory to Toliska, and the line from Salen to Ulva, should be amended and improved at such convenient spaces as would allow the labourers to return at night to their houses, and it would tend to relieve the general committee of much duty of detail and, as far as I can discover, it would be attended with the general approbation of the island if Mr [Murdo] Maclean of Lochbuy was requested to take it upon himself the arrangement of the surveillance of the work upon the roads, in the event of Government choosing to contribute to the mode of finding employment for the people. He is in the habit of taking considerable interest in portions of these lines, and is likely to be resident in the country, and as public money could be better advanced with the view of improving the district, as most of the agricultural produce, manure etc is at present conveyed on horses backs, there being almost no wheel carriages in the islands, and if the roads are improved wheel carriages would follow, and other economical arrangements along with them. He would of course communicate with the factors and others on the larger estates whose concurrence would be necessary and useful in the work. The improvement of the quays has been strongly urged, and particularly the erection of a new quay at Iona. But these works cannot be undertaken at once, and imply an expenditure of time and money for plans and estimates etc.

But there is one work which is more peculiarly fitting for the people of Iona, at which they would work most willingly, and one which no member of the British legislature who has ever seen the spot would think unworthy of being done at the public expense which I will venture to suggest. The ruins of the celebrated Cathedral there are pretty well enclosed, but the Monastery is open to the world and is suffering especially by dilapidation; and the classic ground "which has been dignified by wisdom, bravery and virtue and over which" according to Dr Johnson no frigid philosopher should stand indifferent or unmoved,[85] is open to the constant intrusion of every kind. The cattle, sheep and pigs of the village wander among the tombs of our most ancient Kings and other illustrious men of the oldest ages whose remains lie here. The glebe of the new parliamentary minister comes up to the very bounds of the burying ground; and the former walls of its enclosure are level with the earth. Could the people of Iona make a better return for the public charity bestowed upon them, than by collecting materials for effectually enclosing this sacred ground?

Referring to my last letter when I recommended the formation of separate portions of the country into districts so far as to be more easily managed, and to have the information more concentrated at particular points, I beg to observe that if the system is approved of, a central point might be made at Portree to include communications with Dunvegan, Kyleakin, Isle Ornsay, Loch Broom, Lochcarron, Glenelg, Arisaig etc, etc, and which would comprehend a population of about 45,000. The chain of the Long Island is not well adapted for one committee and, therefore, I should propose that the information relative to Lewis and Harris, a population of 18 or 19,000 should be concentrated at Stornoway, and that of the Uists, Benbecula and Barra (13 or 14,000), at Benbecula. From my information there are efficient men at these stations for forming good committees. These four districts would account for 102,000 of the population of the western Highlands.

The most important point to be considered, if Government is likely soon to begin to forward supplies of meal, is to set these committees to work to form sub-committees for making up correct lists of the heads of families and numbers of each family admitted on the roll of destitute. These lists to be transmitted to the place of depot and centre of the information of each district. I had the occasion to see the utility of that form of lists in checking the cases admitted on the list of Iona. The depots of grain or meal should ostensibly be at one point selected for each district but after the business is in train, probably great facilities might be afforded to local committees by dropping the allotted allowances at different ports on the way to the district depot, or sending them round from thence to the different ports of the district. I have the honour to be, Sir, your most obedient servant.

[85]   S. Johnson, *A Journey to the Western Islands of Scotland* (London, 1775), 346–7.

His Majesty's Revenue Cutter, *Swift*, Loch Tuath, Isle of Mull, 25 March 1837

My dear Alexina,[86] Lord Lynedoch sent me the enclosed note which he had got from Lord Melbourne's secretary . . . .[87]

Pray tell my mother that my toothache is quite gone. We started on the 23rd for Barra; but a foul wind made us take to this side of Mull. We had a happy moment to see Staffa and did our duty at the eastern end of Mull, and in Iona; and we have taken shelter in Loch Tuath for this evening – the weather being rather rough outside. We shall start tomorrow morning for Barra, if the wind will permit. Direct to Portree. Adieu, kindest love to all. Yours ever.

On Board HM Cutter Swift, Loch Tuath 27 March 1837[88]

Sir, Being detained by unfavourable winds in Loch Tuath, we took the opportunity of landing in Ulva and making further inquiries there in reference to the proposition I made as to finding work for the people to enable them to make some return for the assistance afforded them, I was led to believe, from what was stated by Mr Clark the new proprietors of the property,[89] that in the event of any outlay on the roads, the proprietors would be much disposed to go hand in hand with the Government.

Although we have collected some information relative to the islands of Tiree and Coll I have hitherto abstained from stating it in the hope of being able to touch at these islands, and to add to it the results of our own personal observation there, but as that opportunity is not afforded to us at present, I am desirous not to withhold it any longer. These islands being portions of the country which have most materially suffered, not so much from the influence of one bad season as from the loss of the kelp trade and from the excess of population which that manufacture had gradually engendered. Along the coasts of these islands, an immense quantity of kelp was yearly made, which sold at different prices from £10 to £15 per ton on the island of Tiree. The manufacturer was allowed one half, by which the poorer classes had ample employment and were enabled to earn a comparatively comfortable livelihood. Ever since the duty has been taken off salt, there is an alkali made

---

86 Graham's sister Alexina, who was married to her second cousin Anthony Maxtone of Cultoquhey.

87 Two pages from Graham's letter are omitted here: they relate to Graham's efforts on behalf of Alexina's 17-year-old eldest son, James, to procure for him a junior position at the Treasury (on which see Maxtone Graham, *The Maxtones of Cultoquhey*, 164–5). The note which Graham refers to is a letter dated 27 Feb. 1837 from William Cowper to Lord Lynedoch (NRS, Papers of the Maxtone Graham family of Cultoquhey, Perthshire, GD 155/995/8).

88 See 1841 SC, Q 951.

89 Francis W. Clark, a man 'educated to habits of business', was another of Devine's new elite, having purchased Ulva in 1835 ([PP] 1851 XXVI (1397), Appendix (A), 10).

48   THE HIGHLAND DESTITUTION OF 1837

from it at a very small expense which answers all the purposes for which kelp
was formerly used and has rendered kelp of so little value, that it will not
pay the expense of making it.[90] This has thrown many thousands of the poorer
classes totally out of employment. The very great failure of the potato crop for
the last two years, which is the food of the poorer classes, and the loss of their
cattle and horses are aggravating causes of their present destitution. The winter
before last has greatly added to their distress this year, and very many are without
a cow or a horse and such as have no land, of which there are a great number, are
in the utmost distress. On the island of Tiree there is no turf for fuel and they
are under the necessity of coming to the Ross of Mull to make their peats, in all
a voyage of about 20 miles, and to ferry their horses to bring their peats to the
shore to the boating places and afterwards to bring them in boats to the island. All
this cannot be done but at a much larger expense than can be well wrought out of
the small portions of land they possess and for which they pay a rent of 30/- for
from three to four acres of arable land with pasture for a cow and horse. There
is a great number who have a house and small piece of ground that pay no rent.

Ever since the year 1814, the price of all highland produce has gradually fallen
so much in value that black cattle will not pay the expense of rearing and bringing
them to market. Colonel Campbell [of Knock] who has had the charge of this
property for many years stated that another cause of this small subdivision of
the land was that the family of Argyll having raised three or four regiments for
Government during the last war, were anxious to provide with settlements such
of the soldiers as returned to the country. They were induced besides to give
residences to the poorer classes near the sea, in the hopes that they would make
a comfortable livelihood by fishing, and the necessary materials were supplied to
them for that purpose, but after repeated trials, it was found that the occupation
of land did not combine well with their employment as fishers, and their attention
was purposely directed to kelp making which could be undertaken at a period of
the year when their services were not so necessary on the land.

Colonel Campbell considers that the only effectual and permanent relief
which can be given must be by emigration, for which purposes Government
might be inclined perhaps to give free grants of land in America. Upper Canada
he suggests as the best part to which they could be sent and as near Toronto or
Little York as grants can be given. In doing this great care must be taken to afford

---

[90]   Up to the early years of the nineteenth century kelp and barilla were the principal substances
used by the soap and glass manufacturers to provide the necessary alkali for their respective
industries. An alternative to vegetable alkali arose from the possibility of producing alkali
by the synthesis of salt and sulphuric acid. Since the 1780s chemists had attempted to
manufacture synthetic alkali, and between 1778 and 1789 at least six applications for patents
had been made (see L. Gittins, 'The manufacture of alkali in Britain, 1779–1789', *Annals
of Science* 22 (1966), 176–7). The process that became the most important was the Leblanc
method, patented in 1789, which relied on the use of raw salt. The high salt duties had been
a disincentive to this process (see MacAskill, 'The Highland kelp proprietors', 60–82).

no assistance to those who are able to go without assistance: otherwise the most affluent and enterprising will be the readiest to take advantage of the opportunity. Whole families should be transported together and no encouragement given on a principle of selection of individuals. Too many should not be sent at one time, as that would make a glut in the market for employment. The system should be a gradual one extending over a period of at least three years in the course of which the first settlers would in some degree be established before the succeeding sets arrived in the country. He considers that proprietors should be ready to act with Government in this work of benevolence whenever they had the power. From the circumstances of this estate being under trust, it is impossible to expect that any system upon a grand scale for relieving the island of the surplus population can be undertaken simply by the trustees. But it obviously would be an object even for them to do something in this way, if facilities on a grand scale were afforded by the Government. If four of the present crofts could be thrown into one instead of being let, as at present for 30/- a croft, the same portions of land would be at least doubled in value. The proprietor too at present allows some kelp to be made, for the making of which he gives the inhabitants £5 a ton, while the price obtained for it in the market does not exceed £2–5–0 per ton. This he does merely to give employment to the people. Colonel Campbell states that from his own knowledge, there must be a fourth part of the population now destitute on this island. They are going on at present with the assistance of their wealthier neighbours, but by the end of this month, a supply will be absolutely necessary. They will require subsistence from the 1st of April to the end of August as the potato crop will be unfit for use, and unwholesome as food till that period. [He] thinks that at least 700 bolls of meal will be required for the season, and that the amount in addition to such casual assistance as they can procure from the sea and the shore would be sufficient to prevent starvation. He has himself given orders to have all the spare potatoes in the hands of the tenants on the island bought up to save for seed. He thinks there is enough of grain on the island for seed, both of oats and barley. Meal is all that will be required and he considers that the distribution of it should be limited (except in very rare instances) to tenants paying under £5 of rent and those classes (of whom there are many in this island) who have houses and a little potato ground free of rent, and some who have no ground and who consequently must be in the greatest distress.

If the Government should be inclined to propose any work with the view of giving employment to such of the people of Tiree as cannot otherwise make a return for supplies served out to them, probably the best work in which they could be immediately employed would be in constructing a quay on that part of the Ross of Mull where they are obliged to go for their fuel. There is ample material close at hand and probably the same native intelligence which has been considered scientific enough to plan a new quay which Colonel Campbell is constructing on his own account at Tobermory might be resorted to, and might be a sufficient warrant for the extent of the outlay that any money expended under this head would not be wasted for want of knowledge in setting about the work.

The lands belonging to Mr [Hugh] Maclean on this island [of Coll] comprise about 1,200 of the whole population and we were much disappointed in not having an interview with Mr Campbell of Breachacha, one of the principal tacksmen on his property, whom we had invited to meet us at Tobermory. In his answer he stated that however inconvenient he would have made it a point to attend but that it was unnecessary to do so as all the papers relative to the state of destitution upon this island had been transmitted to Mr Nisbet, Mr Maclean's agent in Tobermory. Mr Nisbet, however, has only furnished us with one document, a letter he had received from Mr Campbell of Breachacha dated 20th March, in which the whole information contained is that he finds there are "112 families who will require aid to enable them to subsist during this aggravating season." Mr Nisbet stated that they would require from 100 to 150 bolls of oats for seed, as also the same number of barrels of potatoes; he thinks that all requiring seed would pay in time, but that very few of those requiring meal could pay. We certainly think that between these two gentlemen we have been furnished with but a meagre account of the state of this island, and this makes us more anxious still to have an opportunity, if possible, to visit it. We were led from general circumstances, particularly from its being more divided into large farms than into minute possessions, to hope that the present situation of this island is not really so bad as Tiree and some others, but we regret that the state of the weather in the meantime affords us little expectation that we shall be able to add any more information in regard to Coll to that which the short notices above afford before our return from more distant places.

Mr Nisbet stated that the island of Muck, also the property of Mr Maclean, is much in the same state with Coll, with the additional evil that there is no fuel on the island, which they have to bring a distance of more than 10 miles from Ardnamurchan. He thinks this island much over-peopled. He believes the amount of destitute families is scarcely one third of the population. He thinks there is more need of emigration from this island on account of the smallness of its extent than any other. I have the honour to be, Sir, your obedient servant.

Loch Tuath 28 March 1837 on board the *Swift* ½ past 9 a.m.

My dear Mother, I have plenty of time to write now as we are stationed in this bay of Mull from the severity of the weather outside. Having completed our 3 days in the quiet anchorage we found, nearly up to the narrow part of the sound which is opposite to Ulva house, we made an attempt to get out this morning, the wind having moved about in all directions during the night, but it became so directly against us, and was so squally, that we turned back into the bay again; and we are now lying to, watching for the first opportunity of getting out again. I do not remember if I wrote you that we had visited the old remains of Iona, some parts of which I am sorry to say are getting into a very dilapidated state. Since our arrival in the bay we have been at Ulva which I had visited many years before when Staffa[91] was there. We went to the church and had both a Gaelic and an English sermon.

We have got a capital captain in Mr Beatson who does everything possible to add to our comforts and to forward the objects of our mission. We live well, as he has laid in a good stock of stores. We bought a good supply of fresh fish at Iona and our boats have been out twice for oysters, which are famous in this bay. The new proprietor at Ulva is not as well liked as Staffa was. He is a Stirling writer who does not understand the Highlanders.[92]

The lead is going, so we are coming to anchor – by the deep eleven – [. . .] less eleven[93] – down goes the chain cable, nearly on the spot we have been in for the last 3 days.

1 o'clock. It looks more favourably now, so I take the opportunity of the boat going ashore to send this off, in case we have an opportunity of slipping out of the bay, in which event I may not have the chance of a post. Direct to Portree. Your son, most affectionately.

Loch Tuath 29 March 1837

Sir, A deputation of the Ulva people came on board and a great number assembled opposite the cutter on the shore, on Monday evening, as a demonstration of the general anxiety of the island, that something could be done for the poorer classes in their present distress. In addition to the other grievances which affect generally the interests of the highlands on the occasion of a defective crop, these people labour at present under an accidental and additional disadvantage, in consequence of having changed their landlord within the last 18 months: and an unwonted pressure comes upon them, from the winding up of the concerns of the old proprietor, whose arrears are naturally called up, and the demand for current rent from the new proprietor, who is alleged very rigidly to enforce his rights under his new tenure.[94] Without observation as to the conduct of either party (who both are justified in the strict letter of the law) it is obvious that these double demands, at a time when there is so much less production on the ground, must very seriously affect the welfare of the people. They had suffered, besides, from

91 Ranald Macdonald, who was always known as 'Staffa' (J. Currie, *Mull – the Island and its People* (Edinburgh, 2000), 199–210).
92 Francis W. Clark, a writer to the signet.
93 Graham is writing this letter as his cutter reaches its anchorage; he is describing the use of the sounding or lead line to establish the depth of water.
94 See Currie, *Mull*, 185.

the failure of the crop preceding the last; and in many cases had only been able to sow their ground last year from the kindness of their clergyman Mr [Neil] Maclean who had interposed his own credit to enable them to get the seed for doing so. I understand that in all cases his pledge has been redeemed, though the exertion to do so has contributed to embarrass them further under the effects of the shortening of the crop of last year and they are very badly off for seed for the present season; but I am happy to quote this instance in illustration of what I ventured to suggest upon a former occasion,[95] in the event of any difficulty in procuring other securities, it would be safe, in the general instance, with that class of people to rest satisfied with the assurance of the clergyman, that in his belief they would repay the advances which were made to them. The people who came on board represented themselves as being too poor to adopt of themselves any plan for bettering their condition by emigration but expressed their own willingness, and that of a great many people on the island, to avail themselves of any opportunity offered to them of doing so. Indeed through the medium of their clergyman, they had made an application to the New Brunswick [Land] Company to ascertain if they intended to take out emigrants this year on the terms of a free passage as they had done last season, but their hopes were disappointed by the answer which was to the effect that the company did not intend to carry more emigrants abroad, but at the price of £3 – 10 – 0 per head.

Our detention in Loch Tuath gave us an opportunity of seeing Mr [Alexander] Shiels, factor for Mrs Maclean Clephane[96] who had been prevented from meeting us at Tobermory. He spoke as to a population of about 600 on that estate which is in the parish of Kilmore and Kilninian. He estimated one fifth of the population to be now destitute; and before the crop comes in the numbers will be increased to more than one fourth part. These people are at present supported on the bounty of Mrs Clephane, who has contributed largely to their wants this year, as she has done before. He has lately received £60 from her to be distributed in meal; and, serving it out moderately and from time to time, he thinks this allowance will suffice to keep the destitute population on the estate for the next six weeks. The excess of distress this year is principally to be attributed to the failure of the last two crops; but partly to the excess of population, owing to the failure of kelp making. There is generally a little emigration going on, and many would willingly emigrate if facilities were afforded them. From various causes the population has been reduced upon this estate within these few years, nearly 1/7th part. He thinks there have been more deaths within the last 10 months than during the previous seven years. The people live chiefly on potatoes. He instanced a family of 10 who, at two meals a day, consumed a barrel of potatoes in five days. [He] thinks that between 1 and 1 ½ stones of meal will be equal to

---

95   See p. 22.
96   Mary Ann D. Maclean of Torloisk, who had married William Douglas Clephane of Carslogie.

a barrel of potatoes [and] thinks that a barrel of potatoes is equal to 14 stone weight. These estimates are stated as we received them, but there are different views as to the size of barrels, bolls etc which make it extremely difficult to come to any relative estimate of what would be necessary of the one species of food, from what is known to be a sufficient allowance of the other.[97] In general the relative proportion of potatoes and meal as food, in the rough estimates which have yet come under our observation, varies from 3 to 1 to 4 to 1, in weight. Mr Shiels gave an opinion that emigration was the only permanent cure of the evil. He has known many emigrations during the 14 years he has been factor on this estate; and the rate of transporting them has varied from 50/- to £4 per head, exclusive of provisions on the voyage. This parish (Kilmore and Kilninian) was formerly represented to us as being likely to suffer from neglect in consequence of the state of the health of the clergyman[98] and the circumstance of his assistant not being ordained. We made some enquiries of Mr Shiels, as to the facts of this case. He represents the clergyman as being in an unfit state to take charge of the parish; that he has been so for 18 months, and that previously (at least for 14 years while he has been in the parish) the minister had not appointed one elder; and that consequently there is no kirk session.

We have been detained in Loch Tuath since the morning of Saturday the 25th by heavy gales of wind from the north, accompanied with thick showers of snow. Yesterday morning, an attempt was made to get to sea, but after proceeding a certain length we were compelled to return to an anchorage. This morning, a similar attempt was made. The wind, though light, was very variable, and such a thick fall of snow came on that the Captain did not think himself justified in proceeding, and we were accordingly forced again to put back. I have the honour to be, Sir, your obedient servant.

On Board HM Cutter *Swift* Loch Kishorn 3 April 1837[99]

Sir, We got out of Loch Tuath on the morning of the 30th and the wind not suiting to carry us to Barra we reversed the line of operation we had originally projected and, approaching Skye by the eastern side, we passed through the narrows and anchored in Loch Alsh that night. In passing, we landed in the parish of Sleat and saw the clergyman and some of the inhabitants of that part of Skye; and we have since had an opportunity of inquiring more particularly into the circumstances of this parish and the parish of Strath which form together a considerable population in the southern portion of Skye.

[97] This comment by Graham on the different views on the size of barrels and bolls highlights the difficulties in providing consistent estimates of the daily allowances for food during the famine (see the Introduction).
[98] The Rev. Dr Donald McArthur.
[99] See 1841 SC, Q 951*–955.

We are now approaching those parts of the country where the destitution of the present year seems to exist to the greater extent. In the part of the country just alluded to more than one half of the population are considered destitute at present. The Reverend Mr [John] Mackinnon, minister of Strath,[100] has known that parish for 30 years and never saw it in such a state of destitution. He attributed it almost entirely to the failure of the crop of the last two years, but particularly the last.[101] This was not a kelp country to any extent. We could not discover that its produce in kelp ever amounted to 150 tons; and Mr Mackinnon of Corry[102] stated that the cessation of kelp making left the sea ware available as a manure, and though this was in one view an advantage, it tended indirectly to encourage early marriages and too great an increase of the population. The great population of this part of the country arises chiefly from the minute subdivision of farms and the splitting down of these into still smaller possessions. Of the 1,500 at present destitute in the parish of Sleat, 1,150 pay no rent to the landlord. In ordinary years there is considerable destitution. About 60 are usually relieved in that parish from the sessions' funds. Last year 100 drew relief; but the collections at the church doors, which 10 years ago averaged £10, from the absence of heritors etc. do not now amount to a yearly average of £5. The poorer classes are in general supplied in this parish by the tenants who give to them a portion of meat and potatoes. This year from the failure in the crops, they have it not in their power to do so. The minister of Sleat[103] instanced as a measure of the failure this year what had happened on his own farm. From 16 bolls of oats sown, the produce was only four bolls of meal and that very bad. The minister of Strath planted 46 barrels of potatoes and the return was little more than double that number instead of 8 or 10 returns, which he would consider a fair average crop.

We had an opportunity of enquiring into the details of these circumstances from some of the sufferers themselves; and I select a few cases in different classes as illustrations of the distress which is evidently too general in the district:

[100] Described by Sir Archibald Geikie as 'the best example of a Highland clergyman I ever knew' (*FES*, vii, 183).

[101] See his comments on the destitution in *NSAc*, xiv, 314. Robert Stewart wrote of Strath to his sister: 'this seemed decidedly the worst place we had visited yet. More than half of the people of the whole parish were represented as being [in] starvation. While we were there upwards of 200 people collected around the inn to get their case taken down and really the looks of the poor people indicated great privation and suffering, nor is it confined to the very poorest. Many of the small tenants who have some stock of both cattle and sheep are as ill off as their crops entirely failed and they have no means at present of selling any of their stock to purchase food and having no money are equally ill off with the rest' (NRAS, Stewart family of Ardvorlich papers, 2654/1, box 16, bundle 3, Stewart to Marjory Stewart, 2 Apr. 1837).

[102] Lachlan Mackinnon of Corry, who 'by his gentlemanly bearing, force of character and talent . . . was, in the absence of Lord Macdonald, for many years the most prominent personage in the island' (Mitchell, *Reminiscences*, i, 211).

[103] The Rev. Alexander McIver.

Duncan Martin has a small croft at Kyle, in which he grows principally potatoes; he has a wife and 8 children. His potato crop has almost entirely failed and he has had none in his house for 14 days. He had come out to beg for meal; [he] had nothing but what he could get from his neighbours; sometimes he gets a few fish; [he] says he could pay for 5 or 6 bolls of meal from the next produce of his croft, if he got credit. This last part of the statement seemed not to be implicitly believed by some of the people of the country who were much interested in the general welfare of its inhabitants. This, however, is exactly the case of a small tenant who is in distress, and wants credit. He has the keep of two cows and to a certain extent ought to be able to repay.

Roderick McLeod [of] Kyleakin has 8 children and [a] wife; [he] has neither a croft nor a cow's grass; [he] has had nothing to support his family for the last week but 2d which he got from a person in Kyleakin. [He] has subsisted this year on charity alone; [he] fishes when he is able; [he] has one daughter able to work; [he] can pay nothing; [he] has no ground for potatoes but sometimes gets leave to plant a few in his neighbour's land; [he] planted some last year.

Duncan McKinnon, in the parish of Strath, a cottar, has no croft or cow. [He] sows no grain; [he] has a patch of potato ground [where he] planted last year 3 ½ barrels of potatoes and had only 3 barrels of produce. [He] has a wife and six children and has nothing to support them. No work is to be had here.

Hugh McKenzie, in Strath, planted half a barrel and none of these grew; [he] has no cow and pays no rent. [He] has a wife and five children, one of them is lame. He has not 2d worth of provisions in his house.

These cases are 8 or 10 miles apart from each other. But perhaps the best general view of the state of this district may be taken from the account of John McInnes at Breakish in the parish of Strath, a very intelligent man who has been all his life in the district and 30 years upon the spot he now inhabits. He has a possession of 5 acres of arable land and a cow's grass from Lord Macdonald at a rent of £3.12. He had not a fourth part of an average crop in grain this year and little more than a fourth of potatoes. He has not as many potatoes as will plant his ground, and his grain was quite green when it was cut and is quite unfit for sowing. If he gets seed grain he will be able to pay for it. The year before last was a scarce year. He is 65 years old and never saw any year to be compared with the last in Skye. [He] stated that on the farm on which he resides, which is part of an arrangement on which the arable land is divided among the crofters and the hill let in common, there are 600 souls. The rent of the whole is about £180. Some of these crofters keep no stock but pay their rent by selling their grass to others, retaining the arable in their own hands. Many of them have at this moment nothing to support them. A great proportion of the rents are paid by the labours of the sons of the tenants who go to Dundee and other parts of the low country for 6 or 8 months at a time. Some of the lots no larger than his proportion of the farm have two and three families located upon them and it is that which makes so many of them poor.

In the parish of Sleat, distribution of meal has commenced. 96 bolls of meal have been received for this parish from the committee of Glasgow and have been consigned to the management of the minister. He has divided the district into four classes: 1. Those who can give neither labour nor money. 2. Those who can give labour. 3. Those who can make a partial payment in money on getting credit. 4. Those who can pay cash on credit. The elders are preparing lists with the names of heads of families and the number of individuals in each. The principle of all this is good, but it would require some amendment in the execution. In the first place an issue is made of meal in equal portions to families of every size; [this] is without any relative or apparent computation [of] how long this allowance is to last them. It cannot serve for all these families for the same period; and the next supplies may be wanted much sooner by some families than by others. The want of a fixed standard of consumption with the improvident will be converted to abuse, and even with the best principled will be apt to occasion an expenditure of means which by more prudent arrangements might be kept within smaller bounds. The clergyman most naturally will be inclined to give as much as he can to his people; but in the event of his parish being relieved at the public expense, they should be regarded as one would a garrison in a state of siege or a vessel running short of provisions at sea; a computation of the whole expected period of forced economy should be made, and each class or family should be put on its corresponding allowance. With this view, if the Government interferes it would be highly proper to have, whenever it can be obtained, a mixed local committee for each parish to be responsible for the lists taken up to a general district committee, whose business should be to check these lists and to regulate the supplies. Committees at Edinburgh and Glasgow are too far removed from the spot to be of efficient service in checking the details of the parish lists. But a good deal may be done in this way by the general committees of districts who are not beyond the reach of examining into particular cases where they appear to be doubtful. In the next place it is of great consequence to all parties interested, or likely to be interested, in the expenditure that the amount of this allowance should be fixed as soon as possible and that something like uniformity should exist in the arrangements from the commencement for feeding the destitute generally over the country. Invariably the ministers and those who think only of supplying immediate wants, calculate the proportion of meal which is necessary, with other aids, to prevent starvation, greatly beyond what, on reflection and mature views, they ultimately acknowledge to be enough. We have not yet met with a case, either among the clergymen or among the suffering poor themselves, where in the end they have not expressed themselves perfectly contented if an arrangement could be made to afford the destitute the allowance I formerly stated as being satisfactory for Mull; viz. 2 ½ bolls for a family of 5, or half a boll over head to old and young till the crop comes in. This allowance, although apparently a small one, will in proportion to the apparent destitution require a very considerable outlay, wherever the sources are, from which it has to be drawn.

There is universal want of seed in this district, but it is understood that Lord Macdonald is taking steps in regard to his estate;[104] and we were informed at Broadford that a vessel was at the quay there with part of the seed grains intended for the parish. 650 barrels of potatoes for seed would be required for Strath alone, but we have nowhere yet heard of any markets from which these remote places are likely to be supplied with potato seed, even if the means of immediate payment were more at hand. At Broadford, where we had an opportunity of receiving information from Mr Mackinnon of Corry, Mr Mackinnon minister of Strath, Dr [Norman] Macalister [of Strathaird] and other gentlemen forming the local committee there, a meeting was actually going on to arrange the principles on which the distribution of meal should be made; and we have reason to hope that this part of the business will be satisfactorily attended to there, from the outset; as these gentlemen concurred with the general idea that imperfection might exist in the mode of distribution adopted suddenly in other quarters. About 200 of the poorer inhabitants of the district were in attendance to give evidence as to their wants, and were prepared with sacks and baskets to carry home a supply if the arrangements had been in a state of forwardness. It may not be out of place to state here that they evinced the character of a discreet and orderly population; and though the objects of the meeting necessarily required a continued attendance of most of them for many hours at one time, there was no irregularity of demeanour, and to the best of our observation, no use of whisky. There are no assessments in these parishes. Lord Macdonald and Dr Macalister of Strathaird are the principal heritors. The clergymen have made no special application to them this year, because they consider them always ready to come forward of their own accord when occasion required. They did so last year; and this year they have subscribed to the charitable funds.

We were prevented in consequence of the absence of Mr [Alexander] Beith the clergyman, and Captain Reid, a resident in the parish of Glenelg, from obtaining in our progress to Lochalsh, any minute information as to the state of that parish; but from our conversation with Mr Mackinnon of Corry, factor to Lord Glenelg[105] whose estate comprehended nearly one half of the population of the parish, and from a letter since received from the clergyman, we are enabled to state that it does not differ very materially from some of the adjoining parishes along the coast of the mainland to which I am now going to direct your attention. My present observations then will relate to the parishes of Glenelg, Lochalsh (including the parliamentary parish of Plockton),[106] Kintail and Glenshiel comprising a

---

[104] According to the 1841 select committee, Lord Macdonald imported 800 bolls of seed oats on his own account (Q 951*).

[105] Lord Glenelg, 'probably the only palindromic cabinet minister', was the secretary of state for the colonies (G. Martin, 'Grant, Charles, Baron Glenelg (1778–1866)', *ODNB*).

[106] The church at Plockton was one of the forty-three parliamentary churches built under the authority of the 1823 act for building additional places of worship in the Highlands and Islands of Scotland, 4 Geo. IV c.79 (see [PP] 1831 IX (330), 4, 21 and 42).

population of upwards of 900 souls.[107] We made special enquiries into the state
of each of these parishes separately; but as they are immediately adjoining and
stand in circumstances nearly similar, there is little or no advantage in continuing
the accounts of them apart. None of these parishes are considered quite so badly
off as they are in Skye; but still their destitution is much greater than in former
years; and in all this district it averages ½ of the population; the proportion of
able-bodied men out of work is fully 10 per cent. of the population. The failure of
the potato crop is generally stated at ½ and of the grain crop rather more. There is
a very general want of seed for the district, and a considerable proportion would
be repaid on credit if supplied; but there are no certain accounts of any being in
progress for these parishes; the early Argus is the kind required, and the port of
Dornie on Loch Duich is the best port of arrival for all this district. An immediate
supply of meal is expected from the Glasgow committee for the parishes of
Lochalsh and Glenshiel; but the intermediate parish of Kintail and the adjoining
parish of Glenelg which are equally destitute have had no communication that
any supply is destined for them. In Glenshiel it is proposed to divide the meal
at the rate of 28 lbs to each family. Those who are unable to work are to get it
gratis; those who can work are expected to give work for it. In Lochalsh, no
distribution is yet arranged, but it is intended to divide it as much as possible so
as to save all the potatoes which can be saved for seed. The supply of 80 bolls for
200 families will certainly not be sufficient to keep them for a month. A great
deal has been done by the resident family at Lochalsh[108] who up to the present
time have bought a great deal of meal and have had the great burden of the
population on their hands. Lists of heads of families are making out for all these
parishes, and the form of that adopted for the parliamentary parish of Plockton
seems a good one; and the list itself affords *prima facie* evidence of being fairly
and accurately made up. Its statements are considerably under the average of the
other parishes. All this district is considered to be over-peopled. It has suffered
most materially from the succession of bad crops; but every year there is some
destitution. The distress is attributed besides to the system of letting the lands in
large sheep farms and driving the surplus population into small possessions. The
failure of the kelp making has been to a certain degree injurious, as rents were
then raised and since the failure of kelp making have not proportionately fallen.
It never was much of a kelp district however, and it has not suffered so much
from that cause; but many large farms have been made on the Lochalsh estate,
and the whole parish of Glenshiel is allotted in five large farms and four smaller

[107] See 1841 SC, Q 1001–2.
[108] William Lillingston of Lochalsh, 'a man endeavouring to the utmost of his power to
promote the welfare of the people. He affords indeed a very singular and striking instance
of an English gentleman, accustomed to all the blandishments of refined society, taking up
his permanent residence in a poor and remote country, and among a people comparatively
rude and boisterous, for no other apparent reason than that of doing them good' (Fullarton
and Baird, *Remarks*, 46; see also 1841 SC, Q 1009).

possessions. In the village of Plockton, where the population of the new parish is under 500, there are at least 40 families who have no land; but many of them have a cow's grass; none of these could pay for anything that is done for them, except partially, as they could get employment. If they had fishing tackle, some of them could fish; Loch Duich is an excellent fishing loch. The failure of the fishings is another aggravating cause of the distress. Employment of any kind is very much wanted; unless employment is found, a very great proportion can make no return for any assistance rendered to them. In Lochalsh, work could easily be found by the people in making roads. The same kind of work could be found in Glenshiel where there is a line of road on which the church stands, which wants amendment and is conveniently situated for obtaining the surplus labour of the whole parish. Tools only are wanting to enable the parish committee to set the people to work on this road; and if money was obtained there would be no difficulty in finding tools in the country. The parish of Kintail is differently situated. The only road necessary for the parish is a parliamentary one and is in excellent condition and it seems difficult to find work in which the indigent could be employed. It has been suggested that in these circumstances the people might be employed in making good paths from the public road to their own houses, in draining the ground round their houses and in forming gardens which, besides teaching them habits of neatness, might ultimately be of great benefit in adding to their means of subsistence.

In all this district, there are no assessments; in Glenshiel and Kintail nothing extraordinary has been done by the heritors in consideration of its being an extraordinary year; in one of these parishes there is scarcely a resident heritor or a resident factor; and in both of them the clergymen are decidedly of opinion that the ordinary poor are not well taken care of as if there were assessments. These gentlemen intend still to make a special application to the heritors for the present season and as the question had been put to them, they intend to intimate the answer they have given on the subject of assessments.[109] The ordinary poor roll in the parish of Lochalsh is about 50 and the amount of collections taken at the church doors does not average more than £20. In Glenshiel the ordinary poor roll is 26 and the collections do not exceed £6 or £7. In Kintail the ordinary poor roll is 32 and the collections vary from £8 to £10. The clergymen consider the ordinary poor of these parishes miserably provided for and not in the spirit of the existing law. They are in fact supported by their relations and not by public provision. Emigration is uniformly recommended as the best means of curing the excess of population; but it should be under a proper system to do good to this country, and not on a principle of selection but by removing families in a body. Without this it is reckoned that it could only add to the evil. There is no indisposition to emigrate but the landholders must go hand in hand in the schemes and if they do not make arrangements upon their properties to check the present

[109] No legal assessment is recorded in the 1839 Poor Law Report or in *NSAc*.

rapid growth of population the evil will only be removed in a temporary way and the excess will very speedily recur again to its present amount. Mr Mackinnon the clergyman of Strath stated that if emigration was to go on, on a great scale, it would be of great importance to send some gentlemen or clergymen along with the poorer classes. He would have no objection to go with his whole family on the same allowance he has in this country.[110] None have emigrated from this parish since 1803 but [he] thinks that the people would not be unwilling to go under a proper system. All whom we have conversed [with] on this subject concur in the view that it would be much to be regretted in the event of emigration being adopted on a great scale if circumstances did make it inexpedient to His Majesty's Government to send the surplus population to Canada. In most districts many of the Highlanders have relations and friends in that country who form an existing tie, and would aid and assist the new settlers at the commencement. On this subject it may be right to state that before leaving Mull, an emigrant agent came on board the cutter in his progress in passing to Islay with the object of completing his complement for an export of the surplus population this season. His name is MacNiven and his headquarters is at Tobermory. He has been for sixteen years employed as an agent for emigration. He considers this season the worst he has met with as the people are so much in want of provisions. He never knew a season when they were more inclined to emigrate, but from the bad crop of last year and bad markets they never were so short of means to assist in procuring their transport he has carried out sometimes 1,800 in a year and has been in the habit of advancing to the emigrants what money may be necessary to carry them out, which they repay by instalments when they get to America. Cape Breton is the colony which he is in the habit of taking them to. He has carried out in all 45 ships. The passage has been from 15 days to 6 weeks, the average about 5 weeks. He intends to represent to His Majesty's Government, if he has an opportunity, the number of emigrants he has sent out and that he wishes to settle himself in America, and he hopes to get a grant of land and to employ the people to whom he has advanced money in cultivating this land and encouraging the fisheries. He wishes to go to Cape Breton and he thinks that 30,000 settlers might still be accommodated there. In his practice he has not selected individuals but sent out families entire – when he advances money he takes a bill on entering the ship and an obligation that the emigrants will not burden their grants of land until he is repaid. In general he has found the people ready to pay by instalments. When they had no money, he got produce such as a cow, a pig or a few baskets of wheat. He does not mean to continue in his present line but to go out and settle himself. He thinks he has already sent out 17,000 emigrants besides what he is to send out this year. His rates this year are £3 3s per head furnishing fuel, water bed berths and

[110] Mackinnon encouraged emigration from the parish to Australia and sent his sons there as way of convincing others to go; he wrote about the famine in his contribution to *NSAc*, xiv, 314.

cooking apparatus. If he funds provisions, [his rates are] £4 10s, children between 7 and 14, £1 15s without provisions or £2 10s with; under 7, £1 15s and under 1, nothing. The provisions he lays in are oatmeal, bread and molasses for 7 weeks. This man has probably more knowledge as to the real state of the population of the Highlands than is possessed by any other single individual; and it might be well perhaps for some member of His Majesty's Government to converse with him if he presents himself to their notice. By common report it is said that he has not yet enriched himself by his speculations but I have heard nothing to his prejudice. On the contrary he is supposed to have done more good than anybody else in assisting those who were short of means to emigrate, by making them allowances for their stock in hand and giving them the means of realising the value even of their manure heaps on their departure. Many were thus enabled by his means to depart who could not have otherwise have effected it. He made a direct reference to Mr Campbell of Islay for his character and we have heard that he is not unknown to Mr Stewart Mackenzie and other of the Highland proprietors.[111] I have the honour to be, Sir, your obedient servant.

Portree 4 April 1837

Sir, When at Broadford, I sent to Portree on which point my letters had been directed, and in an enclosure from the solicitor-general, I received a copy of Mr Spring Rice's letter to him[112] and have since had two letters from Sir John Hill. I shall be able to transfer to my correspondence with Sir John Hill a good deal of detail which it is unnecessary for me now to report on: I have stated to him the portions of my route which have not yet been overtaken when I may be able to attend to the arrangements adopted in the distribution of the seed grain, which has been circulated under his authority and I have made some suggestions as to the supply of potato seed which I hope he will approve of,[113] as this is the branch of the seed supply which is likely to be most defective.

[111] Archibald MacNiven dominated the emigrant trade in the Inner Hebrides and along the adjacent west coast, claiming in 1841 that for the previous twenty years he had arranged emigrant ships for 16,000 people from the Highlands and Islands (L. H. Campey 'The Regional Characteristics of Scottish Emigration to British North America 1784 to 1854', 2 vols. (University of Aberdeen, Ph.D. thesis, 1997), ii, 240). Graham writes in warm terms of MacNiven's contribution to Highlanders wishing to emigrate. A rather less complimentary picture is presented in Gaelic poetry, that he deceived and cheated people (Rev. A. Macdonald, *The Macdonald Collection of Gaelic Poetry* (Inverness, 1911), 370) and in a letter in the Canadian Gaelic magazine *Mac-Talla* 2, no. 49 (30 June 1894), 2–3, that he sent people off in unseaworthy boats; see M. Macdonnell, *The Emigrant Experience: Songs of Highland Emigrants in North America* (Toronto, 1982), 13–14 and 200, and C. L. Dunn, *Highland Settler: A Portrait of the Scottish Gael in Nova Scotia* (Toronto, 1953), 18 and 166.
[112] This is the letter dated 18 Mar. 1837, in which Thomas Spring Rice set out the 'steps taken by His Majesty's government for the relief of distress in the Highlands' (p. 264).
[113] There are no express references to this suggestion in Hill's letters to Spearman.

In my former letter,[114] I suggested the names of certain individuals to form a district committee in Mull in the event of His Majesty's Government coming to the determination to interfere directly in the distribution of meal to the poorer part of the population,[115] and I shall continue to do so until I am desired to discontinue it, at the different places which I consider best, as centres of communication, with pretty extensive districts round them. I do so in the conviction that it will be very necessary to have strict scrutinies of the parish lists made up by the local committees and that it is quite improbable to expect that this can be done with advantage even by the ablest and best-intentioned committees at so great a distance as Edinburgh or Glasgow.

I am led from casual reports and private letters received at this place to believe that His Majesty's Government have it in contemplation to encourage emigration to Australia on some principle of selection of individuals, but adapted for the objects of the new colony. I trust that their intentions are not limited entirely to this mode of freeing this country of the surplus population; and I consider it my duty to state that the whole evidence which has been taken by me leads me to the conclusion that no advantage can come to this country by inducing the best and most useful part of the population to go while the feeble and the least enterprising are left behind, and besides that such a plan, if adopted as the only plan of emigration, would probably very speedily defeat itself from the great unwillingness of families to be separated.[116] I have the honour to be, Sir, your obedient servant.

Portree 6 April 1837

Sir, The condition of the people does not improve as we advance into the other parishes in Skye. In Snizort and Portree the destitution is fully as great as any place we have yet visited. We witnessed the distribution of part of the meal supplied by the Glasgow association, at Portree; and we can testify from the statements of the parties and even from their looks and personal appearance, that great misery and even the danger of starvation exists among them.[117]

The destitution is estimated at considerably more than one half; the minister of Portree[118] thinks it amounts to nearer ¾ ths than ½ of the

---

[114] Graham's letter of 22 Mar. 1837 (p. 32).
[115] No such steps were taken by the government, which limited itself to assistance in the supply of seed.
[116] This issue is discussed in the Introduction.
[117] What Graham says here might be contrasted with Hill's journal entry for 2 June 1837 (p. 153), where he described the people as 'clean and healthy'.
[118] The Rev. Coll Macdonald, 'a man of sterling integrity, of clear and discriminating mind, and of a most friendly and amiable disposition' (FES, vii, 174).

population. It is attributed principally to the failure of the crop last year and low prices of cattle; and to the failure of the herring fishery; the cessation of public works in the district; and also the excessive population in a country by no means adapted to support a great population. From these combined causes there is considerable destitution every year. The portions of this district which suffer most from over-population are the neighbourhood of Portree and Skeabost and Bernisdale on the west side of Loch Snizort; also the neighbourhood of Lynedale. In Skeabost and Bernisdale, 40 families were recently located, partly on a moor and partly on small crofts subdivided by Mr [Donald] Macdonald of Kingsborough, the proprietor.[119] He has the contract for repairing the Government roads in Macleod's country in Skye, and he allocated these crofts to the labourers whom he employed on the roads. The teacher of an endowed institution in the parish[120] stated that in making up the list for the distribution of meal, out of a little more than 800 people, 400 were upon the property of Skeabost. Lord Macdonald's proportion of the parish is in valuation one half, but in population greatly under the other proprietors. Mr Maxwell, factor for Lord Macdonald, however stated that on his lordship's estate in Skye there are 1,200 families in the rental book, exclusive of the village of Portree. There are on the land, and not in the rental book, 1,300 families; these are chiefly relatives of the tenants, such as sons and sons-in-law, and sometimes two or three of them are on one lot. In the restricted parish of Portree, which amounts to a population of 2100, there are no tacksmen but one; all the rest of the parish, except two small farms, is divided into crofts and these crofters are subdivided again in numerous instances.

Mr [George] Robertson, the sheriff-substitute of Skye, as a specimen of the kind of tenure commonly held, stated the instance of the portion of ground which he himself occupied. It is one portion of an allotment called Pennyfillar and includes a small pendicle of land called Heatherfield. All this once formed a large farm which was subsequently let off in six lots. The arable land is divided in ridges and the other five crofters occasionally change their ridges, but he does not. The hill grazing is in common and each allotment pays a rent of £6. There are nearly 100 souls upon this joint farm, including the pendicle of Heatherfield, which was let out by the late factor as a piece of poor land to be brought in. The five crofters are not in destitution; they have suffered but they can get something by fishing etc.; but the six families in Heatherfield, who pay a rent among them of £3.10 are very badly off; and there is one cottar, a joiner on the other part of the farm, in a miserable situation. He has a ridge or two of ground for potatoes, and repairs the agricultural implements in the neighbourhood. He has an infirm

---

[119] The Macdonalds of Kingsborough had entertained Prince Charles Edward Stewart on Skye after his escape from Culloden (A. Nicolson, *History of Skye – A Record of the Families, the Social Conditions and Literature of the Island* (Skye, 1995), 150–60).

[120] This was Macdermid's Institution, bequeathed by a native of Borve who had gone to the colonies (Nicolson, *Skye*, 277; *NSAc*, xiv, 294).

father, a wife and 4 children to maintain, and Mr Robertson knows that he worked last year to the amount of £12, and never got a farthing for it owing to the failure of the herring fishery. He computes these 7 families at 57 souls, so that there is this amount out of the 100 certainly destitute.

The failure of the crop last year in this district is estimated at more than 3/4ths in grain and in potatoes about ½. Mr Bethune, a sheriff officer in the parish of Snizort has been in the habit of going about on public business for 35 years and has never known a year to be compared to the present one for destitution. In 1817 the people were not so badly off as now.[121] He pays a rent of £25 to Lord Macdonald. He sowed last year 45 barrels of oats and he had not one half in produce. Of the portion he tried to make into meal, there was not a peck for every barrel.

Except in the case of Lord Macdonald, who has provided seed corn for his own people, nothing appears to have been done for seed grain or potatoes by Mr [Donald] Macdonald of Kingsborough, Mr [John] Maclennan of Lynedale or Mr [John] Macleod of Raasay. The minister of Snizort[122] being absent, we could not ascertain whether any extraordinary application had been made to these gentlemen in consideration of the extraordinary season; but the minister of Portree said he had made no extraordinary application to his heritor, Lord Macdonald, because he had been remarkably generous to his people, both last year and in the present. Last year he had imported for those who directly held under him, 2000 barrels of potatoes and 400 bolls of oats. This year his lordship had imported 800 bolls of seed oats himself and 400 are expected besides from the Edinburgh committee, for which his lordship has given the required security.[123] Mr [Coll] Macdonald, the minister of Portree, stated that the ordinary poor's roll amounted to about 70; the collections at the church door did not exceed £5 a year, and the only other fund for support of the ordinary poor was £13 a year, the interest of some lying money. He thinks the ordinary poor miserably provided for; and that they, at least, would be better off if there was an assessment.

Mr Macdonald and all who spoke on this subject consider the district very much over-peopled, especially as the herring fishery is likely to desert the coast altogether. It has gone back for the last 5 or 6 years, every year getting worse. He considers the making of roads only a temporary relief, and that emigration is the only cure which would have a permanent effect; [he] thinks they would willingly go – [he] never saw them so ready [and] does not know whether

[121] In 1817 Lord Macdonald had obtained government aid for the supply of oats and potatoes to 'relieve the pressing wants of the people living upon my estate in the Isle of Skye' (CDC, GD 221/221, Heritable Bond and Security 1817; see the Introduction).

[122] The Rev. Simon Fraser McLauchlan.

[123] The security required is a reference to the resolutions of the Edinburgh committee that proprietors should guarantee to repay at least half the cost of the supply of seed (p. 245). According to John Cunninghame, Lord Macdonald was 'bawling lustily for relief from all quarters' (p. 257).

or not the landlords would assist them in going; but thinks that they ought, as it would be better, in the long run, for the sake of the large proprietors to contribute towards emigrating their surplus population than to continue to support them.

Mr Maxwell, factor on Lord Macdonald's estate, stated that the increase of population and the subdivisions of crofts has grown on in the teeth of printed regulations made for the management of the estate. Owing to particular circumstances for some time these regulations have not been enforced. Now, however, a determination has been come to enforce them rigorously; and the good effect is already so far apparent that last year there were only two marriages on the estate.

Mr [Duncan] McCallum, the missionary on the island of Raasay[124] thinks that there is no regulation on that estate at present to check the great subdivision of possessions; but that it is likely, when the proprietor[125] comes to live upon his estate (and he is expected soon) that something of the kind may be done.

Mr Maxwell considers emigration as the only permanent cure for the redundancy of the population, but that much temporary relief might be afforded by the making of new lines of road of which at least 150 miles might with advantage be formed in the island of Skye. Were emigration to be promoted by Government on a large scale, he is of opinion that the only way in which effectual relief could be given would be by transporting whole families, old and young, without selection; [he] thinks that much harm would be done to the cause of emigration by selection, as the people are simple-minded and would suppose, or it would be instilled into them by evil disposed persons, that the selection was made with some sinister views either to exact labour from them or make them soldiers. [He] has no hesitation in saying that selection would be fatal to the success of the measure of emigration as a general measure of relief. Should Government see cause to give any aid in the formation of roads [he] thinks it could not be done on more favourable terms than formerly, when the parliamentary roads were made, viz. Government advancing one half and the proprietor the other half. Mr Maxwell thinks that if the redundant population were once got rid of, it would be practicable to keep the subdivision of land within proper limits. The system that has already been adopted on the estate and approved of by Lord Macdonald's trustees is to signify to the eldest son of a family that he is to succeed to the lot held by his father, and it thus becomes his interest to prevent the lot from being parcelled out among the other members of the family. I have the honour to be, Sir, your obedient servant.

---

[124] The parish church at Portree was 'altogether inaccessible to the great body of the people' and so there was a missionary priest in the parish paid for by the Royal Bounty Committee (*NSAc*, xiv, 232).

[125] John Macleod, an officer in the 78th regiment and the last laird of Raasay.

Poolewe 7 April 1837

My dear Mother, I do not think I have written to you since we were in Loch Tuath. We got out of that bay after 4 or 5 days and arrived the same evening in Loch Alsh, from where we crossed to Broadford in Skye and then across again to Loch Kishorn in Ross-shire. From there we made our way to Portree where I got a letter from you of the 4th. We have seen a great deal of wild scenery which looks to good advantage in its present warm coating of snow. We have had occasional falls for the last 10 days – the weather otherwise [is] moderate, but the winds not very favourable. We have seen some wretched habitation and a great deal of want of food in Skye. They are not so badly off for clothing, nor even for fuel any part we have been, though by no means flush of the latter. The failure of the crop accounts for much of this but there is an excess of population in these districts that must keep the [. . .] of them very poor and miserable in an ordinary year. We go from this into Loch Broom and then stand over for Stornoway. I cannot trust in receiving letters in Lewis or Harris; and therefore I have stated Portree to remain as the post town: we can easily come back upon it from Snizort bay in the N. W. of Skye. Adieu. Kindest love to all. Yours ever most affectionately.

Ullapool 11 April 1837[126]

Sir, I omitted in my last letter to mention that Mr Kennedy of Macdermid's Institution, parish of Snizort, whom in the absence of the minister we examined relative to the state of destitution in that parish, stated to us that he had been desired by the minister to report, in illustration of the anxiety of the people to emigrate, that in cautioning some of them not to form too high expectations of what His Majesty's Government intended to do for them this year in promoting emigration, several of them actually wept and said they would much rather take the chance of perishing at sea than be subjected any longer to the privation they endured at home. Mr Kennedy had taken up the lists in this parish and he exhibited an abstract of the number of families willing to emigrate with the amount of months' provisions in the possession of each. He promised to furnish me with a corrected copy of this abstract, but it did not reach me before leaving Portree. I mention the circumstance, in case any measures are being taken at present in regard to emigration, to point out one quarter from which apparently correct information may be required.

Mr Alexander Arbuckle, the surgeon at present practicing at Portree, made an application to me to forward a petition to Lord Glenelg stating his willingness to go from this quarter if any such measures are intended

---

[126] See 1841 SC, Q 1001–2.

for the present season; and he made reference to several gentlemen resident in the place who spoke favourably of him. In my answer I stated that my business was only to correspond with the Home Office and I recommended him to take his own means of laying his case before the colonial secretary. I added, however, that I had no objections to state to you that I had received a communication from him expressive of his willingness to afford the aid of his professional services in the event of His Majesty's Government finding it expedient to encourage emigration on a large scale, and being disposed to provide those who emigrate with medical attendance. I did not see Mr Arbuckle but I understand he is not fastidious as to any particular colony; for although there is great practice at Portree[127] there is very little to induce him to remain.

I have thrown together the several parishes mentioned in the margin[128] because their circumstances are nearly the same. They may be represented as not quite so badly off as the parishes in Skye, but there is a great deal of misery in this country; and in the neighbourhood of Poolewe, in particular, there are specimens of residences among the poorer classes who are besides [being] totally in want of food, which are not surpassed in point of wretchedness and discomfort by the worst instances I have ever witnessed in any country. The amount of destitution in this district appears to be estimated at one half of the population; the failure of crops in comparison with ordinary years may be averaged at ½ of potatoes and more than that of grain; in some of the parishes the whole grain crop is considered lost. The failure of the crop however is by no means the only cause of present misery, and a succession of good crops would not replace this population in a wholesome state. In the parishes of Lochcarron and Gairloch the population is said to have doubled respectively in 25 and 30 years and the whole are considered greatly over-peopled. In Shieldaig the people are represented to be double in number to what the land can support; and in general in the other parishes, the produce of the country is not sufficient to support the population. There is no restriction to the erection of cottages, and the making of small farms into large ones has tended to produce poverty. No part of this district was very much of a kelp country although a few hundred used to be employed in that way. But it has suffered considerably from the failure of the fishings. There was formerly a cod fishing in Gairloch, but for the last 8 years it has been unproductive. The fish seem to have deserted this coast. It never was much of a station for the herring fishery except at Lochbroom; but for several years the fishery has fallen off much

---

[127] Under the practice name of Campbell and Arbuckle.
[128] The marginal notes are: 'Lochcarron, Applecross (including parts of the parish of Shieldaig), Gairloch (including parts of the parish of Poolewe), Lochbroom (including parts of the parish of Ullapool); population 16,000'. The churches at Shieldaig, Poolewe and Ullapool were each one of the forty-three parliamentary churches built under the authority of the 1823 act for building additional places of worship in the Highlands and Islands of Scotland, 4 Geo. IV c.79 (see [PP] 1831 IX (330), 4, 21 and 43; 4, 23 and 44; and 4, 24 and 45, respectively).

there. There has not been what may be termed a good fishery there since 1811. The season 1835 was a total failure. Mr McPhail [the] fishery officer stated that it would take all that the people made last year by the fishing to pay for the meal which had to be supplied to them, previous to its commencement.

It was generally represented that there could be no difficulty in finding employment for the able-bodied poor in making roads in the district if means were afforded for doing so;[129] and the local committees which are appointed in each of these parishes are ready to suggest lines upon which they might speedily be engaged. In the parishes of Lochbroom and Ullapool the recommendation of making roads was earnestly enforced.[130] Emigration however is the only measure which was very urgently pressed in all this district as most likely to afford permanent and efficient relief and as being loudly called for in all these parishes. In general it is believed that the people would be willing to go. Mr [Donald] Macrae, the minister of Poolewe, was somewhat doubtful whether they would willingly emigrate. The only way, he said, in which it could be done would be to emigrate them in families. They would prefer Canada or British North America generally as they have friends there. The same remark as to the colonies was made by Mr [James] Russell, the assistant minister of Gairloch. He thought they would not be unwilling to join their friends in Canada and that some who have no ties in America would willingly go to Australia. Mr Fraser, schoolmaster at Gairloch stated that he had conversed frequently with the people on the subject of emigration and found them very anxious to emigrate if they had the means; most of them would prefer going to Nova Scotia but some of them would not be indisposed to go to Australia, having received favourable accounts of that colony.

No seed corn has yet been imported into the district, which is much in want of it; and in the whole of Applecross, Lochcarron and Gairloch proper, no expectation has been held out of an importation from any quarter. Few of the proprietors seem to have made any exertions about it. At Poolewe had been received of a supply from Sir John Hill and the Edinburgh association of 200 quarters of seed intended for that port which is nearly enough to supply the whole wants of the parliamentary parish there; and expectations are entertained from the same quarter of such a supply for Ullapool and Lochbroom as will be sufficient for the wants of these parishes. Some supplies of meal from the Glasgow association had arrived and have been distributed in small portions at Shieldaig, Lochcarron and Applecross; and similar supplies were daily expected at Gairloch and have just arrived at Lochbroom; but the committee at Poolewe

---

[129] Other work was found – enclosing the burying ground of the parish of Ullapool – for which those employed received payments in meal ([PP] 1844 XXI (564), 424); and p. 168.

[130] Writing in May 1835, the Rev. Dr Thomas Ross had said 'not one parish in Scotland stands nearly so much in need [of good roads and bridges], as the parish of Lochbroom' (*NSAc*, xiv, 88). In February 1837 the complaint had been made that some projected roads 'have been thrown aside to admit of others in the richer and better inhabited parts of the county' (Smith, 'From Isolation to Integration', 160).

have received no intelligence of any supplies of meal being intended for them. All the committees concurred in the view that the allowance of 2 ½ bolls for a family of 5 would be sufficient to prevent starvation for the season. The local committee of Poolewe thought it bare enough, but that they might live upon it. The local committee of Lochcarron remonstrated at first against this allowance as being greatly too small, and finally condescended upon a given number of bolls as being sufficient to support their destitute population until next crop which is considerably under this allowance, if they have given a fair statement of the proportion of destitution in the parish.

Few of the clergymen in any of these parishes have yet made any special application to their heritors in consideration of the extraordinary years. The minister of Shieldaig[131] intends still to apply in consequence of the question having been asked at him. The minister of Applecross[132] will also take an opportunity of communicating with his heritor. The minister of Lochcarron[133] had declined to do so as his heritors, he said, knew the state of the parish, and one of them was a member of the Edinburgh committee.[134] In the parish of Gairloch the only heritor is absent from the country; but steps were to be taken to stimulate the interference of his friends in favour of his people.[135] There is no assessment in any of these parishes. The minister of Shieldaig thinks it would be necessary and that this would be a good year to begin, and that if there was an assessment, the ordinary poor would be better provided for than they are.[136] In Poolewe a voluntary contribution has lately been resorted to, to avoid an assessment. The ordinary poor seem indeed to be very imperfectly provided for. In Shieldaig, the roll amounts to about 30 and they do not receive above 5/- a year over head. In Applecross, among 14 or 15, £4 or £5 are divided within the year. In Lochcarron, 20 or 30 have £6 divided amongst them. In Poolewe, besides the voluntary assessment, the collections at the church doors do not exceed 50/- a year for a poor's roll of 40 or 50. In Gairloch, there is a roll of 70 and they do not receive on the average throughout the year, 3/- a head. In Ullapool, there are 50 ordinary paupers and the average sum to be divided does not exceed £7.

We have now got to the most northerly point on the mainland, to which I think it necessary to proceed in my inspection; and I am now in a condition to make some kind of estimate of the amount of destitution in the portion

[131] The Rev. Colin Mackenzie.
[132] The Rev. Roderick Macrae.
[133] The Rev. John Mackenzie.
[134] In his evidence to the 1844 Poor Law Inquiry (at p. 439), the Rev. John Mackenzie said that there had been an assessment, that both the heritors and their factors were non-resident and neither heritor nor factor ever attended the meetings held for the distribution of relief.
[135] *NSAc*, xiv, 94, states that there were five proprietors, as do Fullerton and Baird (*Remarks*, 48).
[136] No record of a legal assessment is given in the 1839 Poor Law Report or *NSAc*.

of the Highlands which is included in my charge. Although I have not yet examined in detail the circumstances of the western side of Skye, I have no reason to suppose that the parishes on that side differ very materially from those I have examined into on the spot. And although I have not yet touched on any part of the Long Island[137] I am not led to think, from any casual evidence which has met me in regard to them, that these portions are in any more favourable situation than the island of Skye. On the contrary, from the fact that these parts of the Highlands are still more without the advantage of resident proprietors and from the less favourable circumstances under which many of the estates there happen at present to be managed, I am led to believe that the proportion of destitution exists to a still greater extent in the Long Island than in any other portion of the Highlands.

It must be a great object with His Majesty's Government to arrive at some kind of computation of the amount of the evil which it will probably fall upon them mainly to avert;[138] and I therefore proceed to make a general estimate as the result of the observations I have as yet been able to make, subject of course to such modifications as the experience of the remaining part of my tour may suggest. Until the results are more accurately brought out by a strict sorting of the lists of local committees, I am disposed to estimate the destitution of the district which I have included under the name of the Mull district at ¼ of the population. In many of the parishes it was not computed nearly so high; but as in Tiree and Coll, which we had not an opportunity of seeing, it was spoken to as amounting to 1/3ʳᵈ of the population of those islands, it may be safe to average the destitution of the whole of that district at ¼. Of the second district, or that comprehended under the denomination of Skye, I should consider that the parishes on the mainland in Ross-shire and Inverness-shire, which I have added to that district, may be computed as evincing a destitution equal to ½ of the population; and that the destitution of the island of Skye itself cannot be safely computed as under ¾ of the population. At present, in forming a rough estimate for the reasons already given, I am disposed to calculate the probable destitution of the chain of the Long Island at 4/5ᵗʰ of the population.

This must of necessity be but a rude approximation to the fact. The amount itself can only be made up by a strict reference to lists of heads of families; and the truth of those lists must depend upon the integrity of the local committees and the care and vigilance of the district committees in controlling them.

¼ of 25,241 the population of the Mull district
= Number of destitute 6,356

---

[137] Lewis, Harris, the Uists, Benbecula and Barra.
[138] Graham was wrong in this assumption: in the event, the aid was mainly provided from public subscriptions, with the government providing, in financial terms, less than a sixth of the aid.

½ of 24,081 the population of the mainland part of the Skye district
= Number of destitute 12,040

¾ of 23,741 the population of the island of Skye
= Number of destitute 17,806

4/5th of 35,000 estimated population of Long Island
= Number of destitute 28,000

Total number of destitute 64,202

Say of the destitute population of Oban, Fort William and adjoining districts
if not otherwise relieved 5,798

Total number of destitute 70,000[139]

I have been staggered myself once or twice in recurring to the estimate, I have more than once stated to you as being generally admitted to be sufficient to prevent starvation, viz. 2 ½ bolls for the season for every family of 5, particularly in contrasting it with the ordinary allowance in the low country for a working ploughman which is exactly of the same amount, or one stone of meal per week. But it ought to be observed, that in the ploughman's case, it is in some degree a provision for his family if he has one; and when such ploughmen are unmarried, there is commonly a surplus which is bartered or sold as the accumulation takes place. Besides, in the list of the destitute, this allowance is computed independent of all adventitious aids. Many of the families admitted on these lists have cows; many of them will still receive support from landlords and others who are only lying by to see what is to be done first by the public and private charities, and many will be able to pick up some subsistence by fishing and going out to work; and although it seems to be carefully attended to, to exclude from the lists those who have disposable stock, it is impossible to hold as beyond the verge of destitution a family having a single cow, but who are otherwise without food – although this property is certainly an alleviation of their misery and ought to make them satisfied with a smaller portion of aid otherwise. Moreover, this computation has been made on the opinions given by the suffering people themselves, as to the amount which is sufficient to keep their families together; and what I still give greater weight to (for it is the nature of real misery to conceal and disguise its own wants) the clergymen and members of the kirk sessions and those most accustomed to the management and habits of the poor have in every case concurred in the view that this estimate is a fair one on which the experiment might be commenced. Unhappily too, it is a moral lesson which it is necessary to teach to the poor themselves, even in the midst of their affliction, that it is not full meals or plentiful supplies that ought to be served out

[139] This estimate, of course, did not include Sutherland, Caithness, Orkney and Shetland. George Gunn, the main factor for the Sutherland estates, referred to 20,000 people being supported by the countess of Sutherland (Richards, *Leviathan*, 247).

to them. And His Majesty's Government will no doubt have in view, at the same time, that the computation now made is the <u>minimum</u> which these authorities will admit as the basis of this experiment with any prospect of success; and that they will be ready to extend the scheme if, in the progress of the operations, it is found to be insufficient.

In my present situation, I have no sufficient data for forming an estimate of the rate at which the necessary supply of meal could be served out, but supposing the supply to be furnished including all expenses at 25/- per boll (equal to half a sack, or 140 imperial lbs) the amount necessary for the supply of 70,000 souls would be £43,750 or nearly £44,000. How much of this is likely to be saved to the Government by the exertions of the charitable associations, and by the zeal of the meritorious individuals who have been instrumental in drawing forward private subscriptions, you have a better opportunity of judging at present than I have. Much will depend upon the economical arrangements with which this benevolent scheme is carried into effect.[140] I am not sanguine as to much return for money advanced under this branch by the Government; for a few only of those who are to benefit by it have the power of making a return by their personal labour; and if they are made to work, more food must be given to them. Not one-tenth part of the destitute however are able-bodied workmen; and even to set them to work, an additional expense for the implements would be required to be incurred. Still, work should be insisted upon wherever it can be rendered; and I have been the more anxious to make my general statement now, in the expectation that His Majesty's Government may come to a determination on the subject because, in the commencement which has been made of the distribution of meal by the association, although work has in many cases been stipulated for, no arrangement has yet been made for carrying that stipulation into effect; nor do I see that it can very easily be done, unless recourse is had to the system of district committees, as I have recommended, who could very easily put this branch into a well regulated shape. I continue to think, unless Sir John Hill sees cause to think otherwise, that the best form of Government interference is in aid of the charitable associations – by supporting their exertions and feeding them with fresh funds

---

[140] The estimate by Graham of the number of people requiring aid and the amount and cost of meal required (35,000 bolls) excluded Sutherland, Caithness, Orkney and Shetland. The government, as explained in the Introduction, in fact provided very little aid for the supply of meal, concentrating its efforts on seed. The total supply of seed by the committees was around 5,000 quarters of oats, 450 quarters of bear and 1,453 tons of potatoes, at a total cost of around £12,500. The total supply of meal provided by the charitable committees amounted to around 26,500 bolls, and this total included supplies to Orkney and Shetland; the cost of the supply of meal and clothing was around £32,000. The total cost of seed, food and clothing supplied by the committees was around £45,000 (NLS, Lynedoch papers, MS 16147, Report of Edinburgh committee, 21 Dec. 1837 (p. 220); TNA:PRO, Treasury, T 1/4201 Hill to Spearman, 7 May 1838 (p. 194); 1841 SC, 109).

when their supplies fail.[141] A great deal of useful machinery will spring up from the exertions of the gentlemen composing the committees of these associations; who, I take it for granted, are all acting gratuitously;[142] and by that means and in conjunction with district committees, I should hope that an economical arrangement could be devised for doing the greatest possible good with any sum of money which His Majesty's Government may be pleased to place at their disposal for this benevolent object.

I annex, on a separate paper, a list of parishes which, in my opinion may be connected in one district under the name of Skye with the names of the gentlemen who would form a good district committee there, and I intend from Stornoway to send you a similar one for the Lewis district; and before leaving the Long island also one for the Benbecula district. I have the honour to be, Sir, your obedient servant.

List of proposed General Committee at Portree

Skye

John A. Maxwell Esq. Portree, factor for Lord Macdonald, chairman.
Alexander Mackinnon Esq. Corry, deputy chairman.
Rev. Coll Macdonald, minister of Portree.
Rev. John Mackinnon, minister of Strath.
Rev. Alexander McIver, minister of Sleat.
Rev. S. F. McLauchlan, minister of Snizort.[143]
Rev. Robert Macgregor, minister of Kilmuir.[144]
Rev. Alexander Macgregor, son of the minister of Kilmuir, for Stenscholl,[145] at present vacant.
Rev. R. Reid, minister of Waternish.[146]
Rev. R. Macleod, minister of Bracadale.
Rev. S. Glass, minister of Duirinish.
Rev. W. Macdonald, missionary, Raasay.[147]

---

[141] This was, largely, what the government had already decided to do, as explained by Spring Rice in his letter of 18 Mar. 1837 (p. 264).

[142] This was, indeed, the case: the statements of the Edinburgh and Glasgow committees show that remuneration was only paid to the secretaries (pp. 224 and 239).

[143] He was transferred from the parish to Cawdor on 28 July 1837 (FES, vii, 180).

[144] The parish is described as Kilmuir-in-Trotternish in FES.

[145] The church at Stenscholl was one of the forty-three parliamentary churches built under the authority of the 1823 act for building additional places of worship in the Highlands and Islands of Scotland, 4 Geo. IV c.79 (see [PP] 1831 IX (330), 4, 18 and 40).

[146] The parish is described as Hallin-in-Waternish in FES. The church at Hallin was one of the forty-three parliamentary churches built under the authority of the 1823 act for building additional places of worship in the Highlands and Islands of Scotland, 4 Geo. IV c.79 (see [PP] 1831 IX (330), 4, 19 and 41).

[147] In his letter of 6 Apr. 1837 Graham refers to the missionary as being Mr McCallum (p. 65).

George Robertson Esq. sheriff-substitute for Skye.
Hugh McAskill Esq. Talisker.[148]
Edward Gibbon Esq. factor for Macleod of Macleod.
Hugh P. Macdonald Esq. Monkstreet.[149]
Roderick Macleod Esq. agent for the National Bank, Portree.
Henry Macdonald Esq. Portree.[150]
Mr Archibald Stewart, Scudiburgh.[151]

Arisaig

Angus Macdonald Esq. of Glenalladale.
Dr McEachan, Arisaig.
Rev. M. McCallum, missionary, Arisaig.
Rev Angus MacDonald, Roman Catholic clergyman, Arisaig.

Glenelg

Rev. Alexander Beith, minister of Glenelg.
Captain Reid, Glenelg.
Captain Ross, Glenelg.

Lochalsh

Rev. H[ector] Maclean, minister of Lochalsh
Rev. Alexander Macdonald, minister of Plockton.[152]
Mr Macrae, Auchertyre.

Kintail

Rev. James Morrison, minister of Kintail.
Mr Black, Kintail.

[148] Hugh McAskill was a tacksman and grazier who had acquired the lease of Talisker House and the estate from Macleod of Macleod. Having cleared the land of people to make room for sheep, he and Kenneth McAskill established the distillery at Carbost in 1830.
[149] A grazier.
[150] A writer and clerk of the peace.
[151] A grazier.
[152] Described as 'one of the most popular preachers on the west coast of Ross and Inverness-shire' (FES, vii, 162).

Glenshiel

Rev. John Macrae, minister of Glenshiel.
Mr Reid, Ratagan.

Lochcarron

Rev. John Mackenzie, minister of Lochcarron.
Dr Dickson, Lochcarron.
Mr Scott, Lochcarron.

Applecross

Rev. Roderick Macrae, minister of Applecross.
Rev. Colin Mackenzie, minister of Shieldaig.
Mr Pirrie, Keeshorn, factor for Mr [Thomas] Mackenzie of Applecross.

Gairloch

Rev. James Russell, minister of Gairloch.
Rev. Donald Macrae, minister of Poolewe.

Lochbroom

Rev. Thomas Ross, LLD, minister of Lochbroom.
Rev. Alexander Ross, minister of Ullapool.
Mr Hector Mackenzie, Ullapool.
Mr Kenneth Mackenzie, overseer for Mr Hay Mackenzie of Cromarty.
Mr James Noble, schoolmaster of Lochbroom.

Portree District including the following parishes – Population

Isle of Skye

Bracadale 1,769.
Duirinish, including the parliamentary parish of Waternish, 5,200.
Kilmuir, including the parliamentary parish of Stenscholl, 3,415.
Portree 3,441.
Sleat 2,957.

Snizort 3,487.
Strath 3,472.
Total Isle of Skye 23,741.

Adjoining districts on the mainland of Inverness and Ross-shire

District of Arisaig (parish of Ardnamurchan) 1,500.
Glenelg 2,874.
Lochalsh, including the parliamentary parish of Plockton, 2,433.
Kintail 1,240.
Glenshiel 715.
Lochcarron 2,136.
Applecross, including the parliamentary parish of Shieldaig, 3,532.
Gairloch, including the parliamentary parish of Poolewe, 4,445.
Lochbroom, including the parliamentary parish of Ullapool, 5,206.
Total mainland 24,081.
Total population 47,822.

Stornoway 14 April 1837[153]

Sir, The population of the Lewis is nearly 16,000.[154] The state of destitution there is very great, although on the whole it is scarcely to be estimated so high as in Skye. It varies in degree in a striking way according to different circumstances and locations. In the parish of Knock it is estimated only at $1/4^{th}$ part of the population while in Cross it amounts to $4/5^{th}$. In Stornoway parish the amount of destitution is ½ ; in Lochs it is estimated at nearly the whole population and in the parish of Barvas the minister[155] said that he could not name a single family among his whole flock who in the course of a month would have an ounce of meal. This is the more remarkable as we have met with no part of the country

---

153 See 1841 SC, Q 1012–18.
154 There is a marginal note giving the parish numbers: Stornoway 4,400, Barvas 1,880, Knock 1,500, Cross 1,486, Lochs 3,400, Uig 3,300; total 15,966.
155 The Rev. William Macrae; Macrae is 'still remembered with remarkable affection on Lewis . . . a man renowned for his kindliness to people in trouble, and generous with money and provision for the desperate' (J. Macleod, *Banner in the West – A Spiritual History of Lewis and Harris* (Edinburgh, 2010), 127). Thomas Knox in his evidence in the 1844 Poor Law Inquiry said that there was not much suffering in 1837/38 in Lewis and that the meal arrived in time to prevent the people suffering from destitution (1844 Poor Law Inquiry, 380). Knox had written to Stewart Mackenzie in Feb. 1837 reporting on the requirements of meal for the island to carry the people through the famine, which made it clear that 4,400 of meal would be required (NRS, Papers of the Mackenzie family, earls of Seaforth, GD 46/13/199/4, Knox to Stewart Mackenzie, 7 Feb. 1837). According to Hill's journal entry for 6 June 1837 (p. 156), Knox had said he did not, at first, approve of supplies of meal being sent.

to the same extent, where there appears to have been so uniform an arrangement for taking up the lists and apportioning such supplies as have as yet been dealt out to the people. Mr [Thomas] Knox, the factor on the Seaforth Estate, has the chief merit of these arrangements and I can confidently recommend him as being trustworthy for a due and economical management of details as to what has yet to be done.[156] He has had his own difficulties with the clergymen in restricting their views of the amount of supply which should be given to their parishioners;[157] and to strengthen his hands I recommend, on a separate paper,[158] the names of some individuals whom he approves of as members of a local committee – making that list a very special one as it was desirable to admit as few as possible of those who had any connections in the town. I formerly contemplated adding Harris to this district but from their natural features and want of roads, Lewis and Harris are separated not merely as properties, but are sufficiently disconnected to belong to separate kingdoms and it will probably be necessary to leave Harris to be managed by a special local committee for itself. I was much gratified in finding that Mr Knox had computed on different data the smallest amount which was sufficient to prevent starvation and that his result corresponds remarkably with the calculation we had previously arrived at from the information collected in Skye and in Rossshire on the main[land]. In estimating the supply necessary for each family of 5, for 5 months, he proceeded on [the] following principles. He estimated the supply for each adult individual at 1 ½ imperial stones of meal per month; and after deducting 1/3 from the group number to reduce it to the denomination of adults, he finds that the whole quantity required for such a family until the next crop would be 25 imperial stones or 2 ½ bolls.[159] Mr Knox's estimates were verified by reference to the actual ages of existing families and were tested upon an extensive scale. The first supply of meal has come to Stornoway from the Glasgow association for all the parishes of the island and here for the first time we have found a systematic arrangement made for distributing it in proportions corresponding to a provision for a month. Mr Knox has found great difficulty in getting the system adhered to. He is not sure that he has succeeded in every case in getting the supply limited to the scale of 1 ½ stones for an adult, but as yet the other aids are not exhausted and the issue of meal for the month of April at all events has been made, in a proportion rather under than

---

[156] Hill had a similar view of Knox (see Hill's journal entry for 6 June 1837 and his letter to Spearman of 7 June 1837, pp. 156 and 161). Joseph Mitchell described Knox as 'a South countryman, bred an accountant in Edinburgh, and efficient in figures. He was very corpulent, kindly in manner, but I should think very unfit for the rough usage a Hebridean factor must endure if he does his duty' (Mitchell, *Reminiscences*, i, 236).

[157] These difficulties were explained by Knox to James Stewart Mackenzie in a letter of 7 Feb. 1837, in which Knox estimated the supplies needed for Lewis – a total of 4,400 bolls of meal; Knox said that the minister at Cross (the Rev. John Macrae) had estimated a pound of meal a day for each individual (see the Introduction).

[158] Set out at the end of the letter.

[159] This is set out in the 7 Feb.1837 letter from Knox to Stewart Mackenzie.

above this estimate. In this way Mr Knox has still in his hands a certain proportion of the first supply which under a more [. . .] and under a more common management would have been dissipated at once without any computable return; but he entertains great doubts of being able to withstand the urgency of the claimants so as to be able to retain it, and this shows that the supplies afforded even to the storehouses should be periodical, and under arrangements a supply of seed corn has been received from for this district from the Edinburgh association and Sir John Hill. The deficiency of last year's crop has generally been computed at 2/3rds of the grain and ½ of the potatoes. Little or none of the grain is fit for seed, and the inhabitants have opinions or prejudices as to the kind of grain fitted for the country, that makes them fastidious about foreign seed even though they have none of their own to use. The supply of potato seed is very short. There is no difficulty in finding work for the people; but anything like a regular day's work cannot be exacted without a large supply of food and it would be inexpedient, at all times, to supply them so as to interfere with the operations on their portions of land. The uncommon state of destitution in the Lewis this year is generally attributed to the failure of the crop last year, and the bad crop of the preceding year;[160] but there is less or more destitution every year, and there always will be unless the present excess of population can be reduced. The cause of the excess in the village of Stornoway is very much from the people flooding to that place when they lose their possessions in the country. There are instances of small lots which were originally laid out with the view of comfortably maintaining 4 or 5 individuals being subdivided so as to contain three times that number of individuals. In Barvas the population has been increased by early and improvident marriages, and the subdivision of the crofts among the members of families is too great an extent. The population exceeds by about 1/3 the amount of its powers of subsistence. In this parish they have no aids; the coast is completely exposed; there are no bays or inlets and in consequence they have no resource in fishing. There is no employment whatever by which a man can earn 6d; there are only two farms let as high as £20 and one of these tenants lets the half of his possession. The average rent of a possession in this parish is about £3. In Lochs there are only two farms which pay £50. The average rent runs from £2 to £3. The same is about the average in Uig where there is a population of 3,300, so allotted, with the exception of 5 large farms running from £50 to £250. This parish might be made a good cod fishing station, but the people would require to be furnished with tackle and good boats, and a few expert fishermen should be brought from the east coast to teach the art. The parish of Knock is in better circumstances than the rest of the island, chiefly from the natives being engaged

---

[160] A committee in Edinburgh was set up in May 1836 to appeal for subscriptions for the people of Lewis as a result of the 'deplorable scarcity of food' resulting from the weather in the winter and the whole of the spring (NRS, Papers of the Maxtone Graham family of Cultoquhey, Perthshire, GD 155/1347/1).

in fishing. The fishing might be extended in the parish of Lochs if encouragement was given to the art. The minister of Uig[161] (whom we did not see) writes in these terms: "In my humble opinion the people here cannot be comfortable in their circumstances even in good seasons, until the third part of them are removed by emigration or otherwise, and the lands of those that may be removed given to those that remain. I consider that two families in this parish would require all the land that three families now possess so as to enjoy even the necessaries of life."[162] Emigration is said by everyone to be the only permanent cure for the evil. It was recommended that it should take place by families and by farms or neighbourhoods, and that the emigration from one property should be spread over several years so that provision might gradually be made for the occupation of the land by large possessions, that a new population might not immediately spring up. There is no unwillingness among the people to go, if they have the means. They would prefer generally Cape Breton or Upper Canada because many of them have families there; but many of them would willingly go to Australia. One man with a family of 7 sons from 19 years of age downwards was willing to go to Australia or any colony to which he could be sent free. Probably not less than 1,000 persons of the poorest denomination assembled in front of Seaforth Lodge[163] as a kind of demonstration of gratitude for the public feeling so generally made in their behalf and, as far as I could understand through the medium of interpretation, as an expression of their general anxiety for emigration. A kind of deputation from the parish of Uig stated that they could name 40 families ready to go if they had the means, and they believed they could add 40 to that list. The schoolmaster of Uig stated that a great body of people could very soon be got together if means were provided for them; at least 100 families would go. A few individuals who appeared for Stornoway parish stated 11 families there ready to go. In the parish of Lochs the candidates for emigration exceeded the others. The ministers and Mr Knox can without difficulty collect the amount. I have the honour to be, Sir, your obedient servant.

Stornoway district including the following parishes

Parish of Barvas including the parliamentary parish of Cross[164] Population 3,366

---

[161] The Rev. Alexander Macleod, a man described by *FES* as 'greatly beloved' but as 'not all together admirable' by Macleod in *Banner in the West*, 159–61.

[162] A somewhat ironic assessment: the Rev. Alexander Macleod was a 'considerable farmer' who had tenants at Timsgarry evicted to enlarge the size of his glebe (B. Lawson, *Lewis in History and Legend – The West Coast* (Edinburgh, 2008), 216–17).

[163] Where Lews Castle now stands.

[164] The church at Cross was one of the forty-three parliamentary churches built under the authority of the 1823 act for building additional places of worship in the Highlands and Islands of Scotland, 4 Geo. IV c.79 (see [PP] 1831 IX (330), 4, 24 and 45).

Parish of Lochs Population 3,400
Parish of Stornoway including the parliamentary parish of Knock[165] Population 5,900
Parish of Uig Population 3,300
Total Population 15,966

Proposed committee for the district

Thomas Knox, Esq., factor for Lewis. Chairman and Convener
Mr [James]Pitcairn, Supervisor of Excise, Stornoway. Deputy Chairman and Convener
The Rev. William Macrae, Minister of Barvas
The Rev. John Macrae, Minister of Cross
The Rev. Robert Finlayson, Minister of Lochs
The Rev. John Cameron, Minister of Stornoway
The Rev. Duncan Matheson, Minister of Knock
The Rev. Alexander Macleod, Minister of Uig
Mr [William] Fairbairn, Fish curer, Stornoway
Mr [James] McAlister, Fishery officer, Stornoway.

Stornoway 14 April 1837[166]

My dear Mother, I write two lines just to say we are in the land of the living. We go tomorrow, if the wind permits, to Harris; and then to Portree. . . Yours ever.

Loch Tarbert in Harris 17 April 1837[167]

Sir, We arrived in this loch on Saturday evening and yesterday saw a certain portion of the inhabitants at the missionary church,[168] and in the neighbourhood of Tarbert; and this morning we had further communication with Mr [Donald] Stewart of Luskintyre (a gentleman who has known the island for nearly 35

---

[165] The church at Knock was one of the forty-three parliamentary churches built under the authority of the 1823 act for building additional places of worship in the Highlands and Islands of Scotland, 4 Geo. IV c.79 (see [PP] 1831 IX (330), 4, 24 and 45).

[166] Robert Stewart wrote to his sister from Stornoway that: 'to our disappointment . . . we could do nothing that day as the clergy of the island had fixed the day for a fast (as if it had been necessary to appoint a fast when all the people were starving)' (NRAS, Stewart family of Ardvorlich papers, 2654/1, box 16, bundle 3, Stewart to Marjory Stewart, 14 Apr. 1837).

[167] See 1841 SC, Q 1012–18.

[168] At Tarbert; the missionary was supported by the Royal Bounty Committee.

years, and a very extensive tacksman)[169] and his son Dr Stewart who likewise has a farm upon it; and with Mr Mcfee the missionary who has lately come to this place. Mr [John] Maciver, the minister of Harris, resides at the distance of 16 or 17 miles, but in fact is now at Rodel, 25 miles off, taking charge of the landing and distribution of seed oats and meal for the relief of the destitute of the parish; but he sent Dr Clark, the medical practitioner of the district, to attend to us, as an individual well qualified to give any information as to the state of the parish. From these combined sources we have obtained so satisfactory an account of the preparations making for the relief of the destitute inhabitants, that we think it quite unnecessary at present to penetrate further into the interior of the parish.

Dr Clark stated that there had arrived at Rodel for the use of this island, 70 tons of potato seed and 21 tons more expected there, to be sold to the tenants at 5s 9d per barrel and that all this will be required for the island; 219 bolls of oats had arrived from the Edinburgh committee which would all be required; 300 bolls of meal have been sent by the proprietor[170] for the use of the tenants exclusively which he understood was to be sold at 20/- per boll;[171] a further supply is expected from the Glasgow committee for the use of the poor.

With regard to the amount of destitution, Dr Clark stated that there are 450 tenants in the island who pay rent and he does not consider that, of these, 50 families are in comfortable circumstances; that all the rest would require assistance; that there are nearly 400 families more who have no land directly from the proprietor, and who of course are in a state of greater destitution. All the persons we examined concurred in the view that the potato crop had been deficient on the average $1/3^{rd}$ and the grain crop nearly one half; and what was saved was of very bad quality and hardly fit for food. Mr Stewart stated that in the cold, wet, mossy land on the mainland of Harris the potatoes failed to the

---

[169] The Stewarts were said to be 'the greatest curse that ever came upon Harris' and in 1839 Stewart's actions led to the summoning of the army by the factor to assist removals from his farm (B. Lawson, *Harris in History and Legend* (Edinburgh, 2002), 8 and 14–15; and 1841 SC, Q 2647). It has been said that it was the earl of Dunmore who ensured that the crofters were dealt with leniently at the subsequent proceedings (Richards, *The Highland Clearances*, 248) but the letters of the solicitor-general for Scotland, James Ivory, to the lord advocate Andrew Rutherfurd suggest that it was Ivory who persuaded the agents of Dunmore 'to see the matter in the proper light'; Ivory wrote to Rutherfurd of the 'folly and heartlessness' of the earl and that he had sent 'moderating instructions to the sheriff, who happily entertains the same temperate view of the matter'. He told Rutherfurd: 'I believe leniency – if not perhaps even letting them off altogether, with a solemn address as to their duty for the future from the sheriff will do more good to all concerned than any other course' (NLS, James Ivory letters, MS 9654, Ivory to Rutherfurd, 28 June, 21 July, 29 July, and 2 Aug. 1839).

[170] The earl of Dunmore, whose father purchased Harris from Alexander Norman Macleod of Harris in 1834 (Devine, 'New elite', 138).

[171] According to Charles Shaw, the earl of Dunmore provided 1,000 bolls of meal at prime cost and on credit ([PP] 1884 XXXVI [c.3980 IV], *Napier Commission Evidence*, Q 41434).

extent of 2/3^{rds}; in the dry sandy land on the small islands the failure was much
less. Never was a year so bad. The 1816 was a very bad year, but not so bad as last
year; and though in the spring of 1817[172] a supply of oats was sent to the island
by the Government, he considers the people more needy this year than then.
It is probable, however, from the quantity of oats come to the island, that very
little of the ground will remain unsown, although there are many now turning
over their ground in preparation, without being as yet aware from what source
the seed is to come. It is supposed that the proprietor has guaranteed the seed
oats and potatoes to the Edinburgh committee and that such of the poor people
as cannot pay for the potatoes will get them for nothing, and the others at the
rate of what they can pay.[173] The usual supply of potatoes from Skye and Uist
has this year been entirely cut off.

It was represented to us by Mr Stewart, who from his experience and scale of
farming we consider an excellent authority, that in ordinary years the people in
the island cannot supply themselves in consequence of the excess of population,
to which the extent of flat and arable land in the island bears no proportion.
He attributes the excess of population in some degree to the allotment system
and also to a custom which was prevalent during the time of the ballot for the
militia, when many young men were induced to marry because if they had
two lawful children they would get themselves exempted.[174] No person has left
this country for a long period except in 1828 when from 600 to 800 emigrated,
partly from the scarcity of the preceding year and partly from some conditions
which had been imposed by the proprietor as to the management of the lots.
The population has been comparatively in a healthy state since then, until last
year; but he believes it has again mounted up to what it was previous to 1828
and that, as there is so little flat land in the island capable of improvement, there
is as much pressure from over-population here as in any part of the Highlands.
He thinks if something could be done by His Majesty's Government and the
proprietor jointly in promoting emigration, that that would be the best remedy
for the evil. Those left at home might thereby be improved in their condition;
and the recurrence of the mischief might be checked by establishing regulations
on the property to prevent the splitting down of possessions.

---

[172] When Alexander Norman Macleod, together with other Long Island proprietors – Mary,
Lady Hood Mackenzie of Seaforth; Colonel Alexander Macdonald of Boisdale; Roderick
McNeill of Barra; Lord Macdonald; Ranald Macdonald of Clanranald; and Ranald
Macdonald of Bornish – had memorialised the government for a loan to enable them to
purchase 15,000 bolls of meal and 1,000 bolls of seed potatoes (see further in the Introduction).

[173] The resolutions passed by the Edinburgh committee on the supply of seed (p. 245) were
rather more specific as to terms of payment.

[174] It was a law (see Scottish Militia Act 1797, 37 Geo. III c.103). For a discussion of military
recruiting and the Highland estate economy, in particular the concentration by proprietors
on the enlistment of people who would least damage the rent-paying sector of the estate, see
A. Mackillop, 'More Fruitful than the Soil' – Army, Empire and the Scottish Highlands, 1715–1815
(East Linton, 2000), 130–67.

There is no good fishing station on the island but some work might be got to great public advantage by making roads connecting the extremes of the island. Additional piers and quays would be of great use, and the most necessary for this island would be the construction of piers in Skye, Uig and Dunvegan, as there are no facilities there for unshipping the cattle and horses from this island and from Uist. There would be no difficulty in finding able overseers for these works at a trifling expense.

The population directly under the charge of the missionary at Harris amounts to about 1,500; but as he has only been two months settled in his mission, we did not think it necessary to put separate questions to him in regard to his portion of the island. He concurred generally with the views stated by the other gentlemen as applicable to the whole population, and only complained that his portion of the flock were put to some inconvenience from the whole of the seed and meal being landed at Rodel (the south eastern extremity of the island) which was a great distance for the remoter inhabitants to have to send for their share of the supply. I have the honour to be, Sir, your obedient servant.

Portree 18 April 1837

My dear Mother, I have only time to write two lines to acknowledge the receipt of your letters of 24th March and 11th April. My next post office is Tobermory where I expect to be about Sunday, and hope to return home from there. We are going on very well and have been very lucky in weather. Kindest love to all. Yours most affectionately.

Lochmaddy 20 April 1837[175]

Sir, The remaining portions of Skye which have not been reported are the parishes of Kilmuir and Stenscholl, Duirinish and Hallin-in-Waternish and Bracadale including the mission of Miginish[176] comprising a population of about 11,000.[177] The condition of these parishes in regard to destitution does not tend at all to lessen the general average which I made of the state of Skye. That of the parishes on the north east side of the island appears to be estimated at more than ½ of the population and the parishes on the north western sides of the island nearly as high as ¾ ths of the population. Most of the clergymen were absent from their homes attending meetings of the presbytery and synod

[175] See 1841 SC, Q 951*–956.
[176] Supported by the Royal Bounty Committee.
[177] There is a marginal note giving the parish numbers: Kilmuir, 2,275; Stenscholl, 1,736; Durinish, 4,000; Hallin-in-Waternish, 1,337; Bracadale, 1,769. Total 11,117.

at Broadford, but we received information in detail from Mr Macdonald of Kingsburgh and the schoolmaster at Kilmuir,[178] from Mr [Edward] Gibbon, the factor of Macleod of Macleod (who has known the estate for twenty five years) and from Mr [John] Tolmie, an extensive tacksman in the neighbourhood, a native of Minginish and who has held his present farm since 1825. None of these individuals recollected any year at all to be compared to the present since 1816–17. They generally estimate the failure of the grain crops at nearer 2/3rd than ½, and the potatoes much the same. None of them, however, ascribe the present destitution solely to the bad crops, though that has brought the evil to a crisis at the present time. Mr Gibbon stated that when he came to the country twenty-five years ago, there was abundance of work of every kind; and the country was flourishing in a great degree by the making of roads, the manufacture of kelp and the good state of the fishing. Matters are now so much altered, 1st By the peace, which sent many natives to the country and stopped the usual drafts for the army. 2nd By taking off the duty on barilla, which destroyed the kelp manufactory. 3rd The roads have all been completed; and lastly the fishings have failed entirely. The greatest of all these evils was the failure of the kelp manufactory, as when the manufacture was brisk, there was not a small tenant on the estate who after paying his rent had not an abundant supply of meal for his family.[179] [He] thinks that on Macleod's property there are two for one who do not pay rent directly to the landlord; [he] thinks the people on Macleod's estate are better off than on other estates as he has been very indulgent to them in not pushing them for rents during the last year.[180] When he came to this country in 1812 the inhabitants of Skye were 17,000; by the last census they were nearly 25,000, and by the next census may probably be nearly 30,000.[181] At the first period there was plenty of work of every description for the people; and now all public works as well as the manufactory of kelp, have ceased.

To remedy these evils, it was suggested that something might be done to improve the fishery and in making additional roads, but that would only be a temporary relief, and all the individuals expressed their strong conviction that nothing would afford a permanent cure but emigration on a very extensive scale. Restrictions in the management would certainly be necessary in the event of emigration to prevent the population again increasing to the same amount. There might be some difficulty in the cases of smaller proprietors,

---

[178] John MacGregor.

[179] On the importance of kelp on the Dunvegan estate, see Canon R. C. Macleod, *The Book of Dunvegan*, Third Spalding Club, 2 vols. (Aberdeen, 1938–9), ii, 115–17; also MacAskill, 'The Highland kelp proprietors', 60–82; and J. MacAskill, '"The most arbitrary, scandalous act of tyranny": the crown, private proprietors and the ownership of the Scottish foreshore in the nineteenth century', *SHR* 85.2, no. 220 (Oct. 2006), 277–304.

[180] Macleod of Macleod's efforts during the famine in 1847 were roundly appreciated (see Devine, *Highland Famine*, 86).

[181] In Nicolson, *Skye*, 269, the population at the time of the first census is stated as being 16,000 and that it had reached its peak of 23,000 in 1841.

some of whom were rather inclined to encourage the increase of population from mistaken and contracted views, but on the large estates there would comparatively be but little difficulty. Mr Tolmie, on his farm which maintains about 2,000 sheep and some cattle, is bound to submit to 70 families of cottars not upon the landlord's rental whom he found on the farm at his entry and whom he has no right to remove; but he does not allow any subdivision of their lots and he finds no difficulty in maintaining his regulation, which is simply not to allow two families to establish themselves separately on one possession; and it is invariably found that they will not live in the same house if debarred from having separate houses. Mr Gibbon thinks it is not easy to prevent the subdivision of lots in the present state of the population, but if it was once reduced to a healthy state by emigration or otherwise, it would be easy to enforce the regulations afterwards. He thinks too it would be greatly for the interests of the large proprietors to unite with the Government in promoting emigration and believes Mr Macleod would do so. He thinks the people would prefer going in families, in neighbourhoods and districts that they might locate themselves together; [he] thinks, in general, they would prefer emigrating to America.

Every addition to our information strengthens the view as to the present willingness of the people to emigrate. Mr Kennedy, teacher at Macdermid's Institution in the parish of Snizort (whom I had occasion formerly to notice) has placed in my hands the names of 223 families, certainly a population of 1,273, belonging to that parish who are willing immediately to emigrate if they had the means. One third of these families have no provisions whatever; about a third more have provisions for from one week up to a month; and the remaining third, the great majority have not provisions for more than two months; and only eight families are provisioned for three months.

Sixty-four bolls of meal have been distributed at Kilmuir parish among 1,081 individuals; no computation was made as to the time for which this would suffice; but care was observed in apportioning the means to the respective wants of the claimants. Some seed corn had been supplied, but there was still want of it. In the other parishes, the people are badly off for seed. None has come to them, either grain or potatoes; no supplies of meal have yet reached them though it was understood that some had been shipped for them at Glasgow. There is reason to believe that the ordinary poor of these parishes are ill provided for. There are no assessments and the collections at the Church doors which are their chief support are very trifling. In Duirinish there has been no regular distribution of poor funds for some years in consequence, it is alleged, of some irregularities in the proceedings of the kirk sessions. This appears of late to have been put on a better footing, but the present funds are so inadequate that it is considered that an assessment for behoof of the ordinary poor would be a great advantage to them. The ordinary poor are better off in Bracadale parish where there are some separate funds to a small amount under the form of what is called 'mortifications'.[182] These amount to £17 a year but the collections at the Church doors there are a mere trifle. I have the honour to be, Sir, your obedient servant.

Barra 26 April 1837[183]

Sir, I have joined the islands of North Uist, Benbecula and South Uist in one account. They belong to different proprietors[184] but their circumstances are not materially different and they are very much under the same system of management. North Uist is now divided into three ecclesiastical divisions: the old parish,[185] the parliamentary parish of Trumisgarry[186] and the mission of Cairinish,[187] and the original parish of South Uist and Benbecula is now likewise divided under three ecclesiastical charges, viz. the old parish of South Uist, a portion of which is now united to the mission of the island of Benbecula and another mission is formed at the Boisdale on the southern end of the island of South Uist.[188] I have added in this account the island of Barra in order to complete in one view the whole of the southern portion of the Long Island. The united population of these islands amounts to 13,600. The parties whom we have examined in regard to this district all concurred in the view that there is great destitution now, and that there are not many families but will require less or more of assistance before harvest. In Barra, many of the families had actually left their residences in the interior to get nearer the strand where they could pick up shellfish for food.

We first touched upon the islands at Lochmaddy and we made nearly the circuit of North Uist by land, and crossing the strand at low water to Benbecula we made a similar circuit of the western portion of that island from opposite to Cairinish to Creag Ghoraidh, and rejoining the cutter in

---

¹⁸² In old Scots land law this was a kind of tenure whereby lands might be held in perpetuity in return for prayers and masses; it was abolished after the Reformation and the word came to be used to describe charitable foundations (D. M. Walker, *The Oxford Companion to Law* (Oxford, 1980), 857). On the availability of mortifications for poor law purposes, see Dunlop, *Parochial Law*, 375–83.

¹⁸³ See 1841 SC, Q 1012–18.

¹⁸⁴ North Uist was in the sole ownership of Lord Macdonald and in South Uist and Benbecula the proprietors were Ranald G. Macdonald of Clanranald, Hugh Macdonald of Boisdale and Ranald Macdonald of Bornish (the only resident proprietor).

¹⁸⁵ Called North Uist, where the minister was the Rev. Finlay Macrae.

¹⁸⁶ Where the church was one of the forty-three parliamentary churches built under the authority of the 1823 act for building additional places of worship in the Highlands and Islands of Scotland, 4 Geo. IV c.79 (see [PP] 1831 IX (330), 4, 19 and 41), and the minister was the Rev. Norman McLeod.

¹⁸⁷ Supported by the Royal Bounty Committee.

¹⁸⁸ The minister was the Rev. Roderick Maclean. The two established church missions were supported by the Royal Bounty Committee. Roman Catholics formed more than two thirds of the population (*NSAc*, xiv, 196) and there were Roman Catholic mission stations at Ardkenneth and Benbecula and Bornish (or Bornais) and Dalabrog (SSC, 150–1).

Loch Sgioport we proceeded from thence to Lochboisdale and subsequently to Barra. At Lochmaddy we spent a day with Mr Charles Shaw,[189] factor to Lord Macdonald, who is proprietor of the whole of North Uist, and we met there Mr [D.] MacLachlan, the sheriff-substitute in this part of Inverness-shire, and before leaving the island we saw the missionary of Cairinish but the other clergymen were absent at the synod. In the course of driving round the islands we visited several of the cottages to satisfy ourselves from our own observations of the condition of the people, and we had opportunities of witnessing scenes of great misery and wretchedness.

We entered one cottage between six and seven o' clock in the morning which had no latch and no hinges to the door; a yearling heifer occupied the first of two apartments and the other, which was almost without light and where there was only one bed of straw, contained four children – two boys and two girls – nearly quite naked and almost without a bedcover. The mother of the children, who is a widow, had gone 12 miles to Lochmaddy the day before in the chance of getting some potatoes from the factor. There was no food of any kind in the house nor had the children any prospect of a meal before the return of their mother. The cow had been sold in the month of December. This woman was the widow of the son of an adjoining crofter who is also a widow, and who had allowed this settlement on a corner of her small possession. When the one went in search of food for the young family, the other had gone in search of seed to put into the ground.

We entered another cottage by a door about 3 feet and a half high. The inmates were gone, most of them, as we afterwards found from one of the boys of the family, to gather shellfish on the beach as the day's provisions. The family consists of a man and his wife and five children. Nothing in the form of food was visible about the premises, except a sheaf or two of bear. The first apartment here too was arranged as if for a cow, but there was none there. The inner apartment was almost filled up with two beds of straw from which one blanket and a torn coverlet were exhibited to us.

Another group of 17 or 18 relations were settled on the bounds which had once been given by a crofter as a sufficient allotment for containing a single family. This arrangement here expanded to three cottages closely joined together, so as almost to exclude the light, without any land, they are occupied by an old man and two married sons with their families. The old man lives in one wing and has not a morsel to eat and scarcely clothes to cover him. The family of one son consists of a wife and 7 children in two beds. Two or three blankets were all that were displayed to us; and the children were miserably clothed. In ordinary years they

<hr>

189 Charles Shaw had assisted his father, Donald Shaw, as the factor of Harris from Whitsunday 1834 to Whitsunday 1838, and was factor of North Uist for several years, having the chief management of the island from Whitsunday 1835 to Whitsunday 1838, and he was the factor of the greater part of South Uist for many years. He was factor of Barra from Martinmas 1836 to Whitsunday 1838 ([PP] 1851 XXVI (1397), 114).

look for aid to the smaller tenants, or those one degree higher than themselves, beyond such subsistence as can be gained by the occasional work given to the father on the adjoining farm. The other son lives much in the same way. He has a sickly wife whom we saw sitting on the mud floor, and 5 or 6 children. The wife had twins ten weeks ago; she still suckles one, the other died about a week ago and the remaining one seems to have little chance of being reared. They have no potatoes, no meal and never had a cow among them.

Heaps of shells about the doors in all these cases afforded the only symptom of a wretched material for prolonging human life. These are not selected cases; they were the first three we visited in sequence that morning and the latter two were eight miles distant from the former, and perhaps there were a hundred of the same class in the space that intervened between them. The two last were cottars on Mr [James Thomas] Macdonald of Balranald's farm who we saw and who gave us information as to the state of his immediate neighbourhood. He pays altogether a rent of about £400 to Lord Macdonald but this portion of his land is rented at £260 and it contains ten of these settlers who are not in better circumstances than the cases I have noticed and who have no visible means of living but through the kindness of their neighbours and such occasional work as Balranald puts into their hands.

This is not far from the richest part of the island of North Uist which is very thickly peopled and where in the light sandy soil there was last year a tolerably good crop of potatoes. It is comparatively too, more free of these small cottars. In one farm where there is a joint tenancy of 80 small tenants (from £3 upwards to £10) there are not above 40 families not standing on the rental. On two other large farms, held likewise in joint tenancy in a similar way, there is just about a corresponding number of families not upon the rental.

In Benbecula, where we stayed all night, we had our information from Mr Duncan Shaw, factor on the Clanranald and Boisdale estates, and also on Lord Dunmore's estate of Harris, and from Mr Maclean the minister of Benbecula.[190] We met at Boisdale, Mr Chisholm the Catholic priest of South Uist[191] and we had an opportunity of conversing with Mr McClellan, an extensive tacksman there, Mr Macrae, missionary of Boisdale, Mr Finlayson the fishery officer, and other individuals connected with the southern portion of the island. We made observations in an inspection of the cottages in South Uist similar to those already mentioned, but it is endless to repeat details only leading to one uniform result.[192]

---

[190] FES shows Donald Macdonald as the minister appointed in 1837, succeeding Dugald Campbell.
[191] James Chisholm, who was at the Bornish and Dalabrog mission station.
[192] Stewart wrote from Canna to his sister about Lochboisdale (or Boisdale): 'in the course of our work we have come upon the Roman Catholic chapel in the act of being dismissed and really from the respectable look of the people and from their dress would not have been inclined to suppose there was much distress in the country; however we had reason to suppose we only saw the best of people . . . we ascertained that [the people] are now

At Barra, our information was derived from Mr Macdonald, the sub-factor on the estate,[193] Mr [Alexander] Nicolson the minister of Barra, and Mr MacIntosh[194] the Catholic priest there. In the whole district more than one half of the tenants do not pay rent to the landlords. They live chiefly by the toleration, or on the charity, of the tenants, great and small. The present destitution is chiefly ascribed to the failure of the crop which in barley is estimated at ½, in oats a total failure in as far as meal is concerned, the potatoes fully at ½ and in one division of South Uist, viz. the middle divisions at ½ .

The state of destitution over the whole district according to the accounts received by us cannot be stated at less than 4/5ths of the population. A shipment of meal to the extent of 150 bolls has arrived at Boisdale for the use of this district from the Glasgow committee. It appears to have been a second shipment and a previous cargo which had been shipped on the 7th of March has since arrived at Boisdale. The meal was immediately distributed at Boisdale at the rate of 10lbs per head and the proportion allotted to Barra reached it on the 23rd. The tenants on the great proprietors' estates in this district with the exception of Barra, in one way or another will in general be sufficiently supplied with seed corn and potatoes.[195] It is apprehended that the cottars and many others holding indirectly of the landlords will be badly off in all these islands. Under present circumstances this evil appears to be unavoidable. The whole district, though an excellent pastoral district, is not strictly a corn country and the class of people whom I have last alluded to, rest every year for their support in great measure upon those immediately above them, who unfortunately have no the means at present of assisting them. Probably at any hands it might imply a smaller sacrifice to understand the burden of supporting them next season, than to apply the means of enabling them to raise indifferent crops for themselves. It was confidently stated by many

getting fair play in the distribution of the supplies which had come' (NRAS, Stewart family of Ardvorlich papers, 2654/1, box 16, bundle 3, Stewart to Marjory Stewart, 27 Apr. 1837).

[193] The estate of Barra was owned by General Roderick MacNeill of Barra who sold the island to John Menzies in 1839 who, in his turn, sold the island to Colonel John Gordon of Cluny in 1840 (*Inverness Courier*, 13 Mar. 1839 and 30 Dec. 1840).

[194] William MacIntosh (who had been ordained after charges levelled at him for escaping the excise men while smuggling whisky had been dropped – SSC, 129).

[195] On Barra, where the estate had been sequestrated in October 1836, there were difficulties in providing the required guarantee as to payment for seed supplied by the Edinburgh committee because the duty of the trustees was to the creditors and giving such a guarantee would, almost certainly, run counter to this duty. It seems, however, that the Edinburgh committee relaxed the requirement and allowed a small supply (NRS, Court of Session productions in process, CS 96/4274/131–2 and 96/4274/131/102–6, Minutes of meetings of trustees and commissioners, 21 and 27 Apr. 1837). On the problems caused for crofters and cottars when estates were in administration, see S. P. Walker, 'Agents of dispossession and acculturation. Edinburgh accountants and the Highland Clearances', *Critical Perspectives on Accounting* 14 (2003), 815–53; Richards, *The Highland Clearances*, 292; Devine, *Highland Famine*, 185–6; 1841 SC, Q 166–73, 185–6; and [PP] 1884 XXXVI [c. 3980. IV], Q 45462–3.

respectable persons that many of the small farms at present cultivated are unfit for tillage and could only be profitably employed in pasture.

Imported potatoes have arrived, but only at one point and these on private order for Lord Macdonald's tenants. The Messrs Shaws on the estates under their management have taken steps to retain within the island all the surplus supplies wherever it happened to exist and to apportion them among the tenantry to the best advantage. From the particular circumstances in which the Barra estate at present stands,[196] no such advantageous provision has been made for this island.

Over-population is the ruin of the district. If the season had been a good one, the tenants holding directly of the proprietor would not have been in want; but the cottars and smaller householders would have leant almost entirely on those above them for support. The failure of the kelp manufactory which was felt more strongly on Clanranald's estate than on any other, the imperfection of the fishing employment in some cases, the enlargement of holdings in others, the minute splitting down of minor possessions, are all causes (acting and re-acting upon one another) which have contributed largely to the present distress. The numbers still continue to increase very fast and the land is gradually getting worse from the constant and unvaried system of cropping to which it is exposed. The continued use of seaweed with scarcely any other change of manure exhausts the ground; and the people are getting poorer every year. Another circumstance which has caused much hardship to the people is the high prices of wool for the last five or six years, which has prevented them from getting a sufficient supply of clothing and bedding; three-fifths of the small tenants have no sheep, and those that have sell their wool off the islands, the people not being able to purchase it; whenever the tenants have a few sheep they are well clothed. There is no possibility of finding any employment in the islands for the surplus population that would be profitable. There is a work in North Uist for converting kelp into muriate of potash and carbonate of soda, which gives some vent to the manufacture of kelp, but the work itself gives direct employment only to eighteen hands, and having only been in operation for a year and a half it is impossible yet to say whether it will answer. Another work of a similar kind in Barra has now ceased[197] and there are no other manufactures in these islands. The fishing is only good at the southern extremity of South Uist and in the coast of Barra—all along the western coast it is almost impracticable; and on the other portions of the island, upon the authority of the fishery officer and other competent judges, we concluded that no capital should be risked in funding it. The fishery might be improved for the benefit of the people but at Boisdale and Barra they are said to be much in want of good boats. Something might be done in improving the roads which, as far as

---

[196] That is, in sequestration.

[197] In fact both works had failed by 1841 – in the case of Barra with a 'ruinous expense to the speculators' ([PP] 1914 XXXII. 43 [Cd.7564], *Report to the Board of Agriculture for Scotland on Home Industries in the Highlands and Islands*, 32).

they go, are good in the islands. Thirty six miles of roads have been made in North Uist under the statute labour provisions,[198] and twenty more of excellent bye roads have been made by the people themselves giving them neat and comfortable approaches to their houses from the main lines, and access to the interior of the island, from whence they draw their fuel. Further improvement is however still required. The main road from Spronesh to Benbecula, after going twenty-eight miles, comes to a point distant in a line about ten miles from the point of starting. The shorter line is in progress of being made and will be overtaken in time by the present funds, but it can only be done tediously, and this work would afford good employment for the people if funds could be furnished elsewhere. Similar remarks are applicable to the roads in Benbecula and South Uist where, as we have understood chiefly from the exertions of Mr Shaw, the people have done much in making good roads to their houses and the peat bogs.

Emigration, however, was pointed at in every quarter as the only source of ultimate relief. In the southern portion of this island, rents were represented to be much too high even though no labour was exacted. It was recommended to divide the emigration over a period of years and to send the people in families; indeed it was confidently stated that they would not otherwise go. Mr [Charles] Shaw Jnr stated one case of an old man of seventy with 18 followers, all of whom were under the restricted age for Australia.[199] They are all anxious to go, but the children and other descendants will not move without the old man. It is a patriarchal community which by nature and habit they would prefer going as an entire body and from one neighbourhood. There is no indisposition to emigrate, but the contrary. Emigrations have taken place lately both in Barra and South Uist and these are the only places we have visited where the population has diminished since 1831; but the scale is not sufficiently extensive, for the births are annually double the number of the deaths. Mr Charles Shaw has a list of 800 or 900 ready to go to Australia; and Mr [Duncan] Shaw Snr in three days received 700 applications in the neighbourhood of Benbecula, and thinks that in South Uist he might have doubled the number in a week on Clanranald's estate alone.

If the surplus population were once reduced, no apprehensions are entertained as to the difficulties of keeping it within moderate bounds afterwards. The regulations must of course originate with the proprietors, and their participation in the work of taking off the excess would be some guarantee for prudential management afterwards. It is considered that it would tend much to improve the condition of the people if their moral habits were raised by education, as it might be a means of preventing early and imprudent marriages. Want of schools is complained of in several places; but in Barra it may be said there is no school at

---

[198] See [PP] 1836 XVIII (430), *Select Committee on Statute Labour on Roads in Scotland, Report, Minutes of Evidence*, Appendix.

[199] That is, under 35.

all, for although a schoolmaster has been appointed, the schoolhouse is situated widely apart from the population.[200]

There is no regular public provision for the poor in any of these islands. In general they are very unwilling even to go about to beg, and their friends and neighbours make a point of maintaining them on their farms, but this year they are unable to do so. The collections at the church doors, where they are made, are exceedingly trifling and are applicable principally towards the funerals of the poor, in purchasing coffins, etc, etc. Lord Macdonald has an ordinary poor's list upon his estate, and gives from the multures[201] of his three mills from 40 to 50 bolls of meal in the year to the poor whatever the season may be. This practice is said to have been established about 60 years ago as a fund for decayed tenants, but is not strictly appropriated to that object, and has rather been converted into a permanent provision for the poor persons admitted on the roll. Similar arrangements are said to have existed on other estates, and even to have originated in settlements and endowments; but in some instances, from embarrassed states of affairs the management has come into the hands of trustees, and the right application of these funds has been diverted. This is a point which would require further investigation, for if the allegations rest on facts, the poor in these cases have a preference to creditors. At Barra there is an endowed fund belonging to the poor, amounting to £400, but from an embarrassed state of management, the interest has been irregularly paid for many years. Independent of this matter, Protestant and Catholic concur that an assessment for the poor would be advantageous, as it would give the proprietors an interest in looking after the state of the people.[202]

A deputation of fishermen complained of an arrangement on the Boisdale estate by which the people are constrained to give all the fish which is caught, to the factor at a fixed price which they considered very injurious to the people. Mr Finlayson the fishery officer was of opinion that it hurts the fishing by diminishing the number of fish caught, and that he had known cases where, in consequence, the fishermen "did not bait the 3rd hook", which shows the impolicy of the existing regulation. He stated that but for the existence of this rule, there would be no necessity for curing any of the fish caught, as the smacks would take the cod fresh from the fishermen. In such a year as the present it is obvious how much a money price at a ready market would benefit the poor fishermen; and although under ordinary circumstances it is dangerous, if not impossible, to interfere with the contracts of a landlord and his tenants, still, if there is to be any compromise as to the policy in management, and if other interests are forced to make sacrifices with the object of ameliorating the condition of the people, and advancing the

---

[200] According to the account of the Rev. Alexander Nicolson in January 1840 there was no specially built schoolhouse but rather the school was in a 'house which is not fitted to accommodate any tolerable number of the parishioners' (*NSAc*, xiv, 215).

[201] The quantity of grain deliverable to a miller in return for grinding corn.

[202] No record of a legal assessment is given in the 1839 Poor Law Report or in *NSAc*.

general welfare of the country, such points as these should not be left out of the arrangement.[203] The factor on the estate (who is a judicial factor,[204] and on that account perhaps may think it his duty to be more rigid in his regulations) was requested, like the others, to meet us, but he did not attend at the time appointed.

The names of the different individuals most interested in the management of the people in these islands have been specially mentioned in the preceding report. It is therefore considered unnecessary at present to suggest any special committee for regulating the distribution of any supplies which may hereafter be sent. Besides, as the Messrs Shaw represent the whole proprietors of the islands, and are most intimately acquainted with the respective wants of each individual, it is considered that the management of the supplies may best be entrusted to them and to any others they may choose to associate with themselves. The clergymen of the different parishes will of course naturally fall to be of that number, but in consequence of their absence at the synod there were several of them whom we did not see. I have the honour to be, Sir, your obedient servant.

Oban 30 April 1837

My dear Mother, We have just landed here and I cross the country to Inveraray where I expect a steam boat will start tomorrow morning for Glasgow. If I am lucky I may be in Edinburgh before this reaches you; but all events I think I cannot be long after it. . .Your son most affectionately.

Edinburgh 6 May 1837[205]

Sir, Having now finished my inspection of those portions of the destitute Highland districts which I have thought it necessary to visit under the authority of your letter of the 2nd of March; and having made special reports from time to time relative to these districts, I shall conclude my observations on this subject with a short summary or abstract of the information I have gathered in the progress of my tour.

The parts of the country to which I have chiefly applied my attention were the western coasts of Argyllshire, Invernessshire and Rossshire on the mainland, the islands of Mull, Tiree, Coll, the small isles, Skye and the chain

---

[203] As to the reluctance of the government to interfere with contracts between the estate of South Uist and workers on the estate in a modern setting, see J. MacAskill, 'Foreshore', in M. Mulhern (ed.), *Scottish Life and Society – A Compendium of Scottish Ethnology*, 14 vols. (Edinburgh, 2012), xiii, 449.

[204] A person appointed by the court to preserve and administer property, in this case because Clanranald's estates were administered by trustees.

[205] The minute as to the discussion of this letter in the Treasury is set out in Part 5 (p. 283).

of islands from the Butt of Lewis to Barra head and which generally pass under the name of the Long Island.

As I have already reported, most of these parts of the country are in a state of unexampled destitution. The oldest residents in any portion I have passed through were unable to call to their recollection any year which equalled the present one. Many years have occurred in which it was necessary to supply the poorer classes of people both with meal and potatoes but it has hitherto been the practice in the Highlands that the proprietors took measures in years of scarcity to provide supplies for the population of their estates and with two exceptions it is believed that no such appeal as the present for a direct supply has been made to the Government of the country in the memory of any person now living.

The first was in 1782 which was a year of extended famine and when Government had a large supply of pease on hand in consequence of the peace with America which was appropriated to the relief of the Highlands.[206]

The next was in the year 1817 which was a year of scarcity and which was preceded by the unfavourable one of 1816. On an application to the Government a large supply of oats was sent for the support of the districts at this time.[207]

In the same way the present amount of destitute is in a primary way traceable to the occurrence of two unfortunate seasons. The weather during the spring of 1835, though not considered unusually severe in other districts of the country, was in the Highlands very cold and wet; the early part of May in particular was very rainy and in most cases the crop was got into the ground in a very unfavourable state. The summer however turned out dry and warm, and wherever the land was moderately dry the crops turned out a fair average. On wet lands, however, (and perhaps ¾ ths of the land under tillage in the western Highlands and Islands may be stated as of this description) the produce of that year fell greatly short; the potato crop was much under the average, having been very generally affected by disease, and that circumstance, accompanied by a wet late harvest which prevented the ripening of the corn crop and the preservation of it after it was cut down left the people to meet the spring of 1836 with greatly diminished supplies.

Early in February that year the snow fell to an unusual depth all over the country and continued to fall at intervals with alternate rain and sleet until the end of April thereby preventing the occupants of wet lands from getting the crop into the ground in proper time, and in many instances it was not until the dry weather set in about the middle of May that any work could be done. From the low prices the preceding year many people had been induced to keep on an extra stock of cattle which consumed the indifferent stock of potatoes much too rapidly: the disease induced in the former year was continued in the present one, and the seed planted in many cases failed and the plants became

---

[206] See [PP] 1846 XXXVII (281).
[207] See the Introduction.

defective. After a short continuance of dry weather in May, rain again set in and prevailed (as is well known) to an unprecedented extent during the whole summer and autumn; and the potato crop was further overtaken by severe frosts in the month of October. The crop in many places was entirely cut off, and as the staple article of human food in the western and north-western Highlands and Islands is potatoes, the inhabitants were left without their usual means of food almost at the beginning of winter. This loss was not supplied in corn. From the general wetness of the soil, and the late periods of sowing, it was impossible for the grain crops in most instances in the Highland districts to ripen; and even those which partially ripened were beat down and destroyed by the severe gales of autumn, and were thereby rendered unfit for being made into meal, and the straw was almost useless for the cattle.

In most seasons the crops in the Highlands are later than in other parts of Scotland (and that even in situations where the soil and climate are by no means unfavourable.) Late sowing is rendered necessary by the want of enclosures as, until the snow retires, and the grass is sufficiently advanced in the hill ground, besides the impossibility of preventing the cattle and sheep from straying over the low grounds, these portions are often the only sources of keeping them alive during the months of April and May.

From these causes, the state of provisions in the Highlands and Isles has been reduced to a lower ebb than probably ever was known before. The same inclement weather increased the calamity, by preventing the ordinary access to the peat-bogs, and the opportunity of saving and carrying home the usual supply of turf fuel; and to complete the miserable picture, the small sheep stocks which enabled most of the little occupants to make an annual web,[208] have disappeared in the gradual declension of their affairs; and the high prices of wool have drawn all the farmers' fleeces out of the country, and the people have not their former facilities for clothing themselves.

As to the extent of this accumulation of evils, the united population of the destitute districts which have come under my special observation amounts to at least 105,000;[209] and I am more afraid of being under the mark than of overshooting it, in stating my conviction that two-thirds of this amount of population are now, or will be long before the commencement of the next crop, without a supply of either kind of food at home, and will have to look to foreign sources to prevent starvation until that time.

There are two consolatory reflections which come in to relieve the irksomeness of this narrative. By the exertions of some meritorious and spirited individuals, the public attention has been roused to a knowledge of the situation in this country, which was too imperfectly understood at home, and large subscriptions are making, which are likely to afford material relief in the present state of

---

[208] A woven fabric.
[209] This total excluded Sutherland, Caithness, Orkney and Shetland.

distress. The other is that though the crops have been in these districts defective to an unprecedented extent, this by no means is the case all over the country generally; and at few periods, it is believed, has it contained greater stores of grain than at the present time.

The amount of destitution varies in several districts in degree. The islands of Tiree and Coll appear to be worse off than Mull; and the evil does not decrease as you advance northwards along the coast of Inverness-shire and Ross-shire on the mainland; but it is in Skye and the Long Island that the greatest distress prevails.

The immediate and direct cause of the excessive misery which exists at present in the Highlands is already given in the details stated above, as to the failure of the season. The very circumstance, however, of the famine being produced in the Highlands and Islands of Scotland by the failure of one or two crops (and these consisting chiefly of potatoes) indicates not merely great poverty in the people, but seems to imply some great and radical errors as to their condition and management. Important as it is to supply the wants of the people just now, it is infinitely of more importance to enquire by what means the evil is to be prevented from increasing, and how this Highland territory is to be wrested from its present chance of declining, day by day, into a more impoverished and more degraded state, which may gradually extend itself beyond the present limits, and slowly, but certainly, pervade the face of Scotland.

Over-Population

The grand cause of this evil, and in which a variety of minor causes have concentrated their results, is that the population of this part of the country has been allowed to increase in a much greater ratio than the means of subsistence which it affords; that the districts in question are totally incapable of maintaining in comfortable circumstances anything like the present population, must be evident, I think, to any man who has an opportunity of observing them, and who is capable of reflecting and judging on the subject; I may say it is the universal opinion of everyone I have conversed with in that country. This discrepance arises from a variety of circumstances over which the Government have now not much control; and in as far as it has arisen from acts of the legislature, it is almost inevitably the result of attending to the interests of the many, though affecting the interests of the few:[210]

---

[210] This is, in particular, a reference to the lowering of the duty on barilla and the repeal of the duty on salt in accordance with the wish of the government to encourage the advance of science in the interests of the consumer (see MacAskill, 'The Highland kelp proprietors', 78–9).

1. *Consequences of the Peace*

The population has unduly grown up, as a consequence of the peace, which has stopped the regular draft of soldiers and sailors from this country, and has sent back many of its former inhabitants who were lured away by the love of glory and other motives, but who have all a feeling to die a natural death at home.[211] It was indirectly increased during the war, and an encouragement was given to the natural and reckless tendency of the people to early marriages, by a provision of the militia laws, which entitled a man to exemption in consideration of the number of his children.[212] Some of the benevolent and charitable funds too, chiefly connected with the army, most inconsiderately withheld their benefits, but upon the qualification of a sufficient number of children.

2. *Failure of the kelp manufacture*

The kelp manufacture was, during the war, so profitable to the landlords that they encouraged the people to remain on their estates, being well aware that the quantity manufactured depended on the number of people engaged; and that, however high the rents became, they would still be paid, though in the meantime the proper cultivation of the lands might be neglected. The thoughts of all parties were turned to the cultivation of sea-ware, rather than the cultivation of the lands; and the very prosperity which, for a long time, attended the kelp trade, rendered the proprietors and people both thoughtless of other things, until they unexpectedly found themselves in the condition that the one is unable to help the other. Since 1822, the kelp manufacture has been unprofitable to the landlords. By various changes of the law, too hastily applied, perhaps, to be quite consistent with the truest policy, first, by taking the duty off barilla, and then by repealing that upon salt, successive shocks were suddenly given to the situation of the kelp proprietors.[213] The price of kelp bounded downwards, and the fall of the price did not tell so rapidly upon the condition of the people as might have been expected, because considerable quantities were continued to be made long after it had ceased to afford a fair immediate profit, though the employment enabled the labourer to pay his rent. That rent, however, came generally to be paid in work or in the draft of fish, and not in money. The circulating medium of exchange has become greatly

---

[211] Graham suggests here that it was the return of soldiers and sailors which contributed to the problem; but the issue went wider: recruitment of the Highlander to armed service for the fiscal military state of Britain from the 1750s to 1815, especially changes in British recruiting policy, caused its own problems, increasing the redundancy of the Highland population (see generally Mackillop, *More Fruitful*, 234–44).

[212] For example under the Scottish Militia Act of 1797 (37 Geo. III c. 103), married men with two children were exempt from recruitment (J. Western, 'The formation of the Scottish militia in 1797', *SHR* 34.117 (Apr. 1955), 3).

[213] See generally on this MacAskill, 'The Highland kelp proprietors', 60–82.

Tabular View showing the Quantity of Kelp manufactured on another estate, with the expense of manufacture; the price at which it was sold, and the net proceeds received; also the amount of the rental and population of the property for the years 1811–1836, and inclusive. The Kelp manufactured in this District is reckoned of the very best quality, and to fetch the highest prices.

Years	Quantity of Kelp made			Rate per Ton	Net Proceeds exclusive of expense ofManufacture		
	Tons	cwt	qrs		£	s	d
1811	497	13	2				
1812	729	11	—				
1813	365	17	1				
1814	557	5	3				
1815	458	19	3	£10 to £11	3,635	13	4
1816	725	3	2	£8 to £10	4,520	2	8
1817	380	8	2				
1818	559	16	2				
1819	985	9	1	£9 9s to £11 11s	2,356	—	2
1820	627	19	—	£8 to £11 11s	5,486	1	4
1821	441	19	1	£6 10s to £11	3,512	—	6
1822	588	14	—	£4 10s to £9	3,683	4	1
1823	359	10	1	£5 to £10	2,743	12	7
1824	460	12	—	£6 to£8	2,697	10	7
1825	488	12	3	£7	3,014	3	9
1826{	529	12	—	£7 7s }	2,793	8	—
{	201	17	—	£4 to £5}			
1827	376	—	—	£5 to £6	3,730	8	4
1828{	457	10	—	£6}	2,371	2	10
{	89	11	2	£3 7s 6d to £4 15s}			
1829	422	4	3	£4 16s 8d	1,592	4	7
1830	336	13	1	£4 16s 8d	1,265	19	11
1831{	291	19	3	£5}	1,399	5	4
{	121	2	—	£2 12s 6d to £4 12s}			
1832	381	17	1	£5	1,535	18	3
1833	328	17	1	£4 12s 6d	1,213	10	3
1834	414	11	1	£3	1,198	12	1
1835	256	18	2	£3	710	14	11
1836	310	19	3	£3 15s	1,119	7	10

Expenses of Manufacture			Free Net Proceeds				Rental of the Estate exclusive of kelp			Population
£	s	d	£	s	d		£	s	d	
1,593	17	4					10,721	8	10	10,092
2,219	9	2					10,778	12	1	
1,184	4	4					11,390	1	—	
1,720	3	—					11,378	3	—	
1,577	9	3	2,058	4	1		11,649	9	5	
2,358	1	1	2,162	1	7		11,884	—	11	
1,179	16	10					11,856	6	10	
1,794	4	8					11,924	4	5	
1,205	16	8	1,150	3	6		11,964	18	11	
2,129	5	2	3,356	16	1		11,909	12	1	
1,198	—	1	2,314	—	4		11,907	9	6	12,231
1,623	18	10	2,059	5	3		11,976	5	4	
1,049	19	5	1,693	13	1		12,064	4	10	
1,276	14	6	1,420	16	1		11,567	6	—	
1,920	18	—	1,093	5	8		11,507	5	6	
1,058	14	—	1,737	14	—		10,719	11	6	
1,275	8	3	2,455	—	1		9,580	15	2	
1,084	11	9	1,286	11	1		9,809	13	3	
1,641	16	8	49	12	1	Net Loss	9,820	16	—	
1,113	7	1	152	12	9		9,700	—	2	
1,017	17	5	381	7	10		9,706	13	—	14,541
871	1	3	664	16	11		9,823	6	—	
1,211	14	10	1	15	5		9,606	3	3	
803	6	2	395	5	9		9,701	13	3	
1,079	11	6	368	16	7	Net Loss	9,701	13	3	
							9,710	13	3	15,966

diminished in the country, and in many cases the society is gradually going backwards into a state of barter. The effects of this cause of the present distress may be instanced by the produce of one estate where from 1,200 to 1,500 tons of kelp were annually manufactured, £10 per ton was a moderate price during the war. A very small proportion of the produce then required would now meet the natural demands of the district; and the gross price now will not average [£2 or]²¹⁴ £3, more than one half of which must be taken in the shape of work for rent. [so that in many cases the real profit from the kelp will not average even clear £10 per ton.]²¹⁵ (See Appendix.)²¹⁶

3. Failure of the fisheries

The breaking up of the kelp trade has been the principal cause of the general embarrassment of the Highland proprietors, which has had no small influence on the state of their tenantry.²¹⁷ Another cause of the present distress of the people is the failure of the fisheries, partly from artificial and partly from natural causes. At one time great bounties were paid and the fishermen, unwisely enough, but not unnaturally, adapted their manners and habits and modes of life to the advantages they drew from these propped-up resources. These bounties are now totally withdrawn, though the change was effected somewhat more gradually than in the other case;²¹⁸ but, besides, many of the stations have been deserted by the fish, and altogether this source of supply is sadly weakened.²¹⁹

4. Cessation of public works

Various public works, which were instituted in a great measure to advance the Highlands and improve the condition of its inhabitants, have almost ceased. The Caledonian Canal has long been finished.²²⁰ The Commission

---

²¹⁴   The figure and word in square brackets appear in the copy of the letter published as [PP] 1837 LI (501) but not in the copy of the letter in either TNA:PRO, T/4201 or NRS, HD 7/9.

²¹⁵   The words in square brackets appear in the copy of the letter at TNA:PRO, T 4201, but not in the copy at NRS, HD 7/9 or in the letter published as [PP] 1837 LI (501).

²¹⁶   These words appear in the copies of the letter in both TNA:PRO, T/4201 and NRS, HD 7/9, but in [PP] 1837 LI (501) are replaced by the Tabular View set out above.

²¹⁷   The word in [PP] 1837 LI (501) is misprinted as 'tenancy'.

²¹⁸   That is, the changes to the barilla and salt duties. As to the bounties, see Day, *Public Administration*, 236–54.

²¹⁹   Graham makes no specific mention of the problems which the salt laws had caused the crofter-fisherman, although he had expressed the view in 1805 in his notes about Inveraray on a tour of the Highlands that 'severe operation of the [salt laws have been] particularly hurtful to the fishings on this coast' (Robert Graham, 'A Tour of Scotland in Autumn 1805', Private collection of Robert Maxtone Graham).

²²⁰   But, as Graham's letter of 15 Mar. 1837 (p. 20) explained, Graham believed that that the Caledonian Canal works had failed in the object of providing employment for local people.

for Roads and Bridges has been brought into a state[221] that the repairs of existing roads affords comparatively but very diminished means of employment for the people, and there is no other employment where formerly there was a great means of existence, and a good substitute for that employment which landlords in more favoured districts give their tenants, but which the declining means on many of the Highland estates makes it difficult or impossible for their managers to attempt.

5. Want of regulations by landlords

The tendency to over-population is not sufficiently restrained by regulations in the management of properties. In a few well-regulated farms, and in some cases on small properties, especially where they are farmed by the proprietors themselves, there is complete evidence that the thing may be done, and there is every appearance that the subject will soon be taken up on a system by the larger proprietors in general. The over-population has increased chiefly under the operation of the crofting system, or the minute subdivision of possessions, either directly permitted to too great an extent, or connived at by the landlords with the object or in the consideration of taking in muirs and waste land. Some of these hold directly from the landlords, sometimes only from a kind of middle man or greater tenant; in both cases there are instances where the system is not attended with bad effects; but it is the abuse of the system which makes the practice objectionable; and in the general absence of regulations or limitations it is very difficult, with the present habits of Highlanders, to prevent its abuse; these poor people often hold patches of land at two or three times its value of rent. If the allotment has been a fair one once for a single family, it in many cases has been split down to an arrangement for three families. On these spots, as in Ireland, they do what they can to raise potatoes for rearing large families, for whom there is no employment. The rents are paid by that worst of all methods, the work of the cottier and his family. If the superiors are heartless, the amount of wages is entirely in their hands. If the labour on the land is not sufficient, the produce of the fisheries is taken to account of the rent; and having no power to better their condition, these poor people are almost unavoidably consigned to a state of degraded and hopeless slavery; these are the extreme cases which, however, I fear, in complicated managements, are not infrequent. The more common case is without the intervention of the managers, and where the population themselves are chiefly to blame, and arises from the rapid growth of two or more families on a spot which was originally not more than a sufficient adaptation for one. To use the words of a private communication which was handed to me on the subject – "The croft or cottier system in a country where there is no capital, no trade, no

---

[221] The words in [PP] 1837 LI (501) are 'that shape'.

fishing, no manufacture, has been very prejudicial. Indolence and ignorance are fostered; human beings are multiplied in proportion to the increase of poverty, and the people, seeing no prospect of improving their condition, give way to a sullen despondency that incapacitates them for those active and animating exertions which are as necessary to mental enjoyment as they are to bodily comfort and worldly prosperity."

Another cause of crowded population in villages and particular spots (arising sometimes out of the desire of curing the former evil), springs from the determination of the proprietors to abolish joint holdings and to enlarge possessions, or to change the systems of cultivation or management. If this is done with too much celerity, an influx is directed upon some other spot where the means of subsistence, perhaps, are not to be procured; and while improvement goes on in one part, additional and probably permanent misery is inflicted on another part. On the mainland and in the islands of Mull and Skye, and even in some parts of the Long Island, a great change has been produced by the increase in the number of sheep farms. The rearing of black cattle had a direct tendency to support a greater proportion of population; but, since turnips have been so successfully introduced and applied to the feeding of sheep, and since prices of cattle have fallen so low and prices of wool have for some years risen so high, the farmers find it their interest to change black cattle for sheep; and it is alleged that this has been done to an extent not compatible with the welfare of the people, and in some instances without much regard to their feelings and interests as human beings.

6. Non-enforcement of Poor Laws.

The non-enforcement of the poor laws by the kirk sessions has certainly had a bad effect because the want of them has not in general been met, as in other parts of the country, by an adequate substitute in the church collections or voluntary subscriptions of heritors, with the view of forestalling the necessity of assessments. The principle of poor laws has been long and often objected to; and many of those who are much interested in upholding the character of the lower orders, are very averse to the adoption of assessments. Under our modified poor law, assessments need not necessarily be compulsory, if the voluntary contributions are sufficient to maintain the infirm in body or mind, which is the only description of poor who have a *right* to claim a maintenance. The process of enforcing poor laws to this extent is exceedingly simple and, in my opinion, it ought to be enforced if means are not voluntarily taken by the persons interested to separate the claims of those who have a *right* to be maintained, from those who are only appellants to the public charity. I am bound, however, to be cautious in my recommendations when a clerical man tells me that he would rather submit to a sharp touch of famine than an assessment; but he, in his turn, should be satisfied in his conscience in coming to a peremptory conclusion under this head in every case, that he is not looking merely to the evils which may accompany assessments, without giving due weight to the evils they may prevent and the good they may produce. At all events, however, the complete enforcement of the present poor laws, under the authority of the Scotch statutes, would do little to meet the present difficulties. It is not the lame and the maimed and the weaker classes of the community which constitute the great body of the people who are in distress in the highlands; the evil consists in the want of occupation for the great mass of the population in any way which will pay in any quarter. In many large districts, the small tenants could not live as well upon their present possessions as the poorest labourers in the low country, if they were freed entirely from the burden of rent; and the powers of the rent itself are so inadequate to give relief to this grievance of over-population on its present scale, that in the same districts the gross rental would not divide over the population at a rate equal to more than 10s. or 15s. per head, an amount which would subsist them but for a limited number of weeks.

It is evident, then, that though the seasons have brought matters to a crisis this year, other causes have been long and silently in operation; and it is much to be feared, until these causes can be corrected or removed, that no permanent improvement can be expected on the condition of the people in these districts.

Remedies

Unless, therefore, this population is to be allowed to be brought down by natural causes to a level with the means of subsistence, the sooner the attention of His Majesty's Government is turned to other means which exist, either as palliatives for the evil or as permanent remedies, the better. Within a given time, famine and disease would give bounds to the evil, if other means are permanently withheld. This very year, in all probability, if it had not been for the exertions made over the rest of Britain in favour of the Highlanders, these natural cures would have come into operation. A great proportion of this population are supported every year by those above them; the kindness even of the lowest ranks who have the power of assisting those who have not the means of living, is very creditable to human nature; nobody will be allowed actually to starve while a possibility of preventing it exists; but in such a crisis as the present, the means can only be drawn from foreign supplies; and notwithstanding the best exertions having been made to provide against the continuance of this calamity, it is to be apprehended that the effects of these two years will not be speedily forgotten in the country, while it is impossible to expect that the same generous and charitable feelings can be exerted, year after year, to an extent adequate to the probable recurrence of the evil.

Education

Everything connected with the education of the people, which contributes to the elevation of their character and to the cure of the reckless tendency among the Highlanders to early marriages without due provision for the maintenance of a family, to the advancement generally of their civilisation and the improvement of their taste and to rouse them to a sense of the benefits which other portions of the country derive from superior comforts, and better modes of living, must have an obvious and direct effect in ameliorating the general state of society; and what has already been done for the highlands in the establishment of schools cannot be too much applauded, and can scarcely be too forcibly recommended to the attention of the Government to be continued systematically as the best and surest foundation for any internal cure which can now be operated of the present disproportion between the population of these districts and their means of employment.

Works and Manufactures

A few people (but a great minority of those whose opinions on the state of the highlands I had an opportunity of gathering) hold the opinion, that a good deal might be done for the surplus population in getting employment for them at the manufactories in the great towns, or in establishing works for them near their own homes. How far a certain proportion of the population might find employment in this way, it is surely worth while to enquire. The habits and language of the people, however, are much against their reception in the manufactories of the great towns; and it is alleged that there are associations of the native interests in those places against their admission. The ignorance of the people disqualifies them from permanent employments, which they might otherwise obtain by moving southwards. They are rivalled successfully, even in what used to be their own especial work in the harvest season, by the great influx of Irish men and women who now find their way into the south of Scotland.[222] Extensive works in their own country might only tend to increase a population dependent entirely upon their endurance. Several exertions have recently been made to prop up the kelp manufacture still. Establishments have been erected for manufacturing soda, the muriate of potash, and carbonate of soda; the largest of these for the present is inactive, and the next in scale has not existed long enough to establish its chance of success; but

---

[222] Notwithstanding Graham's somewhat gloomy prognosis there was a significant level of both temporary and permanent migration of Highlanders to the Lowlands in search of work (C. W. J. Withers, 'Destitution and migration: labour mobility and relief from famine in Highland Scotland 1836–1850', *Journal of Historical Geography* 14.2 (1988), 128–50, and C. W. J. Withers, *Urban Highlanders – Highland–Lowland Migration and Urban Gaelic Culture 1799–1900* (East Linton, 1998)).

such works must be limited in extent, and the relief they can afford must be but partial. I was casually informed that a house in Glasgow has lately pointed out a new channel for the consumption of kelp, in the production of iodine for manufacturing purposes; but it is probable that this outlet cannot give rise to a great increase in the consumption of the commodity.[223]

Many parts of the highlands are peculiarly adapted for the establishment of manufactures from the extent of water-power, and other facilities; but unless these come chiefly as the results of private enterprise, they have never yet been forced with any advantage in any country.

Roads

It is a more feasible plan that a certain part of the population might usefully, and with general public advantage, be employed in making roads. What has been done by the Parliamentary Commission for the purpose is, perhaps, the greatest boon which the highlands ever received. Several of the islands, and even districts on the mainland, did not avail themselves of the opportunity of these improvements and probably now suffer from the neglect. Many of the districts have received all the benefits from this source which their necessities require; but it was pointed out to me, and earnestly enforced in the respective quarters, that in Morvern and Mull, roads were much required; that in the northern part of Skye some more were still wanting; that new lines from Poolewe and Lochbroom towards Dingwall would be of immense benefit in opening up these portions of the country; and that a more perfect land communication between Lewis and Harris, and some improvements of lines in the Uists, would be most important benefits for these islands. From the want of roads and bridges in many of these districts, the cattle are broken down and maimed in traversing trackless mountains and mosses, and in wading and often swimming through rapid rivers, before being brought to market. The breeders are entirely at the mercy of the dealers who know well the sacrifice of the price which will be made to avoid a repetition of the toil by driving them again over the same ground. Similar inconvenience is experienced in the disposal of fish caught, and the produce of every other branch of industry; and all the articles of merchandise indispensable to the support of families are entirely in the hands of individuals who often dispense their commodities of a second-rate quality, and always at an exorbitant price. All agricultural works are sadly crippled from the wants of wheel conveyance; manure and fuel are transported on horses' backs, or on the backs of women, and in the arms of children, who are thus precluded from undertaking the indoor-duties of the family which more peculiarly belong

---

[223] The main use of kelp did, indeed, become the production of iodine which helped to maintain kelp as a marketable product (A. and N. L. Clow, 'The natural and economic history of kelp', *Annals of Science* 5.4 (15 July 1947), 315; and [PP] 1914 XXXII.43 [Cd. 7564], 118).

to them. To remedy this state of things would be a benefit to the Empire at large, and the formation of new communications, where they are required, would undoubtedly give great occupation to the districts. If the Government should give any aid in the formation of these roads, it could not be done on more favourable terms than formerly, when the Parliamentary roads were made, viz. by the Government advancing one-half, and the proprietors the other half of the expense.[224]

Fisheries

It is the opinion of some people that the cod and ling and lobster fisheries of the west highlands and islands might be much improved by encouragement and assistance, and would be a source of benefit to the tenantry and the people; this is a subject which has attracted public attention from the time of James V downwards, and everything which royal support, and the establishment of associations, corporations and boards could effect, has been done to promote the herring fishery in particular. No branch of industry has repaid the encouragement so ill, from its precarious nature; and upon the whole it may be doubted whether it can be considered as an increasing source of wealth in this country. Its failure generally on the west coasts for several years back has had a very serious effect upon the circumstances of the people; and the migrating character of the fish ought to deter the local fishermen from trusting entirely to that one branch of the art; probably, however, in many situations the general white fishery might be further improved by the countenance and support of Government singly, or by Government conjointly with the maritime and insular proprietors, though all parties should guard against flattering descriptions of the coasts, as if the seas were everywhere full of the finest fish, and as if the demand could be procured for any amount of supply. Many accounts rest on the idea that the fish exist on all the coasts; I have found this frequently contradicted; the greater part of the western coast of the Long Island, from the nature of the shores and the violence of the sea, is almost precluded from the possibility of being fished. Some of what were formerly considered the best stations have greatly fallen off; Gairloch was once a famous station, but for the last eight years it has been unproductive; Lochbroom never was much of a station, except for herrings, and there has not been a good fishery there since 1811; at Arisaig, Tobermory, Ulva and Iona, it was alleged that the people were inactive and did not take the full advantage of their opportunities of fishing. The parishes of Knock and Lochs were the only portions of the Lewis which seemed to be considered as favourable stations; there is said to be none at

[224] On the Sutherland estates, the ducal family had built many miles of roads without parliamentary assistance; between 1814 and 1843 the family had spent £79,414 on roads (see Richards, *Leviathan*, 229).

Harris; and Boisdale and Barra were the only favourable points spoke to in the southern portions of the Long Island. There are none of these stations where the fisheries could be much advanced, but by assistance in procuring for the inhabitants boats and tackle, and perhaps the example of a few more practised fishermen than themselves; but it might be an object of great importance to have the soundings more extensively ascertained, on the west coast of Scotland and north-west of Ireland, to show the fishing banks. The piers and quays would be an improvement at many of the stations, and new ones were suggested, not for the fishery but for exporting fuel, from the Ross of Mull; and at Dunvegan and Uig in Skye, for the traffic of cattle.

Supplies of Food

Even with all the employment which may be given to the people from these sources, it is hardly to be expected, under the present circumstances of the highlands, that in future years the present population can possibly be carried through without adventitious supplies. In spite of all the exertions which have been made, considerable portions of ground among the small holders will probably remain unsown this very season; and similar applications to the present are very likely to be made in future years, and a recurrence of distress experienced, not much less in degree than now. The public will tire of annual subscriptions for local wants; and additional burdens will be thrown upon the Government.

Emigration

The most effectual mode of preventing a recurrence of the present distress, and one which was suggested everywhere as being almost a necessary remedy, would be by emigration. To whatever extent in other ways employment can be found, emigration in one shape or another, must continue to take place. Probably it would, in the long run, be the most expedient, the most efficient and the most economical expenditure of the public money if His Majesty's Government were to assist in establishing a system of emigration on a great scale. To give effectual relief, it must be done generally and on a great scale: if it is done partially and to a small extent, the relief will not be recognised. Good management must always consist in a compromise between the most perfect theory and such occasional and temporary deviations from it as are necessary for the adaptation of theories to practical occurrences in the progress of society; and if this population is not to be starved down to its proper amount; if the barilla and salt duties are not to be restored; if we are not to engage in wars purely with the object of diminishing the number of our people; if our poor laws, such as they are, and even if enforced with rigour, are miserably incompetent to give due relief; and if, as I fear, no system of poor law can be devised which would be adequate for this purpose, at all events on the principle that this territory should be made to support its own poor, nothing very effectual seems to remain but the adoption of that remedy so generally suggested; and as the present state of the highlands is anomalous and extraordinary, His Majesty's Government, if it means to work a cure, should not startle at applying the remedy merely because it may be, on a first view, apparently inconsistent with sound economics; for whenever the surplus population of the highlands should be once drained off, and the landlords as well as tenants shall be thus compelled to adopt a more rational system of managing their lands, the current of regulation may revert into its natural channel, and everything inconsistent with sound principle may cease. Unquestionably, the proprietors must be participators in this scheme, if it were only to ensure regulations in re-letting the lands on their estates: this is an easier matter, I believe, than most highland proprietors have hitherto considered it; resident proprietors, especially those who farm their own lands, find no difficulty in effecting it. The non-residence of proprietors is quoted as one of the misfortunes of the highlands, and one of the causes of the destitution. In the remote islands, constant residence of the proprietors cannot be counted on; but for this purpose resident factors will do just as well; and if they bend their minds to the subject, as many of them seem determined to do, there can be no great difficulty in keeping the population within the proper bounds if it were once reduced to an extent proportionate to the means of subsistence: I would instance the case of Canna as a proof that these arrangements can be made. This island has long been farmed by the gentleman who now possesses it and who became the proprietor by purchase several years ago.[225] The island then contained nearly 500 inhabitants. At his own expense he sent about 200 away, and he made a new arrangement of his land by which the holdings were enlarged and the houses were made more comfortable. The whole island is in his hands. His own stock is chiefly cattle; each of the crofters have as much tillage ground as they can manage and are allowed pasturage for cows and horses, in relation to the tillage ground which they overtake. They pay no rent, but they are liable in services of themselves and horses when required. It is a specimen of the kindly management, and the people live very comfortably and apparently are very happy. He has no interference with those who are inclined to fish; but he is rigid in his regulations as to the crofts. No married pair but one can exist on the same croft; and the only other regulation he finds it necessary to enforce is that no whisky is allowed to be sold on the island. What a contrast does this present to another case to which our observation was directed, where a person not belonging to the county had entered into a speculation to pay £150 a year for the bare walls of three public-houses! And what a consumption of

---

[225] Donald MacNeill, who had succeeded, in 1810, his father as tenant of the whole island, acquired the island for £9,000 in December 1827 from Reginald George Macdonald of Clanranald (Campbell, *Canna*, 150).

spirits among a rural population of 2,000, with a very limited influx of strangers, does not this imply! The best hopes are that this rent cannot possibly be paid; but the case is not cited for its statistics, but as a contrast to the management of Canna, where the island is evidently in good order, and the inhabitants (though perhaps still too lazy) are apparently sensible of their advantageous circumstances. The proprietor of Canna has no doubt facilities in keeping order in his insular situation, and the good quality of his land; but the same system may be followed with modifications in other places; and if the highlands of Scotland could be reduced to a scale of population, and a system of management corresponding to the model in Canna, it would be the greatest public improvement which has yet been made, and which it might be worthwhile to afford some of the public money to effect, as it could not possibly be done without it.

Emigration on a great scale is the first preliminary for this improvement; and if the Government is to embark in this, the sooner it is begun the easier will it be effected. The time is favourable for doing it; and if done, it were well to do it before the undertaking becomes too gigantic. I have the honour to be, Sir, your obedient servant.

Distress in the Highlands[226]

Much of the information requested by the tabular form prepared by Mr R. Stewart is not given in the reports – I have endeavoured to extract the information as far as practicable – in those cases where the <u>amount of relief required</u> is not stated great destitution prevails which calls for immediate remedy, but I think, perhaps, it may not be possible to arrive at any accurate detailed information of the amount of that relief until the local committee (recommended by the reports to be appointed) shall have correctly ascertained the same.

With regard to the <u>causes of distress</u>, it appears to me that over-population is the principal, as this appears to exist greatly beyond what the land will bear. Destitution has, for some years, been gradually progressing whilst the constant and unvaried cropping (and seaweed being in many cases the only manure) of the land has exhausted it. This and the decline of the kelp trade, the fishery and the bad system of allotments etc. (a good deal complained of) has tended to bring the people into a very distressed state, which the failure of the crops has brought to a crisis. The only effective cure seems, on all hands, emigration. Temporary relief may, in some parishes, be given by employment on public works, roads, fishery etc. but unless the surplus population be drawn off, the evil will continue, as it is stated that even if the crops had not failed, a crisis similar to the present would ere long have arrived.

---

[226] This undated note in Graham's hand accompanied the copy of his report of 6 May 1837 sent by the Home Office to the Treasury (TNA:PRO, Treasury T 1/4201, Maule to Spearman, 23 May 1837).

Edinburgh 18 May 1837

My dear Stewart I duly received your packet with the accounts, as your sister would inform you. I think it very likely that I shall be obliged to go to London about this business yet. Maule writes me that they have contrived to mislay my communications previous to the 22nd of March and in the idea that there was only one letter before that, begs me to send him a copy of it. At the same time he suggests my running up.[227] This is a provoking business as there are 5 letters previous to the 22nd of March – I have written to say that if they can make an arrangement so as I shall be sure of seeing Mr Spring Rice, or somebody of equal weight, within a reasonable time of my reaching town, I will come up but as I have nothing due to take me to London and hate dancing attendance at the public offices, I hope they will have the way for getting my business quickly done, if I go there. . ..[228] Adieu. Yours very truly.

[227] Andrew Rutherfurd also suggested to Fox Maule that it would 'be of service' if Graham was to go to London (NRS, Papers of the Maule family, GD 45/14/642, Rutherfurd to Fox Maule, 18 May 1837). See also Hill's journal entries for 15 and 22 May 1837 (pp. 143 and 146), the latter of which says that Graham was to leave for London on 24 May.

[228] The remainder of the letter is omitted as it concerns other matters.

PART 2

THE JOURNAL AND LETTERS OF
CAPTAIN SIR JOHN HILL, RN

Captain Sir John Hill, RN's Tour

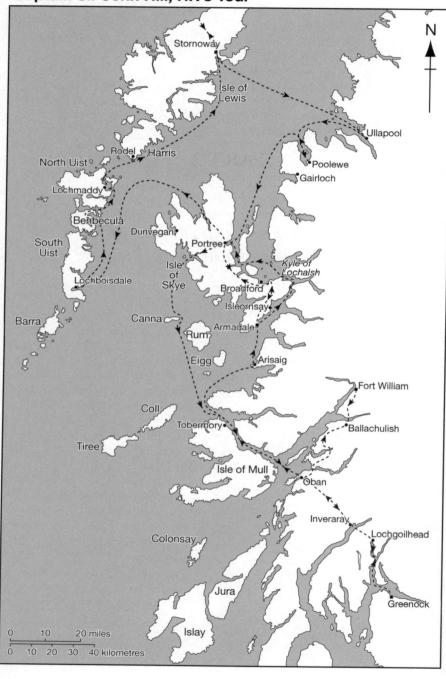

N

Stornoway
Isle of Lewis
Ullapool
Rodel   Harris
North Uist   Poolewe
                  Gairloch
Lochmaddy
Benbecula
        Dunvegan
South   Portree
Uist   Isle   Kyle of
          of   Lochalsh
          Skye
Lochboisdale   Broadford
                  Isleornsay
Barra   Canna   Armadale
          Rum
          Eigg   Arisaig
                              Fort William
Coll   Ballachulish
      Tobermory
Tiree   Oban
          Isle of Mull
                              Inveraray
Colonsay   Lochgoilhead

          Jura   Greenock

          Islay

0   10   20 miles
0 10 20 30 40 kilometres

Tuesday 14 March 1837. Received a note from Mr Spearman last evening to go to the Treasury on considerable important business. Called on him at 11 a.m. when he told me that I was wanted to go to Scotland for the relief of the distressed districts. After staying some time with him, he desired I should wait on him tomorrow. Went to the Admiralty by desire of Mr Spearman and told Lord Minto and Mr Wood[1] that the chancellor of the exchequer wished me to go to Scotland. Returned home in the evening.

Wednesday 15 March. Called again on Mr Spearman who took me to Mr Spring Rice[2] who heard me very kindly and said how useful I have been on former occasions,[3] and that my services should not be forgotten and he wished me to go again but not to Ireland but to Scotland where much distress was said to prevail. I replied I was ready to go anywhere he pleased to send me and would be ready tomorrow. He thanked me and I left with Mr Spearman who said my orders should be sent to Deptford. Employed the remainder of the day in getting ready. Saw Sir C. Adam and Sir J. Barrow.[4]

Treasury Chambers 15 March 1837 [Letter from Spearman to Hill at the Victualling Department, Deptford][5]

Sir, It having been represented to the Lords Commissioners of His Majesty's Treasury that much urgent and pressing distress prevails in certain districts of the highlands and western islands of Scotland by reason of the failure of the crops during the last harvest, their Lordships desire that you will proceed forthwith to Scotland and put yourself in communication with Mr Graham and the committees at Edinburgh and Glasgow and take such steps, in conjunction with them, as may appear necessary in the urgency of the case for the immediate supply of seed corn and potatoes.

---

[1] Lord Minto was the first lord of the Admiralty and C. Wood was the first secretary of the Admiralty.

[2] The Chancellor of the Exchequer.

[3] A reference to the two occasions, in 1831 and 1836, Hill had been sent to the west coast of Ireland to administer famine relief as agent for the government (see the Introduction and Biographical Notes).

[4] Sir Charles Adam was the first naval lord and Sir John Barrow was the second secretary of the Admiralty.

[5] Hill also received a letter from Spearman dated the same day discharging Hill from the duty he had performed in Ireland (NLI, Documents and letters relating to Sir John Hill's involvement in famine relief in Ireland, MS 45004/1, Spearman to Hill, 15 Mar. 1837.) See Introduction as to Hill's mission in Ireland.

For your information and government in this matter I have it in command to transmit herewith a copy of their Lordships' minute of the 14th inst.,[6] and to convey to you their authority to draw from time to time upon Mr Sargent of this office in Bills at three days' sight on account of the service for which you are despatched to Scotland.

My Lords will instruct the Commissioners of the Customs to direct their officers and the commanders of the Revenue cruisers and of the coastguard to afford you every aid and assistance in their power. I am, Sir, your obedient servant.

Deptford 16 March 1837 [Letter from Hill to Lord Lynedoch][7]

My Lord, from the kind feeling your Lordship has always expressed towards me I am sure you will be glad to hear that I have been again selected by His Majesty's Government to proceed on a third mission for the relief of the poor but instead of going again to Ireland I am now going to Scotland and intend setting off this evening by land direct to Edinburgh where I am to meet Mr Graham and the committee for the relief of the distressed districts, and shall go on to Glasgow and perhaps to the islands. Should your Lordship have any commands that way or if I am to be of any service to you or any of your tenants, I shall at all times feel great pleasure in attending to your Lordship's wishes.

I had a long interview with the chancellor of the exchequer this morning who expressed his high approbation of my conduct and read me a letter which he had written to His Majesty to that effect. Lady Hill and all my family beg their kind remembrance, and I have the honour to be, Sir, your obedient servant.

Thursday 16 March. Employed all this day in getting ready. Took my place in the Mail for Edinburgh at the Bull and Mantle. Paid seven guineas. Left home at 5 p.m. and got into the coach at 8 p.m. Found Lord Stormont[8] and Sir H. Campbell, M.P[9] and an officer in the Army in the coach travelling all night.

---

[6] Set out on p. 277.
[7] Lord Lynedoch, who was Graham's cousin (see the Biographical Notes) had known Hill for many years, especially during his time as commander of the British army in the Netherlands in 1814, when Hill was resident agent for transport. In his reply to this letter, Lynedoch told Hill the appointment was 'an additional proof of the justice of the favourable opinion you have long entertained' and invited Hill to visit him at Lynedoch House, 'a place where I have . . . made a great object of my attention' (NRA 44729, Hill papers and correspondence 1792–1855, fo. 68, Lynedoch to Hill, 17 Mar. 1837).
[8] Lord Stormont was on his way to Perthshire to prepare the ground for the next election in which he was to compete as the Tory candidate against Fox Maule, and win the county seat (NLS, Lynedoch papers, MS 16035, fo. 1, Waller to Graham, 28 Mar. 1837).
[9] Sir Hugh Purves-Hume-Campbell, seventh baronet, the Tory MP for Berwick.

Friday 17 March. Fine weather. Stopped at Grantham to breakfast and arrived at York at 5 p.m. where we stopped one hour to dinner and change the coach. Saw York Minster and left at 6 p.m. for Newcastle and Morpeth and on to Belford where we arrived on Saturday the 18th at 8 a.m. and breakfasted and then proceeded on to Berwick on Tweed where Sir H. Campbell left us. The military officer left us at York. We only stopped at Berwick to change horses and went on by the coast road, on for Edinburgh. The country from the Tweed was more or less covered with snow though the day was fine. Got to Edinburgh at 3 p.m. and went to the Royal Hotel kept by Mr Gibbs in Princes Street[10] and dined at ½ past 6. Called on Mr Graham who was absent from home.[11]

Sunday 19 March. Fine weather. Called on Dr Warden[12] and delivered Mr Stevenson's letter to him. Called on Mrs Graham[13] who told me Mr R. G. had gone to the islands about ten days, having left home on the 7th of March and she supposed he was in the island of Mull as a revenue cutter was to be at his disposal at Fort George.[14] She advised me to call on Lord Cunninghame, No. 80 King Street (late attorney general and now a judge).[15] I saw his Lordship who was very civil and recommended my seeing the attorney-general, A. Rutherfurd, Esq.[16] and went with me to his house but he was not at home. Walked all over the new part of the town and also some part of the old town. Received a note at 10 p.m. from the solicitor-general, Mr Rutherford, to breakfast with him tomorrow, to meet Lord Cunninghame.

Monday 20 March. Wrote Mr Spearman and Lucy.[17] Called on Dr Warden and saw Captain of yacht who promised to write out an account of all of the islands. Breakfasted at Mr R and both him and Lord Cunninghame seemed to think that the accounts of the distress were much exaggerated and but very little dependence could be placed in the accounts they had received. They

[10] The original Royal Hotel at 53 Princes Street kept by Moyes Gibbs where Hill stayed was reconstructed by the architect George Beattie in 1870.
[11] Robert Graham had by then started on his own tour of the distressed districts.
[12] This is Dr Adam Warden, FRCSE, MD, of 3 Baxters Place whose wife, Jane, was the daughter of Robert Stevenson, the civil engineer and chief executive to the Northern Lighthouse Board, who lived next door at 1 Baxters Place.
[13] Robert Graham's widowed mother Mary (née Scott of Usan), who lived at 18 Heriot Row.
[14] Hill wrote Fort George but he meant Fort William.
[15] This is John Cunninghame, who had just ceased to be the solicitor-general for Scotland (not the attorney-general as Hill wrote) and had been appointed a judge of the Court of Session (see the Biographical Notes). Cunninghame's letters to Fox Maule about the famine are set out in Part 4 at pp. 253–8 below.
[16] Andrew Rutherfurd, who had just been appointed solicitor-general (not attorney-general as Hill wrote) for Scotland (see the Biographical Notes).
[17] Hill's wife, Lucy (née Swinburne, 1795–1862).

were both extremely civil and went with me to call on a gentleman and also at Mr Stevenson's[18] office where I got a map of the islands and learned that Captain Knight[19] of the Coastguard was looking out for me as he had received notice of my coming. Returned to Mr Rutherfurd where I saw Mr Cheyne,[20] an attorney who had a good deal to do with the relief committee and he said that the committee at Aberdeen had raised about £1,600 and they had undertaken to supply the Orkneys and had freighted a schooner to take a cargo of about 130 tons of meal, potatoes and about 300 qrs of seed corn for which they were to pay £60 freight. Therefore he and the solicitor-general considered that no assistance need be sent by the Government to the Orkneys but our whole attention would be required at the western islands. At 2 p.m. went to a room at the post office and met about ten of the committee, one of whom was a Mr Mowbray of Leith, a corn factor. They showed me their accounts of what was received and what had been laid out and then I said I would ensure £1,500 to be paid to them, to be laid out in purchasing by Mr R. Campbell 1,000qrs of oats which would make up the whole quantity bought 2,300 qrs. Spent two hours with Dr Warden in the evening and saw the master of the lighthouse yacht and received some charts from Mr Stevenson's office.

Tuesday 21 March. Fine weather. Mr Waller[21] arrived at 12 o'clock. Breakfasted with the attorney general and Lord Cunninghame and called on the former in the evening and saw Mr Fox Maule when they all agreed that it was wrong in the Treasury to send the committee the sum which I had put at my disposal. Saw the sub-committee at the secretary's house and desired they would hasten the shipping of the seed corn. Called on Sir E. Lees[22] of post office who gave me every information I wanted and also a map of roads. Received a note from Mr S. Rice to hasten supplies. Occupied all this day in getting information etc.

Royal Hotel, Edinburgh 21 March 1837[23] [Letter from Hill to Spearman]

Sir, I have the honour to acquaint you for the information of my Lords Commissioners of His Majesty's Treasury that I arrived here on the 18th instant at ½ past 3 p.m. and found Mr Robert Graham had left this place for

---

[18] Robert Stevenson, the civil engineer and chief executive to the Northern Lighthouse Board.
[19] Captain G. W. H. Knight, RN, inspector-general of the Coastguard.
[20] Henry Cheyne, of 16 Abercromby Place, who had written to Graham about conditions in Shetland (see p. 7).
[21] George Waller of Portsea, who was to act as Hill's secretary.
[22] Sir Edward S. Lees was the secretary of the General Post Office.
[23] The letter is, in fact, dated 22 Mar., but Hill corrected this in his letter of 25 Mar.

the distressed districts on the 7th instant; in consequence of which I waited, on Sunday morning, on Lord Cunninghame the late solicitor-general who took me to Mr Rutherfurd the present solicitor-general, and from those gentlemen I obtained every information which was necessary respecting the Edinburgh committee which were to meet the following morning (Monday), when I met them and found they had received by public subscriptions about £4,000, £1,500 of which they had remitted to Glasgow and about £2,000 had been expended in the purchase of seed corn. I therefore, from finding their funds nearly exhausted, and from the extreme urgency of the case, decided it advisable to guarantee the immediate supply of 1,000 qrs of seed oats. Having found the purchases which had been made by the committee averaged from 34 to 37 shillings per quarter, which I consider reasonable, I did not think it prudent to disturb the markets by a public advertisement for contracts, and therefore purchased the above quantity on similar terms.[24] By this arrangement about 2,300 quarters of seed oats have been secured and will be shipped off as quickly as possible to the different depots named in the margin.[25] One vessel with 500 quarters is now loading and expected to sail on the 24th instant for Tobermory in the Isle of Mull. It is my intention to proceed to Glasgow tomorrow in further execution of my orders. I have the honour to be, Sir, your most obedient servant.[26]

Wednesday 22 March. Breakfasted with Mr Rutherfurd. Wrote to Mr Spearman. Paid the bill at Royal Hotel and left at 12 o'clock outside the mail coach for Hamilton where we arrived at ½ past 3 p.m. having taken a chaise at Holytown to Mr [Robert] Brown, agent to the duke of Hamilton who has a very comfortable house close to His Grace's mansion which Mr B showed us all over it, and a most splendid thing it is. Dined and slept there and Mr B gave us a great deal of information about the distress, he having lived in the Hebrides fifteen years.[27]

Thursday 23 March. Fine weather with snow occasionally. Left Mr Brown's at ½ past 9 a.m. and arrived at Glasgow at ½ past 11 a.m. at Walker's Hotel on

---

[24] The Treasury was determined to avoid disturbance of prices or markets (see the Introduction). But Hill did, later, advertise publicly for tenders.

[25] Tobermory, Isle of Mull; Oban, mainland; Arisaig, mainland; Oronsay, Isle of Skye (sic); Portree, Isle of Skye; Loch Ewe, mainland; Lochboisdale, Isle South Uist; Rodel, Isle of Harris; Loch Stornoway (sic), Isle of Lewis.

[26] Spring Rice reported the contents of this letter to the king (NLI, Monteagle papers, MS 545, Spring Rice to the king, 26 Mar. 1837). The Treasury minute that discussed this letter is set out on p. 280 below.

[27] Robert Brown had also provided Graham with information (see p. 10 above).

Tontine.[28] Called on Mr [Allan] Fullarton, chairman of committee and also on Collector of Customs[29] who were very civil.

Friday 24 March. Attended the committee which consisted of about 15 members, Mr Fullarton in the chair. They had a copy of the Treasury minute[30] and after a long discussion they would not consent to give any money for seed corn until they received a further sum. I pressed them to spare some of what they had. They parted and I then called on Mr Dirk-Cleland, Mr Maxwell and Mr Hamilton whom I had letters to, who all appeared displeased at the committee not taking my offer, and said they would rather get up another meeting tomorrow which I promised to wait and attend.

Saturday 25 March. Cold weather with snow occasionally. Attended the meeting when Mr Mungo Campbell proposed that the resolution passed yesterday should be seconded, but without effect and when I stated that whatever money I gave them was to be appropriated for seed, and agreeable to Edinburgh printed resolutions dated 2nd of March which I held in my hand,[31] they all declared they had never seen the document but their assistant secretary told Mr Waller that he had a copy of it, at which I expressed my surprise to the chairman and others in the committee, but it appeared quite clear to me that there was jobbery among them and matters which perhaps they did not wish me to see, and were determined not to act cordially with the Edinburgh committee. Reported all this to Mr Spearman and wrote a private note to Mr Spring Rice. Wrote Selby on Friday to purchase 800 qrs of oats for seed.

Glasgow 25 March 1837 [Letter from Hill to Spearman]

Sir, With reference to my letter of the 22nd instant (which should have borne date the 21st) I beg leave to inform you for the information of my Lords Commissioners of His Majesty's Treasury, that I came to this place on the 23rd instant having by the advice of Lord Cunninghame and the solicitor-general called on Mr Brown of Hamilton, agent to the duke of Hamilton, a very intelligent gentleman who resided 15 years in the Hebrides, from whom I gained much valuable information; and he was of opinion that about 7,000

[28] Hill refers later in his journal to this being the Tontine Hotel. This would have been James Walker's Tontine Hotel on Tontine piazza in Glasgow that was built in 1781 by William Hamilton and destroyed by fire in 1911.
[29] D. V. McMurdo.
[30] Of 14 Mar. 1837 (p. 277).
[31] See p. 245 below. These resolutions are discussed in the Introduction.

quarters of seed corn would be sufficient for the distressed districts. A special general meeting of the committee of Glasgow was called on to meet me yesterday when about twenty-three persons assembled. They laid before me an account of the monies they had received amounting to about £6,500 all of which they had laid out in purchasing meal and shipping the same, with the following exceptions, viz. £500 for seed potatoes; £400 for the purchase of blankets; and the remaining £2,300 they had only the day before should be laid out in the purchase of meal; of this latter sum I informed them to take £1,500 and I would meet it with a similar sum to purchase seed corn, by which means they would meet the intentions of His Majesty's Government and comply with the Treasury minute. After much discussion for nearly three hours I saw there was a strong determination not to purchase seed. My proposition was put to the vote and carried against me by 12 to 4 being all that remained at the end of the debate. The following amendment was proposed and carried, to the effect "It is inexpedient to alter our former resolution with respect to the funds received, and that therefore the consideration of providing seed corn and potatoes be delayed until it be seen what amount of funds can be realised. But that as soon as £1,500 additional are received, they will be devoted to the purchase of seed along with the corresponding sum from Government; the committee having every reason to expect that the £1,500 will be soon received." I then determined to remain here another day to see what effect that might have, but as I felt almost convinced that they would not meet me agreeable to my instructions in the purchase of seed, I made up my mind to order 800 quarters of seed oats on my own responsibility from Liverpool unknown to any parties here, by last night's post. Some few individuals who wished to co-operate with me summoned another special meeting this day, which was attended by about the same number of persons and wished to make a motion for guaranteeing the sum of £1,500 on the same terms as I proposed yesterday, but without effect, in consequence as they stated of their ignorance of the printed resolutions of the Edinburgh committee dated the 2nd instant, put into my hands by the chancellor of the exchequer, and which I laid on their table for reference during the discussion. This printed document approved of by their Lordships' minute of the 14th instant, the chairman and the generality of the committee said they had never seen, and immediately proposed and passed almost unanimously a resolution to rescind the above resolution of yesterday, and I have every reason to believe they will memorial their Lordships by this evening's post.[32]

After many members had left I desired Mr George Waller who is with me, to afford the acting secretary a copy of the printed Edinburgh resolutions, when, to my surprise, he said that he had one of those documents in his possession at which I expressed my surprise to the chairman and the few

[32] The Memorial is set out at p. 210 below.

remaining members in the room. From all that I could gather in these two days' discussions there appears to me to be a strong disposition on the part of the Glasgow committee to act independently of the Edinburgh committee, as they positively declared they would not co-operate with me on the resolutions of that document of the Edinburgh committee, although I urged them in the strongest manner to provide seed in the first instance, as time was precious, and to ensure a crop for the poor sufferers to prevent a recurrence of this calamity next season.[33] I have the honour to be, Sir, your most obedient servant.[34]

Glasgow 25 March 1837 [Private letter from Hill to Spearman]

My dear Sir, I have given you a long official epistle this day wherein you will see that I cannot get this committee to take the same view of matters as Government and myself, but I have written a private note to the chancellor to say I shall provide all the seed that may be required in conjunction with the Edinburgh committee which I hope he will approve. We have had more or less snow and frost since I came to Scotland and the weather is exceedingly cold. Believe me, yours faithfully.

P.S. Continue to send my letters to Edinburgh, as I shall return there on Monday.

Sunday 26 March. Very cold with frost. Hired a gig[35] for £1–1–0 and went to Greenock, an excellent road about 21 miles. Passed through Port Glasgow, a small town, but several large merchant vessels and a steamer lying in the pier. Got to Greenock in three hours and called on Mr [Thomas] Saunders, Collector of Customs who was out, but I waited until 5 p.m. when he gave me all the information I wanted about custom house officers at the depots in the Hebrides. Dined with him and Mrs and two Miss Saunders. There is several building yards here and one large steamer just launched and several large merchant ships in the pier. Left at 7 p.m. and got back to Glasgow in two hours and a half.

Monday 27 March. Advertised in the newspapers for tenders for 1,200 qrs of seed oats on Wednesday 29th at Walker's Hotel. Left in the coach for Edinburgh at 10 a.m. Thick snow for two hours. Got to Edinburgh at 3 p.m. at Royal

---

33   The determination of the Glasgow committee not to spend funds on seed is discussed in the Introduction.
34   The Treasury minute that discussed this letter is set out in Part 5 at p. 280.
35   A light two-wheeled one-horse carriage.

Hotel and went to the committee and also the solicitor-general and walked to Calton Hill.

Tuesday 28 March. Cold frosty weather. Met Lord Melville[36] who was very glad to see me and hoped I would spend a day at his castle.[37] Received Mr Graham's third report.[38] Called on Lord Cunninghame who invited me to dine on Friday. Saw solicitor-general in Court and gave him Glasgow resolutions. Transacted business with committee and told them of the purchase of 800 qrs of seed oats for the Hebrides and what the Glasgow committee had done. Visited the library of the Writers to the Signet, a splendid room about 180 feet, also the Court Hall formerly the Parliament House where they entertained George 4th on his visit here.[39] Also saw all the Courts of Justice, etc. Lord Cockburn was sitting at the Justiciary one on the Cromarty Fishery for salmon.[40] Left the Court and called on Dr Warden and Mr Stevenson, who called on me at 9 p.m. At 10 p.m. went to the solicitor-general who appeared much displeased at what the Glasgow committee had done and wished me to apply £150 to meet an equal sum from an offer he had got from a respectable quarter in Edinburgh to provide seed for the Orkneys and Shetland, which I promised. He advised me to go to Aberdeen and said he would write to parties there to meet me and recommended a supply to be sent to a small island which I also recollect Mr Spring Rice said should be done.[41] Supped with him.

Wednesday 29 March. Left at 9 a.m. for Glasgow and arrived at 2 p.m. Fine weather. Received three letters from Selby of his purchases and progress. Visited the quays where there was much business going on and many small vessels and steamers lying. One of the latter, the *Don Juan* of Dublin, about fitting out, 900 tons, engines of 350 horse power. Lt. . .[42] of the Navy, commander, who said the engines were too large to be set going by hand and that a small engine was to be put in to start the large one, and she was going to the Mediterranean. She came from London to Glasgow in four days. At 4 p.m. found that not one tender was sent to me for the seed oats agreeable to the terms advertised and only the

[36] Robert Dundas, the second viscount Melville, whom Hill would have known when Melville was first lord of the Admiralty (see the Biographical Notes).
[37] Melville Castle, situated near Dalkeith. Hill later visited the castle (see his journal entry for 18 Apr., p. 130).
[38] Graham's letter of 13 Mar. 1837 from Fort William (p. 13).
[39] In 1822; the visit which was stage managed by Walter Scott in a pageant of highlandism (J. Prebble, *The King's Jaunt* (Edinburgh, 2000)).
[40] A case in the Court of Session which attracted considerable interest as being of great general importance to the proprietors of salmon fisheries (The Hon. Mrs Hay Mackenzie and Captain Hugh Munro v. Archibald Hare, Colin Mackenzie of Newhall and others, *The Scottish Jurist* 9, no. xxvi (1837), 409–17).
[41] This was Fair Island (see Rutherfurd's letter to Fox Maule of 14 Mar. 1837 (p. 260)).
[42] The name is left blank in the original.

tenderer and one party only attended, where sample was not good and I declined dealing with him. Mr Campbell called, who had offered 400 qrs and said he would try and supply the quantity but I am afraid he is not to be depended on, but he promised to see committee tomorrow in Edinburgh. Wrote to Selby, and Callater of Stornoway and also to Mr Craigie.

Thursday 30 March. At Glasgow, Tontine Hotel, Mr Walker's. Fine, clear, cold weather. Employed arranging papers. Called on Collector of Customs who went with us to Messrs Ewing & May, corn factors. Mr Angus, one of the firm, came to me and said he could not undertake to supply seed corn as it was always customary to purchase from the eastern ports. He said he could supply good oatmeal at £14–12–0 per ton, on board. Called on the Rev. Dr Macleod who was ill in bed. Walked all over the quays round the town, and looked at the gaol. Received a note from the Collector respecting the officers of Customs in the Orkneys and Shetland. Settled the bill at this hotel in Glasgow. The beds were good but attendance not very.

Friday 31 March. Hard frost and clear weather. At 6 a.m. left Glasgow in the coach and got to Edinburgh at ½ past 11 a.m. At Royal Hotel could not get a sitting room. Called on Lord Cunninghame and solicitor-general and also on committee who said they had now got enough of seed corn, and we settled that seed potatoes should be purchased on my return from Aberdeen. Wrote to Treasury. Mr Cheyne went with us to the Court and spoke to solicitor-general who was occupied with the trial on the salmon fishery near Cromarty. Dined with Lord Cunninghame with a pleasant party of about 12 gentlemen. Mrs C was unwell and obliged to put off all the ladies who had been invited. The Col. of Dragoons was of the party.

Edinburgh 31 March 1837 [Letter from Hill to Spearman][43]

Sir, Since my letter to you of the 25th instant from Glasgow, I beg leave to acquaint you for the information of my Lords Commissioners of His Majesty's Treasury, that I have been constantly employed with the Edinburgh committee and at Glasgow from whence I returned this morning. I advertised for contracts for seed oats at the place on the 27th instant and went there to receive the tenders, when only one tender was offered, and that of a very inferior quality which I rejected. I have, however, this morning in conjunction with the Edinburgh committee purchased 400 quarters of seed oats. The total

---

[43]   The Treasury minute of 6 Apr. 1837 that discussed this letter is set out on p. 280 below.

quantity up to this day provided by myself and the Edinburgh committee amounts to 3,450 quarters which the committee unanimously decided was more than sufficient to answer all the demands made upon them up to this day from the western isles and coasts; and should any further demand be made during the next 14 days, which is considered the latest period that the supplies of seed oats should be shipped to arrive at its destination in time, measures will be taken to provide the same. I therefore shall proceed tomorrow to Aberdeen for the purpose of communicating with the committee there respecting a supply of seed corn for the Orkneys, Shetland and Fair Island. But one of the general committee here states that no supplies will be required for the Orkneys.

In consequence of the severe frosts hitherto, and the period for planting potatoes being much later than for corn, it has not been considered advisable to provide seed potatoes to any extent, but my attention will be drawn to that, as soon as I return from Aberdeen. I beg to state that not any remittance has been received by the Edinburgh committee from the subscriptions raised in London, notwithstanding £2,000 has been received by the committee at Glasgow.[44] I have the honour to be, Sir, your most obedient servant.

Saturday 1 April. Cold, clear weather. Employed at committee. Received two letters of introduction from Lord Cunninghame for Aberdeen. Called on Dr Warden and Mr Stevenson and got into the mail coach at 4 p.m. for Aberdeen. Got to Queensferry in about one hour and half where we embarked in a small steam boat and landed at Inverkeithing and got into another mail coach there. The first place we came to was Kinross. The road on towards Loch Leven castle was very hilly. On this loch is a small island[45] where Mary, Queen of Scotland, took shelter and escaped from there with the son of the Earl of Douglas who, they say, threw the key of the castle into the lake; and they say the key was drawn up by a fisherman in 1826.[46] The castle appeared quite in ruins. We got to Perth about 9 p.m. where Captain and Mrs Slater left to go to Inverness. He is employed there surveying and was made a commander last promotion.[47]

---

[44] In the event, none of the London subscriptions went to Edinburgh (NLS, Report by committee in Edinburgh for relief of the destitution in the Highlands and Islands of Scotland, 21 Dec. 1837, Lynedoch papers, MS 16147, fo. 235 (see p. 220)).

[45] Castle Island.

[46] Mary was, in fact, imprisoned in Lochleven castle, escaping with the help of Willie Douglas, a page in the castle and George Douglas, the younger brother of the laird of Lochleven; the key was thrown into the mouth of a cannon (J. Guy, 'My Heart is My Own' – The Life of Mary Queen of Scots (London, 2004), 366–7). But a different version has it that the key was indeed thrown into the loch, recovered in 1805 and presented to the earl of Morton (OGazS, iv, 507). Hill refers to this, again, in his entry for 5 May, in a somewhat different form (see p. 138 below).

[47] Commander M. A. Slater, RN.

Passed through Dundee, Montrose and Arbroath and arrived at Aberdeen at 6 a.m. on Sunday 2 April.

Sunday 2 April. At the Royal Hotel.[48] Breakfasted and went to church[49] and heard an excellent extempore sermon from the Rev. Mr [John] Brown. Delivered letters to the Provost[50] who, with his wife Mrs Milne, was very civil, and immediately fixed Tuesday to dine with them. Called on Mr Bannerman,[51] MP for this place and left his letter. He was not at home. Walked over the town and down to the pier and looked at the harbour which has a bad entrance. There is a lighthouse on the eastern side of it. The trade is principally with the Baltic and Canada, and large shipments of cattle go from here to London in steam boats. Met Sir A. Farquhar[52] who had opposed Mr Bannerman at the last election. Cold with snow occasionally.

Monday 3 April. Received a note and a call from Mr Bannerman, the Provost, Mr [John] Angus, secretary, and Mr Burnett.[53] Met the committee at the town hall at 1 p.m. when I immediately heard what they had done and pledged myself to supply about £1,750. They were all very civil and attentive. Dined with Mr B and met a pleasant party of 15, Mrs B and five other ladies. Mr B drank my health and said how handsomely the chancellor of the exchequer had spoken of me before himself, the duke of Argyle and all the Scotch members who waited on Mr Spring Rice with him before he left town.[54] Mr and Mrs North was of the party.

Tuesday 4 April. Snow and hail, more or less. Received letters from home and Edinburgh. Did business with the committee and dined with the provost, a party of 16 gentlemen and Mrs Milne being the only lady. They entertained us very hospitably and spent a pleasant evening.

---

[48]   The Royal Hotel at 63 Union Street was run by Isaac Machray.
[49]   St Paul's in the Gallowgate.
[50]   James Milne.
[51]   Alexander (later Sir Alexander) Bannerman, who was Whig MP for Aberdeen Burgh and, after his parliamentary career had ended in 1847, lieutenant-governor of Prince Edward Island in 1851, governor of the Bahamas in 1854 and finally of Newfoundland in 1857.
[52]   Rear Admiral Sir Arthur Farquhar. When Hill was the resident agent of transport with responsibility for troop transport ships in the North Sea from 1813, he would have known Farquhar who commanded the frigate Desiree in the North Sea between 1809 and 1814 (J. K. Laughton, rev. Roger Morriss, 'Farquhar, Sir Arthur (1772–1843)', ODNB).
[53]   This is Thomas Burnett, an advocate in Aberdeen and Purse Bearer (see p. 144).
[54]   Alexander Bannerman had been part of the deputation to the Treasury on 13 Mar. 1837 (see the Introduction).

Royal Hotel, Aberdeen 4 April 1837 [Letter from Hill to Spearman][55]

Sir, I have the honour to acquaint you for the information of my Lords Commissioners of His Majesty's Treasury, that I arrived here on Sunday the 2nd instant at 6 a.m. and immediately put myself in communication with the Lord Provost and the secretary of the Aberdeen committee; and met with the committee yesterday, also today when Mr Bannerman, the Member, was present. The committee immediately adopted my suggestions in providing seed corn and seed potatoes and laid before me a statement of the monies they had received amounting to about £2,800, and a donation of meal and potatoes of about £50 value. They had expended about £500 in the purchase of 330 quarters of seed oats and about £850 for meal, all of which was shipped and sent off to Shetland before my arrival; and, I am happy to say, accounts were received this day from the local committee at Lerwick in Shetland of the safe arrival of the vessel and cargo at that port on the 28th ultimo.

Finding that the committee had a balance of about £1,600 in hand, I agreed to meet that amount by an equal sum in the purchase of seed corn and seed potatoes which will make up the whole supply of seed corn for the Shetlands equal to 1,530 quarters, and 200 tons of seed potatoes, all of which will be forwarded to its destination as soon as circumstances will permit. And as the weather still continues here so very unfavourable and the land covered with snow, seed corn has not as yet been sown even in this county; and I therefore trust the supplies to Shetland will arrive in good time. I beg to add that this committee has not as yet received any remittances from London, Edinburgh or Glasgow; the subscriptions at their disposal were raised in this town and neighbourhood and great attention paid to their application. The committee I am happy to say has afforded me every facility in forwarding the views of His Majesty's Government agreeable to my instructions. I have the honour to be, Sir, your most obedient servant.

Wednesday 5 April. Fine weather but still hard frost. Called on Mr and Mrs Bannerman and met the committee. Wrote home and to the Treasury. Went in Mr B's carriage to dine at Sir Michael Bruce's,[56] about 4 miles on the Peterhead road. A noble house and stands on a very large property which he got with his wife, Lady Bruce, who is a very handsome woman, but no family. He also has a large estate in Stirling. She was dressed in a green velvet and velvet head dress with fur tippet and gold ornaments. A very large space of rooms and large billiard table. Everything in a very splendid manner, very handsome gold epergne[57] and solid silver vases. He told me that many of his farmers who

[55] The Treasury minute of 11 Apr. 1837 that discussed this letter is set out on p. 280 below.
[56] Sir Michael Bruce of Stenhouse, eighth baronet.
[57] A centre-dish or centre ornament for the dinner table.

paid him from £100 to £200 a year never had meat in their houses more than once a week, and all his tenants very industrious. The dinner party consisted of 16 – 7 ladies and 9 gentlemen, Mr and Mrs Bannerman, Mr and Mrs North, Mr Cumming and daughter and son, Captain Henderson, RN, Mr Burnett, Jnr. and others whose names I could not recollect. Got home at ½ past 11.

Thursday 6 April. Still at Aberdeen. Called on all parties to take leave. Mr Milne gave me 2 bottles of whisky and every attention was shown to me here. Cold frosty weather. . . .Lord Provost called to take leave. Paid bill at hotel, called on Mr and Mrs North. Took two places on mail coach for Edinburgh. We visited the pier and saw the schooner which had just returned from Shetland. Found freight the same price which committee had paid. Called on Mr Bannerman. This town is well built and bridge across the valley from the old to the new town is a fine piece of architecture being one arch about 130 spans. Union Street is about ¾ of a mile long and well lighted with gas. Mrs Milne, provost's wife, gave me two bottles of whisky.[58] Got into the mail for Edinburgh at 3 p.m. Cold, bleak NE wind. Rode outside about 40 miles as far as Montrose, having passed through Arbroath. Both these places are in a flourishing condition and the suspension bridge over the South Esk from Montrose is a neat bridge, but it gave way soon after it was constructed and has been repaired. Passed through Dundee and Perth during the night and got to the ferry at ½ past 4 a.m. and crossed in an open boat, very cold. Arrived at Queensferry in half an hour and got to the Royal Hotel, Edinburgh at 6 a.m.

Friday 7 April. Had breakfast and went to Leith and called on Capt. Knight who gave me very little hopes of any assistance of cutters. Saw Capt. Arrow[59] and Mr Wentworth, agent for transports. Returned to Edinburgh and met the committee at Mr Bowie's house. This gentleman[60] is the secretary and had returned from London[61] while I was absent. Transacted business with the committee until 4 p.m. Called on Mrs Graham and solicitor-general and dined and went to bed, being much fatigued in travelling all the night before.

Saturday 8 April. Fine clear weather with frost. Employed all this day in writing and copying Mr Graham's reports and sending them off to Mr Fox Maule. Dined

---

[58] It is unclear if this made the gift of whisky a total of four bottles!
[59] Captain John J. Arrow, RN, of 10 Anne Street, the inspecting commander and assistant to the inspector-general of the Coastguard.
[60] John Bowie, a writer to the signet, solicitor to the post office and agent to a number of proprietors including Lord Macdonald, and the man who had managed the later stages of their campaign to save the kelp manufacture.
[61] From his fund-raising mission to England (see further discussion in the Introduction).

at Mr Bowie's, Mrs B and two daughters and Mr Craigie, Mr Russell and Mr Ferguson with ourselves formed the party. Mr B is solicitor to the post office and is agent for large properties in the western islands and agent for Lord Macdonald's property.

Sunday 9 April. Cold weather. Still at Royal Hotel, Edinburgh. Was very unwell all this day and laid in bed until afternoon. Waller went to church with Mr Bowie, who called. Employed writing all the evening.

Monday 10 April. Cold weather with snow occasionally. Capt. [J. H.] Tait, RN called and invited me to Club dinner on 12 April. Declined. Capt. Arrow and Capt. Knight also called and invited me to dine but declined. Transacted business with the committee. We dined with Mrs Graham and her four daughters.[62] Met Sir Thomas Dick Lauder, Bart,[63] who has 7 daughters,[64] Mr and Mrs Grant and Mr Ferguson, writer of the signet. Spent a very pleasant evening, a very good dinner.

Tuesday 11 April. Cold weather with snow occasionally. Met committee and returned visits with Mr Bowie. Lt. Wentworth called. Met Admiral Fleming [sic][65] and called on Mr Murray of Broughton who I met at Killybegs.[66] At Royal Hotel, Edinburgh, employed all this day in writing etc. Dined with Mr [James] Campbell of Northumberland Street,[67] one of the sub-committee who has been married about 3 years and his wife a very fine woman, but no children. Met Mr [James] Dundas of Dundas Castle and Mr and Mrs Douglas, his wife's uncle and aunt and cousin. Passed a very pleasant day.

---

[62] The four unmarried daughters: Eliza, Margaret, Mary and Christian; Mrs Graham's second daughter, Alexina, was married to Anthony Maxtone of Cultoquhey.
[63] Sir Thomas Dick-Lauder of Fountainhall, Haddington, seventh baronet, the notable academic, novelist and writer (H. C. G. Matthew, 'Lauder, Sir Thomas Dick, seventh baronet (1784–1848)', ODNB).
[64] He did, in fact, have two sons and ten daughters.
[65] Admiral Charles Elphinstone Fleeming (1774–1840) of Cumbernauld, the second son of the eleventh Lord Elphinstone and brother of Mountstuart Elphinstone (1779–1859), governor of Bombay.
[66] Alexander Murray of Broughton who had estates at Killybegs in Donegal. Hill would have met him while he was administering famine relief in Donegal as agent for the government in July 1836; Hill and Waller made their headquarters at an Inn in Killybegs, which Graham also stayed in when he toured northern Ireland in autumn 1836 (Heaney, A Scottish Whig, 299).
[67] A spirit dealer.

Wednesday 12 April. Cold weather. Attended committee in consequence of the
Rev. Macleod having come from [. . .] to complain of the Edinburgh regulations[68]
and price of oats etc. and said that the 4 cargoes had arrived and offered for less
money than those sent by committee. He appeared to be a troublesome character
and threatened to write against the committee in the papers. Mr Bowie took
lunch with us. Called on Mrs Graham. Left Edinburgh at 2 p.m. by coach with
Mr Bowie by the road through Falkirk and Cumbernauld. Close to the latter
place is Admiral Fleming's house and his estate. Got to Glasgow at 8 p.m. The
country all the way is well cultivated. Mr Bowie went and called on Dr Macleod.

Thursday 13 April. At Tontine Hotel. Dark, cloudy weather. Received answer[69]
to my letter last evening to Glasgow committee saying they would not alter their
resolution. Called with Mr Bowie on Doctor Macleod and met Mr [Charles]
Baird, secretary to Glasgow committee when they determined on calling another
committee meeting tomorrow, and discussed what had passed during their
absence in London, and begged I would not write to Treasury until the result of
tomorrow's meeting was known.

Friday 14 April. At Glasgow, cloudy with small rain. Went with Mr Bowie to
Doctor Macleod's but no committee was called all this day. There appears a great
deal of mystery about this Glasgow committee and also Doctor Macleod and
Mr Baird, the secretary, as from all that has passed between Mr Bowie and them
and me, I think there is still something kept back. Visited the Bridewell[70] which
is in excellent order and all the prisoners in separate cells. Visited the Exchange
which is a noble room. Mr Baird came in the evening. He is a great Radical and
appears <u>wavering</u> in his decisions.

Saturday 15 April. Fine weather. Wrote to Doctor Macleod who had given me
an order to see the Bridewell. Mr Bowie brought Doctor Macleod to call on me.
They had both been to meet the Glasgow committee and said much discussion
arose and that they expected that all would be brought right with them on Mr
Bowie's return to Edinburgh, where he was to bring matters before them. Left
Glasgow at 6 p.m. by coach, the short road to Edinburgh where we arrived at
11 p.m.

---

[68] The 2 Mar. 1837 resolutions were amended by Macleod and Bowie (see further discussion
     in the Introduction).
[69] See the attachment to Hill's letter of 16 Apr. 1837 to Spearman (p. 130).
[70] The County and City Bridewell on Duke Street, one of two prisons in Glasgow.

Sunday 16 April. At Edinburgh. Went to St George's Church in Charlotte Square with Mr Bowie and heard a good lecture of about one hour. The first Scotch church[71] I ever was in. This building cost £30,000 and is on the west side of the square. Called at Navy Club[72] and saw Captain Arrow of the Coastguard and Mr Campbell. Fine, clear weather. Wrote home and to the Treasury and Mr Spearman and chancellor of the exchequer, also Sir F. Hardy, Sir R. Stopford,[73] etc., etc.

Royal Hotel, Edinburgh 16 April 1837 [Letter from Hill to Spearman][74]

Sir, I have the honour to acknowledge the receipt of your letters of the 5th and 8th instant conveying to me their Lordships' entire approval of the steps taken by me in fulfilment of my instructions, and enclosing a copy of the Glasgow memorial.[75] In obedience to the directions therein contained, I beg leave to acquaint you for the information of my Lords Commissioners of His Majesty's Treasury that I apprised the Glasgow committee of their Lordships' decision in reference to the memorial, and received an answer thereto from their chairman, a copy of which I enclose[76] by which it will be seen they still persist in not meeting me upon the same terms as the Edinburgh and Aberdeen committees have done. I therefore shall take my measures in future with the Edinburgh committee only, agreeable to their Lordships' directions.

Since my return from Aberdeen, I have been occupied with the Edinburgh committee (and in conjunction with them) making arrangements for the supply of seed potatoes, and about 600 tons are in progress of being shipped; and in addition to which I have ordered 200 tons from Ireland which will be considerably more than the quantity originally voted to be purchased by the Glasgow committee for the sum of £500, notwithstanding their standing resolutions to the contrary. This measure I deemed necessary as in the case of the seed oats referred to in my letter of the 25th March last I have also ordered 100 tons of seed potatoes to be shipped from Aberdeen for the Orkneys, and an additional 100 tons for Shetland, making a total of 300 tons for the latter, and shall continue providing the further supply of seed potatoes in conjunction with the Edinburgh and Aberdeen committees until all demands

---

[71] That is, the established Church of Scotland; the minister of St George's was the Rev. S. L. Candlish.

[72] The Royal Naval Club; treasurer Captain J. H. Tait.

[73] Rear Admiral Sir Robert Stopford (J. K. Laughton, rev. Andrew Lambert, 'Stopford, Sir Robert (1768–1847)', *ODNB*).

[74] The Treasury minute of 21 Apr. 1837 that discussed this letter is set out on p. 281 below.

[75] This is the memorial referred to in Hill's letter to Spearman of 25 Mar. 1837 and which is set out at p. 210 below.

[76] See p. 130.

are satisfied in like manner as for the seed corn. I have the honour to be, Sir, your most obedient servant.

Glasgow 12 April 1837 [Copy of the letter from Allan Fullarton, chairman of the Glasgow committee, to Hill which was enclosed by Hill with his letter of 16 April]

Sir, Your communication of the 11th addressed to the secretary was laid before a meeting of our general committee specially called for the purpose of discussing its contents, when it was unanimously resolved "That as the committee see no ground upon which they can with propriety rescind their former resolution on the subject of seed, they decline in present circumstances to enter upon the further discussion of the question, or to dispose of any part of their funds for seed except to the extent formerly stated to you." I have the honour to be, Sir, your very obedient servant.

Monday 17 April. At Royal Hotel, Edinburgh. Met the committee but they had made little progress in providing potato seed. Dined with Mr R. Campbell[77] and met Mr Dundas and his son, and Mr Douglas, Mrs Campbell's father, and a Miss Ferguson, a niece of Mr Dundas.

Tuesday 18 April. Fine, clear weather. Called on Mrs Graham and Lord Cunninghame. Employed all day in writing and arranging accounts. Called on Lord Melville who invited me to dine with him on Friday. Went by the Dalkeith railway which is worked by horses.[78] Melville Castle[79] is a moderate size house, surrounded by a small park with a neat stone lodge at the entrance. Walked back to Edinburgh, about 6 miles. Met Doctor and Mrs Sheriff. Cold and cloudy. Mr Bowie and Mr Douglas called on us and the latter asked us to dinner on Friday. Mr Waller accepted but I was engaged.

Wednesday 19 April. Cold and cloudy, but open weather. Occupied all this day and drank tea and supped with Doctor and Mrs Warden; met Mr Stevenson and his family.

---

[77] This may be Richard Campbell of Achnabreck, a member of the Edinburgh committee.
[78] Also called the Innocent Railway, this was Edinburgh's first railway, opened in July 1831 with passengers first carried in July 1832.
[79] Designed by James Playfair in 1786–91 (see the picture of the Castle contained in *The Traveller's Guide through Scotland, and its Islands*, vol. i (Edinburgh, 1814), 50).

Royal Hotel, Edinburgh 19 April 1837 [Letter from Hill to Spearman][80]

Sir, I beg leave to enclose to you for the information of the Lords Commissioners of His Majesty's Treasury, a copy of a letter I have received from the Collector at Kirkwall in Orkney,[81] in consequence of my having applied to him to inform me if, in his opinion, any seed corn was necessary for those islands, having received many contradictory statements on the subject. By this day's post I have received information from the Collector of the Customs, Stornoway,[82] that a cargo of 400 quarters of seed oats had arrived there, which I had ordered from Liverpool. I have the honour to be, Sir, your most obedient servant.

Custom House, Kirkwall 8 April 1837 [Copy of the letter from the Collector of Customs, Kirkwall to Hill, enclosed by Hill with his letter of 19 April]

Sir, I had the honour of receiving your letter of the 3rd current relative to the supplies of seed corn and potatoes for the inhabitants of the islands of Orkney, and in reply beg leave to state that I concur in opinion with the committees of Edinburgh and Aberdeen that a supply of seed corn is <u>not</u> required for these islands.[83] It appears from documents in this office that since the 1st January last, about 1,000 bolls of meal and bear (the produce of this country) have been <u>sent</u> coastwise, and the operation of malting is still going on. While during the same period there has been <u>brought</u> coastwise 985 cwt. of oatmeal; 270 quarters barley for <u>distillation</u>; 70 sacks flour; 194 quarters seed oats and about 40 tons of potatoes, part of which remain unsold on account of the high price (3s 6d per cwt.) and the actual <u>want of money</u> among the labouring classes arising from the comparative failure for the last two years in the Herring and Davis's Freights fisheries, and no demand for kelp formerly the staple commodity of the country which gave employment to a number of the labouring classes, both male and female during the summer months, who are now almost idle; and in my humble opinion, if some plan is not devised by proprietors and others interested to give them employment, and hence the means of procuring the necessaries of life, particularly those in the towns of Kirkwall and Stromness, where the greater destitution appears, the consequences may be serious, as it is not so much the want of food in the country, but the means of purchasing it, that is more to be feared. From every information I can procure relative to last year's crop in Orkney, I am of opinion that the bear was deficient about one fourth, the oats

---

[80]   The Treasury minute of 25 Apr. 1837 that discussed this letter is set out on p. 281 below.
[81]   Thomas Pollexfen of Cairston.
[82]   A. R. Macleay.
[83]   This was not, however, the conclusion of the Incorporated Trades of Orkney, which petitioned the Treasury for relief (TNA:PRO, Treasury T 1/4201, Petition, 17 Apr. 1837).

one third and the potatoes nearly one half of the average crops of this country, which from the cheap rate potatoes usually sold at in Orkney (1s per bushel) their want is much felt by the poor who chiefly depended upon them, and fish, for their sustenance; and even if a small supply was sent, I do not believe the poor people could purchase them unless at a very reduced price.

Orkney you will please observe, in most seasons, is an exporting country, sending malt, bear and oats to Leith and other places, otherwise from the failure in the crops this year, the country would have been miserably off indeed. If the weather continues favourable, the sowing of oats in Orkney will be finished about the end of next week. Sowing of bear (an inferior species of barley) generally commences early in May and is seldom sown later than the end of the month. Planting potatoes (if the season is favourable) begins about this time and is generally finished about the first of May. I do not suppose that the same quantity of potatoes can be planted this season as formerly, especially in the islands of Stronsay, Westray and Sanday, where the failure appears to have been greatest; other districts will plant their full quantity, although I apprehend few or none will remain after, even in the best supplied parts of the country. A subscription has been set on foot, but from the few resident heritors in the country and the daily demands upon their benevolence, I am afraid the amount will not be much. I have the honour to be, Sir, your most obedient humble servant.

Thursday 20 April. Cloudy with rain at times. Met the committee again this day and pressed them very much to provide the seed potatoes without a moment's loss of time. Wrote to Dublin to provide an additional quantity. Sir Wm Riddell[84] was in the chair but few members attended. Employed writing all this day.

Friday 21 April. Dark, cloudy weather with snow and sleet; cleared up at mid-day. Mr Wigham,[85] the Quaker, called. Gave him a bill on the Treasury for £107 to meet an equal sum he had laid out for Shetland. He appears a very intelligent man and spoke much of his plan for feeding the poor and said they had sent out a woman with ten weeks' provisions for a passage to Canada which cost only 30/- and he considered all the people in the Highlands should be fed principally on barley broth, oat meal and pease on their passage out as they were not accustomed to eat meat. He thought Government might adopt this plan. He also said that the poor fishermen at Shetland only got paid 2/6 for 100 cod fish, and that not in

---

[84] Hill was mistaken: it was Sir *James* Milles Riddell of Ardnamurchan and Sunart who was the chairman.
[85] John Wigham of Salisbury Road, Edinburgh (see p. 7 above).

money but in clothes or tobacco, as all the proprietors have agents who keep a store and deal with the poor in this way. Met with Lord Melville. Met Mr Blair, the banker[86] and Capt. Dundas and Mr Dundas, both his nephews, together with Lady Melville and her two daughters who formed the party. Spent a pleasant evening. His lordship was very pleasant at his table and both Misses Dundas sang and played all the evening. Returned to Edinburgh at ½ past 11 p.m.

Saturday 22 April. Fine, clear, warm weather. Capt. Knight called and said he did not believe there was anything like the distress that was stated, as the commander of his large vessel, a brig, lived at Stornoway and had a farm, and he had never made any representations to him on the subject, which he was sure he would have done if so bad as represented. He also said that the beginning of May the fishing season commences and in June they had plenty of fishing both in the Hebrides, Shetland and Orkneys and all along the coast. Sent a copy of Dr Macleod and Mr Bowie's explanation to Mr Spearman. Met supply committee at 2 p.m. Their accounts were in bad order; I urged them to make more exertions in forwarding the supply of potato seed and begged they would answer all the questions I had put to them. Dined at Mr Bowie's. Met Sir E. Lees of post office and Col. MacLachlan and his wife and two other ladies, aunts of Mrs Bowie, and her elder daughters which was all the party. Spent a pleasant evening. I was not well. Returned home from Mr Bowie's unwell, with sore throat, etc.; took some medicine.

Royal Hotel, Edinburgh 22 April 1837 [Letter from Hill to Spearman][87]

Sir, The enclosed printed document[88] was put into my hands yesterday by the secretary of the Edinburgh committee which I beg to forward for the information of His Majesty's Government, together with a copy of their original resolutions of the 2nd March 1837. The explanations in the document I have every reason to believe has had the effect of causing the Glasgow committee to send back the £1,500 which the Edinburgh committee sent to them as mentioned in my letter to you of the 22nd March last. I have the honour to be, Sir, your most obedient servant.

---

86   Alexander Blair, treasurer of the Bank of Scotland.
87   The Treasury minute of 16 May 1837 that discussed this letter is set out on p. 282 below.
88   This is Bowie's and Macleod's note of 14 Apr. 1837, making amendments to the Edinburgh committee's resolutions of 2 Mar. 1837 as to the supply of corn and potatoes for seed; it is set out at p. 246 below.

Sunday 23 April. Cloudy with constant rain. Did not get up until 2 p.m. when I was a little better. Mr Waller went to the English church and wrote to Mr Cheyne of supply committee.

Monday 24 April. At Edinburgh. Cloudy with rain at times. Called on Mrs Graham and Doctor Sheriff and attended committee where a Mr Spence came and made strong claims for Orkney which I resisted, and on referring to the resolutions from there it was found only 4 bolls of seed was wanted. He appeared a troublesome character and I heard he was very fond of writing to the newspapers about the distress. Wrote to the Collector of Customs and Officers of Excise[89] about cargoes of potatoes ordered from Ireland. Dined with Sir [James] Riddell in Moray Place. Lady Riddell was the only lady present and six other gentlemen. He has an excellent house and appears a man of large fortune. They were going to Leamington and on to London next week. Found myself very unwell with sore throat and slept very little. Mr Bowie called.

Tuesday 25 April. Cloudy but mild weather with SW wind. Sir Donald Campbell[90] with Mr Macpherson, Mr Campbell's[91] agent for Islay came to complain of a small grant being allowed to that island which had been ordered in consequence of an application to me by Mr Bowie and Doctor Macleod at Glasgow by a clergyman residing in Islay. Mr Campbell, the member for Argyllshire and principal owner of Islay had represented to Mr Spring Rice that he required <u>no</u> aid from Government and that the application which had been made was done without the knowledge of Mr Campbell and he wrote a very angry letter to his agent, Mr Macpherson, which they read to me.[92] Paid the bill by a cheque on the Bank of Scotland, No. 1. Took places in the mail coach for Perth. Doctor Warden went yesterday with us and showed us the Royal College of Surgeons and the University College and Museum all of which was in excellent order. Left Edinburgh at 4 p.m., crossed the Queensferry at 5 p.m., got to Perth at 9 p.m. and put up at the Star Inn, a bad inn and a not very clean house.[93]

Wednesday 26 April. Fine, mild weather with fine, warm showers. Took a chaise and drove to Lord Lynedoch's and went over his grounds; it is an old house which has been added to, quite in the cottage style and the way between this and Perth

---

89   James Cornwall.
90   Of Dunstaffnage, Argyll, an Edinburgh committee member.
91   Walter Frederick Campbell of Islay, MP.
92   The Glasgow committee did, in fact, send aid to the parish of Bowmore in June 1837 (p. 236).
93   The Star Hotel on Canal Street, run by Alexander McPherson, catered for commercial and family travellers.

is very good and about six miles from the town. Returned to Perth at ½ past
11 a.m. and got into the *Defiance* coach for Aberdeen which passes through the
interior, all of which is well cultivated. This coach is kept by the famous Capt.
Barclay,[94] the pedestrian and is well horsed. Passed through the small towns of
Forfar, Brechin and Laurencekirk, all small places. Came into the coast road at
Stonehaven. Got to Aberdeen at ½ past 9 p.m. Lord Provost called and found
cards of invitation from Major Taylor[95] who married Lady Jane, sister of Lord
Fife[96] also to dine at the County Club at the Assembly Rooms on Saturday.

Thursday 27 April. Employed with Mr Angus, secretary to the committee in
settling accounts. Several gentlemen called on me. Lord Provost took us to
Gordon's School[97] which is a noble establishment and educates about 140 boys
at no expense to their parents.

Friday 28 April. Fine weather. Met the committee and gave the Lord Provost three
bills on the Treasury for £....[98] Dined with Major Taylor and Lady Jane, his wife,
but she did not sit down at table. We had a party of ten gentlemen to meet us, Sir
J. Forbes and Mr Landowne and the Provost and Mr Duff, his brother-in-law. A
large party of ladies in the evening, and a quadrille dance and cards.

Saturday 29 April. Cloudy with showers of rain. Employed writing and arranging
accounts. Dined at the public rooms with the County Club which has been
established more than 120 years.[99] Sat down with about 36. Mr Grant was the
chairman and Mr T. Burnett, advocate of Aberdeen, was deputy chairman and
secretary. The dinner was by no means good or well served. A great variety of
toasts were drunk and we broke up about 10 p.m.

[94] Robert Barclay Allardice of Ury, known as Captain Barclay, was renowned for his
extraordinary pedestrian performances (L. Stephen, rev. Dennis Brailsford, 'Allardice,
Robert Barclay [Captain Barclay] (1779–1854)', *ODNB*). The *Defiance* coach, carrying four
passengers, two coachmen and a guard, covered the journey from Edinburgh to Aberdeen
in twelve hours and was thought to be the fastest and best conducted coach in Britain.
[95] Major Alexander Francis Taylor of Rothiemay, who had served in the 21st regiment.
[96] James Duff was the fourth earl of Fife.
[97] Robert Gordon's Hospital, now known as Robert Gordon's College.
[98] Blank in the original.
[99] The Honourable, the County Club of Aberdeen, one of two clubs in the city, had its
permanent venue in the public rooms in the city; it was formed in 1718 and dissolved in 1873.
'The Club consists exclusively of noblemen and landed proprietors of the county [and] was
established for the purpose of promoting social intercourse, and of contributing pecuniary
aid to the distressed, it is a society of long-standing and high respectability' (*Pigot*, 164).

Royal Hotel, Aberdeen 29 April 1837 [Letter from Hill to Spearman][100]

Sir, I beg leave to acquaint you for the information of My Lords Commissioners of His Majesty's Treasury that I arrived here on Wednesday night last the 26th inst. for the purpose of completing the arrangements I had made with the Aberdeen committee in regard to the supply of seed corn and seed potatoes for the Shetland and Orkney islands; and the whole supplies of seed corn and seed potatoes for the former place have been sent off with the exception of about 80 quarters of seed bear (a species of barley), and 86 tons of potatoes which I expect will be shipped and dispatched next week, as I applied for and obtained the use of three of the Revenue craft to assist in sending these supplies from this port, which has saved the Crown the expense of freight. The committee of Aberdeen have not been able to procure the additional 100 tons of seed potatoes mentioned in my letter of the 16th instant, but 200 tons will be sent to Shetlands which is deemed sufficient and 50 tons to the Orkneys which latter was all they required.

As the Revenue craft are hourly expected here from Shetland, I intend remaining here until Wednesday next in order to expedite the final shipment of what is to be sent from hence. I have seen the Reverend Mr Barclay, the resident clergyman at Lerwick in Shetland, who left that place on Saturday last the 22nd inst. And he informs me that they have had remarkably fine weather ever since the 4th of this month and that the sowing of the seed oats would all be completed in a few days after he left. By letters which I have received from Ireland to the 24th instant, the whole of the seed potatoes which I have ordered from thence, amounting to about 340 tons, for the west coast of Scotland and the western islands, were in progress of shipping, and I have every reason to believe the vessels will have left Ireland by this time, wind and weather permitting. The supplies furnishing by the Edinburgh committee in conjunction with me, are progressing as fast as circumstances will permit, and I hope will be completed soon after my arrival here.

This morning I received the enclosed copy of resolutions of the Glasgow committee,[101] from the committee of Edinburgh which I beg leave to transmit for their Lordships' information. I have the honour to be, Sir, your most obedient servant.

---

[100] The Treasury minute of 16 May 1837 that discussed this letter is set out on p. 282 below.

[101] Resolutions which provided that potatoes should be provided solely to poor cottars and fishermen; that the distribution should be gratuitous; that no part of the supply should be given to those who had participated in a share of the supply from the government or the Edinburgh committee; and that the supply should be distributed in quantities not exceeding half a boll, or two barrels to each family. There was annexed to the resolutions a series of questions the answers to which would, the Glasgow committee hoped, help the government adopt measures 'for the permanent amelioration of the people' (TNA:PRO, Treasury T 1/4201, Resolutions of the general committee of Glasgow relative to the supply of potatoes).

Sunday 30 April. Cloudy with showers of rain. Went to the west Scotch kirk[102] with Mr Milne and heard a good lecture. In the afternoon went with the provost to the English church[103] where the Bishop read prayers and the clergyman[104] preached. Both were well attended. Dined with Mr Forbes in the family way.

Monday 1 May. Fine weather. The Rev. Mr Barclay of Shetland called and from his manner I really thought the distress was not so great as was represented, as he let they had had a good fishing season for cod, and he also said they had vessels trading with London and the Baltic. But no doubt he calculated having food sent to them until harvest. I pressed him about the people purchasing the same and stated as they caught plenty of fish, they ought to buy it; but he shied this question. Dined with Lord Provost. Sat down 22 at dinner, Capt. and Mrs Shepherd, an East-India director[105] was of the party, Mr Duff and his two daughters and Miss Burnett, etc., etc., etc. In the evening there was a quadrille dance and we spent a pleasant day.

Tuesday 2 May. Fine weather. Walked to Old Aberdeen and saw the Cathedral and the Library at the College. Sir J. Gordon[106] with all his family and Commdr. Dickson arrived in the *City of Aberdeen* steamer and the *Duck* lighter came in with all his baggage from Chatham. Dined with Mr T. Burnett; a pleasant party, Mr Duff and his two daughters, Mrs and Miss Gordon, Sir J's sister. In the evening some more ladies and Sir J. Gordon's son came; they had a dance and we played cards.

Wednesday 3 May. Fine weather. Took leave of Sir J. Gordon who set off with all his family for the country. The three cutters came in and the commanders called on me. Wrote to the Admiralty to say I had ordered *Duck* lighter to Lerwick with corn and potatoes. Dined at the hotel. Employed in getting the potatoes shipped on board the *Duck* lighter and giving orders to the commanders of the cutters.

Thursday 4 May. Cloudy and cold weather with a little rain occasionally. The three commanders of the cutters breakfasted with me and I gave them their final

---

[102] The West Church on Back Wynd; the minister was the Rev. Alexander Davidson.
[103] St Andrew's episcopal chapel on King Street, where the bishop was the Right Rev. William Skinner, DD.
[104] The minister was the Rev. William Downing.
[105] John Shepherd, a member of the court of directors of the home department of the East India Company.
[106] This is probably Sir James Gordon, bart., of Letterfourie.

orders. The *Mermaid*, Lt. Nott, sailed at noon for Berwick, and the *Cheerful*, Lt. Rothesay, with the remainder of the seed, about 82 qrs. for Lerwick in Shetland. She also took about 4 tons of potatoes. The *Duck* sailed at 1 p.m. with about 53 tons. Fine weather, wind from N to NNW. The *Mary*, tender, remained in the harbour but the master promised me to sail on the night tide. Had all the potatoes weighed, about 18 tons, which was left in Mr Forbes' store. Wrote to collector to see them shipped in a vessel which was bound to Archangel. Mr F promised no charge was to be made for the freight as I had allowed *Mary*, tender, and *Cheerful*, cutter, to take meal to the Orkneys. Wrote to the collector of Shetland[107] by *Cheerful*, cutter. Called to take leave of all our friends, Lord Provost Milne and Mrs Milne who were very kind to us all the time we were there. Called on Major and Lady Jane Taylor, Mr and Mrs Burnett and Mr Forbes. Met Mr Gordon at the hotel who had a sick son there. He lives about forty miles in the country. Took places in the Defiance and paid hotel bill. Called on Mrs Morrice.

Friday 5 May. Fine weather. Left Aberdeen at 6 a.m. in Defiance coach, fare £2–10–0, clear of guards and coachmen. Breakfasted at Stonehaven at a very indifferent house at ½ past 7. Passed through Brechin, Forfar, Couper Angus and Perth which is a very fine town, well situated on the banks of the Tay. Here is an excellent set of buildings, which was built for a French prison and surrounded by a wall, now unoccupied except for occasionally housing grain for the farmers.[108] Stopped about twenty minutes at Perth but it was not time enough to dine. Before we reached Perth we passed Glamis castle where the murder of Malcolm, King of Scotland[109] took place, and a gentleman in the coach said that the person that showed the house pointed out the spots of blood. The castle belongs to Lord Strathmore, but he do not reside in it. It is merely kept up as a show place. It lays inland from the road between Forfar and Couper Angus. On the left near the road we passed the hill of Dunsinane on which stood the castle of Macbeth now in ruins.[110] At the foot of this hill is scene described in the play of Macbeth where the witches are seen. On the left we also passed Loch Leven in which there is a small island with a castle in which Mary queen of Scots was confined by Elizabeth but she made her escape with Douglas who was shot when he was stepping into the boat.[111] Four men were drowned in this loch by the boat upsetting under sail last Sunday. Got to the ferry at 6 p.m.. Crossed in the steam-boat, fare 6d. each, but if in the sailing-boat 3d. each. Crossed the ferry and got to the Royal Hotel

---

107   Thomas Fea, at Lerwick.
108   Built between 1810 and 1812 under the supervision of the architect Robert Reid, the prison was a depot for some seven thousand prisoners during the Napoleonic wars.
109   Malcolm II.
110   The story that King Macbeth occupied the fort on Dunsinane Hill arises through Shakespeare's play and local tradition (*OGazS*, ii, 448).
111   See also Hill's entry about this for 1 Apr. at p. 123 above.

in Edinburgh in one hour, viz. 8 p.m. This coach is well managed. Wrote a note to Mr Graham and received letters from home.

Saturday 6 May. At Edinburgh. Fine weather. Called on Mr Graham and he read me his last two reports which were much like the former ones, very lengthy. He also read me a rough abstract of his winding up report which appeared about six sheets of paper. Mr Bowie called, and Mr Cheyne; the latter sent me a copy of the Glasgow printed resolutions dated 29th ultimo which I sent to the Treasury in my letter of this day's date. Employed writing all this day.

Royal Hotel, Edinburgh 6 May 1837 [Letter from Hill to Spearman][112]

Sir, With reference to my letter of the 29th ultimo, I beg leave to acquaint you for the information of my Lords Commissioners of His Majesty's Treasury that I did not leave Aberdeen until yesterday, in consequence of the *Duck* dock-yard lighter having arrived there on Tuesday, which vessel I took upon myself to detain and filled her with about 53 tons of potatoes for Shetland and I hope their Lordships will approve of my occupying this vessel, as I wrote to the Admiralty stating the circumstances. The three revenue craft also arrived here on Wednesday from taking supplies to the Orkneys and Shetland, which enabled me to complete all the seed corn remaining due to the latter; and the *Duck* lighter and *Cheerful* cutter sailed on Thursday morning last for that purpose. The other two cutters I have ordered back to their stations, as Capt. Bowles and Capt. Knight were desirous of having their services. The whole shipment of seed corn and seed potatoes was completed before I left Aberdeen, with the exception of about 18 tons of the latter, for which a vessel was provided. I arrived here last night and this morning have been in communication with Mr Graham. The enclosed document[113] has just come to my hands which I beg to forward for their Lordships' information. I have the honour to be, Sir, your most obedient servant.

Edinburgh 6 May 1837 [Private letter from Hill to Spearman]

My dear Sir, As the time is now so far advanced as to render it no longer necessary to provide any further supply of seed, and if the Government do not intend to come forward for some little time to supply food, but allow the committees to go on with private funds, perhaps I could be spared to return

---

[112] The Treasury minute of 16 May 1837 that discussed this letter is set out on p. 282 below.
[113] This is the interim report of the Glasgow committee of 29 Apr. 1837 set out on p. 227 below.

to Deptford for a short time. But if it is intended that I should be kept in
Scotland during the whole time of supplying the food until next harvest, I
must make some family arrangements for my being absent so long a time,
which I did not calculate upon before I left home. Therefore I shall feel
particularly obliged if you will let me know whether I have any chance of
getting back for a short period, as I could only be spared during the interval
between now and the commencement of the supply of food. I returned last
night from Aberdeen and the weather is now set very fine. I am, my dear
Sir, yours most sincerely.

Sunday 7 May. At Edinburgh. Cold, cloudy weather. Rain at times. Went to
St John's church in Princes Street[114] both morning and afternoon. The Bishop[115]
done part of the morning service. Mr Graham called. Gave him the victualling
of the *John Barry* emigrant ship[116] to copy and he sent me his last two reports to
Fox Maule. Frequent showers of rain. Received letters from home.

Monday 8 May. Cloudy weather. Wrote to Mr Tilly and Drevor and Sons.
Employed copying Mr Graham's reports. Met the committee this day at 3 p.m.
Mr Campbell of Jura[117] invited us to dine with him on Friday; he was in the chair
and only six members present. All the potatoes I had sent off from Ireland I gave
over to the committee at their request and wrote to collectors of Customs and
Excise to do it at all the ports. Gave 30 qrs. of oats from Lochboisdale to Barra.

Tuesday 9 May. Cold, cloudy weather with snow for about two hours. Mr
Graham called and went with him to the Herring Fishery Board's office and saw
Mr. . .[118] the secretary who promised to write to Mr Finlayson about the charge
for hire of store at Lochboisdale. Mr Graham is one of the commissioners of the
Fishery Board. Called on Mrs G and her sisters. Wrote home. After dinner we
went to Mr Stevenson's and drank tea and spent a pleasant evening. Dr Warden
came in and Mr S showed all his drawings of the lighthouse on the Bell Rock
which he constructed more than 21 years ago.[119]

---

[114] St John the Evangelist Church. A Scottish episcopal chapel designed by William Burn,
    construction of which began in 1816.
[115] The Right Rev. James Walker, DD.
[116] The *John Barry* sailed from Dundee and arrived on 13 July 1837 in New South Wales with
    314 emigrants.
[117] Colin Campbell of Jura, an Edinburgh committee member, whose Edinburgh house was
    at 4 Albyn Street.
[118] Blank in the original. The secretary of the The British White Herring Fishery, whose offices
    were at 26 Castle Street, was J. Dunsmore.
[119] The first light shown from the Bell Rock was on 1 Feb. 1811.

Wednesday 10 May. At Edinburgh. Cloudy, cold weather. Employed writing. Mr Graham and solicitor-general called, but I was down at Leith where we dined at the New Ship Inn there and saw the *Clarence* steamer go out for London. Visited the docks and harbour. Called at Mr Stevenson's office and saw the model of the Bell Rock lighthouse. Looked at Wintock's carpet shop in George Street. Returned from Leith at 8 p.m. and Dr Warden called and drank tea with us.

Thursday 11 May. At Edinburgh. Fine weather. Called on solicitor-general who had arrived from London. He said Lord Minto was a particular friend of his and he dined with him twice and he had seen Sir C. Adam and Mr S. Rice who were all pleased with what I had done. He did not appear to know what were the future views of the Government; asked me to dine on Friday week. Met Mr Graham who showed me all over the New Club house in Princes Street which is to be opened on the 1st of July.[120] Paid bill for three shawls £3–9–0. Employed writing. Met the committee at 3 p.m. The vessel from Ireland which Mr Drevor had sent was arrived at Tobermory with 45 tons of seed potatoes. A Scotch dissenting minister came from . . .[121] Orkney and complained that himself and all his brethren were left out of the local committee, and appeared very angry because he could not get hold of some of the supplies. Mr Sheen, a writer,[122] also was disposed to be troublesome about the short supply of potatoes to the Orkneys. I was obliged to call him to order. Mr Craigie read a letter from Tobermory reporting the arrival of the vessel with 50 tons of potatoes which Mr Drevor had sent from Ireland. The letter complained of there being 11 tons short of what I had first named. Dined with Mr Campbell of Jura. Met Sir John and Lady Campbell,[123] Mr and Mrs Lamont[124] and Mr Bowie, with several other ladies and gentlemen, in all 16 at dinner which was an excellent one, and we passed a pleasant evening. Mr Campbell was formerly in business in Glasgow and is supposed to be worth about one hundred and thirty thousand pounds.[125] Paid my bill for the ale £1–4–0.

[120] Graham was a prominent member of the Club, serving on the committee that decided on the Club's move to its new premises on Prince's Street (Cockburn, *A History of the New Club*, 56). According to the Club's history, it opened its doors on 15 May 1837 (M. McCrae (ed.), *The New Club – A History* (Edinburgh, 2004), 140), but Hill's journal entry suggests it was not officially opened until 1 July 1837.

[121] Blank in the original but is probably Kirkwall (see Hill's journal entry for 15 May (p. 143).

[122] There is no record of a writer named Sheen. This may be a reference to W. F. Skene, who was to develop a considerable reputation as historian and Celtic scholar and who was secretary of the Edinburgh section of the central relief board in 1847 (see W. D. H. Sellar, 'William Forbes Skene (1809–92): historian of Celtic Scotland', *Proceedings of the Society of Antiquaries of Scotland* 131 (2001), 3–21; and A. J. G. Mackay, rev. W. D. H. Sellar, 'Skene, William Forbes (1809–1892)', *ODNB*).

[123] Sir John Campbell of Ardnamurchan, whose Edinburgh house was at 25 Rutland Square.

[124] Alexander Lamont of Knockdow, an Edinburgh committee member.

[125] Equivalent to around £9.2 million in 2010.

Friday 12 May. Cloudy, with small rain. Mr Young, a banker of Aberdeen, called on me yesterday and said he was going to London on Saturday. Went down to Newhaven and went on the iron suspension bridge which is a very slender one and appears very weak and is not well constructed. Walked along the shore to Leith and dined at the Ship Hotel on the quay. Several steam boats moving about the Forth. Returned to Edinburgh in the evening. Employed writing.

Saturday 13 May. Cloudy, with showers of rain. Called on Mr R. Graham and Mr Campbell of Jura. Wrote to Mr S. Rice and various other letters. Doctor Warden and Mr Graham called and the Rev. Mr Paterson, a dissenting minister from Orkney who attended the last meeting of the committee and complained that he and all his brethren were excluded from the relief committee and only the kirk clergy of Orkney were allowed to be in the local committee there, and said it was all a political manoeuvre of Capt. Balfour, the member for Orkney, and hoped I would render him assistance in this case. Employed writing. More or less rain and hail all this day.

Edinburgh 13 May 1837 [Private letter from Hill to Spring Rice]

Dear Sir, Since my letter to you of the 16th ultimo, I have been constantly employed in meeting the committees at this place and at Aberdeen as reported in my official letters, and as the season is now too far advanced to render any further supply of seed necessary, I am looking anxiously for letters announcing the arrival of the vessels with the seed potatoes at their destination, though I have every reason to believe that all of them have reached their ports; still I have had as yet only an account of one having done so.

I hope that the sum that I shall have to expend on the seed account will not exceed £6,500, but I have often been hard pressed for more in discussions at the different meetings, notwithstanding a reasonable surplus had been provided at the request of the committees in order that there should not be a deficiency of supply.

There will be a surplus at three depots, viz. Stornoway, Lochboisdale and Shetland, but I have secured it by directing the revenue officers to take charge of it until they receive further instructions from me.

Understanding that a subscription is about to be raised in London by the means of a Ball at the west end of the town, and calculations are already making upon a large sum on that account.[126] I would suggest to you if possible that the

[126] The proceeds of the Grand Fancy Dress Ball, held with royal patronage on 13 July at the Willis Rooms, St James' Square, amounted to £1,012 (*Morning Chronicle*, 31 May 1837), equivalent to around £71,700 in 2010.

money about to be raised should be in some measure controlled and remitted only <u>periodically</u> to check that disposition to an improvident expenditure which I have often times had difficulty in preventing even with the seed question, as I fear there would be more or less jobbing with the money if too lavishly handed over to the committees.[127] As a specimen of the anxiety of some persons to <u>get all they could</u> from me, I was asked for seed oats at this late season to put into the ground as the parties said they would grow sufficiently well to <u>feed the cattle.</u>

I have not had any opportunity of attending to your verbal communication respecting the population being withdrawn by emigration, nor of seeing Doctor Macleod of North Uist[128] on the subject. But as Mr R. Graham has reported so fully on this subject,[129] perhaps you may not now think it necessary for me to make any inquiry. In a conversation I had with Mr R. Graham this morning respecting Doctor Macleod, he did not consider him as having formed any settled opinion on emigration. I have the honour to be, Dear Sir, your most obedient servant.

Sunday 14 May. At Edinburgh. Dull, cloudy weather. Went to the English church[130] in the afternoon and heard a good sermon. Walked over the old town in the evening. Very cold, damp weather.

Monday 15 May. Cloudy weather but not so cold. Met Mr Graham who wanted my copy of his report to send to Fox Maule as they had mislaid his at the Home Office.[131] Attended committee when Mr Mather reported that the 50 tons of potatoes for Orkneys would be shipped at Burntisland that day and the vessel to sail the following day. Read the letter I received from the Rev. Mr Paterson of Kirkwall who complained of himself and his brethren being excluded from the local committee of relief. Went to Leith and dined at the Ship Hotel and returned in the evening.

---

[127] In the event, the Ball proceeds were kept separate from the London subscriptions. The use of the proceeds was still being discussed in 1839 with concerns being expressed that they must be used to give effect to the original object of the contributions (NRS, Papers of the Montague-Douglas-Scott family, dukes of Buccleuch, GD 224/667/6/14, Gordon to Buccleuch, 20 Mar. 1838; Forbes to Buccleuch, 10 Apr. 1838; NRS, Lothian muniments, GD 40/9/385/1, Gordon to Lothian, 22 Dec. 1838; NRS, GD 40/9/385/2, Gordon to Lothian, 1 Jan. 1839; NRS, GD 40/9/385/3, Gordon to Lothian, 30 Jan. 1839).

[128] This is Dr Alexander Macleod (1788–1854), one of the notable doctors in the Highlands. He combined a career of medical practice with that of a factor and a farmer on North and South Uist, Benbecula and Barra, Skye and Knoydart (MacGillivray, 'Medical practice', 284–5; and M. D. Macleod, 'An dotair ban', *The Caledonian Medical Journal*, new series 4 (1901), 4–17). Hill did later meet with Dr Macleod (see his journal entry for 5 June, p. 155).

[129] That is, in his letters to Fox Maule, particularly the last, dated 6 May 1837.

[130] Presumably one of the seven episcopal chapels in Edinburgh.

[131] See Graham's letter to Robert Stewart of 18 May 1837 at p. 110 above on the Home Office mislaying Graham's letters to Fox Maule.

Tuesday 16 May. At Edinburgh. Fine, clear, warm weather. At 9 a.m. went to
Dundas Castle[132] in the Perth Coach as far as Queensferry and walked from there,
as the castle is only about one mile. Saw Mr Dundas and three of his daughters
and three sons showed me all over his gardens, house and grounds. He farms about
500 acres and has a large property round the house, but it is supposed that he has
over-built himself, and as the estate is an entailed one he is more or less involved,
and has not more than £1,200 a year to live on. Walked back from Queensferry
which is 8 miles from Edinburgh. Received a note from Mr Graham to say he
had written to Fox Maule proposing that he and me should go up to Town to
arrange what was to be done about food and to settle his own report. Received
a note to dine with Lord Belhaven.[133]

Wednesday 17 May. At Edinburgh. Fine, warm weather. Major Taylor from
Aberdeen called. Employed writing. Mr [Thomas] Burnett [of Park] from
Aberdeen called yesterday; he is Purse Bearer[134] to Lord Belhaven in the grand
Church procession which is to take place tomorrow from the Palace at Holyrood
House. Dined at the Palace. Took Mr Graham and Major Taylor with us in
the carriage; we sat down about 50 to dinner. The Lord Provost[135] and 9 of the
judges with the solicitor-general, Lord Greenock[136] and the commanding officers
of regiments and artillery and engineers. The Moderator, Doctor Macleod, sat
opposite to Lord Belhaven. The Lord Provost and his retinue were in "state"
and presented the keys of the City to Lord Belhaven on a velvet cushion, this
being the anniversary week of choosing a new Moderator for the Church. The
dinner was served by the master of the British Hotel.[137] We had real turtle, but
it was not very good. After dinner we retired to the drawing room where Lady
Belhaven was with about six other ladies and soon came Lady Greenock, Mrs
Rutherford and Lady Strathmore.[138] The latter has apartments in the Castle. She
is very short and fat. A Mrs Hamilton and Miss H, her daughter, sang and played
on the piano. The Misses Graham and several other ladies also came, in all about
22. Came away about 10 p.m.

[132] Designed by William Burn in 1818.
[133] Robert Montgomery Hamilton, eighth lord Belhaven and Stenton, the lord high
commissioner to the General Assembly of the Church of Scotland.
[134] The purse bearer was an official of the royal household who carried the purse holding the
great seal on state occasions.
[135] The silk merchant, Sir James Spittal, who had business premises on South Bridge. His contest
with James Aytoun for the position of Lord Provost in 1833, the first time the Lord Provost
of Edinburgh was elected by a free vote, was commemorated in a ballad entitled 'Huzza!
For Provost Spittal!!!' (see http://digital.nls.uk/broadsides/broadside.cfm/id/16458).
[136] Major-General Charles Murray Cathcart, second earl Cathcart (who was styled Lord
Greenock) was the commander of the forces in Scotland and governor of Edinburgh Castle
(G. C. Boase, rev. J. Lunt, 'Cathcart, Charles Murray (1783–1895), ODNB).
[137] The British Hotel at 70 Queen Street was run by John Barry.
[138] Marianne, the third wife of Thomas Bowes-Lyon, earl of Strathmore and Kinghorn.

Thursday 18 May. Cloudy, cold weather with easterly wind. Went to the Levee at Holyrood House and took Major Taylor from Aberdeen with us. After the Levee went to the High Church in the Old Town[139] and heard Doctor Macleod, the Moderator, preach an excellent sermon above an hour. From there Lord Belhaven and all the public authorities went to the next Church to appoint the new Moderator Dr. . .[140] who had 250 votes against 59. Strong party feelings exist on this occasion and the Tory party carried the sway. The Church was so full that I could not get in to hear the debates. Dined at the Palace but it was half past 8 before we sat down to dinner. About 220, principally clergymen and the two Moderators. We dined in the Long Room or Picture Gallery. Returned home at ½ past 10 p.m.

Friday 19 May. Cloudy with cold easterly wind. Sir Charles Gordon called and asked us to dinner for Monday next. Mr Graham called. Signed three bills on the Treasury and remitted them to Provost at Aberdeen. Employed all the morning writing. Called on Doctor Macleod and several gentlemen and Mr Burnett of Aberdeen. Left cards at the Palace. Dined at the solicitor-general's – Mrs Rutherfurd, a very pleasant Irish woman from Donegal, has no family. Lord Jeffreys[141] and Mrs and Miss Jeffreys, Lord Cockburn[142] and Mr and Miss Graham with a party altogether of 16 sat down to dinner. Passed a pleasant evening. Lord Cunninghame was also there.

Saturday 20 May. Fine weather. Hired a carriage and took two Misses and Mr Graham to the Botanical Gardens and Craggs Quarry[143] where we saw the petrified tree and drove a little round the country. Received fresh instructions from the Treasury by Friday's post yesterday. Dined with Lord Justice Clerk[144] at Charlotte Square and met Mr and Mrs Smith who are neighbours of Lord Lynedoch. Another gentleman and his wife and the family made up the party. Mrs Boyle, his wife (the second) has four children, the youngest 2 years old. He has a family of . . .[145] grown-up by a former wife. The best house I have been in in Edinburgh. Waller dined with Mr Bowie.

---

[139] On High Street, where the minister was the Rev. Dr G. H. Baird.
[140] Blank in the original. The new moderator was the Rev. Dr Matthew Gardiner, the minister of Bothwell.
[141] Francis Jeffrey, Lord Jeffrey, who had been editor of the *Edinburgh Review*, lord advocate and was a judge of the Court of Session (M. Fry, 'Jeffrey, Francis, Lord Jeffrey (1773–1850)', *ODNB*).
[142] Henry Cockburn, Lord Cockburn, who had been solicitor-general and lord advocate, and was a judge of the Court of Session (K. Miller, 'Cockburn, Henry, Lord Cockburn (1779–1854)', *ODNB*).
[143] This is probably a reference to Salisbury Crags in Holyrood Park.
[144] David Boyle of Shewalton.
[145] Blank in the original. Boyle had six sons and five daughters by his first wife Elizabeth (A. H. Grant, rev. M. Fry, 'Boyle, David, Lord Shewalton (1772–1853)', *ODNB*).

Sunday 21 May. Fresh breezes and cloudy with north wind. Major Taylor of Aberdeen called and wanted me to go to the levee. Received letters from Aberdeen acknowledging receipt of bills and from Stornoway of arrival of a cargo of potatoes. Employed all this day writing. Went to St John's Church and heard a very good sermon. The service is well performed here and some of the first people in Edinburgh and the neighbourhood attend at it. Called on Mr R. Campbell, Mr Bowie, Sir C. Gordon, Lord Justice Grey and the solicitor-general. Saw Mr Craigie who said accounts had been received of the arrival of the potatoes from Ireland at Portree and Lochboisdale. Dined at the Hotel. Received letters from home.

Royal Hotel, Edinburgh 21 May 1837 [Letter from Hill to Spearman]

Sir, I have the honour to acknowledge the receipt of your letter of the 17th instant transmitting a copy of the minute of the Lords Commissioners of His Majesty's Treasury of the 16th instant,[146] approving of my exertions in the immediate and urgent duties of procuring and forwarding seed oats and potatoes to the distressed districts and with further guidance in regard to furnishing supplies of food. In reply thereto, I request you will be pleased to make known to their Lordships the gratification I feel at the expression of their Lordships' entire approval of my conduct and that they may rest assured that no endeavour on my part shall be wanting to fulfil their further instructions to their satisfaction. As soon as I have arranged the final settlement of the seed accounts with the Edinburgh committee, I intend to visit the depots and to inform myself more particularly of the distressed districts that may require my more immediate attention and enable me to control the equable distribution of the food; and also gain some information by personal enquiry whether any supplies may be had on the spot or at nearer points than Glasgow. I have the honour to be, Sir, your most obedient servant.

Monday 22 May. Cold weather. Attended committee who wanted to remit money to Glasgow which I advised them not to do. Mr Campbell of Islay said no distress existed there and it was a shame to send food to that island as all the people had full work and earned five or six shillings a week. Saw Lord Cunninghame who approved of my plan of visiting depots, as I showed him new instructions. Called on Lord Justice Clerk. Sent Mr Drevor a bill for £600 and wrote to Treasury. Dined at Sir Charles Gordon who is a catholic.[147]

---

[146] See p. 282 below.
[147] Sir Charles Gordon of Drimnin; a staunch Catholic, he horrified the local, exclusively Protestant, population by demolishing the sixteenth-century Maclean of Drimnin castle and building a catholic chapel in 1840 (*Press and Journal*, 4 Sept. 2010).

Met Mr and Mrs Hamilton, Mr and Mrs Young and Mr Graham, in all 16 sat down to dinner. Mrs H sang in the evening. Passed a pleasant day. Mr Graham told me he was called up to London and meant to leave on Wednesday by steamer.

Tuesday 23 May. At Edinburgh. Employed all the morning with supply committee and Mr Graham. Drew a bill on Treasury for £1412–16–8 in favour of Mr R. Campbell, chairman supply committee. Mr Campbell called with a clergyman of Islay to prove that no supplies were wanted there. Employed writing etc. Mr Graham called and gave me his route and other information. Waller dined out.

Wednesday 24 May. Fine weather. Breakfasted with the General Assembly and elders of the Church at the Royal Hotel, Mr Nairne[148] in the chair. We sat down about 130. This breakfast was given as a mark of thanks to Dr Macleod the late Moderator and Mr Bowie, and myself and Waller were invited.[149] The chairman paid me a high compliment and so did Doctor Macleod, in returning thanks, spoke very highly of me. Mr Bowie in returning thanks stated that the following supplies had been sent: meal 10,500 bolls; seed oats 4,800 qrs and potatoes for seed 1,200 tons, equal to 144,000 barrels. Doctor Macleod stated that in addition to £10,000 granted by Government, that £40,000 had been raised by private subscription. Saw Capt. Knight yesterday who promised me to order the brig from Stornoway to Snizort or Portree to take me up there on my tour of the islands. Went to Leith to call on Capt. Knight and [William Greene] the Collector of Customs. Employed writing. Dined with Capt. and Mrs Knight and met Col. and Mrs and Miss. . .[150] and Mr Holmes and his wife, the latter is Capt. Knight's daughter. Mr H[151] is paymaster of the 35th [Regiment] at Ceylon where they were going. Went in the evening to the Palace at Lady Belhaven's party where there were about 20 ladies. Two Miss Fergusons sang. Returned home at ½ past 11 a.m.

Thursday 25 May. At Edinburgh. Fine weather with some rain. Called to take leave of all friends. Mr Graham left in the steam vessel for London last evening at 5 p.m. Went to the kirk session but it was so full we could not get in. Employed writing and settling accounts.

---

[148] James Nairne, WS, fiscal to the Society of Writers to the Signet.
[149] According to the very full account in the *Caledonian Mercury*, the breakfast was given by the synod of Glenelg to both the Rev. Dr Macleod and Bowie in recognition of the service they had given to the Highlands by their mission to London seeking public subscriptions, and about two hundred gentlemen were present (29 May 1837).
[150] Blank in the original.
[151] Ensign J. G. H. Holmes.

Friday 26 May. Fine weather. Paid the bill at the Royal Hotel, Edinburgh to Mr Gibbs by cheque on Bank. Left Edinburgh at 9 a.m. in Glasgow coach and got to Airdrie at ½ past 1 p.m. where we met Capt. Cumberland[152] of 42nd Regiment. He took us to his barracks and we had wine and biscuits. Hired a chaise at 1/6p per mile for Cumbernauld which is 8 miles. Got there at 4 p.m. Passed a pleasant country. Saw Mrs Fleming [sic][153] and her two daughters on the road. Put up at the hotel which is about ¼ of a mile from the village which has good beds, but the charge is high.[154] Dined at the Admiral's[155] with his son and Mrs F and two daughters. Spent a pleasant day. The Admiral said that all the highlanders were a lazy set of fellows.

Saturday 27 May. Fine weather. Left Cumbernauld at 8 a.m. by coach and got to Glasgow at 10 a.m. Remained there two hours. Saw Mr Baird, secretary of the Glasgow committee who said they had still a large sum left, and that they had sent two or more gentlemen to the highlands to report on the destitution.[156] Bought maps of the distressed districts and left Glasgow by the. . .[157] steamer at ½ past 1 p.m. Got to Greenock at ½ past 4 p.m. as they call at several places going down. Dumbarton Castle is a fine object. There are also many good houses on the banks of the Clyde. Went to the Tontine Hotel at Greenock which is a clean, good house and charges moderate.[158] Walked around the town in the evening.

Sunday 28 May. Fine weather with some showers. Went to church,[159] a small congregation and not a good clergyman − he preached *ex tempore*. Met Mr [Thomas] Saunders, Collector of Taxes and Mrs S and sat in their seat. Walked out of the town with Mr S. Lt. Engledene dined with us − Mr Waller's friend. Drank tea with Mr Saunders and paid him 8/-. Cloudy with heavy rain.

Monday 29 May. Left Greenock in the *Lochgoil* steamer at ½ past 9 a.m. Squally with rain. Got to the top of this loch[160] at noon. It is about 18 miles from Greenock,

---

152 He was, in fact a Lieutenant G. B. Cumberland.
153 Admiral Charles Elphinstone Fleeming's wife.
154 This was probably the Black Bull, run by William Cowie.
155 Admiral Charles Elphinstone Fleeming.
156 Mr McPhail and John Campbell of Otter, Cairndow (TNA:PRO, Treasury, T 1/4201, Interim report by the committee in Glasgow for the relief of the destitute inhabitants of the highlands and islands of Scotland, 29 Apr. 1837 − see p. 227 below).
157 Blank in the original.
158 The hotel was on Cathcart Street and was run by James Macdonald.
159 The Episcopalian chapel was on Union Street, where the minister was the Rev. Richard Martin.
160 Arrochar on Loch Long.

passing through a most mountainous and beautiful country for scenery and reminded me of Newfoundland.[161] As soon as we landed, an open omnibus with three horses came down to the pier, which they called the coach that runs to Loch Fyne which is 7 miles distant and we passed through a very mountainous road where several fine waterfalls appeared. We were two hours performing this seven mile journey and got out at 2 p.m. at St Catherine's public house close to Loch Fyne, opposite to Inveraray and directly in view of the duke of Argyll's castle, named Inveraray Castle. We got into the Argyll steam-boat of eight horse power, very neat and well managed. It is two miles across the loch and we paid 1/- each and landed at Inveraray about 2 p.m. at Walker's Hotel.[162] It is a pretty village and looks very clean and is surrounded with some fine woods belonging to the duke.[163] Some of the largest oaks are here that I have seen in Scotland. Two Paisley gentlemen joined us and we got post horses and a noddy[164] from Mr Walker and set off at 3 p.m. for Loch Awe. A very hilly road and passed through a very barren country of 12 miles and arrived at the Portsonachan ferry house at Loch Awe at 6 p.m. Had to wait one hour as there is only one ferry-boat and a carriage had just set off before us. No post horses are to be had on either side of the loch, so that we were obliged to take the same horses. 8 miles further on the Paisley gentlemen left us at the loch. These 8 miles was a barren country, but not so hilly. Got to the post house at Taynuilt at 9 p.m. Beds all full, took two fresh horses and arrived at Oban at ½ past 11 p.m. These last twelve miles is a tolerable level road and the latter part a better cultivated country, but it was too dark the last hour and half to see anything. Paid 1/6 per mile. Put up at the Caledonian Hotel at Oban, a clean house.[165] This village is situated close to the shore and forms a sort of semi-circle round the bay. The country round about hilly and poor land. It has a good pier, for the steamers and all the northern boats call here to and from Glasgow. It is much frequented in the summer by visitors and strangers.[166]

---

[161] This was in 1788, when Hill was serving as an able seaman and master's mate on the *Nautilus* (TNA:PRO, Admiralty; Memorandum of the services of Captain Sir John Hill, ADM 9/36, 1868).

[162] According to *Pigot*, 226, there were three inns and posting houses at Inveraray; the George, run by John Walker, and the Argyll Head, run by Robert McKellar, are both described in G. and P. Anderson, *Guide to the Highlands and Islands of Scotland* (London, 1834), 337, as large and commodious; the third, the Inveraray Inn, was run by James McNab.

[163] *Pigot*, 225, describes Inveraray thus: 'Every stranger is struck with the neatness of the town which, though small, is well-built and some of the houses approach to elegance'.

[164] A kind of light two-wheeled cab having a door at the back, and a seat for the driver in front (*Dictionary of the Scots Language*, http://www.dsl.ac.uk/).

[165] The hotel was on George Street and was run by Duncan McArthur.

[166] Oban was described in Anderson, *Guide*, 272, as consisting of about a hundred substantial houses and two excellent inns, 'all whitewashed with lime, and the appearance of the place is extremely neat and cheerful'. *Pigot*, 232, says there were three excellent inns, of which the Caledonian Hotel was the principal.

Tuesday 30 May. At Caledonian Hotel, Oban. This place is always visited by foreigners and strangers going to the islands.[167] Fine, mild weather with some showers. The landlord of this hotel, Mr McArthur, said he was one of the local committee but had declined acting. They had subscribed about £60 for the poor which sum was nearly exhausted and that they had now about 50 bolls of oatmeal in Mr Stevenson's store[168] which had been sent from Glasgow. I sent for Mr Maclachlan (banker)[169] and Mr [Archibald James] Campbell, a bachelor of Kilpatrick who lodges in the town.[170] Neither of these gentlemen, nor the landlord of the inn, were disposed to give me any information. Capt. McDougall RN.[171] called on me and said that the local committee was formed of dealers and jobbers and that a Mr [Campbell] Paterson who is a writer and general dealer managed the whole concern, and he had no doubt he made 40 per cent. of all the supplies sent through his hands. He had now left matters in his clerk's hands and had gone to settle in Mull. We went with one of his clerks to see the oats in the store which was part in an open shed getting damp and eaten by rats. There were also about 10 bolls of potatoes which the clerk said belonged to the committee but he afterwards contradicted it, but I evidently saw it had been tampered with by some persons. 44 barrels of gunpowder were a-lying in store. Part of the oats were in bulk and some Mr Paterson had changed. In short, everything had the appearance of being badly conducted. Mr Caustey, a dealer, also called, off whom the committee at Edinburgh had bought seed oats. Mr. . .of. . . a gentlemen named in Mr Graham's Oban report[172] called, but was not disposed to give any information. Meal was selling from 18 to 22 shillings per boll of 140 lbs and potatoes at 5s. per barrel. Called on Mr Stevenson who is a distiller and general merchant[173] who said not any relief was wanted except to the aged and infirm. Went to the mill where the miller said he would grind all the oats into meal for 10d. per boll and produce an equal quantity, that is for every boll of oats a boll of meal. Total quantity of oats over bought for seed, 428 bolls. Drank tea at Capt. McDougalls's with his wife and sister. He is building a new part to his house and has a large property round the town of Oban extending about three miles. The greater part of the island of Kerrera immediately opposite the town belongs to him. His house is situated on the hill about 1 mile from the town looking up the

---

[167] There were separate connections by steam-boat to Fort William, Inverness, Fort Augustus, Islay, Iona, Staffa, Tarbert, Skye, Stornoway Tobermory, Glasgow, Lochgilphead, Greenock and Liverpool (*Pigot*, 234).
[168] At the Oban distillery.
[169] James Maclachlan, Oban agent for the National Bank of Scotland.
[170] At Main Street.
[171] Captain John McDougall of McDougall, RN. The family estates had been forfeited in 1715 and later restored to McDougall's grandfather, Alexander (*NSAc*, vii, 525).
[172] Blank in the original; it is not possible to identify which of the people interviewed by Graham this individual was.
[173] John Stevenson, the grandson of Hugh Stevenson who, together with his brothers John and James, had established the Oban distillery in 1797–8.

Sound of Mull and a part of a very ancient castle is close to it.[174] He was very civil and sent me his phaeton[175] to take me to the hotel as it came on a very wet night. Wrote a letter to Mr Bowie stating how badly the oats were taken care of and recommending it to be converted into meal.

Wednesday 31 May. Fresh breezes from the westward with showers. An excise cutter came in last evening and sailed this morning. Several steam boats called here yesterday. Paid the bill, the charges nearly as high as Glasgow and about equal to the Tontine Hotel at Greenock. Left Oban at one p.m. in the *Staffa* steam boat. The doctor Mr Graham recommended me to see had left the place and another medical man, Doctor [John Peter] McGregor called on me and said the committee was not well managed and that relief was not fairly afforded. He hinted at jobbery going on and said he was not allowed to interfere but that he knew everyone in the parish as he had lived, and been in practice many years, at Oban. We had about 20 cabin passengers and a great deal of luggage on deck and goods in the hold. This vessel had left Glasgow at 7 a.m. yesterday and came through the Crinan Canal and got to Oban at ½ past 11 a.m. Strong easterly wind and rather cold with some showers. Passed the lighthouse on the point in the island at 2 p.m. which is a guide to vessels going through the Sound of Mull in the night. All through this Sound is a mountainous country on both sides with portions of cultivated lands. A great many cattle and sheep are fed in these districts. The barley and oats both on Mull and on the Argyllshire coast looked very well. We stopped at two places on the mainland and at Salen in Mull to land passengers and got to Tobermory at 7 p.m. being exactly six hours from Oban, a distance of about 30 miles. Here is a good pier and there were about 200 persons on it when we landed, all well clothed and looking healthy. Several coasting vessels in the harbour. Landed and walked all over the upper and lower town. The former is considered the worst part of the place, but their houses is very superior to the Irish in Galway and Mayo.[176] The people are all much better clothed than the Irish. We saw about 15 fishing boats going out to fish. Col. Campbell,[177] Mr Nisbet, a writer,[178] and Mr [John] Campbell [of Cornaig, Coll] called on me and all said they wanted meal. The latter lived at Coll and was on his way to Dumbarton market to sell cattle. He had formerly been a marine officer. Mr Nisbet gave me an account of all the meal that had been sent from Glasgow,

---

[174] Dunolly Castle, the principal seat of the McDougalls, lords of Lorn (see *OGazS*, ii, 443, and *NSAc*, vii, 525).
[175] A species of four-wheeled open carriage, of light construction, usually drawn by a pair of horses and with one or two seats facing forward.
[176] Where Hill had been sent in the summer of 1831 to administer famine relief as agent for the government.
[177] Colonel Donald Campbell of Knock.
[178] Henry Nisbet, WS, who was the Tobermory agent for the British Fisheries Society.

about 72 tons in 10 weeks. They said they would want supplies until the middle of August. Mr Campbell, who had been sent by Glasgow committee, came in the steamer from the popish south end of Mull to this place. He was going his rounds. This looked very much like jobbing away the money. Went to Miss [Barbara Harriet] Cuthbertson's lodgings who keeps the post office and had tea and some whisky punch and went on board the steam boat at 12 o' clock at night.

Thursday 1 June. Fresh breezes with small rain at times. Left Tobermory at 2 p.m. in a heavy swell with the wind against us as far as Ardnamurchan Head; when we passed that we were sheltered by the island of Rum. We passed it and called at Arisaig, a very rocky place and by no means fit for a depot as it is dangerous for ships to enter. We passed the islands of Eigg and Muck which lie at the entrance of the Sound of Skye.[179] All along the main[180] in this Sound which forms part of Invernessshire and Rossshire is very mountainous and picturesque with more or less cultivation, and intersected with lochs and inlets and on the left is eastern coast of Skye where we called at three different places, one of which was Lord Macdonald's castle and Sleat Armadale castle.[181] I hear Oronsay in Skye is where Doctor Boyter[182] means to embark emigrants. [Light breezes and fine weather. On board the *Staffa* steam boat in the Sound of Skye on our way to Portree, calling at various places on the main in Invernessshire and Rossshire and at Glenelg which lately belonged to his Lordship. At Oronsay, a small port in the Sound of Skye is where Doctor Boyter intends to have the emigrant ships to lay.][183] After passing the Sound of Skye we entered Applecross Sound[184] and passed close to the island of Scalpay. We were obliged to go outside this island as it was nearly low water; there is a passage at high water between it and the main, but quite dry at low water spring tides.[185] We passed inside of Raasay island and got to Portree at 5 p.m. The town lays on the side of a hill and the harbour is well sheltered. It was the last day of the fair and we ran alongside the pier where there were about 400 people who all came down to see the steam-boat come in; all of which looked very well and healthy

---

179   The Sound of Sleat.
180   Hill uses the word 'main' rather than 'mainland' throughout his journal.
181   These are one and the same, unless Hill was referring to Duncscaith Castle on the west coast of Sleat.
182   Dr David Boyter, RN, was a naval surgeon appointed by Governor Sir Richard Burke of New South Wales in 1836 as 'colonial emigration agent' in Scotland, with a roving commission to find suitable candidates for emigration and to liaise with T. F. Elliot, the British government's agent-general for bounty emigration (see the Introduction).
183   This section within square brackets appears repetitious. Hill's manuscript journal at this point started a fresh page that seems to have been written some time after the end of the previous sheet.
184   The Inner Sound.
185   Caolas Scalpay leading into Loch na Cairidh.

and well dressed and clothed, not one without shoes or stockings except a few children. There were several booths for whisky exactly like the Irish fairs. The whole population all looked clean and healthy.[186] Two sloops loaded with meal were laying at the quay and several fine boats in the harbour. Visited several of the cabins in the suburbs of the town which were nearly better than in Ireland. Went to the hotel kept by Mr Jamieson but could only get one bed.[187] Mr Waller slept at Mr Maxwell's.[188] Doctor Boyter had made this house his headquarters and occupied the two best rooms so that I had not a very good bed.[189] The house was in confusion in consequence of the fair. There had been a large cattle fair at this place the day before and one this day about 5 miles off. All these people are quite like the Irish on the NW coast both in manners and are as fond of the whisky and a fight after the fair, but they don't fight with sticks.[190] Mr Macdonald the meat-curer called on me. Received a letter from Capt. Oliver[191] of the *Prince of Wales* revenue cutter[192] to say he had arrived at Snizort and sent two men to take care of baggage. Wrote to him that I would embark tomorrow.

Friday 2 June. Moderate breezes and clear, fine, but cold, weather with N.E wind. Mr McDonald of [. . .] called at 7 a.m. and very kindly offered to take us in his gig to Snizort. Hired a cart for the baggage and left Portree at ½ past 7 a.m. Capt. Oliver came in his boat for us and we embarked at 9 a.m. on board the brig. Portree is about 8 miles from Snizort, a poor country and all the cabins like the Irish but better built and all the people better clothed. We waited two hours for our baggage and three hours for the brig's boat which had gone on shore for meat,

[186] This might be contrasted with Graham's letter of 6 Apr. from Portree (p. 62 above), where he said 'from their looks and personal appearance . . . great misery and even danger of starvation exists among them'.

[187] The Portree Inn, run by John Jamieson.

[188] John Argyll Maxwell, Lord Macdonald's factor, who lived at Portree House in the west of the village.

[189] In Anderson, *Guide*, 457, Portree is described as consisting of 'about a score of houses, half of them slated, amongst which is an elegant and comfortable new inn, a branch of the National Bank of Scotland, a neat church, and a good jail – all overlooking the sea'. The Portree Inn is described in *Pigot*, 497, as being 'good and commodius'.

[190] There were three fairs each year at Portree: May and July were for the sale of black cattle and November for hiring servants. John Macculloch advised against visiting Portree at fair-time: 'do not pay it a visit when all sorts of cattle come to be bought and sold; when horn is entangled in horn and drover with drover, and when the whisking of tails threatens to fit you for the one-eyed society of the copper coloured castle' (J. Macculloch, *The Highlands and Western Isles of Scotland*, 4 vols. (London, 1824), iii, 366); and also A. R. B. Haldane, *The Drove Roads of Scotland* (Argyll, 1951), 144–5).

[191] Captain Benjamin Oliver, the commander of the *Prince of Wales*, who lived at Sandwick Cottage in Stornoway.

[192] One of the four coastguard cruisers similar to the *Swift* commanded by Mr Beatson and used by Graham.

etc. Worked out of the harbour and cleared the outer head[193] about 5 p.m. Made all sail for Lochboisdale which is about 50 miles distant, where we anchored at midnight after a pleasant passage.

Saturday 3 June. Fine, clear weather with fresh breeze, about East. Went on shore at 9 a.m. at Lochboisdale where there is only one single house, which sells whisky and where the 170 qrs. of oats were stored. Saw Mr Finlayson, chief officer of the Fishery, who resides 3 miles distant. He appears to be an intelligent man. The *Tartar* schooner from Ireland with 80 tons of potatoes was laying here and discharged her cargo. She arrived the day before yesterday. All the country about here is very rocky and barren. Visited three cabins, very poor but more room in them than in Ireland. There were about 70 persons round the place, all well clothed and the men standing around with their hands in their pockets. The corn and potatoes were generally all full of weeds and cultivated in the roughest possible manner. They all fish more or less about here and catch the finest ling I ever saw, which the factor pays to them only 6d for. I bought four not less than 14 lbs. each for 2s. Gave orders as to disposal of 10 tons of potatoes and 60 qrs. of oats as per letter book to Mr Finlayson. Returned on board again at 2 p.m. and got under way for Lochmaddy in North Uist. McCrae, factor of the Boisdale estate which is in trustees' hands came down and wanted to get hold of more potatoes and some of the corn, but I did not like his appearance, and Capt. Oliver told me he was not a very good character. He looked like a jobber. Working to windward all the remainder of this day under single reefed top-sails and top gallant sails, with the wind right against us but clear, fresh weather. Reefed top-sails; anchored in Lochmaddy in North Uist at midnight. A packet sails from here three times a week with letters and a cargo of cattle or fish, etc. Mr [Charles] Shaw jnr. has a house close to the loch. The land about the shore very barren and a few huts scattered about with some plantations of potatoes and oats.

Sunday 4 June. At Lochmaddy in North Uist. Fine, clear weather with E.S.E. wind. Mr [Charles] Shaw jnr. came on board. This island belongs to Lord Macdonald, and Mr [Duncan] Shaw senr. is factor for this island and Harris. Went on shore at 10 a.m. to Mr Charles Shaw's house and saw his father and his mother. At noon the sheriff, Mr MacLachlan,[194] came, who with the two Mr Shaws formed a quorum of local committee. Employed with the local committee in making arrangements with them about the future supplies until next harvest. They all said that the supply of seed oats which I had sent were excellent and had come up and looking far better than their own oat seed. Dined with Mr C. Shaw,

---

[193] Waternish Point.
[194] D. MacLachlan, the sheriff-substitute.

his father, mother and aunt and the sheriff. It came on heavy rain, with S.S.W. wind. Went on board at 9 p.m. Walked out about two miles before dinner. This loch is filled with a number of small islands and there is a manufactory of soda. In this loch is also large quantities of seaweed for kelp.

Monday 5 June. Fine weather with NW wind. At 8 a.m. Doctor Macleod, whom the chancellor of the exchequer wished me to see,[195] came on board as I had sent an express for him. He is the only medical man on the island and wishes much to emigrate either to America or Australia, but prefers the former. He is willing to go on the same terms as a surgeon in the navy. He appears quite a man qualified for this undertaking as he has great influence over all the people and says he could take any number with him.[196] He went with me to Rodel as we weighed anchor at 9 a.m. and got to Rodel at 11 a.m. and landed as the brig could not get into the harbour which is very confined and a ridge of rocks runs across the entrance. It is only fit for boats and small craft. Saw Doctor Clark and Mr Stewart, who is factor for Lord Dunmore[197] who bought all this island (Harris) for £60,000[198] and the rental pays him more than five per cent. Mr S was serving out meal to the tenantry and more than 150 people had come in from all parts of the island for meal, with horses and boats, all of which were well clothed and looking healthy and well. Rode four miles across the island and visited many cottages all of which were superior to the Irish and two and three separate rooms besides an outhouse. The men were all dressed in blue jackets and trousers and all stand about with their hands in their pockets and all are more or less idle, indolent and lazy. Several of the cottages had looms in them and the spinning wheel, and some of the women knit stockings and mitts.[199] All along these islands from Barra to Stornoway and the north end of Lewis more or less fish is caught, of ling, cod, turbot and herrings, also crabs and lobsters. The corn and potatoes all looked very healthy and every prospect of good crops if the weather proved favourable. The Rev. Mr Maciver, minister of this island, and [. . .] who lives about 6 miles

---

[195] See Hill's letter to Spearman of 13 May 1837 (p. 142).

[196] This entry in Hill's journal sheds new light on Dr Alexander Macleod; there is no record in any of the published information about him that he had any interest in emigration. As to his being a person with great influence over all the people, this is certainly the case. He was praised in poetry by the Skye poet Mairi Mhor nan Oran and he had the reputation of being the most popular factor in the Highlands (MacGillivray, 'Medical practice', 285).

[197] Donald Stewart had, in fact, been the factor before Lord Dunmore acquired the island, when Duncan Shaw was appointed estate factor.

[198] George Murray, fifth earl of Dunmore, acquired Harris in 1834 from the bankrupt proprietor, Alexander Norman Macleod, but owned the island for only two years before his death in Nov. 1836, being succeeded by his son Alexander, the sixth earl (on the Dunmore family and Harris, see J. Hunter, *The Islanders and the Orb – The History of the Harris Tweed Industry 1835–1995* (Stornoway, 2001), 27–46).

[199] Tradition has it that the Harris Tweed industry started on the island in around 1840 (Hunter, *The Orb*, 23).

off came to meet me. He and Doctor Clark and Mr Stewart form the local committee here. Transacted business with them and they gave me an account of what would be required until 15ᵗʰ August after which time they would not require any further supply. Gave Mr Maciver a cheque for £15 to purchase 4 tons of potatoes out of the *Tartar* at Lochboisdale. Here is a very ancient church with several monuments inside, and there were three skulls and many human bones lying near one of them. The whole was in a dilapidated state.[200] The land was very good immediately about the church. Took leave of Doctor Macleod and the Rodel committee and went on board at 3 p.m. and made all sail for Stornoway. Passed close to Glass lighthouse near Loch Tarbert;[201] we had a fine breeze off the land and ran close to the shore for 20 miles. Anchored in Stornoway harbour at midnight. Hazy with rain.

Tuesday 6 June. Fine weather with small rain about one hour. Landed at the quay at Stornoway at 10 a.m. with Capt. Oliver and called on Collector of Taxes, Mr [Alexander] McLeay,[202] who showed his accounts of the distribution of the oats and also the oats remaining on hand which were placed in a new house on the quay at 20s per week. He said the house would be let for £14 a year. Walked round the town which has many houses and a large population, as they cure large quantities of fish: ling and cod; and the whole beach was covered with their apparatus.[203] At Capt. Oliver's house, where there is now several hundred tons laying. Saw Mr Knox who is Stewart Mackenzie's factor for all the island of Lewis. He appeared an intelligent man and said he had received 814 bolls of meal from Glasgow committee and had about 30 remaining. He did not approve of meal being sent at first[204] but as it has begun they would now require 800 more bolls to carry them through. He thought the people would not go to Australia but some would go to America. He did not seem disposed to give any more information than he could help, but as there is no other person at Stornoway who could be depended on all supplies had better be sent to him. There must be some merchants here making

---

[200] The church, dedicated to St Clement, of the old Augustinian Priory at Rodel, was restored at the end of the nineteenth century.

[201] Eilean Glas on Scalpay, one of the four original lights commissioned by the commissioners of the Northern Lights; the light was first displayed in 1789 and the original tower was replaced in 1824 by Robert Stevenson.

[202] A. R. McLeay, who was also Captain Oliver's son-in-law.

[203] Stornoway was described in 1834 as being a place which 'the stranger is surprised at finding so considerable and flourishing a place in so remote and uninviting a corner. It is a fishing establishment with several streets of substantial and slated homes, and numerous shops' (Anderson, *Guide*, 482).

[204] This comment is odd because Knox had written to Stewart Mackenzie in Feb. 1837, reporting on the requirements of meal for the island to carry the people through the famine, which made it clear that large supplies of meal would be required (NRS, Papers of the Mackenzie family, earls of Seaforth, GD 46/13/199/4, Knox to Stewart Mackenzie, 7 Feb. 1837); see also Graham's letter of 14 Apr. 1837 (p. 76).

money, and although the population is great round the town they must have plenty of employment in curing the fish, of which there were large quantities and I do not consider this place so much in distress. The parsons about here are large farmers and I do not think them better than the priests.[205] Very avaricious in getting all they can lay their hands on. Dr Millar[206] told me they had a very good fishery season this year and more fish had been caught than for some years before.[207] Drove out 7 miles across the island and saw the western ocean, but it was quite a waste, boggy land all the way and we saw only one herdsman's cottage and had a glass of whisky and returned to the town and dined at Capt. Oliver's with his wife and daughter and son and son-in-law, the Collector of Taxes. Eggs are sold at 2 ½ d per dozen, fowls from 4d to 6d each and mutton at 2 ½ d per lb. Fish is in great abundance here. We returned on board at 11 p.m.

Wednesday 7 June. At Stornoway. At 10 a.m. weighed and made sail for Ullapool; light breezes and fine weather with N.E. wind. Dr Millar came off at 8 a.m. Gave him an order for 6 qrs. of oats for meal for sick. Made all sail for Ullapool which lays up a deep loch in Rossshire. Anchored at 8 p.m. off the village which is on an isthmus on the North-east side of the loch. Went on shore and saw Mr Ross, the clergyman.[208]

Stornoway, Isle of Lewis, Hebrides, 7 June 1837 [Letter from Hill to Spearman]

Sir, Since my letter of the 21st ultimo, I beg leave to acquaint you for the information of my Lords Commissioners of His Majesty's Treasury, that I left Edinburgh on the 26th ultimo and passed through Glasgow and Greenock and left the latter place at 9 a.m. on the 29th for Oban, one of the depots in Argyllshire, passing through the highlands by Lochgoilhead, and Loch Fyne, Loch Awe and by Inveraray and Taynuilt to Oban where we arrived

---

205   It has been said that it may have been a justifiable complaint of the evangelicals that the moderate ministers may have been more interested in farming than religion, an example of whom was the Rev. Alexander Macleod of Uig (Lawson, *Lewis*, 216–17; and see also Fullarton and Baird, *Remarks*, 26, on the minister in one of the Uists).

206   Dr Roderick Millar of North Beach Street, Stornoway, who had conversations with Hill about emigration and Hill asked him to make enquiries as to the disposition of the people to emigrate and to report back to Hill with the result (see Hill's letter to Spearman of 7 July 1837 and enclosure, p. 181 below).

207   In a letter to Alderman Pirie in the City of London, who had asked for information as to how the people of Lewis could be helped, Stewart Mackenzie had spoken in positive terms about the prospects for the fisheries – 'the sea round the island teems with fish, and the great cod banks on the west is supposed to equal that of Newfoundland' (NRS, Papers of the Mackenzie family, earls of Seaforth, GD 46/13/199/6, Stewart Mackenzie to Pirie, 13 Jan. 1837).

208   The Rev. Alexander Ross.

at midnight. I found a surplus of about 321 quarters of seed oats which I suggested to the Edinburgh committee should be converted into meal, as I visited a mill at the place and the miller was willing to make this conversion at a moderate expense; the oats were not so well stored or taken care of as I could wish. There are two whisky distilleries[209] at this place and oatmeal was selling at 21/- the boll of 140 lbs. Captain McDougall of the Royal Navy who resides about a mile from Oban, informed me that he did not consider the distress so great as was represented and that very little or no aid would be required. I also saw a medical man, Doctor McGregor, who was of the same opinion. The master of the hotel where I put up[210] was one of the local committee and others who were dealers in meal were not of the same opinion, and were very reluctant in giving me any information except a Mr Stevenson who showed me 50 bolls of oatmeal which were the remains of a supply sent by the Glasgow committee, and who said that supplies of food in times like these tended to demoralise the people by encouraging idleness and their habitual indolence. All the population in and about the places we passed through, and in Oban, were looking very healthy and well clothed, far superior to many of the poor in the remote parts of the western coast of Ireland.

I left Oban on the 31ˢᵗ ultimo at noon by steam boat and passed through the Sound of Mull and arrived at Tobermory, another of the depots, at 7 a.m. and on entering the harbour there were not less than 300 of the inhabitants, men, women and children, came down to see us land, all of which appeared healthy and well clothed and there was not the least appearance of want or famine depicted in their circumstances. We walked around the town and saw most of the inhabitants. There is a whisky distillery at this place.[211] Colonel Campbell of Knock, chairman of the local committee, called on me and stated that they had received all the seed corn and potatoes and they were all planted and the former looking well. He also stated that they had received a large supply of meal (72 tons) from the Glasgow committee, but that much more would be required before harvest time. I told him I should see the committee on my return as I was obliged to avail myself of the steam boat proceeding on, to go by Portree. In passing through the Sound of Mull we observed the cultivated lands on the Argyllshire coast and on the Sound of Mull were all looking in a very flourishing condition and more or less cattle and sheep are fed in these districts. We also observed 15 fishing boats going out to fish.

[209] The two distilleries were New Cleigh distillery, owned by Angus McInnes, and Oban distillery, which was founded by Hugh, John and James Stevenson in 1797–8 (J.R. Hume and M.S. Moss, *The Making of the Scotch Whisky Distillery Industry* (Edinburgh, 2000), 320; *Pigot*, 233). The distillery industry also suffered from the weather conditions which had contributed so much to the famine: the wet weather made it impossible to dry the peats, making malting and distilling very difficult (Hume and Moss, *Scotch Whisky*, 93).

[210] Duncan McArthur of the Caledonian Hotel, Oban.

[211] Tobermory distillery established by John Sinclair in 1795.

We left Tobermory at 1 a.m. on the 1st of June,[212] passing round by Ardnamurchan Head and between the islands of Muck, Eigg and Rum, and through the Sound of Skye, calling off Arisaig, another of the depots, but as the steam boat would not wait for me, I could not land. But this place is so surrounded with rocks I consider it a very improper place to send vessels to, and on my return to Glasgow and Edinburgh shall recommend the depot to be discontinued. From Arisaig we passed through the Sound of Skye calling at several places on the eastern side of the island and at Glenelg. The cultivated parts of Skye and the coast on the mainland in Invernessshire and Rossshire were all looking in a very thriving condition and the few of the population that we saw in the several boats and places we touched at, looked well and healthy.

We passed through parts of the Sound of Applecross and arrived at Portree in the Isle of Skye at 5 p.m., another of the depots. This town is situate at the head of a good harbour and has a pier; and a fair had been held there which gave us an opportunity of seeing a greater portion of the population than we otherwise could have had, and not less than 400 persons came down to the pier to see the steam boat, all of which were well clothed and looking in the most healthy condition. The little whisky booths which were pitched for the fair were exactly similar to what are used in the fairs in Ireland, and these people resembled very much the inhabitants on the shores of the north west coast of Ireland, in the county of Donegal where I was last autumn.[213] I was also informed they had no dislike to a little fighting before parting for home. We walked in the town and passed the suburbs and visited several of the cabins which are similarly constructed to those in the county of Donegal, but more internal comfort as they have two or more apartments in them. There were two sloops lying there at the quay, loading with meal which was selling at 21/- per boll. Doctor Boyter was here at the only public house in the place, and only one spare bed could be got which obliged Mr George Waller to accept of one at the house of a Mr Maxwell who resides here. The *Prince of Wales* revenue cruiser had arrived at Loch Snizort the day before at which port I requested Captain Knight of the coast guard to place this vessel for me.

At 6 a.m. on the 2nd of June we left Portree and crossed the island of Skye and arrived at Loch Snizort at 9 a.m. and went immediately on board the brig. Captain Oliver then got under weigh [sic] and made all sail for the Long Islands or Hebrides and we arrived at Lochboisdale in South Uist at midnight where I found the *Tartar* had anchored the day before with the last cargo of potatoes of 80 tons which I had ordered from Ireland. Went on shore on the morning of the 3rd of June and saw Mr Finlayson the fishery officer stationed here, who gave me

---

[212] In his journal, Hill records leaving Oban at 2 p.m. on 1 June (p. 152).
[213] This refers to when Hill was sent by the government to Donegal in Ireland to establish the state of distress on the north-west coast and to ensure that government relief was limited strictly to that necessary for the preservation of human life (see the Introduction).

every information I wanted and showed me the surplus of seed oats, about 161 quarters remaining in store here. He was employed in unloading the *Tartar* and distributing the seed potatoes agreeable to previous arrangements; and there were about 80 of the country people and some boats which had come in from various parts with their creels and ponies, all of whom looked comfortably clothed and looking healthy. We visited several of their cottages which were similar to what I had seen in Donegal. The country on this side of the island is rocky and barren, but Mr Finlayson stated the western side was much more fertile. More or less fishing is carried on here and very fine ling and cod are caught in abundance. The factors allow the people sixpence each for the former and four pence for the latter. The men are more or less indolent and lazy and fond of hanging about with their hands in their pockets, instead of being industrious and keeping their potato grounds clear of weeds.[214] Mr Finlayson stated, and so did several other persons I saw, that all the seed corn had grown and had given great satisfaction and was looking in a very flourishing condition. After placing four tons of surplus potatoes at Mr Finlayson's disposal for the poor, I returned on board the brig. Mr Finlayson stated that 400 bolls of meal would be required for this island to carry them through until harvest time, the latter end of August.

At 3 p.m. we got under weigh [sic] and made all sail for Lochmaddy in North Uist where we arrived at midnight, and on the following morning went on shore (Sunday) to Mr Charles Shaw where I met his father who is the factor for all the island and Benbecula, and all the estates in these islands. The sheriff substitute Mr McLauchlan came to meet me and these three gentlemen formed a quorum in the local committee. They stated they had received all the seed corn and potatoes which had been sent and all had been planted except the *Tartar's* cargo, and the corn was much liked and was looking very well. They stated that they had received supplies of meal from the Glasgow committee and had enough to last around 20 days but they would require 500 bolls to carry them through until harvest time. They appeared to have managed their business well. There is a manufactory of soda here.[215] The country about this is rocky but on the west coast, they stated, was a much more fertile and productive country. I waited here all the remainder of this day and night to see Doctor Macleod on the subject of emigration, agreeable to the wish of the chancellor of the exchequer, and to whom I have written this day on the subject. He did not arrive until the morning of the 5th when we immediately weighed anchor and made sail for Loch Rodel in Harris island, but the harbour was too small for the brig to enter and I desired Captain Oliver to lay to and we went on shore where I met the Rev. Mr Maciver, Doctor Clark and Mr Stewart, all of the local committee, and the latter was serving out meal to Lord Dunmore's tenantry to whom he is factor, which

---

[214] In his report on his mission in Donegal in 1836, Hill had made similar comments on the people (see the Introduction).

[215] See Graham's letter of 26 Apr. 1837 on p. 90.

gave us a good opportunity of seeing about 150 of the peasantry who had come in from various parts of the island with ponies and in boats, to get their supplies, all of which looked healthy and decently clothed. We obtained a horse and cart and drove about 4 miles into the country which gave us a good opportunity of seeing the growth of the oats which had been imported, and there was a marked difference in the strength and health of the plants over those raised from the seed of the islands; and Mr Waller who is with me and has some knowledge of farming, assured me he never saw finer oat plants in his life; and the clergyman and the above named gentleman were of the same opinion it would be of the greater benefit to the island for some years to come, provided they had a good harvest. We visited several of the cottages, most of which were roomy and some had looms and spinning wheels, but the men were standing about idle as usual, and the committee told us they were as lazy and idle as those we had seen in the other islands. The committee had about 12 bolls of meal remaining of the last supply sent by the Glasgow committee, and they stated that they would require 350 bolls to carry them through up to harvest time. I gave the clergyman Mr Maciver £15 to purchase four tons of potatoes out of the *Tartar* at Lochboisdale which the master of her had to dispose of. The committee appeared to have managed their district well and gave us every information I wished, and I left them and returned on board at 3 p.m. and made all sail for Stornoway in the isle of Lewis where we anchored at midnight.

We went on shore yesterday morning the 6th and saw the Collector of the Customs[216] who had charge of about 98 quarters of surplus seed oats which I looked at and found in good condition, and which I shall order to be converted into meal hereafter. We also saw Mr Knox, factor to Mr Stewart Mackenzie and all the island of Lewis; he said they had received 814 bolls of meal from Glasgow all of which had been issued except about 30 bolls, but more was expected. He said that they would require about 800 bolls of meal to carry them through until harvest time. At this place is a great quantity of fish; ling and cod are cured and there were several hundreds of tons laying on the beach nearly cured; and its being the capital of the Hebrides, I considered that many of the people ought to have the means of purchasing meal at a reduced price, and after much perseverance and pointing out the impropriety of giving meal *gratis* and my offering to send 400 bolls of meal to be sold at 20 per cent. under prime cost, Mr Knox said he thought purchasers might be found for that price, but I told him I could not send it unless he guaranteed to me the return of the money at that rate, which he did, and in passing along all these islands at the three different depots, viz. Lochboisdale, Lochmaddy and Rodel, all the committee men approved of my suggestions of sending some meal to be sold. I saw the clergyman of the parish but I learnt that he and the committee had not acted cordially together.[217] Mr Knox appeared

---

[216] In his journal entry Hill referred to meeting Mr Macleay the collector of taxes.
[217] It is not clear to which of the Lewis clergymen Hill is referring here.

to me to be the best person to entrust the future supplies to. We drove about 9 miles across the island and saw the western ocean but it was a perfect waste of bog and moss land the whole way. Doctor Millar, who is the only medical man in the island,[218] said the population were all very healthy and he had little beyond his allowance of £40 per annum from his present practice and would be glad to emigrate. I gave him six quarters of the surplus oats to convert into meal for the sick, and having walked through the town and suburbs returned on board to sleep at night as there was not any accommodation in the town; and this morning we weighed anchor and made all sail for Ullapool, Rossshire, another of the depots where we anchored at 8.45 p.m. and shall make my inspection tomorrow after which I shall proceed to Loch Ewe and on to Portree and the remainder of the depots, when I will make a further report. Their Lordships will see that I have lost no time and that we have used every exertion in getting through the visitations of the Hebrides in the time herein stated. I omitted to state that there is a large distillery for whisky in Stornoway.[219] The *Hercules* of Aberdeen of 232 tons [. . .], with 166 emigrants on board sailed from Stornoway this morning for Cape Breton and Quebec. We visited this vessel and the master stated he had received these emigrants from the following places, viz. Aberdeen 39; Stornoway 9; and Rossshire 118. I have the honour to be, Sir, your most obedient servant.

Thursday 8 June. Fine, clear weather with light winds. At 10 a.m. went on shore to Mr Ross's house and Mr. . .[220] who told me they wanted meal and gave me an account of all the seed corn and potatoes they had received and also of all the meal. Showed me some of the fishery stores. Saw Mr. . .[221] the fishery officer. Walked all over the town and went to the Inn which appeared clean and had several beds. The people were building a wall round the churchyard. Mr. . .[222] the excise officer told me the meal was not given out fairly and that the postmaster[223] and others of the committee were jobbers and dealers in meal, and the clergyman was as bad as any of them. At 3 p.m. went on board and weighed and made all sail for Loch Ewe with a fine breeze. Saw several boats out for herrings. Anchored in Loch Ewe at ½ past 12 at night. Fine, clear weather.

---

[218] *Pigot*, 742, says that there was another doctor, Alexander McIver of South Beach Street in Stornoway.

[219] Described as being 'on a grand scale' (*NSAc*, xiv, 126); the distillery came into operation in 1829 or 1830 and ceased operations around 1840.

[220] Blank in the original.

[221] Blank in the original, but the fishery officer was said to be Mr McPhail in Graham's letter of 11 Apr. (p. 68 above).

[222] Blank in the original.

[223] Mrs Mackenzie.

Friday 9 June. At Loch Ewe. Mr. . .and Mr. . .[224] from Dingwall came on board and took breakfast, but both said they knew nothing about the distress. Went on shore at 10 a.m. and saw the Reverend Mr Macrae, the clergyman of the parish,[225] who is the only person who does all the business of the local committee here. He gave me the accounts of all the seed corn received and also all the meal which had been sent from Glasgow, but appeared very reluctant for any being sent for sale, but consented at last. He appeared very avaricious for more meal and said all his whole population wanted it *gratis*, as they had no money. The houses and cottages both here and at Ullapool was worse constructed than any we had seen, but all the crops of oats were looking well. The master of the Inn and other men told me that meal would sell if sent, and the former said that the postmaster at Ullapool was a jobber and retailer of meal. There is not a medical man living within 50 miles of Loch Ewe or Ullapool. The clergyman at the latter place has resided there 15 years and the one at the former, seven years and is married to the parson's daughter at Gairloch.[226] He has one child nine months' old and appears desirous to emigrate. Visited several cottages and went up to the head of Loch. . .[227] which is eighteen miles long. At the head of it there is a good road for a carriage to Dingwall.[228] At Loch Ewe they make pickled salmon. We went into the curing house and saw the large copper where they boil the salmon about half-an-hour before it is put into the [. . ..] It is cut up into pieces before it is boiled and vinegar only is put into the [. . ..] Gairloch is only 5 miles from here by land, where there is a good house belonging to. . .[229] which lets for £100 a year and a party of gentlemen come down for about 3 months to fish and shoot every season. All the men about here are very indolent and well clothed. The women do all the hard work. At 5 p.m. got under weigh [sic] and made all sail for Portree. Light breezes and variable winds, several small vessels in sight.

Saturday 10 June. Squally with heavy rain. At ½ past 2 a.m. anchored in Portree Harbour, Island of Skye, about a cable's length from the shore. At 10 a.m. went on shore to the inn which is kept by Mr Jamieson, a very clean, comfortable house.

---

[224] Blank in the original in both cases.
[225] Rev. Donald Macrae, the minister of Poolewe.
[226] Jessie, daughter of the Rev. James Russell of Gairloch.
[227] Blank in the original but Hill is referring to Loch Maree.
[228] The road from Poolewe (the port through which all communications with the island of Lewis had passed) to Dingwall had a somewhat tortured history (see A. R. B. Haldane, *New Ways through the Glen* (Argyll, 1995), 107, and Smith, 'Isolation to Integration', 155–9).
[229] Blank in the original; Hill may be referring to Sir Francis Alexander Mackenzie, bart., the twelfth laird of Gairloch and Conon, and his mansion, Flowerdale House. On the death of Sir Francis in 1843, the estate of some 192,000 acres was managed by Dr John Mackenzie, who became a prominent figure in Highland farming and estate management and a firm opponent of emigration as a solution to the Highland problem (MacGillivray, 'Dr John Mackenzie', 81–100).

Mr Macleod the banker[230] and Mr Macdonald of the local committee called and gave me an account of all the seed corn and seed potatoes they had received and also how they had disposed of the same. Called on Mr Maxwell, factor to Lord Macdonald, but he was from home collecting rents. Saw Miss Maxwell and Miss Macleod, the former his sister and the latter daughter of Doctor Macleod, Moderator. Drove out 8 miles on the road to the Cuillin mountains where we had a splendid view of the wild scenery about them. The road was quite as good as in any gentleman's park in England, but quite barren land all the way with large quantities of cattle and sheep feeding. There were not six cottages the whole way. Returned at 5 p.m. Capt. Oliver and Mr Bell dined with us and we all drank tea with Miss Maxwell. Miss Macleod played on the piano and there was another lady of the party. The clergyman of Harris[231] called who lives near Tarbert and said they were much in want of supplies of meal, and quite agreed it would be a good plan to send some for sale which the local committee here also wished to have some. Mr Macleod the banker said that many of the people went away from this island to seek work in the south and east of Scotland and were constantly remitting money to their relations and friends, even from London and other parts of England. But they were all very indolent in the island. The committee did not think that Doctor Boyter was doing any good in selecting the people for emigration, as he would only take mechanics and men fit for shepherds, and refused sailors. Everywhere that I have been it was the general wish that the people should be taken away by families. Miss Maxwell said persons had been tampering with the people and telling them if they went to Australia they would be eaten by serpents and cannibals and would be constantly at war, and many had declared off from going.[232]

Sunday 11 June. Fine weather with showers; the country looking very well. At 10 a.m. drove to Snizort church. The Rev. Mr McLauchlan[233] performed the service in Gaelic and English. We were 3 hours in church. It was quite full, not less than 700 persons, all decently clothed and very attentive. The poor people sat on stones in the aisles and round the pulpit.[234] Mrs McLauchlan was there. After church, went to his house and he said all his parish was in distress and that

[230] Roderick Macleod, the agent in Portree for the National Bank of Scotland.
[231] The Rev. John MacIver.
[232] Bowie wrote to Lord Glenelg at the Colonial Office about the great ignorance of Highlanders about Australia and prejudices of 'the most absurd description' which prompted him to write his Notes on Australia (TNA:PRO, War and Colonial Department and Colonial Office: Emigration original correspondence, CO 384/44/25, Bowie to Glenelg, 8 Nov. 1837).
[233] The Rev. Simon Fraser McLauchlan, the moderator of the presbytery of Skye. When Graham had visited, he had not been able to interview the clergyman as he was away from the parish.
[234] The church was originally intended to seat 450 people, but with the increase in population was later enlarged by 300 seats (NSAc, xiv, 294).

200 bolls of meal per month would be wanted. The father of the Macdonalds was there and lives near Snizort church. Visited several cottages and saw a bag of potatoes in one and cooking potatoes in a pot in another cottage. Drove 16 miles today. Sent all our baggage on board the brig and requested Capt. Oliver to go to Loch Bracadale where I promised to meet him on Tuesday morning. Kept the carpetbag and umbrella only. Paid the bill at the inn (£. . .).[235] Wrote to postmaster to send letter to Tobermory.

Monday 12 June. Cloudy weather. At 6 a.m. left Portree in a gig from the inn and at ½ past 8 arrived at a public house at Sconser,[236] 12 miles from Portree. Passed close to the Cuillin mountains. At 9 a.m. left Sconser and arrived at Broadford at 12 o'clock which is 13 miles distant from Sconser. Through all this land very little of it is cultivated and few inhabitants. The last seven miles very hill and we were obliged to walk a good deal. The clergyman[237] has a good house here which is close to the sea, as is also the inn kept by Mr McInnes, and at the entrance of the Sound of Scalpay which island lays opposite. Took lunch and got a fresh horse and drove on to Sleat which is a small village at the head of the harbour of Isleornsay, the Sound of Skye, where the first ship is to come to take off the emigrants.[238] Doctor Boyter makes Broadford his headquarters and comes over here to collect the emigrants from this and the coast opposite. He was away at Sleat. Fine weather. Called on Mr [Colin] Elder who keeps a shop and is a general dealer. He had a vessel alongside the quay[239] with about 900 bolls of meal which he was selling at 23s per boll. He was one of the local committee and like others said much meal was wanted but no money. All the crops were looking very fine, particularly the oats and potatoes. Drove on to Armadale Castle which is 9 miles from Sleat and about 16 from Broadford. All this 9 miles which is along the Sound of Skye is well cultivated and much better farmed than what we had seen. Got to the Castle at 4 p.m. where we met Mr Bowie, Mr Maxwell, Mr Maclean and Mr. . .[240] Dined at the Castle which is a modern building and cost about £20,000 which the late Lord Macdonald built.[241] It is well surrounded with plantations

---

[235] Blank in the original.
[236] Run by William Smith.
[237] The Rev. John Mackinnon.
[238] This was the *William Nicoll* on 6 July 1837 with 321 emigrants to Sydney, Australia, from Sleat, the neighbouring parish of Strath and the adjoining mainland (Macmillan, *Scotland and Australia*, 276). Embarkation took three days to complete and so many people wanted to emigrate that more people turned up than the ship could actually accommodate (*Edinburgh Evening Courant*, 10 July 1837). The surgeon and superintendent on board was G. Roberts and his medical and surgical journal for the voyage from 3 July to 8 Oct. 1837 is at TNA:PRO, Records of the Admiralty, ADM 101/79/7.
[239] At Isle Ornsay.
[240] Blank in the original.
[241] 'a Gothic edifice of 1815' (C. McKean, 'Graham, James Gillespie (1776–1855)', *ODNB*) after a design by the 'romantic historical architect' James Gillespie Graham (*OGazS*, i, 73).

and faces into the Sound. Mr B. and Mr Maxwell were here collecting the rents and looking about getting the emigrants off. Doctor Boyter had gone over to the mainland. Various opinions seem to exist about emigration. At 9 p.m. left and drove back to Broadford and got there at 11 p.m. Went to bed which was tolerably comfortable but charges high; they charged me 12s for one horse for the day.[242]

Tuesday 13 June. Squally and cloudy weather. At 7 a.m. left Broadford in the Portree gig and drove back to Sconser where Mr [Edward] Gibbon[243] had sent his man and horse and gig the night before. Got into it, drove through the road that lays among the Cuillin mountains and along a very hilly road on the one of the branches of Loch Bracadale and got to Mr Gibbon's house at 4 p.m., a snug cottage.[244] Mrs G. and her son and two nieces were of the party at dinner. We spent a pleasant day and slept there. Mr Gibbons and Capt. Macleod,[245] late paymaster of 27th Regiment, who lives near him, came in the latter's gig to meet us 7 miles on the road, which is good for sheep and cattle and some good cultivated land close to their houses. All the crop looking well.

Wednesday 14 June. At Mr Gibbon's and Capt. Macleod's. Squally with rain at times. Left Mr Gibbon's at 7 a.m. and breakfasted with Capt. Macleod at Drynoch in Loch Bracadale. The former told me he had bought 300 bolls of meal and expected Glasgow committee would pay for it and said 200 bolls more would be wanted, but he also said that it would be better if none had been sent and only a supply of seed was wanted, as it only made people lazy and indolent. He was for emigration by families. It appears quite clear to me that they do not want to increase the population here as they all like to keep them in ignorance and bondage and the clergymen equally the same and are quite as bad as the priests in Ireland as they keep up the Gaelic schools which tends to keep the people in ignorance. Capt. Oliver arrived at the loch yesterday (Tuesday) at 5 p.m. Sent his man to Dunvegan post office for my letters. Went on board the brig at 11 a.m. in Loch Bracadale, strong gale at southwest, could not get to sea. Capt. Macleod

---

[242] Broadford is described in Anderson, *Guide*, 456, as consisting 'of only three houses and the inn which is a comfortable one. The charges, as in most part of Skye, are moderate.'
[243] Factor to Norman Macleod of Macleod, twenty-fifth chief of the Clan Macleod.
[244] At Feorlig.
[245] Hill writes McDonald in his journal, but in the next day's entry for 14 June he had crossed out McDonald and written in Macleod. It is undoubtedly captain and paymaster Martin Macleod of the Macleods of Drynoch, who were among the most prosperous and respected tacksmen on the Macleod estate; Captain Macleod received a silver medal for his services in France with the 27th regiment, and he had retired on half-pay in 1830. He lived at Gesto House until 1845, when he and his wife and children emigrated to Canada (*The Clan Macleod Magazine*, Edinburgh, January 1939, 145; and Lieut.-Col. J. Macinnes, VD, *The Brave Sons of Skye* (London, 1899), 115–16).

has a family of six children and holds a large farm belonging to Mr Macleod[246] for which he pays £700 a year rent to Mr Gibbon who is factor of all Macleod's country which is all laid out in large farms. Very large flocks of sheep are fed on the hills and much fish is caught in the loch and last week 87 young whales came into the loch and Capt. Macleod got all the boats out and drove them all ashore where they were all secured and divided which will give them a good supply of oil. He was boiling the blubber and securing the oil. They all catch plenty of small cod now and plenty of herrings in July and August. Dined at Capt. Macleod's. His mother is sister to General Sir John Macleod, late of the 78th Regiment who was with me in Holland at Williamstadt.[247] Capt. Oliver dined with him. He has a family of seven children and is a pleasant gentlemanly man. Mr Waller went up the loch to fish. Wrote letters home and returned on board at 11 a.m.

Thursday 15 June. Light breezes and fine weather. At 10 a.m. weighed and worked out of the harbour when it fell calm until 8 p.m. The people about Capt. Macleod and Mr Gibbons' farms are not badly off. Moderate breezes. Passed between Canna and Rum islands at midnight.

Friday 16 June. At sea with light winds and fine weather. Passed Ardnamurchan Head and worked up to Tobermory where we anchored at ½ past 12 at noon. At 2 p.m. Col. Campbell[248] and Mr Nisbet[249] came on board and informed me what they absolutely required to last them through the harvest, and as they formed

---

[246] Norman Macleod of Macleod.
[247] Captain Macleod's mother was Alexandrina, whose father was Donald Macleod of Bernera – 'the Old Trojan' – by his third marriage, to Margaret Macleod of Grishornish. Donald Macleod of Bernera was something of a Skye institution; he was born in 1693 and died at the age of 90 in 1783. He was married three times and so numerous were his descendants that they were known as the 'Bernera tribe'. His third wife, who he married at the age of 75, was Margaret, daughter of the Rev. Donald Macleod III of Grishornish, minister of Duirinish, and who was a young lady of 16; she had nine children by the Old Trojan, three sons, the eldest of whom was General Sir John Macleod, and six daughters, the eldest of whom was Alexandrina, who married Norman Macleod, VIII of Drynoch (Macinnes, *The Brave Sons of Skye*, 115 and 120); one of the other daughters, Anne, was the mother of Mary, the wife of Dr Alexander Macleod of Uist (see p. 155 above). Hill's knowledge of General Macleod came from Macleod serving with the 78th regiment in Holland in 1814 when the regiment was sent from Scotland to reinforce, as part of the second brigade, the army commanded by General Sir Thomas Graham (as he then was). Hill was responsible for the transport of the regiment that disembarked at Williamstadt. The regiment took part in the attack on Merxem on 13 Jan. 1814, during which Colonel Macleod (as he then was) was wounded 'but did not quit command of the brigade till he became weak from loss of blood' (A. Bamford, *The British Army in the Low Countries, 1813–1814*, http://www.napoleon-series.org/military/battles/).
[248] Colonel Campbell of Knock.
[249] Henry Nisbet of the British Fisheries Society.

the local committee here I did not think it necessary to land at the town. The former is factor to the duke of Argyll's property in the island and the latter is writer and factor for the British Fishery Society. Mr Gregorson,[250] sheriff-substitute for the district, who resides in Morvern on the mainland opposite, came on board and said they did not want any supplies there, and he seemed not to approve of sending supplies. I do not consider what these gentlemen said was much to be depended upon, as the people cannot be so badly off as represented, as there is plenty of fish to be caught; but the people are too indolent and lazy to work, which the two gentlemen from Loch Sunart and Mr Gregorson said was absolutely true, and all throughout the long islands and on the mainland and in Mull and Skye no man would work under 1s/6d or 2s per day. Mr McNeil, the victualling contractor, came on board and he said he had been in the habit of supplying all these islands with meal and buying their kelp and cattle these last 16 years, and he said it was all a farce about the famine and starvation, as they were not worse off this year than usual, and that the committees were giving meal to those who could afford to buy it, and said he knew of one instance where they had given ½ a boll of meal to a man who was building a house in the island of Skye and many other instances, and it was also reported that the people would not work for the meal as they told the committee they were entitled to it for nothing. At 6 p.m. went ashore to Mr Maclean of Coll's house which is pleasantly situated opposite to Tobermory which he built about 10 years ago.[251] He bought his estate in this island from the duke of Argyll. The garden and fishpond and woods are well laid out and in good order. He has let the house for one year to Lord Orkney.

Tobermory, Isle of Mull, 16 June 1837 [Letter from Hill to Spearman]

Sir, Since my letter to you of the 7th instant, I beg leave to acquaint you for the information of my Lords Commissioners of His Majesty's Treasury that I visited Loch Ullapool on the coast of Cromarty-shire on the 8th instant where I met the clergyman of the parish[252] and some of the local committee and obtained from them an account of what they had received and their remains of meal, and what further supplies would be actually wanted until harvest. They were employing some of the poor to whom they had given meal, in re-building a wall round the churchyard. We visited several of the cottages which were

---

[250] John Gregorson (or Grigorson) of Ardtornish.

[251] Aros House, or Drumfin, which was designed for Hugh Maclean of Coll by William Burn in 1825. It was demolished in 1960.

[252] The Rev. Alexander Ross; the church at Ullapool was one of the forty-three parliamentary churches built under the authority of the 1823 act for building additional places of worship in the Highlands and Islands of Scotland, 4 Geo. IV c.79 (see [PP] 1831 IX (330), 4, 24 and 45); the parish was declared *quoad sacra* by the Act of Assembly, 25 May 1833.

nearly similar to those in the Long Islands, except a few which were not so well constructed; but all the population looked healthy and comfortably clothed. This is one of the fishery stations under the Fishery Board[253] and they have a tolerable good supply of fish here, but the men are as indolent as those in the Long Island. At 5 p.m. I returned on board and sailed for Loch Ewe on the coast of Ross-shire where we arrived at midnight, and on the 9th instant we visited the place which contained only a few houses. I saw the clergyman of the parish[254] who was the only person who conducted the business of the local committee. He gave me all the information I required as to the supplies sent and which would be required until harvest time or the end of August. There is a good salmon fishery here and an establishment for the pickling of salmon which is sent off to the London market via Aberdeen. At both Loch Ullapool and this place I was assured that the supply of seed was of the greatest benefit to them and that all the crops of the same were in a very flourishing condition, and all that we saw were looking very fine. We returned on board in the evening and made all sail for Portree in the island of Skye where we arrived at 2 a.m. on Saturday the 10th instant and went on shore at 10 a.m. and met two of the local committee, Mr Maxwell the chairman who is factor to Lord Macdonald being absent. Having learnt from the former gentlemen what they had received and what further supplies would be wanted, we drove 8 miles into the country and inspected several of the cottages and all the population that we saw, and with those in and about Portree, were all looking healthy, and the young oat plants and potatoes in flourishing condition. On Sunday the 11th we went 8 miles in a contrary direction to what we had been the day before and went to the parish church of Snizort where we had a good opportunity of seeing not less than 700 of the population, all of which looking very healthy. The clergyman[255] was three hours in performing divine service, having first preached in Gaelic and then in English. After the service we went to the clergyman's house, who gave me all the information I required as to the supplies sent and to what would be required, and said his whole population was in absolute want, upon which I remarked that from the specimens I had seen I could not imagine the case was as bad as he stated; and after leaving him I entered several cottages not very far distant from his house. The first I entered had a bag of potatoes and the inmates appeared in their usual state, all healthy and well clothed; and in the second they

---

[253] The fishing village at Ullapool was constructed by the British Society for Extending the Fisheries and Improving the Sea Coasts of the Kingdom (founded as a joint stock company in 1786) between 1788 and 1790 (see Dunlop, *The British Fisheries Society*, 46–65).

[254] The Rev. Donald Macrae; the church at Poolewe was one of the forty-three parliamentary churches built under the authority of the 1823 act for building additional places of worship in the Highlands and Islands of Scotland, 4 Geo. IV c.79 (see [PP] 1831 IX (330) 4, 23 and 44); the district, which was part of the parish of Gairloch at the time, was declared *quoad sacra* by the Act of Assembly, 25 May 1833.

[255] The Rev. Simon Fraser McLauchlan who was transferred to Cawdor on 28 July 1837.

were cooking their pot of potatoes. We returned to Portree in the evening and I requested Captain Oliver to move his vessel round to Loch Bracadale, another port in the island, while I should be visiting the several following places; and on Monday the 12th instant at 6 a.m. we left Portree for Sconser and Broadford passing through a country of about 26 miles, the greater part of which is more or less barren and few inhabitants, but such as we saw were all looking healthy, and on the plots of ground which were cultivated, the oats and potato plants were in a most healthy and flourishing state. At Broadford the clergyman[256] was absent but I made such enquiries as I wanted to be satisfied upon, and then drove to Sleat and Armadale Castle, a further distance of about 18 miles. This part of the island is better cultivated and the plants of potatoes and oats were all looking in remarkably fine condition. At the latter place we met Mr [John] Bowie who had come from Edinburgh, and Mr Maxwell from Portree was also here. Doctor Boyter had fixed on having the first emigrant ship at Isleornsay in the parish of Sleat, and Mr Bowie informed me he had gone over to Ross-shire on that day, but they expected to have the ship from Glasgow ready next week. We left Armadale Castle at 9 p.m. and got back to Broadford at midnight where we slept, and started again at 6 a.m. on Tuesday the 13th instant for Teorlich, passing through the Cuillin mountains' road to Mr Gibbon's house, a distance of about 16 miles. This gentleman is factor to the Macleod property, which is all let out in very large farms from £500 to £1,500 a year rent. Many parts of this country are well cultivated, considerable herds of cattle and thousands of sheep are fed throughout. Having obtained all the information we required from Mr Gibbon, and myself and Mr Waller accommodated with beds at his house (as there was no public house in the district) at 6 a.m. on the 14th instant we left Teorlich and arrived at Loch Bracadale at 9 a.m. where we found Captain Oliver had arrived the day before with the *Prince of Wales*. Captain Macleod, late of the 25th Regiment[257] who has a farm here for which he pays £700 a year rent, received us very hospitably and gave me every information I wanted respecting the supplies sent and what would be wanted until harvest. Both he and Mr Gibbon did not think the people were so well disposed to go to Australia as to America. As it was blowing so hard that the vessel could not sail, I remained with Captain Macleod until the evening. Some of his people were occupied in boiling the blubber of an extraordinary catch of young whales which came into the loch last week consisting of 89 of these fish. From 18 to 27 feet long, all of which he with his people and the boats of the loch succeeded in driving on shore and securing the whole. At 10 a.m. yesterday we left Loch Bracadale. The factor and other persons holding property in this island seem disposed not to cultivate much of the soil,

---

[256] The Rev. John Mackinnon, described by Sir Archibald Geikie as 'the best example of a highland clergyman I ever knew' (*FES* vii, 183).

[257] Captain Macleod was, in fact, late of the 27th regiment – see Hill's journal entries for 13 and 14 June (p. 166).

but prefer converting the farms into sheep walks and grazing lands, vast ranges of which are now in progress of conversion, which I consider is a great cause of the want of employment for the people, and tends to multiply their wants, from their inability to purchase them. We arrived here at 1 p.m. this day, and I shall endeavour to see the local committee tomorrow and obtain all the information I want respecting this island, and then proceed to Oban and Fort William and the two remaining depots, and from the latter place, proceed to Glasgow and Edinburgh, when I will address you again. I have the honour to be, Sir, your most obedient servant.

Saturday 17 June. In Tobermory Harbour on board *Prince of Wales*, cloudy and light airs with rain at times. At 8 a.m. weighed for Oban. Mr [Hugh] Maclean [of Coll] came on board to breakfast. He came down in the steam boat last night to meet Doctor Boyter about emigration.[258] Doctor Boyter came from Armadale last evening to Tobermory but finding Colonel Campbell on board the steam boat the Doctor did not land but went on in the steam boat with Colonel [Donald] Campbell [of Knock] to his house. Calm and hazy with rain. At 11 a.m. the tide came against us. The steam boat that came from Glasgow sailed at 6 a.m. this morning for Staffa and Iona and was to get to Oban in the evening. A breeze sprung up; made sail again at 6 p.m.; anchored for the tide off Scallastle. Went ashore and saw the Rev. Mr Clark[259] who was very civil and offered us beds. Visited several of the cottages which was all comfortable and the people looking healthy. There is a very good road all along the island of Mull on this side. Mr Clark stated what quantity of meal he had received and what would be wanted. Returned on board at 9 p.m. Light airs and fine weather. All the crops looking well.

Sunday 18 June. Light breezes and hazy with rain. At 5 a.m. weighed and made sail down the Sound of Mull for Oban and anchored in Oban at ½ past 11. Sent letters on shore. Paid Captain Oliver by cheque £15 and £1 to steward. At 6 p.m. landed and went to the Caledonian Hotel. Called on the miller[260] who

<hr/>

258 Maclean of Coll was to have extensive correspondence at the end of 1837 and in 1838 with the Colonial Office about emigration; his plan was for the government to grant him a large tract of land in Australia and advance him £42,400 over five years for the transfer of 1,500 emigrants and he would send, at his own expense a further 1,500. He was, he said, 'a Highland proprietor who having lost one third of his income by the annihilation of kelp manufacture, have consequently a large surplus population which must either ruin me, starve or emigrate' (TNA:PRO, War and Colonial Office: Emigration original correspondence, CO 384/44/180, Maclean to Glenelg, 25 Nov. 1837, and CO 384/44/185, Maclean to Grey, 4 Dec. 1837).
259 The Rev. Duncan Clark (or Clerk), the minister of Torosay.
260 Neil McCulloch, a corn miller and wood turner at Oban Mill.

was grinding the oats into meal. Took leave of Captain Oliver and drank tea at Captain McDougall's [of Dunolly castle] who said there was no distress about them and it was all humbug got up by Edinburgh lawyers and others and the first he heard of destitution was in an Edinburgh paper.

Monday 19 June. At Oban, Caledonian Hotel; cloudy with small rain. At 9 a.m. left Oban in a gig and one horse which I engaged for 30s to go to Fort William and back. About 5 miles from Oban we crossed Connel ferry and paid 2s 6d. At the end of 5 more miles we crossed Shian ferry and paid 3s 6d and drove 16 miles and then crossed Ballachulish ferry and paid 1s 6d. All along this road which is an excellent one, very level, the scenery is very fine and all the crops are looking in the most flourishing condition. The canal boats are all bad and the passage boats very small. The tides run very strong up and down these ferries, and when blowing hard it must be difficult to cross. Went to the Caledonian Hotel in Fort William[261] where we arrived at 6 p.m. Not a very good house. Had tea and sent for the principal officer of customs[262] who gave me an account of meal, corn and potatoes sent here. Mr [James] McGregor, an advocate[263] and factor to Lord Huntley, and the Rev. Mr Swanson[264] both of the local committee, called and the former promised to send me an exact account of all the seed corn and potatoes sent here and how it was disposed of. He said he would send it to Edinburgh. Saw a sloop alongside the quay with 300 bolls of meal on board her. Walked all round Fort William where there was a subaltern party of thirty men of the 76th Regiment. Mr Swanson did not wish to have any more meal sent, but Mr McGregor pressed hard for thirty more bolls which he said would be quite enough.

Tuesday 20 June. Fine, clear weather. At 6 a.m. went in a gig to the entrance of the Caledonian Canal where there is 9 pairs of gates and one swing bridge and 5 pairs of gates at the entrance near the sea. All the people looking well and healthy and the crops very fine. Returned to Hotel to breakfast and left Fort William at 10 a.m. It is a small town with a population of about 1,200. Ben Nevis, the highest mountain in Scotland, is close to it. Very fine weather. Got to the ferry at Ballachulish at ½ past 11, went over and fed the horse. Both these ferry houses has beds but the one on the Oban side is the better, and has a good open brake[265] and a car to let with horses.[266] The other man has only a bad gig and a cart. Met the 8 ladies who left Oban in the two cars who were going to Fort William and

---

[261] Run by Donald Cameron.
[262] Charles Reid.
[263] He was, in fact, a writer to the signet.
[264] The Rev. John Swanson, the minister of Fort William.
[265] Or break – a large wagonette.
[266] The inn at South Ballachulish is described in *Pigot*, 217, as being 'very comfortable'.

by the canal to Inverness. Set off again and got to the ferry house at Loch Creran at ½ past 3. Strong gales and squally. Fed the horse and crossed the ferry and at 5 p.m. got to Connel ferry and crossed that and got to Oban at 7 p.m. All this road is remarkably good and a variety of mountain scenery. Passed Glencoe which is nearly opposite the first ferry coming from Fort William. Saw Mr [Campbell] Paterson who wanted to send the oats to Mull, but I told him I would not allow them to be taken from the miller who was ordered to convert the whole into meal. He also wanted to get some supplies sent to Mull where he was about taking up his residence. He is a lawyer, a dealer in grain and merchandise and appears to be a regular jobber and by no means fit to have the management of the distribution of the meal. Mr [John] Stevenson, the distiller here, appears a very respectable man and did not approve of what was doing as neither he nor Captain McDougall thought there was any necessity for it. Captain Oliver was still laying here and called on us.

Wednesday 21 June. Cloudy with warm showers of rain. Left Oban in the coach for Inveraray (fare 15s) at 10 a.m., passing by Taynuilt which is 12 miles from Oban and a tolerably good road. Changed horses there and got to the ferry house at Loch Awe, Portsonachan at 1 p.m.[267] This house keeps a chaise, a gig and an Irish car, but no horses or carriage can be had at the ferry house on the Inveraray side of the ferry. Crossed the ferry in a boat, where we found the coach from Inveraray waiting and the passengers they bring take the coach left by us, to go to Oban, and we got into the Inveraray coach, and the road from there to Inveraray is not very good. We changed horses about half way and got to the Argyll Head Inn at 5 p.m., a good house kept by Mr Walker who charges very high – 2/6 for a bed.[268] Dined and slept there. Walked over the grounds of the Duke of Argyll's castle which is close to the inn. A fine building and the grounds well laid out and well planted with fine trees, and the mountains all around this place gives it a very splendid appearance, with the fine Loch Fyne which is about 2 miles broad here and a very neat steam boat of 8 horse power is stationed here. They are now carrying out the pier so as to admit the steamer alongside at low water. You pay 1s to cross this ferry.

Thursday 22 June. Left Inveraray at 9 a.m. Fine weather. Crossed the ferry and got into the coach at 10 a.m. for Lochgoilhead which is about 7 miles from the ferry house. There being 8 more passengers than the coach would hold, an Irish

267 The inn and posting house was run by Archibald Carmichael.
268 According to *Pigot*, 226, there were three inns and posting houses at Inveraray: the George, run by John Walker, and the Argyll Head, run by Robert McKellar are both described in Anderson, *Guide*, 337, as large and commodious; the third, the Inveraray Inn, was run by James McNab.

car was filled with the 8 to follow the coach. All this road is very mountainous and it takes nearly two hours to go the 7 miles with four horses in the coach. Got to Lochgoilhead at noon where the steam boat was waiting, with flag half-mast which was the first intimation we had of the King's death.[269] The passengers who came from Glasgow in the steamer got into our coach and we left in the steamer at 1 p.m. They had got a large catch of herrings in this loch, part of which we took on board the steamer for Glasgow. Called at two places going down the loch and at Gourock, Greenock, Port Glasgow and several other places on the banks of the Clyde to land and take in goods and passengers. Dined on board, paid 2s for dinner and arrived alongside the quay at Glasgow at ½ past 5 p.m. and went to the Tontine Hotel and got all my letters, about 14. The fair of the steamer from Loch Goil to Glasgow is 4s.

Friday 23 June. At Tontine Hotel, Glasgow. Fine, warm weather. Called on [the Rev.] Doctor [Norman]Macleod last evening who promised to call a meeting of the committee this day, but I never heard anything from him. At 1 p.m. called at Mr Baird the secretary's office and saw his brother and met Mr Fullarton the chairman of the committee who said the supply committee would meet at 9 a.m. tomorrow which I promised to attend when they said they would be ready to show me what they had done. Wrote my third and final report of my visitation to the islands and Highlands and also to solicitor-general. Fine warm weather, employed writing etc.

Glasgow, 23 June 1837 [Letter from Hill to Spearman]

Sir, Since my last letter to you of the 16th instant from Tobermory, I beg leave to acquaint you for the information of my Lords Commissioners of His[270] Majesty's Treasury that I visited Tobermory in the isle of Mull and saw Colonel Campbell of Knock and Mr Nisbet of the local committee there; the former is factor to the Duke of Argyll's property and the latter is a writer. These gentlemen gave us every information that I required respecting the supplies that had been sent, and what they would absolutely want until harvest. Mr Gregorson the sheriff-substitute for this island and the adjoining coast of Rossshire who resides at Morvern on the mainland opposite, was also at Tobermory and came on board the *Prince of Wales* to see me. He said they were not so much in want of supplies on the mainland as in the islands, and that all the crops in his circuit were in the most promising condition, and both Colonel Campbell and Mr Nisbet said the

---

[269] King William IV died in the early hours of the morning of 20 June 1837.
[270] Hill still refers to 'his' despite the death of the king and the accession of Queen Victoria, but she had not been proclaimed by then.

same of the crops in the island of Mull.

Having completed what was necessary to be done here, we got underway and made sail down the Sound of Mull but as the wind was baffling[271] and the tide against us, we were obliged to anchor at 7 p.m. when we landed at Scallastle bay in Mull and went about 4 miles into the country and visited several cottages, and all the population we saw were looking healthy and their dwellings similar to those we had seen before. The Rev. Mr Clark, the minister of the parish whom I sent for, came to meet me, and I obtained from him what supplies he had received for the parish and the adjoining one, as also what would be required until the harvest, and returned on board again at 10 p.m. On Sunday the 18th instant at 5 a.m. we weighed anchor and made sail for Oban where we arrived at 1 p.m. when we landed and I acquainted Captain Oliver, the commander of the *Prince of Wales*, that I had no further occasion of his services at present and that he might return to his station. I beg to state that during the time we were on board the *Prince of Wales* Captain Oliver rendered me every assistance in his power, and the expedition he made in conveying me through so extensive a district, and rapidly visiting so many ports, is the best eulogium I can give of his perfect knowledge of the navigation of all these seas and ports, and the good order of his vessel, and which I reported to Captain Knight, the inspector-general of the Coastguard.

On Monday the 19th instant we left Oban by the highland road to Fort William, crossing the ferries of Connel, Shian and Ballachulish and arrived at Fort William at 6 p.m. when I sent for the minister of the parish, the Rev. Mr Swanson and Mr McGregor, a writer and the factor to the Marquis of Huntley, both of the local committee. They gave me an account of what they had received and what was wanted until harvest. We then made a tour of the town and suburbs. All the population were looking in a very healthy state and no appearance of absolute want in these quarters. At 6 a.m. on the 20th instant we drove to the entrance of the Caledonian Canal and all the cottages on and about that road were looking uncommonly well. We returned to Fort William at 9 a.m. and set off again by the same road back to Oban where we arrived at 8 p.m. Through all this tract of about 50 miles of this part of the Highlands, all the crops of corn and potatoes were never known to look better than they do at this season of the year, and the whole population we saw were extremely healthy and their cottages in good condition. Having seen Mr [Campbell] Paterson, the principal manager of the local committee at Oban, I got every information I wanted from him,[272] and at 10 a.m. on Tuesday the 20th instant we left Oban by the mountain road to Inveraray, crossing Loch Awe, and slept there that night; and at 10 a.m. yesterday left Inveraray, crossing Loch Fyne and by the mountain road to Lochgoilhead, and arrived in Glasgow at 6 p.m.

---

[271] Shifting or variable winds making straight sailing impracticable.

[272] It is interesting that Hill did not pass on to the Treasury his private views of Mr Campbell Paterson and his suitability to be in charge of the local committee as reflected in his journal entry for 20 June 1837 (p. 173).

Having gone through so great a tract of sea and land in 28 days, I trust that their Lordships will feel assured that every exertion was made to effect the visitation of the distressed districts in so short a space of time; as great bodily fatigue and exertion through such a country was necessary for its accomplishment. Throughout the whole of the places that we have visited and the country we have passed through, the people were all looking healthy and well; the prices of meal at the various ports were not generally more than 2/- per boll above the ordinary prices at this season of the year, and I am happy to say that I did not find the destitution so great as had been represented by many local parties; and if a proper supply of meal be sent until harvest time, which I shall impress on the minds of the committee here and at Edinburgh, using my aid in support of the same, the people will have the means of subsistence through the season and I trust will prevent any further alarm of destitution. I have the honour to be, Sir, your most obedient servant.

Friday 23 June. At Tontine Hotel, Glasgow. Fine, warm weather. Met the supply committee which only consisted of Mr Fullarton and Doctor Macleod and the secretary Mr Baird. Gave them an account of all that remains at the depots and what had been sent, but as the Queen was to be proclaimed, no business could be done until Monday. Went to the Town Hall and saw the Lord Provost and all the troops, etc. and heard the Queen proclaimed and at 1 p.m. the procession came to the Council Chambers at this Hotel where there were about 500 gentlemen of the city met to drink the Queen's health, and the Lord Provost drank also the health of the Army and Navy which I returned thanks for. Mrs Fleming and four daughters called. She is the wife of a ship owner who owns the ship which is to take out the first batch of emigrants and was to leave Greenock for Skye today; her name is the *William Nicoll*.[273] The sheriff for the county, Mr Alison[274] invited us to dine to meet Captain Basil Hall[275] and Doctor Macleod. Mr Fleming called on me and invited us to dine on Monday. At 6 p.m. went to Mr Alison's where we met Captain and Mrs Basil Hall and Captain and Mrs Trotter,[276] Dr Macleod and 3 other gentlemen. Passed a very pleasant day at his house about two miles out of the town called Fossil House. Received letters from home to say they were coming to Scotland.

---

[273] See Hill's journal entry for 12 June 1837 (p. 165).
[274] Archibald Alison, esq, advocate.
[275] The naval officer and author (see J. K. Laughton, rev. Roger Morriss, 'Hall, Basil (1788–1844)', *ODNB*).
[276] This is probably Captain Henry Dundas Trotter, RN (J. K. Laughton, rev. Andrew Lambert, 'Trotter, Henry Dundas (1802–1859)', *ODNB*).

Sunday 25 June. Fine, warm weather. Went to church morning and evening. Mr Fleming, Captain Hall and Captain Trotter called and Mr. . . .[277] Walked over the cemetery which is a very fine thing with a monument of Mr Knox. Walked round the old cathedral. There is a very fine view of the city from the top of the cemetery. Although the population is so great, all are very clean and orderly of a Sunday and no shops or public conveyance of any sort moving, except the mail coaches, and not a drunken person to be seen. The police appear to be well regulated. Found my lock of my portfolio out of order and could not open it.

Monday 26 June. At Tontine Hotel, Glasgow. Fine, warm weather. Employed with the supply committee and calling on the several authorities, also on the Sheriff and Mrs Alison at Fossil and on Captain and Mrs B. Hall and Captain Trotter. Dined with Mr and Mrs Fleming who has a very handsome house about 2 miles out of town called Claremont.[278] He has 8 daughters and 3 sons. Met the Lord Provost with about 9 other gentlemen and passed a very pleasant evening. A Mr Lumsden was of the party who is principal proprietor of the newly invented steam-boat.[279]

Tuesday 27 June. Still at Tontine Hotel. Fine, warm sultry weather. Employed with the general committee who told me they had still ten thousand pounds in hand (£10,000) and they all agreed it was necessary to send supplies until latter end of August. Called on Mr Fleming and Lord Provost. Received a letter from Mr Binstead to say he had forwarded the King's Warrant the post before which I had never received.[280] Wrote to him on the subject to make enquiries. Went on board the new steam-boat with Mr Lumsden. Received an invitation to go down the Clyde with the Corporation. Employed all day on business and dined at Mr Fullarton's, the chairman of the committee, with ten other gentlemen among whom was Mr Fleming, Rev. Mr Rose, Mr Baird, secretary, etc. returned at midnight. Merchants complained much of the great failures, etc.

[277] Blank in the original.
[278] Claremont (or Clairmont) House, which was built by John Fleming, a well-known Bombay merchant, and hence dubbed 'Bombay Castle', long stood in its own beautiful grounds, isolated and conspicuous. People wondered that it should have been built so like a street house, but Mr. Fleming firmly believed that Glasgow would come out to Claremont, and planned his house for the centre of a row. And it now forms, just as he built it, no. 6 Claremont Terrace.
[279] Hill may be referring here to the first regular steamship service on the Clyde, operated by the paddle-steamer *Comet*, which was designed by Henry Bell and launched at Port Glasgow in 1812. James Lumsden, later lord provost of Glasgow, was on the *Comet*'s maiden voyage.
[280] This was the king's warrant dated 27 Apr. 1837, under which, for his services in Ireland and Scotland, Hill was awarded a civil list pension of £150 per annum to take effect on his ceasing to hold the office of captain superintendent of the victualling yard at Deptford (NRA 44729, Hill papers and correspondence 1792–1855, fo. 72, King's warrant, 27 Apr. 1837).

Wednesday 28 June. At Tontine Hotel, Glasgow. Fine weather. Employed writing. Received two books, specimens of the printing of the Blind Institution. Paid the bill by cheque at the hotel to Mr Walker £6–4–0. Paid 30s for a pair of black cashmere trousers. Left Glasgow at noon by the regular coach by the Airdrie road for Edinburgh. This coach carries six. Mrs Fleming and another lady inside. Very hot and dusty. Got to Royal Hotel, Edinburgh at ¼ before 4. Received a letter from my . . .[281] but no account of missing letter. Drank tea with Mrs Graham; Mr G and his sister not at home.

Thursday 29 June. Fine, clear weather, very hot and dusty. Called on Graham and told him all about the visitation. He said he had read my reports in London and saw Mr Spring Rice and Spearman. Called on the solicitor-general but he was not at home. The Lord Provost Spittal called and invited us to dinner to meet Mrs Fleming and her two daughters. Employed writing and looking after lodgings. Engaged Mrs Hastie's lodgings at 4 Glenfinlas Street, Charlotte Square. Dined at the Lord Provost at No 3 Minto Street, Old Town.[282] Mrs Spittal, a very fine woman and has three children. She is his second wife. With his son, Doctor Spittal, he has a large linen draper's shop on the South Bridge in the Old Town.

Friday 30 June. Fine, warm weather. Paid bill at Royal Hotel and went to the lodgings. Called on Sir C. Gordon and Lord Provost. Saw Mrs Spittal and gave her an order to see the Yard and to Mr Munro. Saw Mr Spittal at his shop and also his son. Called on Mr Wigham the Quaker, who said that nothing but enforcing the poor laws would put a stop to these starvation cases. Received letters from home to say they had not left, also of Fanny's having a [. . ..] Saw Mrs Fleming and her two daughters in the Glasgow coach and took leave of them. Met Mr Trotter and a young man from near Canterbury, Mr Kendrick, who was with him on a trip to Scotland. Dined with them at the Royal Hotel and Mr Cummings, an advocate. Returned home at 11 p.m. Wrote to Emma[283] and Mr Munro.

Saturday 1 July. Fine, hot weather. Wrote to Messrs T & E. Edwards and to Sir G. Westphal[284] and Mr Munro. Employed writing and paying visits.

---

[281] Blank in the original.
[282] The house has a large stained glass window bearing Sir James's arms. Ceremonial lampposts marking his provost ship survived until 1935.
[283] His daughter, who was married to Captain William Castle, RN, and who died on 25 Oct. 1837 from typhoid fever, aged 31.
[284] Captain Sir George Augustus Westphal, RN (J. K. Laughton, rev. A. Lambert, 'Westphal, Sir George Augustus (1785–1875)', *ODNB*).

Sunday 2 July. Went to St John's Church. It was Sacrament Sunday. The Bishop and three clergymen were present but no sermon. Called on Major and Lady Jane Taylor who introduced me to General Sir . . .[285] Went to afternoon church and heard a good sermon. Received Mr Binstead's letter to say he had seen Mr Spearman and had delivered letter himself which was lost. Called on Mrs Graham and Mr and Mrs R. Campbell. Wrote to Treasury and my brother, Captain John and Mr Binstead. Fine, warm weather.

Edinburgh, 2 July 1837 [Letter from Hill to Spearman]

Sir, Since my letter to you of the 23rd ultimo I have met the Glasgow committee on the 24th ultimo and finding that there were ample funds in their hands at present, amounting to about £9,900 for all the calls they had on them for the supplies of meal, I did not consider it necessary for me to render any Government aid, since my last instructions, until I had exhausted the seed oats that I had found at the different depots in my late visitation, amounting to about 500 quarters, which I informed the committee I would hand over to them as may be necessary hereafter; and it is not my intention to make any further offer of money until I can see how far the same may be necessary; as by frequent attendance on the movements of the committees of Edinburgh, Glasgow and Aberdeen from time to time, it will enable me to form my judgement how far, and to what extent, supplies of meal in aid from me may be necessary.

I yesterday met the Edinburgh committee. Sir James Riddell was in the chair and Mr Balfour, the member for Orkney, was present. And as it appeared that the committee had about £5,000 in hand and there was still about £15,000 in the hands of the London committee, I did not consider it necessary to grant any aid at this meeting. And as the whole sum now remaining in the hands of the various committees amounts to about £30,000, after some discussion they resolved that their secretary should write to the London committee stating that, considering the great distress that existed in various manufacturing districts and the large sum remaining, they did not deem it advisable to make any further call on the public for subscription.[286]

A deputation of this committee had been to Glasgow and reported their proceedings, which appeared very favourable. I have the honour to be, Sir, your most obedient servant.

---

[285] Blank in the original.
[286] At the conclusion of the public fund-raising exercise, there was a total surplus left unspent of around £20,000 (see the Introduction).

Monday 3 July. Cloudy with some warm showers. Gave Mr Waller black coat, blue trousers and 1 pair worsted stockings and three neckerchiefs to take to Deptford in his trunk. Called on Mr Nairne, Mr Young and Captain Knight. Received letters from home. Went to Leith at 2 p.m. and the steamer arrived with my family at 3 p.m. Showed them round the town in the evening.

Tuesday 4 July. Fine, warm weather. Mr Stevenson and Doctor Warden called and several other of our friends. Employed settling accounts with Mr Waller and other writing. Walked over the New and part of the Old Town.

Wednesday 5 July. At lodgings, 4 Glenfinlas Street, Edinburgh. Fine, clear, warm weather. Drove all over the New and Old Town. Visited Holyrood House and the Castle and Statuary on Calton Hill and attended the Examination of the Deaf and Dumb.[287]

Thursday 6 July. Fine weather. Went to Portobello and dined at Mr Campbell's. Three officers of the 79th and ourselves formed the party.

Friday 7 July. Fine weather. Family visited the Botanical Gardens and the Museum etc. with Mr Waller. Employed writing all the morning. Dined with Mrs Graham. Met Dr and Mrs Graham,[288] Mr and Mrs Scott and Mr Buchanan.

Edinburgh, 7 July 1837 [Letter from Hill to Spearman]

Sir, I beg leave to transmit to you for the information of my Lords Commissioners of Her Majesty's Treasury a letter I have received from Mr Millar, the surgeon who resides at Stornoway in the isle of Lewis (Hebrides), whom I saw when I was there, and from the conversation I had with him, he seemed much inclined to emigrate and having more or less influence with the poor on that island, I desired him to make enquiries as to the disposition of the people to leave the country, and to write to me the result which

---

[287] The annual examination of the pupils of the Institution for Deaf and Dumb Children founded in 1810.
[288] Dr Robert Graham was the regius professor of botany at Edinburgh University (A. McConnell, 'Graham, Robert (1786–1845)', *ODNB*).

the accompanying letter will show.[289] I have the honour to be, Sir, your most obedient servant.[290]

Stornoway, 26 June 1837 [Letter from Dr Roderick Millar to Hill][291]

Sir, In reference to the conversation I had the honour to hold with you on the 8th and 9th instant[292] respecting the emigration of the peasantry of this island to New South Wales. I beg to acquaint you that I have gone a good deal among them since making enquiry of their inclination to emigrate. I found among them a great degree of [. . .] about going to Australia, but on the other hand a great desire to emigrate to Americas.

Upon my acquainting them of the advantages of Australia and of my own wish to accompany them as medical attendant, I find I would have no difficulty in getting from three hundred to four hundred people to accompany me, restricting the age to 45 years. I have practised in this island for the last seven years as surgeon, this simple people have formed an attachment for me and being able to speak their language would accompany me sooner than a stranger.

May I respectfully request of you to represent to Government the crowded and growing up state of the paupers of this island, uncared for and uneducated in industrial habits or trade and the only recourse of these wretched beings is to beg, to rob, or starve.

Were Government pleased to grant me the allowance normally made to navy surgeons for attending emigrants, I would willingly accompany them as surgeon, or intrust me as their agent at this port for examining and procuring emigrants, I promise to direct my anxious attention to their advantage. I am a licentiate of the Glasgow Faculty of Physicians and Surgeons and refer you to Dr Robert Hunter, professor of anatomy in Glasgow,[293] as to my medical attainments and to the Hon. A. J. Stewart Mackenzie, governor of Ceylon still at London, and Thomas Mackenzie, Esq., MP for Ross-shire as to my character.

---

[289] See Hill's journal entry for 6 June 1837 (p. 156).

[290] Spearman forwarded Dr Millar's letter to James Stephen, the permanent under-secretary at the Colonial Office, and asked him to lay it before Lord Glenelg, the colonial secretary, 'with reference to the communication already made to his Lordship by this Board from the district in question' (TNA:PRO, War and Colonial Office: Emigration original correspondence, CO 384/43, Spearman to Stephen, 15 July 1837).

[291] This letter from Millar to Hill is included because of its significance: it prompted the newly appointed agent-general for emigration, Thomas Elliot, and Dr Boyter to 'push on with the selection of emigrants and the arranging of the first vessels to sail from the Hebrides in July and August 1837' (Macmillan, Scotland and Australia, 278–9, and see the Introduction).

[292] According to Hill's journal, Hill left Lewis on 7 June 1837 bound for Ullapool, so Millar seems to have mistaken the date of his conversations with Hill.

[293] At the Andersonian University.

I am the more confident in undertaking the charge of emigrants to a tropical climate as I have been in the East Indies as surgeon of an Indiaman. May I mention the peasants of this island would be content with a very moderate and plain diet on the voyage – say ¾ of a lb. of oat meal, half a gill of [. . .], ¼ a lb. of beef and ¾ lb. of biscuit per day, for sake of variety a salt herring occasionally in lieu of the beef. I am, Sir, your most obedient servant.[294]

Saturday 8 July. Fine weather. Paid several visits. Waller left me for England at 5 p.m. on his appointment as secretary to Sir F. Maitland.[295]

Sunday 9 July. Still at Edinburgh. Fine weather. Went to St John's Church in the morning. Drove round by Leith and Newhaven in the evening and spent the evening with Mrs Graham.

Monday 10 July. Fine weather. Went to Dalkeith, the Duke of Buccleuch's house, Newbattle Abbey, the Marquis of Lothian's and passed under the Midlothian Railway Bridge to Hawthornden, and from there to Roslin Castle where we had tea and fruit and returned home after a pleasant day.

Tuesday 11 July. Fine weather. Mr Dunbar called on me about Caithness and Stroma. Mr Trail who put up as a member for Caithness called on me on Saturday for the same purpose. Employed writing and met the committee.

Wednesday 12 July. At Edinburgh. Family went to the Convent to see the nuns.[296] Went to a large party at Mrs Ramsay's whose husband is the parson of St John's.[297] He has a brother, a commander in the navy who knew Castle.[298] He was there with about 100 more.

Thursday 13 July. At Edinburgh. Visited model of lighthouse at Mr Stevenson's. Drank tea with small party at Mrs Graham's.

---

[294] A note is written on the letter as to the actions taken by Thomas Elliott: '24 July. As regards Dr Millar's application, this letter will be disposed of by a communication I have made this day to Dr Boyter. As regards the Treasury itself, it will be answered by a Report I have also made this day on their former letter dated 21 June. T. Fredk. E.'

[295] George Waller was rewarded for his efforts after Hill's mission ended with his appointment as the secretary to Rear Admiral Sir F. Maitland, KCB on his succeeding to the command in the East Indies (*Caledonian Mercury*, 20 July 1837).

[296] This was probably St. Margaret's (Ursuline), founded in 1835.

[297] The Rev. E. B. Ramsay, AM.

[298] Captain William Langford Castle, RN, who was married to Hill's daughter Emma.

Friday 14 July. At Stirling. Squally with rain, thunder and lightning. At 7 a.m. embarked[299] on board an iron steam-boat *Ben Ledi*[300] where we arrived at ½ past 11 a.m. and went to Gibb's Hotel[301] where we dined and visited the castle and the church. View very fine from former place. Left Stirling at 6 p.m. and posted to Glasgow by Cumbernauld. Got to the Tontine Hotel in Glasgow at ½ past 10 p.m. and slept there.

Saturday 15 July. At Tontine Hotel, Glasgow and Mrs Stephen's lodgings in George Square. Fine weather. Walked all over the town and the Exchange Rooms.[302]

Sunday 16 July. Fine weather. Mr and Mrs Fleming called. Went to the English church in the Trongate.[303] Visited the cemetery in the evening.

Monday 17 July. Fine weather. Still at Glasgow. Visited the Cathedral, Blind Asylum,[304] University, etc. Mr Strang, City Chamberlain,[305] and Mrs and Miss Fleming with their carriage accompanied us. Drove out in the evening.

Tuesday 18 July. Cloudy with showers of rain. Met the committee and received a letter from Mr Cheyne. Family visited a cotton mill.[306] Dined with Mr and Mrs Fleming at their house at Claremont: a large party, Lord Provost, Mr and Mrs MacGeorge, Mr Strang, etc.

Wednesday 19 July. Fine weather. Left Glasgow at 5 a.m. in the *Tarbert Castle* steam-boat.[307] Got to Greenock at 8 a.m., called at Gourock, Dunoon, Rothesay, Tarbert, Ardrishaig. Went ashore at the two last places and looked at the locks of the entrance to Crinan Canal. Arrived at Inveraray at 7 p.m. The fare from

---

[299] For Stirling.
[300] Run by the Glasgow and Southwestern Railway Company.
[301] The Golden Lion on King Street, run by John Gibb.
[302] This was either the Royal Exchange or the exchange otherwise known as Tontine Buildings (*Lumsden*, 75 and 68).
[303] The church in the Trongate was, in fact, the church of Scotland, St Mary's.
[304] Described in *Lumsden*, 73, as being 'an institution well worthy of a visit'.
[305] Dr John Strang, who was appointed the sixth city chamberlain (one of the city's principal officers) on 29 May 1834.
[306] This was probably the factory of Messrs R. Thomson & Son in Rose Street, recommended in *Lumsden*, 79, as being one of the 'manufacturing establishments which have tended to raise [Glasgow] to its present state of opulence and splendor'.
[307] The hundred-ton boat was wrecked in a gale on Loch Fyne in 1838.

Glasgow to it was 5s.[308] We had some rain while passing through the Kyles of Bute. Walked through the park. Slept at the Argyle Hotel kept by Mr Walker,[309] a good house but charges 2/6 for a bed.

Thursday 20 July. Fine, warm weather. Walked all over the park and grounds. Met Mr Campbell of Islay and Sir Donald Campbell.[310] He told me that the party against him said that he had not done well for the poor, and the *Scottish Guardian* newspaper had a long paragraph against Mr Graham and myself being employed at great expense by Government. Islay went off in the steam-boat for Dunoon to see his constituents.[311] At 12 o'clock left Inveraray in an Irish inside car and got to Portsonachan at ½ past 2 p.m.[312] Crossed the ferry and hired another car and went to Taynuilt and then hired another car and arrived at Oban at 7 p.m. Fine weather. Had a good view of the effect of the tide at the entrance to Loch Etive[313] and also of Dunstaffnage Castle.[314] Walked all over the town. The steam-boat came in from Staffa with a few passengers.

Friday 21 July. Fine weather. Hired a car and left Oban at 9 a.m. for Taynuilt where we arrived in about two hours and a half but could not get another car, so fed the horse and took Oban car and horse on to Portsonachan, and no car was to be had there as the man only keeps one and a gig, and the former had not crossed Loch Awe. Got into the stage coach on the Inveraray side of the loch and arrived at Inveraray at ½ past 4 p.m. At the Argyle Inn which was very full and could not

---

[308] The tour from Port Glasgow to Inveraray of 109 miles is described in detail in *Lumsden*, 102–16.

[309] See the footnote referring to inns at Inveraray to Hill's journal entry for 29 May on p. 149.

[310] Of Dunstaffnage.

[311] See the *Caledonian Mercury*, 27 July 1837, for a report of this election meeting, which took place the next day and at which Campbell of Islay referred to the criticism from his opponent, the evangelical Tory, Alexander Campbell of Monzie, of the alleged creation of unnecessary commissions, viz. the sending of Robert Graham and Hill to the distressed districts, which Islay defended saying that neither Graham nor Hill had received one farthing for their services, having given them gratuitously. Hill was, in fact, to drop a broad hint with the Treasury when he finally submitted his accounts that as he had received a payment of £200 on completing his services in Ireland in 1831, he hoped the Treasury would 'deal liberally with me' on the present occasion and the Treasury responded by authorising Hill to retain £200 'as a special remuneration to you for your services upon the occasion in question' (p. 194 below).

[312] Hill had not chosen the 'scenic' route for his family. The route to Oban via Portsonachan was 10 miles shorter than, but did not have the 'interesting grandeur' of, the route via Dalmally.

[313] 'from the narrowness of the passage and a reef of sunken rocks a very turbulent rapid is occasioned at particular states of the tide, especially at half ebb, when the agitation and noise of the shelving current are not a little striking' (Anderson, *Guide*, 330).

[314] Which was mostly in ruins (see the description given in Anderson, *Guide*, 329).

get a sitting room. It was the day of the great wool market fair and Campbell of Islay addressed his constituents on a platform close to the Inn under his colours. Sir Donald Campbell of Dunstaffnage was his chief supporter. He made a good speech in favour of the Government and spoke very highly of Mr Graham and myself and said the duke of Wellington was my friend who placed me where I was, and my known integrity was the cause of the Government employing me. He left Inveraray in the steam-boat for Dunoon at 6 p.m. Walked all over the Park and left a card at the Castle. Cloudy with some showers.

Saturday 22 July. At Inveraray. Cloudy with small rain. Left this place at 8 a.m. on the road from Inveraray to Loch Lomond in the Loch Lomond coach which carries six inside and six outside, fare 8s in and 7s out. Arrived at Cairndow 10 miles distant at ½ past 9 a.m. A small inn[315] where we changed horses and had a good breakfast for 1s 6d each. This house is situated close to the head of Loch Fyne on the Tarbet side of the loch. After we left this we passed through between very high mountains, a glen called Glen Kinglas about 4 miles when the road turns to the right and goes up a very high mountain at the top of which is a stone placed by the soldiers of the 23rd Regiment when they completed the road in 1768. 'Rest and be thankful' was inscribed on it and we all sat down on it and walked down the hill which runs through Glen Croe.[316] Two very high mountains form the glen and only two shepherds reside in these remote parts. This is one of the wildest parts of the Highlands, and close to Ben Arthur[317] and Ben Lomond, the finest mountain scenery. After passing these we went round the head of Loch Long and arrived at Tarbet, an excellent inn,[318] on Loch Lomond at 1 p.m. Lunched there and walked about 2 miles up the loch and had a good view of Ben Lomond. At ½ past 2 p.m. the iron steam-boat the . . .[319] came down the loch and we embarked and found about 30 passengers on board. Paid 3s each. The scenery down this loch is considered as fine as any in the Highlands. Landed on the small island Inchmurrin where we walked up and had a fine view both ways. Arrived at the end of the loch at ½ past 5 p.m. where we got into a large flat barge which was shoved up the entrance of the River Leven about 1 mile, by men with long poles as there is only about 18 inches of water. We landed at

---

[315] The Cairndow Inn run by Dugauld Paul, described in *Lumsden*, 120, as being 'a very comfortable house where the greatest attention and civility is met with'.

[316] The stone was, in fact, inscribed in 1748 when the road was built and an addition was made in 1768 – 'Repaired by the 23rd Regiment, 1768'.

[317] Better known as The Cobbler.

[318] The Tarbert Inn, run by Lewis Colquhon.

[319] Blank in the original, but the boat would have been the fifty-four-ton *Loch Lomond*, built by David Napier of Glasgow and launched in 1835, which entered service on Loch Lomond in 1836.

6 p.m. at Balloch Castle about 5 miles from Dumbarton. Two coaches were ready to take the passengers. Paid 1s 6d each. Passed through the villages of Alexandria and Renton. At Bonhill is a plain stone monument of Smollett.[320] Got to the Elephant Hotel at Dumbarton at 7 p.m. kept by Mr [Alexander] McDougall.[321] Had tea and walked down to the Castle. Showery weather.

Sunday 23 July. Showery weather. At the Inn at Dumbarton, the Elephant. Went to church and heard a good sermon. Visited the Castle where we ascended 340 steps. It commands a fine view of the River Clyde both up and down. You see Port Glasgow and Greenock, also Ben Lomond and other mountains. Walked all round the town and through the suburbs in the evening.[322] Fine weather.

Monday 24 July. At Elephant Hotel at Dumbarton. Cloudy weather with rain. Left in the steam-boat[323] at ½ past 7 a.m. and got to Glasgow at ½ past 9 a.m. Called on Mrs Fleming at Claremont. Received a large package of letters which had lain here all the week. Fine weather. Employed writing. The town is in a bustle about the election as Lord W. Bentinck had arrived.[324]

Tuesday 25 July. At Mrs Stephen's lodgings in George Square, Glasgow. At 9 a.m. went to the committee but Mr Macpherson was the only one present, Mr Fullarton being ill at home. Requested him to summons a committee but he said it would be of no use until the election was over. Mr and Mrs Fleming took us to see the carpet manufactory,[325] also the Exchange and Port Dundas, the entrance of the canal to Edinburgh. Fine weather. Called on Lord W. Bentinck and Mr Dennistoun.[326] Changed my hat.

---

[320] The sixty-foot-high monument is, in fact, in Renton. It was erected in 1774 to commemorate the author Tobias Smollett, who had been born at the nearby Dalquhurn House in 1721.

[321] The hotel was given the name Elephant after the prominent Dumbarton Rock, a volcanic plug which is said to resemble an elephant. The poets William Wordsworth and Samuel Taylor Coleridge are said to have stayed in the hotel, on the south side of High Street and west side of Quay Street, when they visited the town in 1803.

[322] Dumbarton is described in Anderson, *Guide*, 347, as consisting 'chiefly of a long, crooked, and irregular street, at the upper end of which a bridge of four arches is thrown across the stream'. There were several ship-building yards and three large glass-houses 'forming one of the most extensive and celebrated establishments for cut-glass in the kingdom'.

[323] Run by the Dumbarton Steam Packet Co.

[324] Lord William Henry Cavendish-Bentinck, the army officer, diplomatist and governor-general of India, who was elected MP for Glasgow in Feb. 1836 and again in 1837 (D. M. Peers, 'Bentinck, Lord William Henry Cavendish- (1774–1839)', *ODNB*).

[325] Probably the Port Eglinton Carpet Company at 85 Buchanan Street.

[326] John Dennistoun, who was one of the two MPs for Glasgow (replacing James Oswald at the 1837 election) from 1837 to 1847.

Wednesday 26 July. Fine, warm weather. Went to the Town Hall and saw the candidates proclaimed. About 15,000 persons were assembled and all went off quietly. Mr and Mrs Fleming and family and Mr and Miss Lumsden took lunch with us. Went to see the Bridewell[327] and the new house for the destitute. Dined at Mr Fleming's and met Mr and Miss Lumsden and went to election Committee after dinner.

Thursday 27 July. Squally with constant rain. Town all in confusion about the election. Lord W. Bentinck and Mr Dennistoun were returned again and they dined at Mr Fleming's. Employed writing.

Glasgow, 27 July. [Letter from Hill to Fullarton, chairman of the Glasgow committee][328]

Sir, Having by the command of Her Majesty's Government for some time back been in communication with the committee of which you are the chairman, as well as with the committee in Edinburgh, and having visited those parts of the Highlands and Islands of Scotland in which great destitution was stated to prevail and contributed, so far as I saw it to be necessary, supplies of seed oats and potatoes to the inhabitants, I am exceedingly desirous of having the opinion of your committee as to the necessity of anything further being at present done in the matter on the part of Government.

I have been given to understand that from the amplitude of the funds now under your control there is little danger of your not being able to furnish supplies to the necessitous districts, till the produce of the present crop, which promises to be very abundant, shall be fit for use. And as I feel it to be my duty to make an early communication to Government on the subject, I request you may do me the favour to put that in my power by furnishing me with a written statement of your opinion. I have the honour to be, Sir, your obedient servant.

Friday 28 July. Fine weather. At 8 a.m. put my family aboard the canal boat for Edinburgh and Miss Green for Stirling.[329] Met the committee at 3 p.m. Doctor Macleod and Mr Fullarton and Mr Baird were present. Wrote them a letter and transacted other business. Found they had a large sum in hand. Paid

---

[327] Described in *Lumsden*, 70: 'there is perhaps no Institution in the empire better managed than this, nor one which is more worthy of the consideration of the philanthropist'.

[328] A copy of this was sent by Hill to the Treasury with his letter of 29 July 1837 to Spearman (p. 188).

[329] Both run by the Forth and Clyde Canal Co.

my lodgings bill and bill at Tontine Hotel. Called on Mr Fleming at Claremont. Left Glasgow at 6 p.m. in the coach for Edinburgh where I arrived at 4 Glenfinlas Street at 11 p.m. Cloudy with rain at times.

Saturday 29 July. At lodgings in Edinburgh. Cloudy with constant rain all day. Employed writing to Treasury and Admiralty.

Edinburgh, 29 July 1837 [Letter from Hill to Spearman][330]

Sir, Since my letter of the 2nd instant I beg leave to acquaint you for the information of my Lords Commissioners of Her Majesty's Treasury I have been in constant communication with the Edinburgh and Glasgow committees and as they have had ample funds for providing all the supplies that were wanted up to this time I have not deemed it advisable to make any grants to them in aid of those supplies. I yesterday met the Glasgow committee and they found they still had about £4,000 remaining in their hands and that they believed there still remained a large sum in the London committee. Having taken into consideration the large sums that still remain, I deemed it advisable to write to the chairman of the committee, and enclosed is the copy of my letter to him[331] and which I request you will be pleased to lay before their Lordships and from what passed when I was present at the committee yesterday, I have every reason to believe that no further aid will be required from me, but as soon as I receive the answer to the enclosed letter, I shall immediately transmit a copy of it to you for the information of Her Majesty's Government.

It is my intention to write a similar letter to the Edinburgh committee and meet them on Monday or Tuesday next, when I shall report the result in order that their Lordships may judge how far my services are any longer required in Scotland. I have the honour to be, Sir, your obedient servant.

Treasury Chambers, 29 July 1837 [Letter from Spearman to Hill]

Sir, I am commanded by the Lords Commissioners of Her Majesty's Treasury to convey to you their Lordships' approval of the several steps take by you, as reported in your letters of the 7th, 16th and 23rd ultimo and 2nd and 7th instant, and to express to you the satisfaction with which my Lords have received the information communicated in your letter of the 2nd instant, from which, and from your previous reports, their Lordships have no doubt that

---

[330] The Treasury minute which relates to this is set out on p. 285.
[331] See the entry for 27 July above (p. 187).

the arrangements made by you, and by the local authorities, have produced all those results, the expectation of which induced this Board to dispatch you to Scotland to give the assistance of the Government in aid of local exertions in relief of the distress in those districts to which the attention of their Lordships was so urgently called, and that you are now therefore at liberty to return to London to report finally upon your proceedings. I am, Sir, your obedient servant.

Sunday 30 July. At Edinburgh. Cloudy with some rain. Went to St John's Church, called on Misses Graham and they called on us in the evening. Employed writing etc.

Monday 31 July.[332] At Edinburgh. Cloudy with rain at times. Delivered my letter to Mr Bowie for Sir James Riddell of Edinburgh committee. Occupied with him for two hours on the emigration subject. He called and invited us to dinner on Wednesday at Newhaven. Called on Lord Provost and Lady Spittal. This day the candidates for the county were nominated; town all in a bustle. Received orders to return to England.[333] Employed about my accounts and other writing. Showery all day.

Edinburgh, 1 August 1837 [Letter from Hill to Spearman][334]

Sir, I have the honour to acknowledge the receipt of your letter of the 29th ultimo conveying to me the approval of the Lords Commissioners of Her Majesty's Treasury. In reply thereto, I request you will be pleased to make known to their Lordships the gratification I feel at the expression of their Lordships' entire approval of my conduct and of the several steps taken by me since the 7th of June; and of the satisfaction my letter of the 2nd ultimo gave to their Lordships; and I feel confident that all the results expected therefrom will be fully realised.

I shall return to England as soon as I have finally arranged such matters as I have to complete regarding my accounts, when I will immediately report my return and, agreeable to their Lordships' directions, present the final report of my proceedings. I have the honour to be, Sir, your obedient servant.

---

[332] This is the last daily entry in Hill's journal.
[333] See Spearman's letter to Hill of 29 July at p. 188 above.
[334] The Treasury minute that relates to this letter is set out on p. 285 below.

Edinburgh, 4 August 1837 [Letter fom Hill to Spearman][335]

Sir, With reference to my letter of the 29th ultimo, I beg leave to acquaint you for the information of the Lords Commissioners of Her Majesty's Treasury, I wrote a similar one to the letter which I had written to the chairman of the Glasgow committee, to Sir James Milles Riddell, chairman of the Edinburgh committee. I now beg leave to enclose a copy[336] of the answer I have received from the secretary of the committee, which I request you will be pleased to lay before their Lordships. I have the honour to be, Sir, your obedient servant.

Highland Destitution

Edinburgh, 1 August 1837

At a meeting of the Edinburgh committee held here this day, Sir Charles Gordon of Drimmin in the chair.

There was laid before the meeting a letter from Sir John Hill of date 31st July addressed to the chairman in which Sir John states that having visited those parts of the Highlands and Islands in which great destitution was stated to prevail, and contributed so far as he saw it to be necessary, supplies of seed oats and seed potatoes to the inhabitants, together with such sums of money as was required from him by the committee, he was desirous of having the opinion of the committee as to the necessity of anything further being at present done in the matter on the part of Government.

The committee having maturely considered the letter above referred to, desire in the first instance to record their sense of the great obligations they were under to Sir John Hill for his cordial, zealous and energetic cooperation in the great and important matter in which he has been engaged. The task imposed on Sir John was in many respects not only irksome, but from the first laborious in the extreme. Throughout the whole course of Sir John's interference, he has so transacted the important duties assigned to him not only in the most efficient manner possible, but also in a way which has secured to him the esteem and respect of all who came in contact with him, and the committee now beg leave cordially and sincerely to tender to Sir John Hill their best and most grateful thanks.

With reference to the wished for further interference on the part of Government, the committee beg to observe that the liberal aid of Government with reference to the supply of seed oats and potatoes, is likely to lead to

---

[335] The Treasury minute of 11 Aug. 1837 that relates to this letter is set out on p. 285 below.
[336] Set out below.

the greatest possible benefit to those to whom such aid was extended, and from the funds now at the disposal of the several committees, there is every reason to hope that the committees will be enabled to furnish the inhabitants of the destitute districts the necessary supply of oatmeal, till such time as the ensuing crops become available.

There is one point, however, as to which the committee have earnestly to request Sir John Hill's further kind aid and assistance. Sir John has already visited great parts of the Highlands and Islands, and the committee are inclined to hope that from their personal inspection, Sir John must be equally satisfied as the Edinburgh committee are, that nothing but emigration, and that on a most extensive scale, can tend to ameliorate the condition of the overgrown population in these interesting districts. The committee feel grateful to Her Majesty's Government for the part they have already acted with reference to emigration to Australia, and the committee trust that the Government will see fit to continue this emigration on an increased scale. While, however, many families will have emigrated to Australia in the course of this summer and while there are many more anxious to follow as speedily as possible, still the committee are well aware that there are many thousands in the Highlands and Islands of Scotland who though reluctant to proceed to Australia are no less anxious to emigrate to Canada. The committee therefore earnestly and respectfully request of Sir John Hill to bring this matter under notice of Her Majesty's Government, and the committee sincerely trust that measures may be speedily arranged so as to ensure early next season an extensive emigration not only to Australia, but also to Canada, and the committee would further take leave to impress on Sir John Hill the necessity which exists of early intimations being given of the intentions of Government with respect to the emigration to these two colonies, particularly as to the numbers which can be sent out to each.

It is highly important that the emigration should take place before the month of May next, and it will be necessary that it be known as early as possible, who are to emigrate, so that the intending emigrants may have full time given to them to dispose of their little property and make all necessary arrangements for leaving their native shores.

John Bowie, secretary.[337]

---

[337] An extract of the part of this minute relating to emigration was sent by Spearman to James Stephen, permanent under-secretary at the Colonial Office, requesting that it be laid before Lord Glenelg and that his attention be drawn to the opinion expressed by the Edinburgh committee on emigration (TNA:PRO, War and Colonial Office: Emigration original correspondence, CO 384/43/337, Spearman to Stephen, 18 Aug. 1837). A copy was also sent to Elliot, the agent-general for emigration on 29 Aug. 1837.

Victualling Yard, Deptford, 19 August 1837 [Letter from Hill to Spearman]

Sir, With reference to my letter of the 29th July enclosing a copy of a letter addressed by me to the Glasgow committee, I beg leave to transmit for the information of the Lords Commissioners of Her Majesty's Treasury, a copy of the letter I have received in reply to the same,[338] in which it will be seen the Glasgow committee differ on the subject of emigration from the Edinburgh committee. I have the honour to be, Sir, your obedient servant.

Extract from minutes of meeting of committee in Glasgow on the fund for the relief of the destitute inhabitants of the Highlands and Islands held at Glasgow on the 9th August 1837.
Allan Fullarton, Esq., in the chair.

It was moved, seconded and unanimously resolved that as Captain Sir John Hill, the Government commissioner for superintending the supplies to the destitute inhabitants of the Highlands and Islands of Scotland, is now on the eve of taking his departure from this country, this committee cannot allow the opportunity to escape of recording the very high sense they entertain of the zeal, energy and ability with which he has discharged the duties of his important, and in many respects, delicate and difficult mission; as also of the generous and well-timed aid afforded by Government to a class of Her Majesty's subjects, as remarkable for their patient and peaceable endurance of suffering as they are for their steady and devoted loyalty. They further resolve that their most cordial thanks be tendered to Sir John Hill for the frank, courteous and kindly manner in which he has uniformly co-operated with them in their interesting labours, now happily near a close.

And should Sir John Hill in reporting his proceedings to Government think it his duty to allude to the necessity of applying a permanent remedy to that state of misery, at which the great mass of Highland population has now arrived, this committee respectfully request of him to state it as their decided opinion that emigration, on an extensive scale, affords the only rational means of cure, but that this cure can only be temporary unless some regulation be enforced in the country with regard to the lettings and subdivision of lands: a regulation which can only be established by the landowners themselves, or by the legislature.

Extracted by Charles R. Baird, secretary.[339]

---

[338] In fact this was an extract of a minute of a meeting of the Glasgow committee.
[339] A copy of this minute was sent by Spearman to James Stephen requesting that it be transmitted for the information of Lord Glenelg (TNA:PRO, War and Colonial Office: Emigration original correspondence, CO 384/43/341, Spearman to Stephen, 31 Aug. 1837).

Victualling Yard, Deptford, 19 August 1837 [Letter from Hill to Spearman]

Sir, I have the honour to transmit to you for the information of the Lords Commissioners of Her Majesty's Treasury, a copy of a resolution of a general meeting of the Aberdeen committee of the 7th instant which I have received from the Lord Provost of that City since my return to Deptford.[340] I have the honour to be, Sir, your obedient servant.

At a General Meeting of the Aberdeen committee for managing the subscriptions for the relief of the destitute Highlanders and Islanders of Scotland, held within the Town Hall this seventh day of August, Eighteen hundred and thirty seven years.

James Milne, Esq., Lord Provost in the chair.

On the motion of the Lord Provost, seconded by Alexander Webster, Esq., It was unanimously resolved that as Sir John Hill, who was appointed to superintend the application of the relief fund granted by Government, has now fulfilled the objects of his important mission, this committee feel themselves called upon before his leaving this part of the country, to bear their unanimous and willing testimony to the very zealous and efficient manner in which he has discharged the arduous and, in many respects, difficult duties committed to his charge. They would at the same time beg leave to tender to Sir John Hill their best thanks for his valuable and judicious co-operation in the benevolent work in which they have been mutually engaged, and for the uniform kindness and courtesy which marked his intercourse with the committee at all times.

The committee would respectfully request Sir John Hill to make offer of their acknowledgements to his secretary Mr Waller, Lieutenant Rothery of the *Cheerful*, Lieutenant Nott of the *Mermaid*, Mr Brooman of the *Mary*, and to Mr Nutter of the *Duck*, commanders of the Government vessels employed in the transmission of supplies from Aberdeen to Orkney and Shetland, for their active exertions in the departments under their charge.

The committee further request the Provost to sign and transmit in their name a copy of this resolution to Sir John Hill.

James Milne, Provost and Chief Magistrate of the City of Aberdeen.

[340] In the covering letter the lord provost sent to Hill, he thanked Hill for his 'zealous exertions and active co-operation in this benevolent and charitable undertaking, and also for the kind and courteous attention paid by you at all times to every member of our committee' and gave Hill his own 'personal acknowledgements' (NLS, Sir John Hill, 1837: diary and papers, Acc 12738, Milne to Hill, 7 Aug. 1837).

Deptford, 7 May 1838. [Private letter from Hill to Spearman]

My dear Sir, I have written you officially and sent in my accounts this day, which I hope will be correct as heretofore.

I think both the Chancellor and yourself will be agreeably surprised to find so small a sum expended when you consider how hard the Treasury was pressed by the Scotch Deputations who calculated upon getting at least £20,000 out of you; and the saving shows the advantage of having a person on the spot on such occasions.[341]

On my return from Ireland in 1831, the Treasury gave me two hundred pounds over and above all my expenses. As I have been put to considerable and unexpected expense by my removal from here, I trust you will deal liberally with me.[342]

I cannot quit this without assuring you that I feel most grateful for the very essential services you have rendered me, and if in my new situation[343] I can in any way be of use to you, I beg you will command me. I am, my dear Sir, your much obliged.

Deptford 7 May 1838 [Letter from Hill to Spearman]

Sir, I have the honour to transmit to you for the information of the Lords of the Treasury an account of my proceedings on the occasion of my mission to Scotland with such vouchers as the peculiar circumstances would admit.

The delay in forwarding the documents has arisen from the difficulty of collecting several sums due to the Crown by the sale of oats and potatoes since my return to England upon which I have been occupied more or less during that period,

In all my transactions I acted conjointly with the Edinburgh committee for Highland Destitution and the enclosed printed copy of Resolutions dated 2nd March 1837 show the principle on which the assistance was afforded.[344]

The sum of £71 12s 2d remitted last March from Messrs Drever & Co, Dublin was owing to my discovering the freight of the *Industry* as for voucher No. 10 had been paid at Stornoway and which I called on them to refund which they did less postage. I have placed that sum to the credit of the Crown, but should any claim be made hereafter for any part of the same by the parties in Scotland, I must beg to be allowed to refer them to the Treasury. I have the honour to be, Sir, your most obedient servant.

P.S. I beg to request any further communications may be addressed to me at Her Majesty's Dockyard, Sheerness as I leave Deptford this day.

[341] Hill was given £10,000 by the Treasury and his account shows a total of £7,065 13s 11¾ d was spent, of which £5,938 went on seed and supplies and the balance on administrative expenses.

[342] The Treasury responded by authorising Hill to retain £200 of the balance in hand 'as a special remuneration to you for your services in question' (NLS, Sir John Hill 1837: diary and papers, Acc 12738, Spearman to Hill, 16 July 1838).

[343] Hill was moved from Deptford in somewhat unhappy circumstances as mentioned in the Biographical Notes above, to be captain superintendent of the dockyard at Sheerness.

[344] The resolutions are set out on p. 245 below.

Vouchers Date and No.	Sir John Hill in Account with Her Majesty's Treasury Disbursements	Seeds Bear , Oats Potatoes	Amount of costs and charges £-s-d
1837			
April 7 No. 1	By – Purchased of Messrs I.M.J. Tilby as per his Bill of costs and charges for	799 7/8t qrs oats	1475-8-0
April 21 No. 2	By – Purchased of Messrs Grey & Son of Dalkeith and Mr Wigham Jnr for their bill of cost and charges (for moiety) _____	54 qrs oats	107-9-6
April 28 No. 3	By - Purchased at Aberdeen as per account & statement of Provost Milne being moiety of the same_____	2 qrs bear, 562 6/8 qrs oats, 1 2/20 tons potatoes	938-6-0
April 28 No. 4	By – Ditto _____Ditto_____ *_____	7 qrs bear, 57 tons potatoes	193-9-4
April 28 No. 5	By – Ditto _____Ditto_____	66 7/16 qrs bear	122-8-6
May 18 No. 6	By – Ditto _____Ditto, part of above *__	123 2/8 qrs oats	210-4-11¾
May 18 No. 7	By – Ditto _____Ditto_____	40 qrs bear, 37 4/20 tons potatoes	192-12-8
May 18 No. 8	By – Ditto _____Ditto_____	24 15/20 tons potatoes	83-19-0
May 24 No. 9	By – Purchased by committee of Edinburgh as per account & statement of Rd. Campbell Esq being the balance of the moiety of the same _____	1178 4/8 qrs oats, 140 2/20 tons potatoes	1412-16-8
June 5 No. 10	The Revd J. McIver, Rodel, Isle of Harris for the purchase of potatoes _____	4 tons potatoes	15-0-0
June 25 No. 11	Purchased of Messrs Drever & Son of Dublin as per their bill of costs and charges for _____	321 16/20 tons potatoes	1191-2-6
March 15 No. 12	By – Stationery _____		14-8-0
	By – Carriages to attend on Chancellor of the Exchequer		2-2-0
	By Newspapers etc. _____		1-10-0
	By – Given to the poor in mall sums at various times _____		9-0-0

Vouchers Date and No.	Disbursements	Seeds Beer , Oats Potatoes	Amount of costs and charges
1837			£-s-d
April 13/ May 27 No. 13	By -Advertisements _____		1-2-6
May 22 No.14	By — Pilotage of *Duck* lighter from Aberdeen to Shetland		1-0-0
	By — Carriages hired at Edinburgh _____		24-0-0
	By — Carriages hired at Aberdeen _____		4-18-0
	By - Carriages hired at Glasgow _____		8-0-0
	By — Postage and carriage of parcels _____		15-13-3½
	By - Captain Oliver of *Prince of Wales* cutter _____		15-0-0
June 19 No. 15	By - Crew of *Prince of Wales* cutter _____		2-0-0
	By - Passages in steam-boats, ferries & boats hired at various times _____		2-18-6
	By — Office rent		35-15-6
	By - Stationery		7-11-0
	By - Stamps		4-10-9
	By — Expenses for travelling from Deptford to Edinburgh, Glasgow, Greenock, Aberdeen thro' the Highlands to Fort William and back to Glasgow to Deptford, 1560 miles at 2s 0d per mile _____		156-0-0
	By — Various journeys taken between Edinburgh, Glasgow, Aberdeen and the distressed districts to examine into the state of the country and visit the depots during five months — 755 miles at 2s 0d per mile _____		75-10-0
	By — Subsistence for 150 days at 35s per diem _____		262-10-0
	By — Ditto and expenses of Clerk _____		142-19-0
	By — Carriage to attend on the Chancellor of the Exchequer _____		1-1-0
	By — Thirty days employment of myself & Clerk since my return from Scotland last August _____		30-0-0
		115 7/16 qrs bear, 2718 3/8 qrs oats, 585 19/20 tons potatoes	6760-6-8¼
	Balance due to the Crown _____		305-7-3½
			£7065-13-11¾

Date of Bills	From where and on whom drawn	Amount
1837		£-s-d
4 April	To my Bill at 3 days sight on Wm. Sargent Esq., Paymaster of Civil Services in favour of Mr I.M.J. Tilby of Liverpool at Aberdeen _____	1475-8-0
19 April	To Bill on Treasury in favour of Bank of Scotland ___	300-0-0
21 April	To my Bill in favour of Messrs Grey & Son of Dalkeith, Edinburgh _____	107-9-6
28 April	To my Bill in favour of Jas. Milne, Esq., Lord Provost of Aberdeen _____	938-6-0
28 April	To my Bill in favour of Jas. Milne, Esq., Lord Provost of Aberdeen _____	193-9-4
28 April	To my Bill in favour of Jas. Milne, Esq., Lord Provost of Aberdeen _____	122-8-6
18 May	To my Bill in favour of Jas. Milne, Esq., Lord Provost of Aberdeen at Edinburgh _____	210-4-11¾
18 May	To my Bill in favour of Jas. Milne, Esq., Lord Provost of Aberdeen _____	192-12-8
18 May	To my Bill in favour of Jas. Milne, Esq., Lord Provost of Aberdeen _____	83-19-0
24 May	To Richd. Campbell, Esq., of Edinburgh _____	1412-16-8
22 May	To Messrs Drever & Son of Dublin at Edinburgh ____	600-0-0
25 June	To Messrs Drever & Son of Dublin at Glasgow (Balance of their Account) _____	591-2-6
11 July	To Bill on Treasury in favour of Bank of Scotland ____	500-0-0
13 Sept	To sale of oats not wanted at Lochboisdale _____	161-16-6
9 Oct	To sale of oats and potatoes at Stornoway _____	24-14-0
8 Feb	To sale of oats at Lerwick _____	68-17-2
18 March	To sale of potatoes at South Uist _____	11-0-0
20 March	To recovered from Messrs Drever & Co for freight of *Industry*_____	71-9-2
		£7065-13-11¾

PART 3

PETITION, MEMORIALS, RESOLUTIONS AND REPORTS

This Part contains, in Section 1, the Petition to the Treasury from the provincial Synod of Shetland and the Memorials to the Treasury from the Edinburgh and Glasgow public meetings concerning the need for Government aid; in Section 2 the resolutions of the Edinburgh, Glasgow, Aberdeen and London public meetings which set up committees to appeal for public subscriptions and Government aid; in Section 3 the Reports by the Edinburgh, Glasgow and London committees; and in Section 4 the resolutions of the Edinburgh committee which regulated the terms for the supply of aid for seed and which were adopted by the Government to regulate the use of the funds made available to Hill, and an explanatory note written by the Rev. Dr Norman Macleod and John Bowie.

Section 1

Petition to the Treasury of the Provincial Synod of Shetland dated 12 January 1837[1]

To the Right Honourable the Lords Commissioners of His Majesty's Treasury, the Petition of the Provincial Synod of Shetland

Humbly sheweth

That your petitioners, feeling a deep interest in the temporal as well as the spiritual welfare of the people committed to their care, deem it their duty to lay before your Lordships a statement of the deplorable circumstances in which the poor inhabitants of these islands are at present placed in consequence of the failure of their crops and their fishings for two successive seasons.

That the accompanying report to which the Synod earnestly beg your Lordships' attention, is founded in a minute, careful and anxious investigation into the circumstances to which it relates, and that the distressing facts which are embodied in it, far from being exaggeration of the truth are studiously represented in the least unfavourable light that truth will warrant.

That the present case is manifestly beyond the reach of either private or public benevolence and that your petitioners do most sincerely believe, that, unless His Majesty's Government interpose and grant speedy assistance, multitudes of people in these Islands must die of famine.

May it therefore please your Lordships to take petition and the accompanying report into your Lordships' favourable consideration, and to grant to the poor inhabitants of Shetland such aid as your Lordships may judge sufficient to save them from the impending miseries of famine, and your petitioners shall ever pray etc.

Signed at Lerwick this 12th day of January, 1837, in name and presence, and by appointment, of the Synod of Shetland, by William Stevenson,[2] Moderator.

At Lerwick, the twelfth day of January, one thousand eight hundred and thirty seven years The Synod met, session secunda, and was constituted.

The Committee for Overtures agreeably to the instructions delivered by the Synod at their formal meeting gave in a Report, the tenor of which follows:—

---

[1]   A copy of the petition and the report contained in the petition was sent by Henry Cheyne to Graham in a letter dated 6 Mar. 1837, in which Cheyne stressed to Graham the urgency of the situation in Shetland.

[2]   Minister of Northmarine and Ollaberry.

'At Lerwick, January 11th 1837. Your Committee having maturely considered the report submitted to the Synod on the state of the several parishes in Shetland, lament to find that in some districts the scanty produce of the late harvest is already consumed, that in a few months the whole food at present in these islands will be exhausted; and that from various conspiring causes the great body of the labouring classes are destitute of the means of purchasing the necessaries of life.

Of the fourteen parishes into which the Shetland islands are divided, it appears that in one parish, containing 2,909 inhabitants the present crop, including grain and potatoes, will not furnish sustenance for a longer period than two months; that in six parishes containing 11,891 inhabitants there is sustenance for only five months; that in three parishes containing 4,900 inhabitants there is sustenance for only four months; that in the parishes containing 6,548 inhabitants there is sustenance for only six months; that in one parish containing 950 inhabitants and that from the remaining parish containing 2,194 inhabitants, no report has been laid before the Synod, though it is well known that in it also there is a great deficiency. With reference, however, to thirteen parishes, the foregoing abstract shows this appalling result – that, when the produce of the crop is averaged, 27,198 people have not food sufficient to support life during five months of the year.

The inability of the people to purchase grain for their maintenance during the remaining seven months of the year, arises from a combination of unpropitious circumstances, by which their earnings have been abridged and their means exhausted in the course of the last two years. In 1835 the crops in Shetland were as deficient as those in the Hebrides; the ling fishing failed; the herring fishing along the whole east coast of Shetland was unproductive; the whale fishing was worse than unproductive and during the succeeding winter an unprecedented mortality among the sheep, horses and cattle swept off nearly the whole of their stocks. In 1836 the ling fishing was again unproductive, while the herring fishing and the whale fishing were total failures; and thus all who engage in these pursuits, that is nearly the whole male population of these islands, instead of improving their circumstances, which the preceding year had so grievously impaired, were involved in still greater difficulties, and rendered altogether unable to help themselves under this second failure of their crops which has taken place.

Looking therefore to the deficiency of crops, and to the impoverished condition of the people your Committee are fully persuaded that not less than twenty thousand bolls of meal will be required to preserve the lives of those who have not the means of purchasing food for themselves.'[3]

---

[3]   In the event it appears that a total of 5,457 bolls of meal were sent to Shetland by the relief committees (p. 226).

Said report having been carefully considered by the Synod was unanimously approved and adopted as their report and the Clerk was instructed to forward an authenticated copy of it, along with the Synod's petition for aid, to the Lords of the Treasury.

Extracted from the Record of the acts and proceedings of the Provincial Synod of Shetland, on this and the three preceding pages, by T[homas] Barclay,[4] Synod Clerk.

Memorial to the Treasury of a committee appointed by public meeting in Edinburgh dated 20 February 1837

Unto the Right Honourable the Lords Commissioners of His Majesty's Treasury, the memorial of a committee appointed by a public meeting, held at Edinburgh on the 25th January last, to consider and take steps to relieve the distress prevailing among the inhabitants of the Highlands and Islands of Scotland;

Humbly Sheweth,
    The memorialists are induced to present themselves to the notice of your Lordships, for the purposes of making known to you the destitution which at present pervades a great part of the Northern and Western Districts of Scotland, including the Orkney and Shetland Islands, and which cannot fail, unless speedy and effectual steps be taken to arrest its progress, to reduce to a state of absolute starvation an extensive population, which has hitherto, under circumstances of extreme suffering, maintained a high character for industry, morality, and submission to the law.
    The meeting by which the memorialists were appointed a committee was numerously and respectably attended and was presided over by the marquis of Huntly. It unanimously adopted the following resolutions. . .[5]

The meeting was attended by several faithful ministers of the Gospel, who had travelled from the remotest districts to bear testimony to the frightful extent of misery to which many thousand families were reduced. From their statements it appeared that in many instances two families united under the roof of the one in order that the materials of the dwelling of the other might be used as fuel; that the blankets of the one were cut up for clothing, while those of the other afforded to both but an inadequate covering for the nights

4   Minister of Lerwick.
5   The memorial contained only resolutions 1, 2, 3 and 5, omitting resolutions 4, 6, 7, 8 and 9. The resolutions are not included in the above text of the memorial but are to be found in full in Section 2 below.

of an unusually severe season. Many hundred families were not possessed of food sufficient for a single meal, nor could they procure employment as a means of obtaining it. Scarcely a family had more than a few weeks' supply, and even that was of the most miserable and unwholesome description. This was amply verified by the samples exhibited at the meeting, – the exhibition of which produced a stronger feeling of sympathy than the affecting details laid before them; yet even in such a state of wretchedness, those who had little were found sharing their all with those who had none, in the hope that ere that was exhausted, relief would be extended to them, without which they must starve.

The distress which prevails to so great an extent, your memorialists apprehend is to be attributed to a superabundant population, acted upon by a variety of causes, and at present more immediately by the extensive failure of the two last harvests, the deficiency of the fisheries,[6] and the unusual loss of sheep and cattle, amounting in some districts, as in Orkney and Shetland, to one half.

But the most important cause affecting the over-abundant population of a great part of the distressed districts, is to be found in the almost entire cessation of the manufacture of kelp.

This manufacture, which existed for nearly a century, not only gave employment and subsistence to a population, consisting of more than 50,000 souls, in the Hebrides and West Coast of Scotland, besides those of Orkney and Shetland, but also yielded very large profits to the proprietors of the estates upon which it was carried on. For a great length of time this manufacture met with the encouragement of Government, by a protection against the various articles which might have competed with it in the market, – a protection which, while it encouraged this manufacture, tended to increase the population engaged in it. In the year 1822,[7] however, the protection began to be, and has now been altogether withdrawn; as a consequence, the almost entire extinction of this manufacture has ensued. These measures, however beneficial to the nation generally, have caused severe distress, if not ruin, to many of the landed proprietors, and the destitution of a population, amounting, as has been previously stated, to more than 50,000 individuals.[8]

In order to understand the connection between the nearly total extinction of the kelp manufacture and the consequent destitution of such an extensive population, it is necessary to explain to your Lordships what was the relative situation of landlord and tenant in the kelp districts, while kelp could be

---

[6] James Stewart Mackenzie had wanted the memorial also to point out that the reduction of the fishing bounty in 1826 had had a serious effect on the crofter/fishermen (NRS, Maclaine of Lochbuie papers, GD 174/1975, Copy note to John Bowie, 15 Feb. 1837).

[7] 3 George IV c. 109 – an act which lowered the duty on barilla from £11 a ton to 5 guineas a ton.

[8] See MacAskill, 'The Highland kelp proprietors', 60–82.

manufactured without loss to the proprietors. A piece of ground, called a *lot*, was held by each tenant, from which, with all his skill and perseverance, even in the best seasons, he could barely provide the necessaries of life; by the manufacture of kelp, however, he was enabled not only to pay his rent, but also to realise a sufficiency for the comfortable maintenance of himself and family.

When the manufacture of kelp as a profitable employment was extinguished, two thirds of the incomes from kelp estates were annihilated; and the proprietors could not afford to allow the small tenants to possess their lots without payment of rent. They were therefore compelled, in many instances, where it could be done without absolute ruin to the people, to resort to the system of letting their land in large farms; a large population was thus thrown out of employment, and being unable, by any exertion of their own, to relieve themselves from the destitute condition into which they were thrown, not in consequence of idleness or immorality, but by the force of circumstances over which they had no control, they became a burden on the soil which they had been in the habit of cultivating. They have not the means of emigrating; and unless relief is extended to them, they and their families must inevitably perish.

Petitions to both houses of parliament, and memorials to Government, urging the necessity of protecting the manufacture of kelp, were presented in the year 1831,[9] not only by those whose local knowledge and personal interest had given them access to the best means of information on the subject, but by the suffering population themselves.

These memorialists were, however, unsuccessful in their objects. Misery and disease, the usual accompaniment of famine, have been the consequence, and have reduced the population of these districts to a state of wretchedness unexampled in the history of this country. In the midst of destitution the most appalling, the national character has been maintained – the people have not forgotten the moral and religious principles in which they were educated – not a tumult has occurred, nor even a single infraction of the law, to call for the interference of the civil authorities.

Your Lordships are aware, the poor law of Scotland does not afford relief to the able-bodied – it is only the aged and infirm who are entitled to parochial aid. Thus the greater part of the population in whose behalf the present appeal is made to your Lordships, have no legal claim upon the parishes in which they have acquired a settlement. At the same time, your memorialists beg to assure your Lordships, that the landed proprietors in those districts have not been indifferent to the distress of their suffering people – their utmost exertions have been used, and great sacrifices made in order to alleviate a calamity which in fact it is not in the power of individual exertion wholly to obviate.[10] These exertions, however,

---

[9]   See MacAskill, 'The Highland kelp proprietors', 75–6.
[10] As to the special pleading of the proprietors, see MacAskill, 'Public response', 169–206; and

if they could be continued, would be unavailing, either to meet the present crisis, or to provide a permanent remedy for an evil of so extensive a character. This will at once be evident to your Lordships, when informed of the relative proportion of population and rent in some of the districts referred to. In an extensive and contiguous tract of country in the Hebrides, the population of which is not less than 55,000, the rental, in round numbers, is £43,000, being about 15s. of rent for each individual, and this amongst a population who, with few exceptions, have derived their sole means of existence from the resources of the district within which they reside.

An appeal has been made to the public, in order that means might be procured to supply the immediate wants of this starving population. Meetings have been held in Edinburgh, Glasgow, Leith, and other towns in Scotland, and large sums have already been subscribed, which will afford a temporary assistance. The object of the present application to your Lordships is for the purpose of obtaining, in the first instance, a grant of money in aid of those subscriptions; and secondly, to obtain the means of emigration to those who are willing to quit their native shores. A precedent for what the memorialists now humbly crave, is to be found in what took place in the year 1782, when the member for Caithness (the late Sir John Sinclair), earnestly besought the interposition of parliament, to relieve the severe distress then prevailing over a great part of the north of Scotland. The case was referred to a committee of the House of Commons, on whose report the house presented an address, recommending the calamitous state of the north of Scotland to His Majesty's gracious consideration, and promising to make good the expense incurred.[11] Great and appalling as was the distress in the year 1782, that of the present season is not less so, in the districts to which reference is here more immediately made.

The memorialists humbly entreat your Lordships to take the deplorable condition of these unfortunate people into your most serious consideration, and to grant such relief, in the circumstances of the case, as shall to your Lordships seem meet.

Signed, in name and on behalf of the committee, by
James Milles Riddell, Bart. Convener.
John Bowie, Secretary.
Edinburgh, 20th February 1837.

the Introduction on the lack of legal assessment and the failure of the poor law.
[11] See J. Knox, *View of the British Empire, More Especially Scotland* (Edinburgh, 1784), 78–80; Sir J. Sinclair, *Analysis of the Statistical Account of Scotland*, 2 vols. (London, 1826), ii, Appendix, 40–4; and [PP]1846 XXXVII (281). It is interesting that no mention was made here of the aid provided by the government in 1817 (see Introduction).

Memorial to the Treasury of a committee appointed by public meeting in Glasgow dated 27 February 1837

Unto the Right Honourable the Lords Commissioners of His Majesty's Treasury, the Memorial of a large committee, appointed by a public meeting of upwards of four thousand of the more Influential Inhabitants of Glasgow, which was held on the 6th instant, for the Relief of the Destitute Inhabitants of the Highlands and Islands of Scotland,[12]

Humbly Sheweth,

That your memorialists have abundance of the most unquestionable evidence (part of which they hope to have the honour of presenting for your Lordships' consideration) that destitution of the necessaries of life prevails to an appalling extent in some large and populous districts of the Northern and Western Highlands and Islands of Scotland; and as the case is too urgent, and the calamity too extensive, for the tedious and even hopeless task of collecting from individual benevolence anything like an adequate relief, the memorialists venture to pray that your Lordships may be pleased to administer speedily and liberally a supply out of the National Funds, as was done under the pressure of a similar calamity in 1782, and adopt other measures for the permanent relief of the sufferers.

The most needy districts are –

1. The Long Island or Outer Hebrides, population 34,000
2. The Isle of Skye, population 24,000
3. The Islands of Eigg, Muck, Rum, and Canna, population 1,000
4. The Islands of Tiree and Coll, population 6,000
5. The Isle of Mull, population 10,000
6. The Island of Jura, population 1,300
7. Iona, and some smaller Islands, 1,000
8. The West Coasts of Ross, Inverness, and Argyllshire, comprehending the parishes of Lochbroom, Gairloch, Applecross, Lochalsh, Lochcarron, Kintail, Glenshiel, Glenelg, Ardnamurchan, and Morvern on the mainland, population 30,000
9. The Orkney Islands, population 30,000
10. The Shetland Islands, population 30,000

Total population 167,300[13]

---

[12]   An extravagant description of the meeting is contained in the *Glasgow Herald*, 10 Feb. 1837: 'One of the most magnificent assemblies of ladies and gentlemen ever collected for one special object – undoubtedly the most splendid that ever met within the walls of any structure in Scotland . . . the spacious hall was filled in every corner by an assembly which, whether we take into account its numbers, respectability, or talent, never was surpassed by any in any kingdom, and the remembrance of which a length of time cannot efface from the memories of those who witnessed the thrilling and animating spectacle.'

[13]   This total did not include Sutherland and Caithness.

With the Orkney and Shetland isles your memorialists are not much acquainted or connected, so as to be able to state positively what may be their relative destitution; and in the observations, which they humbly take the liberty of making to your Lordships, the memorialists beg it to be distinctly understood that they have not yet sufficient proof as to them. But with respect to the Western Highlands and Islands the memorialists have no hesitation in stating that at least one-third, if not a larger proportion, of the inhabitants are at present destitute of food, seed corn, and fuel, many of clothing and of the means of procuring them; and that four-fifths of these inhabitants will be destitute of these articles before next harvest.

These countries must have been always comparatively poor, owing to the want of roads, manufactures, trade, capital and education. The more immediate cause of the present destitution was the uncommon inclemency of the two past seasons. The potato crops, on which the people in general depend for subsistence, failed to an appalling extent both in quantity and quality. The same has been the case with the corn crops. The wetness of the summers prevented the drying of the peats, their only fuel. There is no firewood growing, and coals are out of the question with them. Besides, the tempestuousness of the weather has been so great that their ordinary access to a supply of fish has been denied them. But other, though more remote, causes contributed and added greatly to their distress.

The memorialists do not mean to trouble your Lordships with a long and elaborate account of the more remote causes of the present calamity, though the memorialists consider them easily developed, and worthy of a nation's investigation. The memorialists, however, may briefly enumerate the following as appearing the most prominent of these causes, – viz. 1st, the cessation in the manufacture of kelp. This manufacture gave employment to a great proportion of the population, and yielded large revenues to the proprietors; but, in consequence of the protection given by Government against various articles which competed with it having been withdrawn, it has been almost entirely extinguished. 2nd, during the late war, the money given as pay to those enlisted was of essential service to the people at large; but that of course is now at an end. 3rd, emigration to America took away many that had money enough to pay their passage,[14] while it rendered poorer still those that remained. 4th, the herring fishing, which was very profitable for some years, has almost entirely failed of late on the west coasts of Scotland. 5th, there are no public works going on in the districts referred to, the making of the Crinan and Caledonian canals, and of the parliamentary roads, bridges, and piers having been finished long ago. 6th, the Trades' Unions in Glasgow and other towns are a bar in the way of the employment of such as might be inclined to

---

[14] See T. M. Devine, *Clanship to Crofters' War – The Social Transformation of the Scottish Highlands* (Manchester, 1994), 180–4.

come south.[15] 7th, ignorance prevails to an awful extent in the said districts, as is proven by the answers of the different clergymen to the queries of the General Assembly's committee on education; and your Lordships need not be informed that poverty and distress usually accompany ignorance. 8th, the Memorialists may also remind your Lordships that the poor law of Scotland does not afford relief to the able-bodied, but only to the aged and infirm. Besides a number of the landowners are not resident, and several of the large estates are under trust.

The memorialists might easily state other circumstances which have combined to cause the present destitution; but, in the respectful yet confident hope *that your Lordships will enter on an investigation of the case*, they forbear troubling your Lordships at greater length at present.

Your memorialists consider the sending immediately of a temporary supply of food to the destitute people necessary to the preservation of their lives. But this, without some radical amelioration, might only tend to perpetuate their poverty. Your memorialists therefore beg leave humbly to suggest to your Lordships that, besides a grant of public money and allowing a quantity of grain to be taken out of bond free of duty,[16] there is a necessity for your devising and executing some plan for the permanent amelioration of the condition of the parties on whose behalf your memorialists now address you, and who, amidst unparalleled hardships and distress, are distinguished for their peaceable, loyal, moral, and religious character.

May it therefore please your Lordships to take the condition of these truly destitute people into consideration, and to grant such relief as to your Lordships shall seem proper.

And your petitioners shall ever pray.

Signed, in name and on behalf of the Committee, by
Allan Fullarton, Chairman.
Charles R. Baird, Secretary.
Glasgow, 27th February, 1837.

---

[15] The migrant from the Highlands, unused to urban life and without industrial skills, found serious obstacles in his way when trying to obtain work or training for work in towns such as Glasgow where the unions were keen to ensure that the supply of labour was strictly limited (see T. C. Smout, *A History from the Scottish People 1560–1830* (London, 1969), 412–13, 428–9; [PP] 1837–8 VIII (488), *First Report of the Select Committee on Combinations of Workmen*, Q 2117–22; and Withers, 'Destitution', 128–50).

[16] This was also suggested by Sir Colin Mackenzie of Kilcoy to Lord John Russell (see NRS, Papers of the Mackenzie family, earls of Seaforth, GD 46/13/202, Mackenzie to Stewart Mackenzie, 27 Mar. 1837); and by the earl of Strathmore (*The Manchester Times and Gazette*, 27 May 1837).

Memorial of the committee in Glasgow for the relief of the Destitution in the Highlands and Islands of Scotland, 25 March 1837[17]

Unto the Right Honourable the Lords Commissioners of His Majesty's Treasury. The Memorial of the committee in Glasgow for the relief of the Destitution in the Highlands and Islands of Scotland.

Humbly sheweth

That your memorialists are a committee appointed to administer a charitable fund raised by voluntary contribution for the relief of the distress at present existing in the above-mentioned districts, the reality of which distress has been incontestably established by evidence both written and parole.

That the primary and principal object of the contributors was to furnish the indispensible necessaries of life to the sufferers and accordingly of the funds, six thousand five hundred pounds which have come under the control of the memorialists. Three thousand three hundred pounds have actually been expended in purchasing food and two thousand seven hundred pounds have been appropriated to a similar purpose, the remaining five hundred pounds having been set aside for the purpose of purchasing seed potatoes for the cottars or very poorest class of highlanders. These grants have been made without any stipulation for repayment or return of any kind.

That your memorialists have attentively perused your Lordships' minute relative to this destitution dated the fourteenth instant[18] together with the regulations of the Edinburgh committee approved by your Lordships as to the distribution of seed corn and potatoes[19] and they lament to find that no part of the ten thousand pounds which your Lordships have so kindly appropriated for the latter purpose can be dispensed to the needy districts unless the memorialists shall expend a corresponding sum for similar purpose on the terms prescribed by the Edinburgh committee.

That the sum already realised by the memorialists is wholly expended or anticipated and they can by no means flatter themselves that the contributions to be received hereafter shall be at all commensurate to the great and all-important object of supplying the people with the immediate necessaries of life for any considerable length of time. That the memorialists consider it a duty equally due to themselves, to the contributors of the fund and to the sufferers to look in the first place to a supply of food, fuel and raiment in the hope that Government and the proprietors of the soil may so arrange matters as to supply them with seed potatoes and oats.[20]

[17]   This memorial is referred to in Hill's letter to the Treasury of 25 Mar. 1837 (p. 119).
[18]   See p. 277.
[19]   See p. 245.
[20]   In 1847 the Central Board of Management determined that none of the public subscriptions

The memorialists are in hopes, therefore, that your Lordships will issue instructions to Sir John Hill authorising him to devote the ten thousand pounds at his disposal to the purchase of seed oats and potatoes, leaving it to the memorialists to expend their funds in the manner they originally contemplated in furnishing food and fuel and clothing to the starving population of the highlands.

May it therefore please your Lordships take the memorialists' case and the condition of the truly destitute persons into your consideration and to grant them such relief in the premises as to your Lordships shall seem proper.[21]

And your petitioners shall ever pray.

Signed in name and behalf of the committee by:
Allan Fullarton, Chairman
I. H. Muirhead, Assistant Secretary.

Section 2

Resolutions of a public meeting held on the 25 January 1837 in the Hopetoun Rooms, Edinburgh, the marquis of Huntley in the chair, for the purpose of taking into consideration the present unprecedented and alarmingly destitute state of the poor in the Highlands and Islands of Scotland, on the motion of the Rev. Dr Norman Macleod, seconded by Hugh MacLean, Esq., of Coll

The following Resolutions were unanimously agreed to

1. That a great proportion of the inhabitants of the western coasts of Argyllshire, Inverness-shire, and Ross-shire, together with the islands connected with these counties, are at the present moment in circumstances of the most appalling destitution, in regard to the want of fuel, clothing and the most ordinary necessaries of life; and that if an immediate supply be not provided, famine to a most awful and unprecedented extent, with its usual accompaniments of disease, must ere long lay waste those extensive and populous districts.

2. That the exertions of the Highland proprietors to relieve the destitution of the people resident on their properties, in the course of the year 1836, were great and praiseworthy, in as much as their benevolence was exercised

---

should be spent on the purchase of seed. Funds spent this way would, the board resolved, be a diversion from the express purpose of the fund which was to meet destitution and, the board said, the provision of seed was, in any event, more properly the duty of either individual proprietors or the government (NLS, Highland Destitution Reports (1846–51), Resolutions of the Central Board, 23 Feb. 1847).

[21] The Treasury minute of 31 Mar. 1837 setting out the government's response is set out on p. 280.

in behalf of a class of people from whom they derive little or no advantage; but the very general extent of destitution which now unhappily prevails, owing to the great deficiency of the herring Fishing, and the almost entire failure of the crops during the last inclement season, renders an appeal to the country at large absolutely necessary.[22]

3. That of so extensive a character is this destitution, arising not more from the scantiness of the produce, than from the inferior quality of the crops of every description in the Highlands and Islands, that it is essentially necessary not merely to send a supply for the *immediate preservation of life* but also for the purpose of seed for the ensuing crop; otherwise, whatever be the nature of the next season, it can only be followed by a destitution, if possible still more lamentable, because more permanent than at present unhappily prevails.

4. That while this meeting cherish the most grateful recollection of the liberal exertions which were made by the inhabitants of Edinburgh, Glasgow, Paisley, Greenock, and other places, in the course of the last year, in behalf of the suffering poor in the Highlands and Islands of Scotland,[23] they are constrained to declare, that there is now an imperious call for greater and more extensive exertions; and with a view to these, this meeting is of opinion that local committees should forthwith be appointed in all these towns, who shall act in concert in this great cause of suffering humanity; and further, that a correspondence be immediately entered into with such influential individuals in London, Manchester, Liverpool, and other cities throughout England, as are known to be well disposed to the object of this meeting; and that, with a view to holding public meetings in these cities, a deputation from Scotland shall be sent, who shall make known the facts of the case, and use their utmost exertions to procure subscriptions.[24]

5. That while the meeting feel the necessity which is imperiously imposed upon them, of doing all in their power to alleviate the existing evils, and provide for the fearful destitution which at present exists and is daily increasing, they cannot avoid a declaration of their firm and decided opinion, founded upon an intimate knowledge of the state of the Highlands and Islands, and of the causes which

[22] John Bowie's address to the meeting (see *Edinburgh Evening Courant*, 28 Jan. 1837) expands on this sensitive issue for the proprietors that they were not perceived to have done enough to assist their tenants and that the public would consider the appeal to be a self-serving exercise on behalf of the landed proprietors.

[23] NRS, Papers of the Maxtone Graham family of Cultoquhey, Perthshire, GD 155/1347, Island of Lewis – Deplorable scarcity of food, 19 May 1836; *Inverness Courier*, 23 May 1836; and *The Scotsman*, 18 June 1836.

[24] The deputation comprised the Rev. Dr Norman Macleod and John Bowie form Edinburgh and Charles Baird from Glasgow. Apart from the public meetings held in Edinburgh, Leith, Glasgow, Aberdeen, Inverness and London, public meetings were held in a number of English towns and cities, including Manchester, Hull, Exeter, Bristol, Ipswich, Newcastle, Liverpool, Leeds and Sheffield (see generally MacAskill, 'Public response', 169–206).

have led to the present lamentable crisis, that the same evils must occur year after year in greater or less degree, except extensive national remedy is applied to alter the condition of a population thus reduced to poverty, chiefly from the great decrease, and, in many places, total annihilation of the manufacture of kelp, which constituted almost their sole dependence.

6. That, under these circumstances, the deputation proposed to be sent to England shall be instructed to communicate with His Majesty's Government on the subject of emigration, as well as on the means of relieving the present destitution of the Highland population.

7. That for the purpose of carrying these resolutions into effect, the following committee be appointed, with power to add to their number, viz. – Sir James Milles Riddell of Ardnamurchan and Sunart, Bart; Sir John Campbell of Ardnamurchan, Bart; Sir John Stewart Forbes, Bart; Sir Reginald Macdonald S. Seton, Bart; Sir Donald Campbell of Dunstaffnage, Bart; William Gibson-Craig, Esq.; The Rev. Dr Norman MacLeod, Moderator of the Church of Scotland; Hugh MacLean, Esq. of Coll; Colin Campbell, Esq. of Jura; Alexander Lamont, Esq. of Knockdaw; Thomas Mackenzie, Esq. of Applecross; Richard Campbell, Esq. of Achnabreck; Charles Gordon, Esq. of Drimnin, Secretary of the Highland Society; William Robertson, Esq. Younger of Kinlochmoidart; John Ferrier, Esq. WS; James Archibald Campbell, Esq. of Inveraw; Alexander Hunter, Esq. WS; James Macinnes, Esq. SSC; James Mackenzie, Esq. WS; John Bowie, Esq. WS; Archibald McNeill, Esq. WS; and Alexander Hutchieson, Esq.

That Sir William Forbes & Co be requested to act as treasurers, and John Bowie, Esq., WS as secretary; that any three of the committee shall form a quorum; and that the committee be authorised to send copies of these resolutions to all presbyteries in Scotland and England; to communicate with all local committees in Scotland and England; and also to appoint district committees throughout the Highlands and Islands, not only for the purpose of procuring subscriptions, but also for ascertaining and determining the relative destitution, and ultimately distributing the supplies that may be furnished.

8. That this meeting learn with the highest satisfaction, that several influential individuals in England, and especially Alderman Pirie of London,[25] have taken a deep interest in the circumstances which have led to this meeting. They direct that copies of the foregoing resolutions be transmitted to them, as also to

---

[25] John Pirie was the largest shipbroker in the city of London and later became lord mayor. He was a founder director of the South Australian Company and a supporter of the colonisation of South Australia and later New Zealand. He had written to Thomas Knox, the factor in Lewis, at the beginning of Jan. 1837 with a questionnaire as to the distress in the island (NRS, Papers of the Mackenzie family, earls of Seaforth, GD 46/13/199/6, Seaforth to Pirie, 13 Jan. 1837).

all noblemen and gentlemen connected with Scotland, who may be present in London, and particularly members of parliament, that their attention may be early directed to this most momentous subject.

9. That subscriptions will be received by Sir William Forbes & Co. Bankers, Edinburgh, the treasurers; Mr Bowie, the secretary, or any other member of the committee, or by any Bank in England or Scotland.[26]

Resolutions of a public meeting held on 6 February 1837 held in the Great Pavilion, Buchanan Street, Glasgow for the purpose of adopting measures for the relief of the destitute inhabitants of the Highlands and Islands of Scotland, including the Orkney and Shetland Isles

On the motion of principal Macfarlan,[27] it was resolved that, in the absence of the lord provost[28] (from whom a letter was read, regretting that pressing official business prevented him from attending, and expressing his cordial acquiescence in the object of the meeting) the honourable the sheriff of Lanarkshire[29] was requested to take the chair.

The meeting having been opened with prayer by the Rev. Dr Smyth[30]

The following resolutions were thereafter moved, seconded and unanimously carried:−

1st. Moved by [the Rev.] Dr [Norman] Macleod and seconded by Mr [John Robertson] Glass of Durinish −

That there is incontestable evidence that a great proportion of the inhabitants of the Highlands and Islands of Scotland are at present in circumstances of the most appalling destitution, in regard to the want of fuel, clothing and the most ordinary necessaries of life; and that if an immediate supply be not provided, famine to a most awful and unprecedented extent, with its usual accompaniments of disease, must ere long lay waste those extensive and populous districts.

2nd. Moved by Mr [Finlay] Macpherson of Tobermory (in the absence of Professor J. P. Nichol)[31] and seconded by James Lumsden, Esq. of Yoker − That of so extensive a character is this destitution arising not more from the

---

26   The total of the subscriptions raised by the Edinburgh committee, including from events organised, amounted to £16,553, of which £13,515 was spent (p. 224).
27   Duncan Macfarlan, DD, principal and vice-chancellor of the University of Glasgow.
28   The Hon. William Mills. The lord provost was the city's chief magistrate.
29   Archibald Alison, esq., advocate.
30   The Rev. Dr John Smyth, DD, minister of St George's Church.
31   Professor of practical astronomy at the university of Glasgow.

scantiness of the produce than from the inferior quality of the crops of every description in the Highlands and Islands, that it is essentially necessary, not merely to send a supply for the *immediate preservation of life*, but also for the purpose of seed for the ensuing crop; otherwise, whatsoever be the nature of the next season, it can only be followed by a destitution, if possible, still more lamentable, because more permanent, than at present unhappily prevails.

3rd. Moved by the Rev. Nathaniel Patterson of St Andrew's and seconded by Sir Reginald Macdonald Seton, Baronet[32] –
That the moral character of the highlanders, and of the services they have rendered to the country in times of danger, give them a special claim on the sympathy and assistance of their fellow-countrymen under their present distresses.

4th. Moved by Allan Fullarton, Esq., and seconded by William Campbell, Esq. of Dunoon Castle –
That as the general and fearful extent of the destitution which now prevails imperiously calls for great and extensive exertion all over the country, a correspondence should be opened by the several committees in Edinburgh, Glasgow, Greenock and Paisley, with those individuals who are known to be friends to the cause, and deputations sent to the principal cities and towns in Scotland, to make known the character and extent of the destitution which prevails.

5th. Moved by the Rev. Lewis Rose[33] and seconded by Robert Oak, Esq. –
That the meeting learn, with much pleasure, that the Rev. Dr Macleod and John Bowie, Esq. of Edinburgh have agreed to proceed to London for the purpose of furthering the objects for which this meeting has been called, and with a view of aiding them in that important mission, that the committee to be appointed at this meeting shall name a deputation who may be requested to accompany Dr Macleod and Mr Bowie for the purpose of obtaining subscriptions to meet the present destitution and, above all, to act along with them in bringing the whole facts of the case, and the various causes which may have contributed to occasion the distress, under the notice of His Majesty's Government, with a view to some great measure to prevent the recurrence of a destitution under which so overgrown and unemployed a population frequently suffer.[34]

6th. Moved by M[atthew] M[oncrieff] Pattison, Esq. seconded by Mr Macdonald –
That this meeting respectfully request the Right Honourable Lord William Bentinck and James Oswald [of Shieldhall], Esq. the representatives of the city

---

[32] Second baronet of Seton-Stewart of Allanton, Lanark.
[33] Minister of the Gaelic church, Duke Street.
[34] Charles Baird was the appointee from Glasgow.

of Glasgow, to aid the deputation to be sent from Glasgow in their mission, and particularly to impress on His Majesty's Government the propriety and necessity of immediate and effective assistance being rendered to our destitute fellow-countrymen in the Highlands and Islands.[35]

7th. Moved by Baillie [John] Bain and seconded by the Lord Dean of Guild[36] – That a large subscription should now be raised, and the committee acting in charge of the fund raised for the relief of the destitute inhabitants of the Western Isles[37] be re-appointed (with power to add to their number) to procure additional subscriptions, and to take charge of the application of the funds now to be raised and that Mr John Macpherson be requested to act as treasurer, and Mr Charles R. Baird as secretary with power to them to employ a suitable person to act under them.

8th. A vote of thanks was then given to the deputation from Edinburgh.

9th. A vote of thanks to John Gordon, Esq. for the use of his premises, and to the gentlemen who kindly granted the use of the Pavilion for this meeting.

10th. And a vote of thanks to the chairman for his conduct in the chair.[38]

Resolutions of a meeting held on 17 February 1837 within the Court-House of Aberdeen, provost James Milne in the chair, for the purpose of considering the course that may be deemed most advisable for calling forth the sympathy and benevolent aid of our fellow citizens for the relief of the incontestably fearful destitution of many of our countrymen in the Highlands and Western Islands of Scotland.

On the motion of the Rev. Mr [William K.] Tweedie[39] seconded by Baillie Harper[40] the following resolutions were unanimously agreed to:

35   Lord William Henry Cavendish-Bentinck and James Oswald were the two Glasgow MPs. On the dissolution which followed the king's death, Oswald ceased to be an MP. Neither of them were present at the meeting with the Chancellor of the Exchequer on 13 Mar. 1837.

36   William Brown. The five baillies and the Lord Dean of Guild, who belonged to and was nominated by the Merchants' House, were part of the city's town council.

37   In June 1836 an appeal had been launched in Glasgow (which followed the appeal in May, in Edinburgh) for subscriptions in aid of the destitute inhabitants of the Western Isles and a committee had been formed; the balance of funds remaining from the subscription, £458–15–4, were made available to the re-appointed committee in 1837 (1841 SC, 109).

38   The total of the funds raised locally by the committee was £5,000, but the committee received funds totaling another £31,511 (which included remittances from the London, Edinburgh and other committees). The surplus remaining with the Glasgow committee after all its disbursements was £2,950–12–3 (1841 SC, 109).

39   Minister of the South Church on Belmont Street.

40   Aberdeen's municipal government was vested in a body corporate consisting of the provost,

1. That this meeting hears, with deep concern, of the appalling destitution, as regards fuel, clothing, food, and the most ordinary necessaries of life, which at present prevails over a wide extent of the Highlands and Islands of Scotland, under the destructive pressure of which, aggravated by two successive inclement seasons, and by prevailing sickness, the numerous inhabitants of these districts have been, and still are, exposed to the extreme of human misery; that the meeting feels deeply convinced that this misery must go on increasing in extent and fatality, unless prompt and effectual measures be adopted to meet the urgent necessities of the district thus visited by an afflictive providence, and that not only for the present, but until the existing destitution be alleviated or removed by the return of a bountiful harvest.

2. That while this meeting recognises the hand of God in these sore calamities, it also feels it to be the duty of all who, by the blessing of providence,[41] possess the means, to contribute for the alleviation of these suffering; and therefore this meeting, desirous of seconding the efforts which are being made in other quarters of the kingdom for this purpose, resolve individually so to contribute, and to solicit, on behalf of the famishing sufferers, the benevolence of the inhabitants of Aberdeen and the adjoining country.

3. That a subscription be accordingly opened, under the management of the following gentlemen as a committee: the lord provost, James Milne; Sir Michael Bruce of Stenhouse; Baillie Harper; Baillie Simpson; Mr Lewis Crombie, city treasurer; Mr Smith, jun., dean of guild; Mr [Alexander] Webster, advocate; Mr [Alexander] Forbes, wine merchant; Mr Alexander Gordon, advocate; Mr [David] Chalmers of Westburn; Mr [Alexander] Jopp, advocate; the Rev. John Murray;[42] the Rev. James Foote;[43] the Rev. William K. Tweedie; the Right Rev. Bishop [William] Skinner;[44] the Rev. John Brown;[45] the Rev. Charles Gordon;[46] the Very Rev. Principal [William] Jack;[47] the Very Rev. Principal [David] Dewar;[48] Mr [Thomas] Sangster, advocate; Mr James Edward, advocate; the convener of the incorporated trades; the president of the Shipmaster's Society; collector [Alexander] Fiddes; collector [James] McLaren; Mr Duncan Davidson, advocate; Mr John Angus, advocate; Mr [William] Keith, surgeon; Mr Henry Lumsden, advocate; Mr Leslie Clark, merchant; Mr [James] Ferguson, advocate [and notary]; Mr John Gibb, engineer; with Mr Alexander Webster, advocate, Mr

4 baillies, a dean of guild and a treasurer, with a council of seven deacons of the incorporated trades.
41 See the Introduction as to the use of providentialist language.
42 Minister of the North Church, King Street.
43 Minister of the East Church, Union Street.
44 Of the episcopal chapel, St Andrew's, King Street.
45 Minister of the episcopal chapel, St Paul's, the Gallowgate.
46 Minister of the roman catholic chapel, Chapel Court.
47 Principal of King's College, Old Aberdeen.
48 Professor of church history at Marischal College, Broad Street.

David Chalmers of Westburn and Mr James Edward, advocate, as joint treasurers and Mr John Angus, advocate, as secretary; 5 to be a quorum. That subscription papers be placed in the various banking offices in Aberdeen, also in the hands of the members of the committee, and distributed throughout the country.

4. That the committee be requested and authorised to transmit, from time to time as collected, the sums so subscribed to the secretary or treasurer of the Glasgow committee, to be applied in terms of these resolutions, under the direction of that committee; or be otherwise disposed of as the committee now appointed shall direct.

5. That these resolutions be published in the Aberdeen newspapers.[49]

Resolutions of a meeting held on 11 March 1837 at the Egyptian Hall, Mansion House, London in behalf of the destitute in the Highlands and Islands of Scotland, the Right Hon. The Lord Mayor[50] in the chair

The following resolutions were proposed and carried unanimously:

1. It appears to this meeting, from the facts now stated, that there is incontestable evidence that many parts of the Highlands and Islands of Scotland are at present in circumstances of the most appalling destitution, in respect generally of food, and in particular districts also of fuel and clothing; and that if an immediate supply be not provided, famine to a most awful and unprecedented extent, with its usual accompaniment of disease, must ere long lay waste these extensive and populous districts – that great exertions are, therefore, imperiously called for in order to meet the extreme urgency and necessity of the case.

2. That this meeting hereby resolve that subscriptions be immediately commenced in aid of their destitute and suffering fellow countrymen. That the bankers of London, and the following booksellers – Messrs James Nisbet and Co., Berners Street; Messrs Hatchard and Son, Piccadilly; Messrs Seeley, Fleet Street; Messrs Smith, Elder and Co., Cornhill; be requested to

---

[49]   In addition to subscriptions in money, the committee gave notice that it would thankfully receive donations of grain, meal, potatoes, or other provisions, which would be transmitted to the most necessitous districts. Such donations would be taken charge of by William Walker or George Lyall, town sergeants; and, in the meantime would be deposited in the cellars of the meal market, which the tacksman had generously allowed the use of for this purpose. No custom would be charged on victual so lodged, on the same being certified by either of the above officers. The subscriptions raised locally by the committee amounted to, at least, £5,680 (*Aberdeen Journal*, 10 May 1837).

[50]   John Cowan, who was of Scottish descent and acquired a considerable fortune as a wax and tallow chandler.

receive subscriptions and that the sum collected be transmitted to the joint committees of Edinburgh and Glasgow.

3. That the following be appointed a committee for carrying the object of the meeting into effect, with power to add to their number:– The Rt. Hon. The Lord Mayor; The Rt. Hon. Lord Teignmouth; Sir George Sinclair., Bart, MP [for Caithness]; Sir Andrew Leith Hay, MP [for Elgin district]; Sir Charles Forbes, Bart; The Hon. Fox Maule, MP [for Perthshire]; The Hon. Col. F. W Grant, MP [for Elginshire and Nairnshire]; Colonel MacDougall; Major C. L. C. Bruce, MP [for Inverness district]; Thomas Balfour, Esq., MP [for Orkney and Shetland]; Alex[ander] Bannerman, Esq., MP [for Aberdeen]; Walter F. Campbell, Esq., MP [for Argyll]; A. W. Chisholm, Esq., MP [for Invernessshire]; J. A. S. Mackenzie, Esq., MP [for Ross and Cromarty]; Roderick Macleod, Esq., MP [for Sutherland]; Mr Alderman Pirie; The Rev. John Crombie, DD; The Rev. J. R. Brown, DD; The Rev. P. McMorland; Nadir Baxter, Esq., James Bonar, Esq.; John Campbell, Esq.; Alexander Elder, Esq.; Robert Forman, Esq.; Alexander Gillespie, jun., Esq.; Captain Gordon; Alexander Haldane, Esq.; William Hamilton, Esq.; John Hodge, Esq.; Mr Alderman Lucas; James Marshall, Esq.; Kenneth Macrae, Esq.; James Nisbet, Esq.; William Skirving, Esq.; and William Waugh, Esq.

That Alderman Pirie be appointed treasurer, and the Rev. Peter McMorland and James Nisbet, Esq., be appointed secretaries to the committee.

4. That the cordial thanks of the meeting be given to the Right Hon. The Lord Mayor for his readiness in granting the use of the Egyptian-hall, and his kindness in presiding at this meeting.[51]

In publishing the resolutions the committee also made the following statement: The committee, in publishing the proceedings at the Mansion House, and the list of subscriptions already received, respectfully call the attention of the public to the facts that in certain districts in the Highlands and Islands of Scotland, including the Orkney and Shetland Isles, containing a population of 167,200 inhabitants, no less than 86,000 persons are in positive want of food, raiment, and fuel, and of the means of procuring them, in consequence of the deficient harvest of late years, the unusual mortality of sheep and black cattle, the almost total failure of the crops of last year, and other causes pressing on a redundant population, left, by the destruction of the kelp manufacture (in which the majority of the people were formerly engaged) without any means of employment.

[51] The subscriptions received by the London committee amounted to £30,486 (p. 244). A little over £19,000 was remitted to Scotland, virtually of all of which went to the Glasgow committee for food and clothing (1841 SC, 109). There was an unspent surplus left with the London committee of £11,752. As to the controversy over how the surplus should be used, see MacAskill, 'Public response', 186–8.

It may be observed, that many of the inhabitants of these districts have been allowed by the landlords to remain on their estates although they pay no rents; any sums, therefore, which the benevolent may contribute to alleviate the distress of the poor inhabitants will not be misapplied to the payment of rents to the landlords, who, notwithstanding the great diminution of their incomes from the stoppage of the manufacture of kelp, have come forward in a liberal manner – many of them beyond their means[52] – for relief of the distress of the population.

The amount required to relieve the present destitution is calculated at not less than £100,000;[53] but notwithstanding that great exertions have been made in Edinburgh, Glasgow, and generally throughout Scotland, it has been found impossible to raise such a sum there; an appeal has therefore been made to the English public which the committee doubt not will be instantly and liberally responded to, so as to prevent thousands dying from starvation.

Section 3

Report by the committee in Edinburgh for relief of the destitution in the Highlands and Islands of Scotland – 21 December 1837

At the first public meeting, held in Edinburgh on the 25th January 1837, to take into consideration the lamentable destitution then existing in certain districts in the Highlands and Islands, this committee was appointed for the purpose of giving effect to such measures as might be deemed most advisable for alleviating the distress in those districts.

The great object contemplated by the meeting, as set forth in the resolutions,[54] was not only to provide for the immediate relief of the destitute population, but at the same time to prevent, so far as possible, a recurrence of their sufferings. With this view, while a committee appointed at Glasgow for similar objects undertook the immediate charge of the supply of food, it was left more particularly to the Edinburgh committee to attend to the procuring of proper seed for the ensuing crop; as also to consider the best means of permanently ameliorating the condition of the over-peopled districts.

Following out the above arrangement, this committee, after ascertaining by returns from the resident clergy and others that in most of the distressed districts there was not a sufficiency of grain and potatoes for seed, immediately took means of placing a supply within the reach of tenants paying low rents and

---

52 On the special pleading of the proprietors, see MacAskill, 'Public response', 189–95.
53 The London committee had to defend this estimate and the fact that it continued to seek subscriptions at a time when, it was alleged, it must have been known that the sums already subscribed were more than adequate (see MacAskill, 'Public response', 185).
54 See p. 211.

also cottars paying no rents, such persons not having the means of supplying themselves. Aware, however, of the duty of the proprietors to aid in this matter, the committee required a guarantee of a partial payment by them at Candlemas 1838 of the seed distributed in their lands; and the district committees appointed to distribute the supplies were empowered, in their discretion, to afford gratuitous relief only to those paying under £5 of rent. The committee have to report that, from returns received from the district committees, the supplies of seed appear to have been confined, with few exceptions, to tenants paying under £5 of rent, and a great proportion distributed to persons paying no rent. These supplies of seed were partly furnished by Government, who evinced the greatest readiness to cooperate in the important matter in which the committee was engaged, having first ascertained through the commissioner Mr Graham, that the destitution was even greater than had first been reported.

At a very early stage of the proceedings, it was resolved that a deputation should proceed to London, not only with a view of procuring subscriptions, but for the further object of bringing under the notice of Government the extent of the destitution and the various causes which had led to the same, in the expectation that Government would come forward liberally in aid of the subscriptions, and also arrange with reference to an extensive emigration from the distressed districts. The deputation consisted of the Rev. Dr Macleod, Mr Bowie WS and Mr Charles R. Baird of Glasgow, to whom the Government evinced every disposition to meet the objects they had in view, and here the committee deem it their duty to record their sense of the indefatigable exertions of the deputation.

From the very full and able reports published by the Glasgow committee and which have shown the urgency and the extent of the destitution, as well as the principles and nature of the joint operations of the two committees, this committee feel it to be unnecessary to go into any detail on these subjects; they therefore confine this report to the more immediate objects of their own labours.

From the annexed abstract state, it will be seen that very large supplies of seed were forwarded to the Highlands and Islands, including Orkney and Shetland; and here it is right to state that, with reference to the supplies sent to Orkney and Shetland, this committee were greatly assisted by a committee established at Aberdeen for the purpose of more immediately attending to these distant districts. From the returns received, the committee feel themselves warranted in assuring the public that the supplies of food, clothing and seed which were furnished by the several committees have proved of the most incalculable benefit to the poor people who were so relieved; although the committee regret to state that in some districts of the country, and particularly in Shetland, a north-east gale and a severe frost materially injured some of the crops.

The committee subjoin a statement of the funds, from which it will be observed that a balance of £3,084 -6–2 ¼ remains in their hands. That statement seems to call for few remarks. The committee have endeavoured to conduct their operations at the smallest possible expense, and no member of it has, directly or indirectly, been remunerated for the labour undergone. That their deputations, which proved so necessary and so useful, should have been allowed to bear their own expenses (and no more was allowed) would have been unjust. And while the committee early found it necessary to employ a responsible and competent person to act as their assistant and cash secretary, on the express understanding that he was to be remunerated, they have fixed that remuneration less in relation to the fidelity and amount of his labours, than to the nature of the fund out of which it had to be granted.[55]

That this balance should remain can be easily accounted for. In almost the words of the London committee "to the scanty distributions which were made during the early part of the season when the charitable supplies were coming in slowly, and the ultimate amount of them altogether uncertain – and to the bounties of a gracious Providence, furnished not only at the last, in an early and very plentiful supply of the usual fruits of the earth throughout most of the distressed districts, but also to an unusually abundant supply of fish", to which this committee may add the imperative duty they felt to be imposed on them to confine the supplies within the narrowest possible limits, for the reasons so well set forth in the Glasgow report, are to be attributed the amount of the expenditure being so much smaller than was anticipated. At the same time, the committee beg to state that they took the earliest opportunity of closing the subscription, which circumstances, in their judgement, justified.

That such balances as are in the hands of the several committees should be left, the committee feel most grateful for; and the question now remaining for consideration is the mode of employing the surplus funds, so as best to accord with the views of the donors and most effectually to promote the permanent welfare of those districts where the distress has prevailed.

The committee have no hesitation in stating that, looking to the terms of their original appointment and bearing in mind that in one and all of the appeals to the public, emigration was held out as the obvious means of preventing a recurrence of the evil, and having also in view that several large contributions from distant lands have been sent home for the purpose of aiding in the permanent amelioration of the over-populated districts, this committee do most cordially concur in the views of the Glasgow committee that the surplus funds would be most fitly appropriated for the purposes of emigration from the districts referred to.[56]

[55] The remuneration was £150, which might be contrasted with the salary paid by the Glasgow committee to the assistant secretary of £73–10–0 and by the London committee to its clerk and occasional assistants of £37–14–0.

[56] See MacAskill, 'Public response', 184–8, where it is suggested that this statement is something of a masterpiece of manipulation of the facts.

The committee believe that it is well known to all connected with the Highlands and Islands of Scotland that the Government, in the course of the last summer, commenced a system of emigration to Australia; and the committee are rejoiced to have it in their power to report that the same facilities of emigrating are again to be offered to the inhabitants of the distressed and over-peopled districts. But the experience of the past has shown: 1st That many who were willing to emigrate to Australia could not be taken out free of all expense because of their advanced years; and 2nd That while thousands are anxiously imploring that they may be removed from their present state of poverty and dependence, it appears from the returns made by the local committees that Canada is in most instances the place to which they would prefer going.

The committee are therefore of opinion that the remaining funds in the hands of the several committees may be most beneficially employed, not only in assisting some of the old people to accompany the younger members of their family to Australia, but also in aiding a *very large* emigration to Canada. With reference to the latter emigration, the committee entertain a very confident hope that the Government may be induced to aid liberally. Farther assistance can be given from the surplus funds of this and the other committees; the remaining proportion, the committee are of opinion should be made up by the proprietors whose estates are to be relieved. This burden the committee are aware must fall very heavily on many proprietors; still the committee are of opinion that in a matter to them of such importance, they ought to bear a share.

But the committee, having ascertained in the course of their inquiries that the destitution in its worst form existed chiefly in those places where *crofting* or a division of the land into small allotments and the formation and extension of villages had encouraged an increase of population, think it right to express their conviction that great evils have resulted from that system and that greater evils may be apprehended from a continuance of it in situations where there is little or no demand for productive employment. The committee believe that the proprietors are fully aware of these evils and very desirous to provide a remedy; and in proposing to contribute therefore, by means of the surplus funds at the disposal of the committee to an object so important in all its bearings as emigration, they feel themselves at the same time called upon to state it as their opinion, that unless local regulations calculated to diminish the present population in these districts and to check its future progress, be adopted and strictly enforced, emigration or any other measure of relief which could be devised, must prove in the end unavailing.

In conclusion, the committee trust that, having brought so far to a termination their labours, it will be found that their efforts have been faithfully and zealously directed to accomplish the great objects in view. The committee deem it right to record their sense of the zealous and cordial cooperation at once of the officers of Government, the London and Glasgow committees, the committees formed at Aberdeen and Inverness, as well as all the local committees established in the different districts. By the splendid liberality of the public, the different committees have, under Providence, been enabled to relieve the immediate wants of the destitute, and happily a large surplus fund remains, by the judicious application of which, together with the support of the Government and the cooperation of the proprietors in these districts, the committee trust the recurrence of such an amount of misery as they have been called upon recently to contemplate will be effectually prevented, and the condition of a large and valuable portion of the community[57] permanently improved.

By order of the committee,
J. Milles Riddell, *Chairman*.
John Bowie, *Secretary*
Edinburgh, 21st December 1837.

General state of receipts and expenditure of the Edinburgh committee, with a subjoined abstract of the supplies of seed, food etc., furnished by the committees of Edinburgh, Glasgow and Aberdeen.

Charge

Amount of subscription, collections etc., £13,554–12–11 ¾
Proceeds of Ball, deducting expenses, £335–11–0
Ditto of Concert, ditto, £106–3–3
Ditto of Promenade, ditto, £46–17–6
Ditto of Exhibition of Paintings, £8–0–6
Received from Government for seed,* £1,412–16–8
Bank interest to this date, £89–13–8
Remittance from the London committee (for Aberdeen committee), £1000–0–0
Amount of charge £16,553–15–6 ¾
Note: the Paintings presented to the committee are yet undisposed of.

Discharge

Cost of seed purchased by the committee for the West Coast, including freights etc., £7,589–10–6
Remitted for food to ditto, £49–13–0
Remitted to the Aberdeen committee at various times for Orkney and Shetland and Stroma in Pentland Firth, of which £250 for seed, £3750–0–0
Remitted to Ditto (sum received from London committee), £1,000–0–0

---

[57]   After, presumably, the emigration of that part of the community which the 25 Jan. 1837 resolutions of the Edinburgh public meeting referred to as 'a class of people from whom [the proprietors] derive little or no advantage' (p. 211).

Remitted for food for Tingwall in Shetland, £50–0–0
Ditto ditto for Latheron in Caithness, £50–0–0
Ditto ditto to Tain for Croich and Kincardine, Ross-shire, £150–0–0
Ditto ditto to Inverness for Creich in Sutherland, £20–2–1
Paid for 50 tons of seed potatoes for Orkney and freight etc., £237–18–10
Miscellaneous expenses:–
Paid expenses of two deputations to Glasgow, £16–15–0
Ditto ditto ditto to London, £144–19–0
Ditto printing account, £31–13–0
Ditto advertising account (list of subscriptions, etc.), £122–0–4
Ditto for writings, copies of accounts etc., £35–5–6
Ditto for collecting subscriptions in Edinburgh, £10–17–0
Ditto framing paintings presented to committee, £30–5–0
Ditto postage and parcels, £61–7–5 ½
Ditto stationery, £6–0–0
Ditto incidental expenses, £3–14–9
Ditto postages and stamps, paid to bankers, £5–3–5
Allowance voted by general committee to Assistant and Cash Secretary, £150–0–0
Amount of discharge £13,515–4–10 ½

Balance £3,038–10–8 ¼
    Add value of seed refunded to this committee, £40–12–06,
    Subscriptions for clothing, £5–3–0

Leaving a Balance, as of this date, in the hands of Sir Wm. Forbes & Co. Bankers, £3,084–6–2 ¼

Edinburgh, 16ᵗʰ December 1837
Henry Craigie, *Assistant and Cash Secretary*

Edinburgh, 19ᵗʰ December 1837. In terms of minute of committee of 18ᵗʰ current, we have examined the above account and compared the same with the vouchers and found it correct.
Richard Campbell, 11 Northumberland Street.
Henry Cheyne, 25 Abercromby Place.
Alex. Hutchison, 10 Drummond Place.
James Kinnear, 9 Doune Terrace.

★The aid afforded by Government appears to be :–
1. The above sum of £1,412–6–8
2. Sum paid to Aberdeen committee £1,741–0–5
3. Expended by Sir John Hill £2,666–10–6
£5,819–17–7

Abstract of total supplies transmitted by the committees of Edinburgh, Glasgow and Aberdeen, as appearing from their several accounts.

Sent by Edinburgh committee direct:

To West Coast (including 800 quarters oats and 340 tons potatoes purchased by Sir J. Hill), seed oats 3,784 qtrs.; seed bear 220 ½ qtrs.; seed potatoes 858 tons.

To Tain for Croich and Kincardine in Ross-shire, £150 money.

To Inverness for Creich in Sutherland, £20 money.

To Orkney for seed, seed potatoes 53 tons.

Sent by and through Glasgow committee:

To West Coast, including Inverness, seed potatoes 301 ½ tons; 18,601 ½ bolls meal;[58] 188 2 cwt. sacks of flour; £725 money; 3,315 pairs blankets.

Sent by and through the Aberdeen committee:

To Orkney, seed potatoes 49 ½ tons; 2,128 bolls meal;[59] 53 2 cwt. sacks of flour; 122 1 ½ cwt. sacks of rice.

To Shetland (including 45 ½ bolls special donation from Mrs Hope, Granton, to Tingwall), seed oats 1,372 qtrs.; seed bear 238 qtrs.; seed potatoes 192 tons; 5,457 bolls meal;[60] 525 2 cwt. sacks of flour; 320 1 ½ cwt. sacks of rice.

To Stroma, in Pentland Firth, 60 bolls meal.

To Latheron, in Caithness, 92 ½ bolls meal.

To Strathdon (besides some other supplies to Highland parishes), 100 bolls meal.

Total of supplies: seed oats 5,156 qtrs.; seed bear 458 ½ qtrs.; seed potatoes 1,454 tons; meal 26,439 bolls; flour 766 2 cwt. sacks; rice 442 1 ½ cwt. sacks; £895 money; 3,315 pairs of blankets.

Notes: – it is right to explain that large sums were remitted by the London committee to those of Glasgow and Aberdeen (£15,000 to the former, including £1,000 remitted through the Edinburgh committee, £1,300 to the latter), and that the whole of the flour and rice supplied by these committees were furnished to them by the London committee.

The full quantity of 800 qtrs. of oats sent to the West Coast by Government is included in the above Abstract, and the cost and freight of it are also

---

[58]   On the basis of Graham's estimate of half a boll per head for the season (p. 56), this suggests 37,202 people on the west coast and islands were supplied. By comparison, in 1847, during the first three months of its existence, the Glasgow section of the Central Board distributed 14,723 bolls of meal (7,047 bolls of wheatmeal, 5,696 bolls of oatmeal and 1,980 bolls of peasemeal) (Devine, *Highland Famine*, 129, and Hunter, *Crofting Community*, 64).

[59]   On the basis of Graham's estimate of half a boll per head for the season (p. 56), this suggests 4,256 people in Orkney were supplied; see [PP] 1844 XXI (564), 246.

[60]   On the basis of Graham's estimate of half a boll per head for the season (p. 56), this suggests 10,914 people in Shetland were supplied.

included in the sum of £2,666–10–6 stated to have been expended by Sir J. Hill, of which quantity, however, only 480 qtrs. were placed at the disposal of this committee. A part of the remainder was, it is believed, not distributed.

The potatoes sent by the Glasgow committee to the West Coast and stated above as 301 ½ tons are stated in the Glasgow report as 3,617 barrels.

Interim Report by the committee in Glasgow, for the relief of the destitute inhabitants of the Highlands and Islands of Scotland – 29 April 1837

As it may be satisfactory to the committees at a distance, as well as to the public in general, to learn the proceedings of this committee, it has been deemed proper to publish the following brief report.

In the month of June last an appeal was made to the citizens of Glasgow on behalf of the destitute inhabitants of the Western Islands, when a public meeting was held, a committee named, subscriptions raised and the committee (in conjunction with similar committees in Greenock and Paisley) sent considerable supplies of meal from time to time to the destitute districts.[61]

The committee in Glasgow having great cause to fear, from the reports which reached them and especially from the report of a gentleman (Mr McPhail) who had kindly proceeded to the Islands with a supply of meal to superintend its distribution and to bring back intelligence regarding the actual condition of the people, that the majority of the inhabitants of the Islands, as well as many of the Highlanders of the mainland, would be in a state of still greater distress during the current year; and being anxious to obtain definite information as to the extent of the destitution and the character, employment and wants of the people, issued circulars, with relative queries, to the clergy and other gentlemen of the districts, to which queries such answers were received as impressed the committee with the conviction that their exertions behoved to be greatly extended, and that they ought to call for the aid of the public in general.

Accordingly, a second public meeting was held in Glasgow on the 6th February last, when the present committee was appointed, extended measures resolved upon and a new subscription (which now amounts to about £4,000) was commenced.

It having also been resolved that a deputation should be sent to London and other cities and towns in England, the secretary, along with the Rev. Dr Macleod and Mr Bowie (the deputation named by the Edinburgh committee for the same purpose) proceeded thither, and the cause having been generously and promptly

---

61   In June 1836 an appeal had been launched in Glasgow (which followed an appeal in May, in Edinburgh) for subscriptions in aid of the destitute inhabitants of the Western Isles and a committee had been formed; the balance of funds remaining from the subscription, £458–15–4, was made available to the re-appointed committee in 1837 (1841 SC, 109).

taken up, most liberal remittances have been received from London, Liverpool, Newcastle, Sheffield, Stockton, Halifax, Plymouth, Exeter, Sunderland, North Shields etc., etc., besides many congregational collections. The committee have also received similar remittances from Perth, Inverness, Paisley, Kilmarnock, Kilsyth, Dumbarton, Rothesay and other towns in Scotland, besides congregational collections. These remittances have from time to time been advertised in the public papers and shall be specifically detailed in a future report. In the meantime it may be mentioned that the funds received by the treasurer in Glasgow amount to £15,022 but the committee are aware that large sums have been collected in Manchester, Bristol, Oxford, Birmingham and other places besides those above named, in aid of the general fund.

As soon as the necessary arrangements were made, particularly the establishment of the local committees in the different parishes or districts where destitution prevailed, the committee resolved to send off supplies of provisions, and accordingly they have, on *three* different occasions, allocated 6,887 bolls of meal in addition to 500 bolls sent from the Inverness committee for distribution, and about 4,000 barrels of potatoes, among 63 parishes[62] or districts according to the population and number of destitute persons in each, all of which meal and potatoes has been dispatched to the places of destination, except a small quantity now in the course of being shipped. The committee have also in several instances placed small sums of money at the disposal of the local committees for the purchase of meal and potatoes where such articles can be got in the districts at a cheaper rate than they can be purchased and shipped from Glasgow.

The committee have already received very minute and interesting accounts of the distribution of the supplies of meal in some of the parishes, with which they are highly satisfied. These reports state the number of persons who have been assisted, their names, the quantities received by each person etc., etc.; but the committee will for the present only exhibit the following abstract of a few of the reports, viz.:–

First supply of meal sent

Where sent	Quantity	Number of persons to whom distributed	Average quantity to each person	Certified by
Snizort	128 bolls	1,430	12 ½ lbs.	A. C. Kennedy
Kilfinichen	96 bolls	636	21 lbs.	A. Maclean and D. McLachlan
Barvas	60 bolls	661	13 lbs.	Rev. William Macrae
Cross	48 bolls	482	14 lbs.	William MacGregor
Kilmuir	64 bolls	1,081	8 lbs.	Robert MacGregor
Colonsay	40 bolls	400	14 lbs.	John McNeill
Poolewe	100 bolls	1,550	9 lbs.	Donald Macrae

---

[62]   The final number of parishes assisted by the Glasgow committee was 76 (1841 SC, 110).

(Additional supplies of meal and a supply of potatoes have been sent to each of these and other parishes. A supply of meal and potatoes has been sent to Mr MacGregor for the parish of Stenscholl.)

In acknowledging receipts of the supplies of the clergy and other gentlemen of the local committee, while they convey to this committee the grateful intelligence that they have been instrumental in saving many valuable lives, give the most heart-rending accounts of the circumstances of the people; and the committee think they need only refer to the following (out of a number of letters) to convey to a generous public some idea of the fearful state of destitution in the Highlands and Islands, and to demonstrate the necessity of the committee continuing their exertions. . . .[63]

Though this committee have every reason to put confidence in the reports which have reached them from the destitute districts, as well as to suppose that the supplies will be wisely and impartially administered, yet, at the suggestion of several parties (and especially as this committee have been intrusted with such large sums from committees at a distance), it was thought proper to get Mr McPhail (who kindly undertook a similar mission last year) and Mr Campbell of Otter,[64] gentlemen intimately acquainted with the language, customs and manners of the Highlanders, to visit the districts to ascertain how the supplies had been administered, how far they had answered the intended purpose, what supply of food and clothing would still be required, and to report on these and many other points (which need not be specified here) to the committee and also "to embrace every opportunity of stating to all parties in the Highlands and Islands, in the strongest terms, that as it was evident that the liberal subscriptions which have been raised have greatly proceeded from a feeling that no such call on the public benevolence would be repeated, the people should be warned of the absolute necessity of making the most strenuous exertions for their future maintenance, as they could not expect the public to come forward again."

The committee have not yet sent off any supply of clothes or blankets (excepting some parcels forwarded with special instructions) but have provided a lot of both, which they mean to despatch to the places where such articles are most required, so soon as the committee receive answers to additional queries which they have made, or when they get the reports expected from Messrs. McPhail and Campbell.

In consequence of an arrangement between the committees in Edinburgh and Aberdeen (in both of which cities very large subscriptions have been raised) and this committee, the charge of sending supplies to the Orkney and Shetland Isles has been left with the committee in Aberdeen, it being understood that both of the other committees should assist the Aberdeen committee as much as possible.

---

[63] The extracts of the letters from the ministers of Kilmuir, Lochbroom and Poolewe which are set out in the original are omitted here.
[64] John Campbell of Otter, Cairndow.

Accordingly, although this committee have great cause to fear that the funds placed, or to be placed at their disposal, will fall much short of meeting the wants of the population of which they take immediate charge, still, as they cannot, so long as they have funds, think of withholding their aid from any necessitous districts, they have, at the request of the committee in Aberdeen, remitted to them the sum of £500 for the purchase of food to be sent to Orkney and Shetland, and desired that committee to return a particular account, or schedule, of the distribution of the food or seed sent to these Islands, in order that the necessity of making them a farther grant from the funds at the disposal of this committee should be taken into consideration.

As above noticed, the committee at Inverness have remitted their funds to Glasgow (in all the very liberal sum of £320). But as there have been several applications for aid from parishes and districts which lie much nearer Inverness than Glasgow, this committee has requested the one acting in Inverness to take such places under its charge, at least to the extent of distributing the quantity of 500 bolls of meal to the most destitute.[65] This committee would have preferred putting a sum of money at the disposal of the Inverness committee, confident that it would be most judiciously applied, but it was found that meal could be purchased in Glasgow and sent to Inverness on more favourable terms than it could be bought for in the latter place.

The committee have thus stated generally the quantities of meal and potatoes dispatched, but although they have prepared tables of the population and numbers destitute in each parish, with the exact quantities of meal and potatoes allocated to each, the committee refrain from publishing these tables, as they could not be fairly appreciated unless with the evidence laid before the committee, and which is much too *voluminous* for publication.

All who have taken any interest in this subject are aware that the committee some time ago presented a memorial to Government[66] setting forth the extreme state of destitution existing in the Highlands and Islands, the remote and immediate causes thereof and praying that Government would take the case into consideration, and grant such relief as might seem proper. To this memorial the deputies from Edinburgh and Glasgow received a verbal answer, that Mr Robert Graham of Redgorton had been sent to the Hebrides for the purpose of investigating the reality and extent of the destitution, and subsequently a copy of a Treasury minute was received[67] in which, after stating reasons why Government were averse to interfere in the matter, it proceeds: "But as the necessity of procuring the supplies of seed is urgent and as it would be inexpedient to allow any delay to occur, Lord Melbourne and the chancellor of the exchequer recommend that Captain Sir John Hill, superintendent of the

---

[65]   The Inverness committee took responsibility for 17 parishes (1841 SC, 110).
[66]   See p. 207.
[67]   See p. 277.

Victualling Department at Deptford should at once be directed to proceed to Scotland to put himself into communication with Mr Graham and the committees at Edinburgh and Glasgow and to take such steps in conjunction with them as may appear necessary in the urgency of the case for the immediate supply of seed corn and potatoes." And, "In order to give effect to the recommendation of Lord Melbourne and the chancellor of the exchequer and to the intention of their Lordships it will be proper that Sir John Hill should be authorised to enter into contracts on the most favourable terms for the supply of seed oats, barley and potatoes at such of the ports and places in the distressed districts as may seem most advisable to the extent of such sum as may be necessary not exceeding £10,000 which My Lords will place at his disposal for this object a proportionate contribution being furnished by the charitable committees and that he should report his proceedings in this matter from time to time to this Board taking care that no time is lost making the purchases and dispatching the supplies so as to ensure their reaching the distressed districts before the proper period for the due cultivation of the soil shall have passed away." "My Lords reserve the question of the supply of food for consideration when by the reports expected from Mr Graham they shall be made acquainted with the actual state of the population in the districts in question in that respect."

As the grant by Government was to be applied solely for *seed* and only on the conditions above stated, and as this committee were aware that all their efforts, coupled with those of the various committees throughout England and Scotland, would scarcely enable them to fulfil the primary and all important purpose of furnishing food to the famishing population, they did not feel themselves justified in applying any of the funds committed to their charge to the purchase of seed, but left the Edinburgh committee, with the assistance of Government and of the proprietors of the soil, to adopt such measures, on this head, as they should think proper, and this committee are aware that the Edinburgh committee have turned their attention to the question of seed.[68]

This committee may add that their resolution to confine their operations to food and raiment are entirely in accordance with the opinions of the committees in London, Liverpool, Manchester as well as with those of other cities and towns who have taken the point into consideration.

The committee have not yet received any intimation from Government of the proceedings of their commissioner, Mr Graham, but they are happy to state that, by a letter received from Sir George Grey,[69] it appears "that Dr Boyter, R.N. who has recently been engaged in the selection of emigrants for New South Wales in the East of Scotland and has discharged this duty with great zeal and efficiency, has been directed by the Secretary of State for the Colonial Department personally to visit the Highlands in order to ascertain the number

---

[68] See the memorial dated 25 Mar. 1837 on p. 210.
[69] The under-secretary of state for the colonies.

of families of a suitable description who may be anxious to avail themselves of a free passage to that Colony", *and to make the necessary arrangements for their conveyance thither.*

This committee cannot conclude the present report without expressing the deep sense of gratitude they entertain towards the committees in the different cities and towns in England and Scotland, as well as toward the many congregations and individuals in both countries who have so generously and nobly assisted this committee in their endeavours to discharge the arduous but interesting duty devolved upon them, and they congratulate these parties upon the fact that they have, by the blessing of the Almighty giver of all good – to whom be all the praise – been instrumental in not merely promoting the comfort, but even in saving the lives of many of their fellow creatures. Much, however, remains to be done. Many thousands have still to be provided for and several months must elapse before any subsistence can be derived from a new crop, even should that crop be an average one, of which great fears may reasonably be entertained.[70] The committee therefore most earnestly entreat their friends in every quarter of the Empire to continue their exertions in aid of a cause which they cannot but feel to be one of the best in which human beings can possibly engage – a cause involving their duty to God as well as to man.

Signed in the name of the committee by
Allan Fullarton, Chairman
Charles R. Baird, Secretary
Glasgow, 29th April 1837

Second Report by the committee in Glasgow, for the relief of the destitute inhabitants of the Highlands and Islands of Scotland – 27 June 1837

Circumstances have lately occurred to induce this committee to publish a second report sooner than they intended. Several persons, perhaps in ignorance and a few, it is feared, actuated by malicious motives, have stated that the destitution in the Highlands and Islands of Scotland was by no means as great as had been represented by this committee; and it has even been insinuated that the supplies which have been so liberally bestowed by the public, have in many instances been misapplied.[71] This committee (having no more interest in the matter than any other committee or individual in the United

---

[70] By the time of its second report on 27 June 1837, however, the committee was able to report the promise of a 'very abundant crop' (p. 237).

[71] An example of this is in *The Scotsman*, 24 May 1837. Charles Baird wrote letters at the same time as this report making the same point as the report (see, for example, his letter published in *The Belfast News-Letter*, 27 June 1837).

Kingdom, no more than what Christian humanity dictates) might be justified in stating their own proceedings which they flatter themselves cannot be impugned; but they are even willing to take upon themselves the task of showing that the liberal subscriptions of the public were most *urgently* required, that the distress of the people in the Highlands and Islands has been much *greater* than was first stated, and that the supplies sent by this committee have, upon the whole, been fairly and judiciously applied.

Since laying their former statement before the public, the committee have received very minute and valuable Reports from Messrs McPhail and Campbell (the gentlemen who, at their desire, investigated personally the state of the distressed districts) which the committee, but for their great length, would be well pleased to print for distribution. This has been deemed inexpedient, on account of the expense, but copies of these Reports will lie with each of the committees of London, Edinburgh and Glasgow, where they may be inspected by anyone feeling an interest on the subject. In the meantime, the committee cannot help quoting the following remarks by Messrs McPhail and Campbell. As to the state of the destitution:– "In submitting the present Report, the Reporters take it for granted that the committee are fully satisfied of the great extent of destitution which actually exists; *but which, they observe, can hardly be properly estimated except by personal observation.* The Reporters were previously acquainted with many parts of the Highlands, particularly those nearest to the low country, and they thought they had a pretty accurate idea of the average amount of distress which generally prevailed; but they must now confess that, compared with what they have witnessed during their visit to the districts reported upon, any distress which they were previously acquainted with could hardly be complained of. They have not detailed individual cases of suffering because their movements were, in general, too hurried to make them properly acquainted with them; and also because they believe the committee have had these already amply detailed. They have, however, no hesitation in stating that, but for the benevolent exertions which have been made to relieve the distress, *a very great and general famine would have prevailed.*" As to its cause:– "The causes of destitution which have been operating for some years may be shortly stated to be the great increase of population, the failure of the herring fisheries, the almost total suspension of the manufacture of kelp, the small demand and very low price for inferior stock, and a progressive improvement in sheep farming which has led proprietors to encourage tenants of capital to increase the extent of their possessions which has had the effect of dispossessing a large number of small tenants, who do not leave the country, but locate themselves along the coasts wherever they can get a footing. And the particular causes of the existing distress are the almost total failure of the crops for the last two years; and a general falling off, from the scarcity of provender, in the quality of inferior stock for which there has been almost no sale." Regarding the conduct of local committees:– "On the whole, considering the difficulties which some committees have had to contend with and the novelty of the circumstances under which they have been called upon to act, the Reporters are satisfied that the local committees showed an anxiety to discharge their duty impartially, and they have been as successful in their endeavours as could have been expected." And as to the means of permanently improving the condition of the people:– "After having given the best consideration in their power, the Reporters are satisfied that nothing will tend to the permanent relief of the people but Emigration, and that on an extensive scale such as will enable whole families to emigrate together. In general, they are anxious to go anywhere, but they cannot themselves command the means; and if Emigration is to be carried into effect, extensive assistance must be obtained from Government. The Proprietors, however, should be called upon to assist, as it is their interest to do so. The sooner the matter is set about the better, because considerable preparation is necessary, seeing that cots and crofts are taken from Whitsunday to Whitsunday, that each of these poor people has something to arrange and that, in order to enjoy the full benefit of the boon, they ought to have intimation given them long before of the probable time of departure."

There are also subjoined some extracts from the Reports on the particular parishes visited by Messrs. McPhail and Campbell.

Besides the very important information received from these gentlemen, the committee have continued their correspondence with the clergymen and gentlemen residing in the destitute districts; and from some of the very numerous and interesting letters they received, they annex a few extracts.

Convinced as well by the Report of Messrs. McPhail and Campbell, as by the letters referred to, of the necessity of continuing their supplies, the committee have allocated and dispatched an additional quantity of oatmeal, besides 138 sacks of flour, forwarded by the London committee; and now direct the public attention to the following general statements of their proceedings.

It will be in the recollection of all who have perused the former Report, that at the date of issuing it (29th April last), the committee had received funds altogether amounting to £15,022, that on three different occasions the committee had allocated among sixty-three parishes or districts, according to the population and proved destitution in each, the quantity of 6,887 bolls of oatmeal in addition to 500 bolls sent to the Inverness committee for distribution in the districts in their neighbourhood. The committee had also dispatched about 4,000 barrels of potatoes besides, in some particular instances, placing small sums at the disposal of the local committees for the purpose of purchasing food when that could be done on better terms than those on which it could be forwarded from Glasgow. The Aberdeen committee, who have taken the exclusive charge of supplying Orkney and

Shetland, having expressed their great fear of famine in these islands, this committee had also advanced to them £500 for the purchase of supplies.

Since the date of their first Report, the committee have had returns from nearly all the districts of the distribution of their various supplies. These returns are all more or less interesting and in every instance show the necessity that existed for the extension of the public bounty to these districts, as well as the care and judgment which the local committees generally have exercised in the distribution of the supplies. An abstract of the details will be published by the committee in their final report, but in the meantime it may be stated generally that the quantity of meal furnished to each family has varied from 8 to 20 lbs. and that the potatoes were doled out in quantities varying from two pecks to half a boll to each family.[72]

The number of parishes or districts in which the supplies are now in the course of being distributed has increased to eighty-one, a circumstance which necessarily entails upon the committee a great increase of trouble and expense. To meet this expense, however, Providence has kindly placed more adequate means than formerly at their disposal. The funds received by the Treasurer up to the present day amount in all to £23,821–19–2. In that sum is included £1,500 received from the Edinburgh committee at the outset, to assist in sending an instant supply of food to the Highlands *but which sum this committee have seen proper to repay*;[73] and the balance now in the Treasurer's hands amounts to £9,965–2–9 but from which there will fall to be deducted some outstanding accounts for freight, insurance, printing etc. (not yet ascertained), as well as the price of the supplies which the committee are continuing to send. The total quantity of potatoes sent has already been stated. Additional supplies of oatmeal, however, to the extent of 3,822 bolls have, since the date of the former Report, been purchased and shipped by the committee, making in all 14,315 bolls including certain supplies specially voted to districts which had been too late in their application to be included in the general allotment. Two supplies of 500 bolls each have been sent to the Inverness committee in reference to whom it may be stated that they have not only placed the whole of their funds at the disposal of this committee, but taken an active and efficient charge of the destitute districts in that part of the country. Of the distribution of the first of these 500 bolls, this committee has received a very satisfactory report, the statements in which were the immediate cause of their transmitting the second supply.

In every instance of purchase of oatmeal, the committee have not only been careful that it should be of the very best quality, but that the stock and sample should be compared before completing a bargain; and this they easily effected

---

[72] No indication is given of the period which this supply was supposed to last for and so it is not possible to compare this to the estimate of a daily allowance of half a pound per person per day given by Graham (p. 56).

[73] See Hill's letters to Spearman of 21 Mar. and 22 Apr. 1837 (pp. 116, and 133).

from the circumstance of several of their members being competent judges of the article. The samples are retained and lie in the committee-room for inspection. The same attention has been paid to the quality of the potatoes.

As stated in the former Report, the committee have entirely confined their operations to the supplying of food and they can see no reason for any future change in their plan. This is indeed the less necessary, as they understand that His Majesty's Government have, by their Commissioner, Sir John Hill (a gentleman to whom the Highlands of Scotland is deeply indebted), in conjunction with the Edinburgh and Aberdeen committees, furnished an ample supply of seed oats and potatoes to the destitute districts. Independently of the consideration just stated, the extracts from the correspondence about to be given, will show the wisdom of the course this committee have prescribed to themselves, and a comparison of the extent of the funds at their disposal with the number of the destitute, and the length of time before the new crop can come into play, will prove it to demonstration.

In regard to the article of clothing, the committee have not found it necessary to do much, and the genial weather which happily has continued for so long a time back, has justified their moderation. Having, however, had an opportunity of doing so on most favourable terms, they have purchased blankets to the value of £400, which will be distributed in time to meet the rigour of the approaching winter, along with a valuable parcel of blankets sent by "An Old Cameronian" and several parcels of clothes forwarded by Henry John Porter, Esq. of Tandragee Castle[74] for whose exertions and donations this committee feel deeply grateful.

Such is a brief sketch of the proceedings of this committee since the publication of their former Report. They have refrained from entering into particular details, both because this will come more naturally to form their final Report,[75] the period for issuing which is not very far distant, and because their whole proceedings of every kind are upon record *and open at their committee room to every one who chooses to inspect them.*

As the preceding Report was going to press, Mr Ferguson (who had kindly undertaken to inspect and report on the state of Islay) has returned to Glasgow and has reported to the committee that, although Mr Campbell's donations and exertions in giving meal and procuring work for the people in that island have been most munificent, and although the inhabitants of several of the parishes might, with his aid, have sustained the poor without asking supplies from the committees, still it appears that many of the inhabitants, especially in the parish of Bowmore, are in a state of extreme misery. This committee, therefore, while they express their admiration of Mr Campbell's liberal conduct, think it right to

[74] In County Armagh.
[75] It has not been possible to trace the final report if, indeed, it was ever issued. However, the final financial figures (taken from 1841 SC, 109) are given below and the details of the supplies provided through the Glasgow committee are given in the Edinburgh report above at p. 226.

send some additional supplies to Islay, the more particularly as the parties they meant to supply are chiefly very poor villagers, having no claim whatever on Mr Campbell or any other landlord, and that it appears but just to aid Mr Campbell in his generous exertions.

The committee cannot close this Report without adverting, with feelings of the deepest gratitude, to the generous contributions they have received from many parts of England, Scotland and Ireland, especially from London, Liverpool, Manchester, Alnwick, Birmingham, Bristol, Durham, Exeter, Gateshead, Halifax, Hartlepool, Hull, Hutton Rudby, Newcastle, North Shields, Oxford, Plymouth, Sheffield, Stockton, Sunderland; Atholstonfold, Belfast, Carriden, Castlegate, Comber, Co. Down, Cork, Drogheda, Dublin, Galway, Tyrone; Bowness, Inverness, Kilrenny, Fifeshire, Ormiston, Perth, Pinpoint; Isle of Man; St Kitts and Tobago, West Indies. They are also exceedingly grateful for the cordial co-operation they have met with on the part of the committees of the different towns in the United Kingdom. They beg leave again to felicitate themselves and their friends and well-wishers everywhere, on the fact of their having been the humble instruments of saving a great and interesting portion of their countrymen from the combined horrors of famine and pestilence and death. And they trust that, by a judicious use of the public bounty, they will be enabled to support these poor people till the maturity of a crop which Providence seems to promise will be very abundant, they shall be placed in circumstances of comparative independence.

By order of the committee,
Signed,
Allan Fullarton, Chairman
Charles R. Baird, Secretary
Glasgow, 27th June 1837.

★

Extracts from letters referred to in preceding report[76]

Additional extracts from Messrs. McPhail and Campbell's Reports

"Barvas. It appears, after examining the foregoing statements together with the Reporters' observations, and considering the population and division of lands in Lewis, together with very bad quality of soil of those portions which are cultivated, and on the produce of which the great mass of the population depend for their subsistence, they are in a most destitute state. The chief

---

[76] The extracts of the letters from ministers and others relating to Eigg and the parishes of Ulva, Sleat, Lochbroom, Kilmuir, Barvas, Ross in Mull, Cross, Ullapool and Barra which are set out in the original are omitted here.

subsistence must have been potatoes of an inferior quality, even in pretty good seasons. For the last two seasons that crop was a failure; and although they have cattle and a few sheep, in general there is a great proportion of the population that have none. The quality of the stock they do keep is very inferior and at present in such a poor condition that it is impossible to get any market for them; and it is a well known fact that there has been no demand for the inferior qualities of stock for the last two or three years. The Reporters are quite aware, from the examination they made, that there are many wholly destitute at this time who could pay in the course of three or four months, provided there was anything like a market for stock, or the fishings springing up on the coast. The Reporters are further aware, from their examination, that this destitution came gradually on, although the last two seasons have been so very bad. The increase of population, the immense decrease in the value of kelp and the failure of the herring fisheries for many years, must have eventually brought it to its present state. The Reporters had an excellent opportunity of seeing a great portion of the destitute population, from their being getting their distributions from the stores in Stornoway while they were there."

"Portree. It appears to me that the destitution is now great in the four preceding parishes and that June and July will be the worst months, that the supplies were sent rather soon and that they would not have required above the one-half till now. The local committees appear to have paid attention to a proper distribution. I am satisfied that the crofters, lotters and cottars must be very ill-off from the failure of the last two crops, and the small quantities they have in cultivation, although the lands here are much superior to what they are in the former parishes. A medical man who I met here, stated that there was a considerable deal of fever in that neighbourhood; and several times, when he asked for gruel for his patients, there was no meal in the house; and they are very ill-off for bed clothes."

"Tiree. The small tenants are all in arrear and the factor stated that he could not collect as much money as would pay the minister and schoolmaster. There are now destitute in the island about 700 families who would require 500 bolls of meal to keep them alive. The clergyman was very particular in making his survey. The destitution is daily increasing. From the great population in Tiree, the want of employment and mode in which the lands are divided, it appears to me that there must be a considerable deal of destitution. Although I believe the soil is fertile, the small patches which the poorer classes have in such a season as the last, could not support them."

Abstract of Treasurer's account with the Glasgow Highland Destitution Fund, 25 February 1841

Receipts:	£.	s.	d.
Balance of old fund transferred[77]	458	15	4
London committee, remittances at sundry times	19,706	8	8
Glasgow and neighbourhood, collected in, say	5,000	–	–
England, Ireland and the colonies – ditto	9,845	16	–
Edinburgh committee, received from them[78]	1,500	–	–
	£ 36,511	–	–

Disbursements:			
Oatmeal, amount of shipments to Highlands for distribution	22,303	2	5
Potatoes etc., ----------ditto--------------ditto	1,043	18	6
Blankets------------------ditto----ditto	2,218	15	8
Outfit for emigrants furnished to Glasgow and shipped to Highlands	298	16	10
Freights, amount on shipments to ditto-------------ditto	1,160	15	4
Marine insurance-----------------ditto-----------------ditto	452	6	5
Remittances to particular localities, to purchase meal and potatoes	1,846	9	1
Distributions by sub-committees in Glasgow at sight of general committee	806	10	4
Emigration; this sum, to which the committee are pledged, part of which is drawn from treasurer	918	5	–
Deputations; expense of, to England £57–1–6; to Edinburgh£5–11–6; and to Highlands, £85–7–10	148	–	10
Edinburgh committee, returned to them	1,500	–	–
Special sums voted by general committee	280	12	–
Advertising, stationery, printing reports etc.	250	5	5
Salaries; assistant secretary £73–10–0; clerk of committee rooms £29–10–0; and for copying necessary documents £60–10–6	163	10	6
Postages, per secretary, treasurer, and Dr Macleod	79	3	7
Incidental expenses, including public meetings, carriage of parcels, Freight of clothing, and rent of office, etc.	87	15	10
Balance, exclusive of interest, at disposal of committee	2,950	12	3
	£ 36,511	–	–

(Errors and omissions excepted)
Glasgow, 25 February 1841
John Macpherson, Treasurer, Glasgow Highland Destitution Fund.

---

[77] The fund set up after a public meeting in June 1836 (see p. 227).
[78] This sum is referred to in Hill's letter to the Treasury of 21 Mar. 1837 (p. 116) and was returned to Edinburgh after the Glasgow committee resolved not to be party to the arrangement with the government regarding sums to be spent on seed (see the Introduction, p. xxix). The returned sum is shown in the disbursements.

Statement on the closing of the London committee appeal – 17 July 1837

The London Committee for the Relief of the Destitute Highlanders, in closing their labours, desire to render sincere thanks, first to Almighty God, "whose is the silver and the gold," and next to a liberal public (especially to many excellent Clergymen) for the promptitude with which they have come forward to the aid of the poor Highlander in the day of his necessity.

The Committee have the happiness of informing their generous contributors that the funds placed at their disposal have already been the means of saving thousands; and as some relief has recently been obtained from fishing and field labour, the Committee trust they have almost enough in reserve, deposited at interest in the Bank of Scotland, to supply the wants of those who will continue to look to them for bread until the days of harvest, which, through the Divine blessing, promises to be abundant.

The Committee might have continued their exertions a little longer, and have thereby converted the above hope into certainty; but whilst from commercial depression, and consequent manufacturing distress, there are so many loud calls for help from the towns and villages of England itself, the Committee feel that they would not be justified in taking for one shilling more than the most frugal and barely competent supply of the Highlander's necessities requires; and their trust is, that this will be accomplished by means of the funds which they have on hand, together with the sums collected in various parts of the country, but not yet forwarded – the anticipated fruits of sermons already announced, and of public meetings already intimated, all which the Committee will receive with sincere thankfulness.

The Committee beg to offer their grateful acknowledgements to the bankers of London and Westminster, and to the various parties who have kindly received the subscriptions, and who have thereby efficiently aided them in the accomplishment of their benevolent object.

Considerable expense has been unavoidably incurred in printing addresses, and advertising the subscriptions in the public papers; but, throughout the whole of their proceedings, the Committee have paid the strictest regard to economy, and they have not expended one shilling more than was absolutely necessary; the honorary secretaries, aided occasionally by a few active members of the Committee, having gratuitously done the work.

By order of the Committee, John Crombie, D.D, Peter McMorland, James Nisbet and William Skirving, Hon. Secretaries.

N.B. Future communications are requested to be made to the Honorary Secretaries, at 21 Berners Street, Oxford Street.

July 17, 1837

Final report of the London committee – 24 October 1837

Highland Destitution Committee's Report.

The London Committee appointed to promote a subscription for the relief of the lately existing destitution in the Highlands and Islands of Scotland, feel it to be their duty once more to address their fellow-citizens and countrymen, not as formerly (blessed be the giver of all good) to solicit their aid, but to thank them for their generosity, and to render an account of the important stewardship wherewith the Committee was entrusted.

When at a Public Meeting held at the Mansion-house on the 11th of March last this Committee was appointed, it was then stated that 86,000 persons were in a state of utter destitution; that 14,000 more, it was feared, would be ere long added to the number, and that £100,000 would be necessary, from first to last, for the supply of their wants; that the large towns of Scotland had already done their utmost, and that consequently the Scottish Committees were compelled to apply to England for aid in this emergency. To this appeal the meeting above-mentioned heartily responded, appointed this Committee, and instructed us, first, to use such exertions in obtaining subscriptions as the urgency of the case demanded; and, secondly, to "transmit the sum collected to the joint Committees of Edinburgh and Glasgow."

This Committee may be permitted to say that they lost no time, and spared no effort, in carrying the first of these resolutions into effect; and that, in compliance with the second, they remitted from time to time, according as they were needed and sought, considerable sums to the Scottish Committees; and that the whole sum obtained by this Committee amounted to £30,486–2–6; that the sum remitted and otherwise disbursed, according to the subjoined account, is £18,733–8–11;[79] and that the sum in hand, deposited in the names of the treasurer, Mr Alderman Pirie, and four members of Committee. Messrs. Crombie, Nisbet, Hamilton, and Skirving, is £11,752–13–7, part thereof in the Bank of Scotland bearing interest, and the remainder in the Bank of England.

This Committee not being as yet in possession of any full or final account from the Scottish Committees, are unable to state either the amount of their receipts, or the extent and variety of their distributions; but have reason to believe that the gross amount of all that has been contributed for this object, including £10,000 from Government, is about £70,000. And that so vast a multitude has been brought through its period of destitution by the expenditure of a sum so much smaller than that which was at first anticipated is mainly owing, this Committee believes, to the scanty distributions which were made during the earlier part of the season, when the charitable supplies were coming in slowly, and the ultimate amount of them altogether uncertain, and to the bounties of a gracious

---

[79] Glasgow reported that it received, at various times, from London £19,706 (1841 SC, 109).

Providence, furnished not only at the last in a plenteous supply of the usual fruits of the earth, but also in an unusually early and abundant supply of fish, affording both food and profitable employment to the inhabitants of the distressed districts. All this goodness from the hand of a merciful God, this Committee could hope and pray for; but to have reckoned upon it, so as to have thereby limited their exertions and diminished their receipts from the outstretched hand of charity, would have been to tempt God, rather than to trust in his providence.

Those, therefore, who have, from the circumstances of there being a surplus in our hands, drawn the conclusion, that this Committee "continued to appeal to public benevolence for some weeks after they knew they had enough to meet the exigencies of the case,"[80] may rest assured that their suspicion is altogether unfounded. Those members of the Committee who did the work, though worn out with their labour, and especially with the anxiety attending that labour, were indeed willing to persevere to the utmost of their strength, and of the necessity which required its exercise; but were at the same time, most earnest and diligent to ascertain the earliest period and the lowest estimate at which they might close their labours, being very unwilling to stand, one moment longer than was absolutely needful, in the way of other charitable subscriptions which were then soliciting public support. Far distant as this Committee were from the scene of the distress, and receiving as they did, from the enemies and from the friends of the cause in which we were engaged, contradictory, and therefore perplexing accounts, their situation was one of no slight difficulty; and though now it is evident that they did continue to urge their claims a little longer than was absolutely necessary, yet this they did not, could not know at the time, yea, nor until they obtained the accounts, very recently brought them, of a plentiful harvest being generally secured; but which a sudden change in the weather and a single storm might have materially injured.

While the hostility of a few writers, in some of the northern newspapers, created in the south a prejudice against the subscription, and retarded its progress, this Committee authorised an extensive correspondence with the clergymen in the distressed districts, by which they were enabled to refute many mis-statements and to arrive at the conviction of its being their duty to persevere, and in which conviction they were strengthened by the corroborating report of the Government Commissioner.[81]

This Committee, in laying before the public an account of the expenses incurred, while they rejoice in being able to say that not one farthing thereof has been disbursed so as, directly or indirectly, to accrue to the profit or advantage of any one of them (but have, on the contrary, borne their own personal expenses), have, at the same time, to regret that the obligation under which they were

---

[80]   This quote was taken from a critical leader in *The Times* of 18 Oct. 1837 to which John Crombie had responded in a letter to the editor published on 21 Oct. 1837.

[81]   Robert Graham.

imperatively laid to publish in the newspapers frequent and very minute lists of subscriptions, have proved so heavy an item in the expenditure as to constitute fully three-fourths of the whole;[82] and we would call the public attention to the fact, that the amount of what is properly speaking the Committee's expenditure is no more than £237–11–5.

This Committee have further to add, that they are now in course of correspondence with the Scottish Committees concerning the application of the money still in hand, they being better judges than we can possibly be of the present state and future prospects of the Highlands and Islands; and to assure our generous contributors that the Committee will spare no pains to find out and to accomplish such a mode of employing this residue as will best accord with the views of the donors, and most contribute to the welfare of the objects of their charity – of which also a full and faithful account will hereafter be rendered.

John Crombie and Peter Macmorland, Corresponding Secretaries, By Order of the Committee, Oct. 24, 1837.

---

[82] *The Times* reported that complaints had been received that the advertised lists of subscriptions had not included the gifts of a number of contributors: 'where a large amount of the fund has been contributed by individuals who in the true spirit of Christian benevolence conceal their names or distinguish their donations merely by initials, it is unfair (to use the mildest term) to withhold the only acknowledgement by which the respectable class of subscribers can ascertain that their money has been properly applied' (23 May 1837). On the importance of subscription lists, see B. Harrison, 'Philanthropy and the Victorians', *Victorian Studies*, 19 (June 1966), 364–5: 'through the subscription list one could display one's wealth to public view'.

TREASURER'S ACCOUNT.
RECEIPTS.

Amount of subscriptions from March 11th to October 2nd, 1837.

	£30,486	2	6

EXPENDITURE.

Remitted to the Glasgow committee.					£15,000	0	0[1]		
Ditto, in flour.					£154	1	6		
Remitted to the Edinburgh committee for Shetland and Orkney.	£1,000	0	0						
Ditto to the Aberdeen committee for ditto.	£300	0	0						
Ditto, in flour and rice.	£1,072	4	5						
					£2,372	4	5		
Advertising in the London newspapers.					£969	11	7		
Expenses of public meetings and postages etc. incurred previously.	£19	11	4						
Printing addresses, lists of subscriptions, circulars, etc., etc.	£92	11	6						
Rent of offices at 15s. per week and room for general committee meetings.	£18	10	0						
Cleaning office and coals.	£3	17	2						
Clerk's salary and occasional assistants.	£37	14	0						
Messenger.	£28	15	0						
Fifty collecting boxes.	£2	0	0						
Office expenses: viz., stationery, postages, porterage, carriages of parcels to and from all parts of England and Scotland, and other incidental expenses.	£34	12	5						
					£237	11	5		
								£1,207	3	0
								£18,733	8	11
In Bank of Scotland at interest.					£11,000	0	0		
In Bank of England					£752	13	7		
								£11,752	13	7
								£30,486	2	6

Signed:
       JOHN PIRIE, Treasurer
       JAMES NISBET, Cash secretary
       WILLIAM SKIRVING, Cash secretary
       WILLIAM WAUGH, Auditor
       WILLIAM HAMILTON, Auditor
       JOHN HODGE, Auditor
       ALEXANDER GILLESPIE, Jun., Auditor

---

[1]   The figure given by the Glasgow committee in 1841 shows a much higher amount of £19,706 8s 8d (see p. 239).

Section 4

Resolutions dated 2 March 1837 of the Edinburgh committee of contributors for the relief of those suffering from destitution in the Highlands and Islands of Scotland relative to a supply of corn and potatoes for seed.[83]

I. That it seems to be absolutely essential to render assistance (and that as speedily as possible) to the distressed districts in the Highlands and Islands, in the shape of *corn and potatoes for seed*.

II. That in order, as far as may be, to ascertain what the wants of the people are in that respect, inquiry to be made immediately (by circulars to the proprietors, or their factors, and the clergy), as to the quantity of seed required, and the time before which it is indispensable, that the seed should be furnished.

III. That it be at the same time intimated that such assistance can only be given:

1. On condition that the proprietor, or someone authorised by him, guarantee the repayment to the committee, in money, in the course of the year 1838, of at least one half of the cost of the supply, transmitted to the individuals on his estate, who are relieved by the committee.

2. That it shall only be forwarded upon receipt of a list from the local committees, of the names of those requiring it, and of the rent paid by them, for their farms or holdings.

3. That it shall be confined to tenants paying under £20 yearly of rent.

4. That it shall be distributed according to the following scale:

1st. Tenants paying from £20 to £10 of rent, at prime cost, in money.

2nd. Ditto paying from £10 to £5 of rent, at prime cost, or ¾ ths, according to circumstances.

3rd. Crofters and others paying under £5 of rent, to make a return for the seed in money or labour, and that, to such a proportional extent in either, as shall by the local committees be deemed advisable.

IV. That the local committees, immediately after the distribution, shall report to the committee in Edinburgh, the amount promised to be repaid, in the course of the year 1838, by the tenants on each estate in money, – if it shall exceed the half guaranteed by the proprietor, the excess is to be remitted by the local committees, as soon as collected.

Note – The local committee will take notice, that all members of the general committee are, *ex officio*, members of the local committees.

---

[83] The Edinburgh committee had also issued earlier resolutions and general instructions to local committees dated 21 and 27 Feb. 1837 (see 1844 Poor law Inquiry, 245).

Covering letter of 2 March 1837 sent with the resolutions

Edinburgh, 2 March 1837.

Sir, The committee, in consequence of communications from different quarters, being impressed with the conviction of the great importance of affording a supply of seed, whether in grain or potatoes, to those standing in need of it, beg to send you a copy of certain resolutions, which they have come to upon the subject. The committee feel assured that you will enter into the spirit by which they are actuated, entrusted as they are with the management and distribution of a strictly charitable fund, and that you will therefore, in carrying their resolutions into effect, look only to the relief of the poor sufferers and to their interest and well-being; and, in as far as is consistent with such interest and well-being, to the husbanding the funds entrusted to them.

In that assurance the committee leave the making up of the lists, and the whole details, with confidence, to you, and to the different local committees, as to those, upon whose exertions the useful carrying into effect, and working of the benevolence of the public must mainly depend.

The committee would urge, that, from the season being so far advanced, no time should be lost in making up the lists, and procuring the necessary guarantee. The committee has sent a copy of this circular to those through whom it conceives it likely to attain the object in view; but in a matter of so much urgency as to time, it would request your personal co-operation in making this communication known, in such quarters as you may conceive it ought to be made known to.

We are, Sir, your most obedient servants,
James Milles Riddell, Bart. Convener.
Henry Craigie, Assistant Secretary.

A copy of this has been sent to the following persons, believed to be connected with your district:

Note of 14 April 1837 by Macleod and Bowie relating to the resolutions

Glasgow, 14 April 1837.

We the undersigned having met this day, after our return from England[84] and having taken into consideration the various explanations required from and given by us to His Majesty's Government, and to the public, with reference to

---

[84]   This was the fund-raising deputation referred to in the Introduction.

the appropriation of the funds for the relief of the destitution in the Highlands and Islands of Scotland, collected by us, deem it necessary to submit to the joint committees of Edinburgh and Glasgow:

1. That, in terms of the resolutions of the general meetings held in Edinburgh and Glasgow,[85] we urged the necessity of raising funds for procuring provisions to be sent to the destitute districts for the immediate preservation of life, and also for the purpose of purchasing seed for the ensuing crop.

2. That, in terms of the arrangements made betwixt the Edinburgh and Glasgow committees, it was agreed that the former should purchase and allocate the distribution of the seed, leaving it to the latter to send immediate supplies of food for the preservation of life; and that in effecting these objects, the two committees should communicate to each other their respective proceedings.

3. That the funds collected in England and Scotland should be transmitted to either committee, and be considered as one common fund for accomplishing the objects which the committees have in view.

4. That, on our return, we found with regret that some misunderstandings and differences of opinion exist, particularly with reference to the supply of seed to be forwarded to our destitute countrymen; and with the view of obviating all such misunderstandings, we beg respectfully to state that, in all our appeals to the public, we distinctly explained, that the relief we sought, whether in the way of provisions or seed, was only for the *poor*, and those who were considered by local committees to be fit objects of relief, leaving it to their discretion to apply that relief according to their knowledge of individual cases.

5. In reference to the resolutions issued by the Edinburgh committee, relative to a supply of corn and potatoes for seed, we think it proper to state, that we had no knowledge of these resolutions until a copy of them was forwarded to us while in London, with instructions to submit them to His Majesty's Government.

We have given these resolutions our best attention and, in consequence, beg leave to observe that while we would have been better pleased if no mention whatever had been made of tenants paying above £10 of rent as *a class*, and that a full discretionary power had been vested in the local committees to grant a supply in all cases of destitution at their discretion without reference to classes, still we are well aware, that there are in the Highlands and Islands of Scotland, very many persons paying £20 of rent who need relief as much as persons paying a rent of £5, and therefore that it was proper that relief should be extended to them, they having been reduced not only by the entire failure of last year's crop, and the very low price of cattle, but also in consequence of their benevolent and extraordinary exertions in behalf of their destitute neighbours.

It will be observed, that the accommodation thus afforded to the first and second classes in the printed regulations, will not trench much on the general

---

[85] 25 Jan. and 6 Feb. 1837.

fund, from the arrangements made for the repayment of certain proportions, according to their abilities, and by the guarantee granted for the repayment of the one half by their respective proprietors; while a very extensive good to the whole district will result, from affording good sound seed to so numerous and deserving a class of the community.

With reference to the third class, viz. crofters and others paying under £5 of rent, it is stated in the resolutions, that these parties are to make a return to such a proportional extent, in labour or money, as shall by the local committee be deemed advisable.

In our answer to various enquiries put to us in England and since our return as to this condition, we stated, that in our opinion the distribution of seed gratis would have an injurious effect on the parties receiving aid, while we distinctly declared that such labour was not to be for the individual benefit of the proprietor,[86] but on works of general *public utility* and that at the discretion of the local committees, who were to require it or not, in part or in whole, as they may deem advisable, from their knowledge of the peculiar circumstances of the individuals constituting this class, and to whom it had been extended.

We distinctly stated, and we now declare as our opinion, that the local committees are, in the exercise of sound discretion, to extend this aid to all poor cottars and possessors of small patches of land, whether they pay a rent of £5 or no rent at all, well knowing that this class constitute a vast proportion of the destitute population in behalf of whom the present appeal has been made. We are aware, that for this class, who are in extreme indigence, no guarantee could be procured, and if not relieved at the discretion of the local committees, their small patches of ground must remain unsown, and the evil of destitution by this means perpetuated.

These explanations do not, in our opinion, trench to any degree on the arrangements to which His Majesty's Government have come and we are sanguine in our expectations that the same will be approved of, not only by His Majesty's Government, but also by the general committees, and by the local committees, to whom the distribution, on those principles, is entrusted.

We have only further to observe, that while it is our confident belief, that while no proprietor in the destitute districts will be found capable of taking any undue advantage of this charitable fund, still we are of opinion, that it should be distinctly set forth, that in any case where needy persons have been relieved by a supply of seed, and are afterwards either sequestrated or removed before reaping the crop, the landlord shall be held bound to pay to the local committee, the full value of the seed supplied; and we doubt not, the respectable local committees will pay especial attention to this important matter.

We have considered it our duty to make these observations for the reasons stated in the outset, and although we have gone more into detail than we first

[86]   See MacAskill, 'Public response', 189–95.

thought to be necessary, we shall not regret having done so if our explanations tend to remove misconceptions, secure an efficient distribution of the funds which a generous public have put at our disposal, and promote the harmonious co-operation of all parties concerned in these important arrangements.

Norman McLeod.
John Bowie.

Extract from minutes of a meeting of Edinburgh committee, held at Edinburgh on 20 April 1837 relating to the resolutions

The committee having considered the preceding statement by Dr Macleod and Mr Bowie, and as they understand that the circulation of the same will tend to remove doubts and misconceptions which have arisen in various quarters, they authorise the secretary to print the same, and to furnish copies to the different local committees.

Henry Craigie, assistant secretary,
Edinburgh, April 1837.

To the local committee of —

Gentlemen,

Upon applying to the committee in charge of seed oats and potatoes deposited at   you will receive   bolls of oats, and   bolls of potatoes, to be issued for the use of the tenants on the under mentioned estates, conform to the lists forwarded to this committee, and in accordance with the foregoing resolutions – taking proper vouchers for the seed issued, and transmitting the same, along with the bags, to the keeper of the depot at   .

The average price of the oats is   per boll; but in the event of present payment being made, a deduction (equal to the freight) of   per boll will be given.

I am, Gentlemen, your obedient Servant.

PART 4

GOVERNMENT CORRESPONDENCE AND OTHER DOCUMENTS

This Part contains, in Section 1, Government correspondence relating to the appointment of Graham and Hill, and in Section 2 the report of T. F. Elliot, the agent-general for emigration, on Graham's suggestion for an extensive emigration to the colonies and the formal response of Lord Glenelg, the secretary of state for the Colonies, to the Treasury's request that he consider Graham's suggestion.

Section 1

Edinburgh 29 January 1837 Cunninghame to Fox Maule[1]

My dear Maule, I learnt a conversation yesterday, which it is right for the Government immediately to know.

You wrote me a few days ago to make enquiry about the distressed districts of Scotland – and the extent and kind of relief most suitable. I am doing so. But I fear we are likely to encounter some tory jobbing, unless immediately counteracted. It seems there has been a private meeting[2] of some north country lairds and they have resolved to send a deputation to London, consisting of that sly old fox Macleod, moderator of last general assembly – and Bowie the agent of Lord Macdonald expecting 1st that they will have the conduct of the suggestion 2nd that if refused it will raise a clamour amongst the whigs or 3rd that if aid be granted they and their subordinates will have the administration of the fund or of the corn and meal sent. I am the more satisfied of their underhand views, from this, that when it was suggested to take, or ask Macpherson-Grant[3] to go as one of the deputation, they refused.

Now we can easily counteract this vile intriguing way of setting about a laudable object. I know of no use a deputation can be. You have in London the members of parliament and most of the lords lieutenants who can communicate with Lord Melbourne and Lord John Russell just as easily as Macleod. But in order to show these people, that they are completely anticipated, I wish much that you would write me an official letter as either from Lord John or yourself, desiring me as soon as possible to take all prudent means to collect information as to the state of the poor in the districts of Scotland likely to be most distressed by the late unfavourable season and to ascertain from intelligent and disinterested persons the extent of aid and the manner and time of dispensing it which it would be most prudent for Government to afford. I should also be authorised if necessary to send a well-qualified person to the districts to ascertain on the spot the situation of such districts and to make a report as soon as possible to Lord John.

Then when the deputation arrives, Lord John would be in a situation to say, Gentlemen you are anticipated. The affairs have been sometime in the hands of Government and we shall take the most effectual means of affording such relief, as is expedient – though this is not a matter fitted for public discussion.

---

[1] This is taken from NRS, Papers of the Maule family, earls of Dalhousie, GD 45/14/625/48 and 49.

[2] This appears to be the meeting in Edinburgh of 25 Jan. 1837 which, while comprising mostly landed proprietors and their agents, was in fact a public meeting.

[3] George Macpherson-Grant of Ballindalloch, who was created first baronet in 1838. The Macpherson-Grants were one of the main Whig families in the eastern Highlands (Hutchison, *A Political History of Scotland*, 44).

You will observe there is time for this[4] – as no one I have conversed with thinks the aid should be afforded before May. . . .[5] Ever yours most sincerely.

Edinburgh 3 February 1837 Cunninghame to Fox Maule[6]

My dear Maule, In order to show you the nature and style of the private and confidential letters I have been writing to such friends as I could trust in distant parts of the country, I enclose a copy of this private dispatch;[7] I happen to know some trustworthy person in almost every district – and I shall collect a body of information that will be most important.[8]

I shall look early for your official despatch. The nature of the job the Tories want is every day more and more apparent so we should lose no time.

I hardly think that there is any occasion for the great concealment, as formerly thought necessary. You may show my letter to Lord John if you think it will be necessary when discussing this subject.

How would it do, to request me, if necessary to confer with Lord Lovat,[9] Mr Macpherson Grant, Sir Donald Campbell,[10] Mr Fletcher,[11] Mr George Trail,[12] Sir James Riddell[13] (this to prevent an insinuation that we are all Whigs) and to correspond with such of the sheriffs as we think may have useful information. . . .[14] Ever yours.

---

4 This was a misjudgment; within a month it became policy that immediate supplies of seed should be supplied (see Cunninghame's letter of 22 Feb. 1837 below).
5 The remainder of the letter is omitted as it refers to other matters.
6 This is taken from NRS, Papers of the Maule family, earls of Dalhousie, GD 45/14/625/51.
7 Set out at the end of this letter.
8 It has not been possible to trace any of these replies if, indeed, there were any. There is no evidence to suggest any information that was received was used by the government.
9 Thomas Alexander Fraser, created first baron Lovat on 28 Jan. 1837, a leading Whig aristocrat.
10 Sir Donald Campbell of Dunstaffnage.
11 Angus Fletcher of Dunans, an eminent advocate and JP for Argyllshire, who played a prominent part in county affairs.
12 George Traill had been Whig MP for Orkney and Shetland from 1830 to 1835.
13 Sir James Milles Riddell of Ardnamurchan and Sunart who was the convener of the Edinburgh committee; a man who gained some notoriety as a minor but still reviled actor in the highland clearances and was immortalised in one of the few direct attacks in gaelic poetry on a named landlord (L. A. Ritchie, 'The floating church of Loch Sunart', *Records of the Scottish Church History Society* (1985), 22: 159–73; D. E. Meek (ed.), *Tuath is Tighearna – Tenants and Landlords* (Edinburgh, 1995), 59–60; W. Gillies (ed.), *Ris a' Bhruthaich – The Criticism and Prose Writings of Sorley Maclean* (Stornoway, 1985), 55).
14 The remainder of the letter is omitted as it refers to other matters.

Edinburgh February 1837[15]

Dear Sir, I have been requested by the secretary of state to collect, in a judicious and confidential manner, such information from the different districts of Scotland as may be useful to ascertain the situation of those districts which have been most sincerely affected by the late unfavourable harvest, and the means of affording some aid in the shape of temporary loans of money, or of meal and seed corn to those districts where there is such a number of destitute poor as cannot be relieved by ordinary assessments or the bounty of landlords and neighbours.

The points to which I should wish more particularly to direct your attention are these:

I.   Be pleased to specify the districts within your own knowledge in which there is an amount of population likely to be in a state of want and which cannot be relieved by local assessments or by voluntary contributions likely to be given by neighbours, or sent from a distance.

II.   Specify, as nearly as possible, the number of destitute population in each district, the proprietors in those districts, and what measures they have adopted to relieve the distress.

III.   Have you known public aid given in former seasons in these or any other districts? In particular: 1. In what form and to what extent was it given? Was it in money? Or meal? Or corn? Or potatoes? 2. Was the aid afforded in shape of gifts? Or in loans? 3. Who administered the aid? Was there any check or guarantee that it would reach the destitute objects and be applied to their use?

IV.   Did any defects appear to you in the administration of such aid at the time? Or has subsequent enquiry or reflection satisfied you of any error therein? If so, be pleased to explain this and favour me with your views: 1. As to the districts to be assisted. 2. As to any conditions which ought to be imposed on the proprietors and residenters in the parish before relief is afforded. 3. As to the best mode of doing so. If in corn, meal or money and if by loan, how the vouchers can be taken to be made available afterwards? 4. As to the most seasonable time of sending relief.

Any other particulars which occur to you on the subject of this investigation will be most acceptable. Or, I shall feel obliged to you if you can refer me to any other judicious person likely to give me information on the important subject of enquiry on which I now write.

---

[15]   This is the private dispatch referred to above. It is taken from NRS, Papers of the Maule family, earls of Dalhousie, GD 45/14/625/50.

But I beg again to impress on you the necessity of great delicacy and privacy in regard to this communication, as publicity would aggravate the evil, increase applications from many places where it would not be expedient to interfere, and deter private dealers from sending provisions and produce to the neighbourhood in the ordinary course of trade. My object is chiefly to obtain your <u>own</u> sentiments and I beg that the views or wishes of Government on the subject may not, at present, be communicated to any other individual whatever. I am, dear Sir, yours very faithfully.

Edinburgh 22 February 1837 Cunninghame to Fox Maule[16]

Private and Confidential

My dear Maule, You will get a full despatch I think by this post from Rutherfurd as to Highland distress; collected from a private meeting of four or five of our own best and most judicious friends including Ballindalloch,[17] Robert Graham,[18] Sir Donald Campbell[19] and Angus Fletcher[20] – all intimately acquainted with the subject.

You will see that the clergy and the lairds headed by that old cunning dog Macleod late moderator and Lord Macdonald's agent,[21] intend to make a complete job of the affair if not promptly checked – Lord Macdonald's agent will be with you on Friday or Saturday – as he sets off this morning – and the Rev. Dr Macleod follows on a begging excursion through the great English towns such as Liverpool, Manchester, York, Hull etc., etc.

The consequence of this deputation and clamour, will for the time be a monstrous demoralisation of the Highlands. The whole population will become beggars; and the proprietors will do nothing – nay they will get <u>payment of enormous cottage rents, from the contributions</u>, for example, the minister and lairds' committee[22] have already reported that <u>one half</u> of the population in the parishes reported on are in destitution – some that the whole are so – and a great many that they will <u>all</u> be so, before the months of May or June. I believe there is not a season in which the same may not be said.

[16]   This is taken from NRS, Papers of the Maule family, earls of Dalhousie, GD 45/14/625/60 and 61.
[17]   George Macpherson-Grant of Ballindalloch.
[18]   Graham refers, somewhat obliquely, to the fact that he has been party to the discussions of Cunninghame and others as to the state of the Highlands, and that he is being put forward as the person to undertake a review, in his letter to Robert Stewart of Ardvorlich of 22 Feb. 1837 (p. 5).
[19]   Sir Donald Campbell of Dunstaffnage.
[20]   Angus Fletcher of Dunans.
[21]   John Bowie, WS.
[22]   This is the Edinburgh committee.

At the same time, there is truly and bona fide some dreadful cases; and they must be encountered – and the subject must be taken up, promptly and energetically, as the seed time is at hand.

Now what I would suggest to Lord John and you is this – to give up the expectation of lawyers sitting in Edinburgh such as Rutherfurd or me doing real good in such an enquiry. If I were you, I would at once employ such a man as Robert Graham (a man conversant in county affairs and totally unconnected with the Highlands) to proceed to the spot, – accompanied by Ardvorlich[23] as his colleague and secretary, who is acquainted with Gaelic – and I would request them to prepare such a despatch, as might be laid before parliament.

You have an excellent precedent in the commission given and despatch written by Lord John to Mr George Nicholl on 22 August 1836 directing him to proceed to Ireland and enquire into the State of the poor there whose Reports are now in the course of printing and distribution.[24]

In short, *coute qui coute*,[25] I would have you just instantly employ Graham. The very idea of a representation coming to you that 20,000 – (or it may be more likely 50,000 as the clergy are going on) are in a state of starvation is dreadful. Their system cannot be exposed just now when the famine is going on, as it might check private charity; but the public must be enlightened as to the causes of the distress – and the very different way in which it is met by different proprietors. I believe that Campbell of Islay[26] and Lord Breadalbane[27] will not take our shilling – while Lord Macdonald and Clanranald[28] are bawling lustily for relief from all quarters.

I enclose the rough sketch of a despatch which I would propose to be written to Graham, but of course you can alter and correct it to your view. You know I proposed Fletcher to go – but he will not move in case his aid be wanted on behalf of Islay at a general election. Would the same objection apply to Ardvorlich? At all events, he might go with Graham on his first excursion – and he could find another interpreter in April if you were then electioneering.[29]

---

23 Robert Stewart of Ardvorlich.
24 [PP] 1837 LI (69); and Collison Black, *Economic Thought and the Irish Question*, 109–11.
25 Presumably coute que coute – at all costs; see the similar use of the expression by Benjamin Disraeli in a letter of 25 Jan. 1838 to his sister Sarah (M. G. Wiebe *et al.* (eds), *Benjamin Disraeli Letters: 1838–1841*, 8 vols. (Toronto, 1982–), iii, 13–14).
26 W. F. Campbell of Islay, Whig MP for Argyllshire.
27 John Campbell, the second marquess of Breadalbane had represented Perthshire as a moderate Whig from 1832 (when Robert Graham had been chairman of his election committee) to 1834 when he succeeded to the marquessate, the seat then being fought by Robert Graham who was heavily defeated by the Tory candidate. He was then responsible for the Whig party organisation in the constituency.
28 Ranald Macdonald of Clanranald, proprietor of South Uist and Benbecula. The empire of the Macdonalds of Clanranald had included Arisaig, Moidart Eigg, Canna, Muck, South Uist and Benbecula but Clanranald was financially distressed and this lead to the empire vanishing in a series of sales between 1813 and 1841 (Devine, 'New elite', 109, 139).
29 The ill-health of the king made the need to hold a general election in the event of his death

To have an <u>immediate</u> report will be proper to know where seed corn should be sent. Ever yours most sincerely.

P.S. I think Graham will accept; but pray keep my name secret as having suggested anything, even to Rutherfurd, in case I might now be thought an intruder.[30]

Tell Robert Steuart[31] to be on his guard about the Highland <u>deputation</u>. I am not sure but they may go first to the Treasury and Lord Melbourne. They should therefore be apprised of the real state of the case. I know they have introductions to Steuart.

Instructions should be sent down to have a revenue cutter at the service of Graham and Ardvorlich to be at Fort William forthwith.

King Street 28 February 1837 Cunninghame to Rutherfurd[32]

My dear Rutherfurd, Along with this I now send you the whole of the little bundle I had collected about the scarcity.[33] I was keeping them up (not wishing to bother you with all your work) until it was fixed – what missionary should be dispatched to the spot (as in the case of Nicholls in Ireland) to ascertain and report on the distress. I sincerely hope it will be Graham as I think he would face it – and that he likes it.

   If you can read them, look particularly at Bowie's letter and that of Traill's factor; they are most judicious. Ever yours.

London 2 March 1837 Fox Maule to Rutherfurd[34]

Private

My dear Sir, I send you officially a letter I have written to Graham desiring him to go to the distressed districts and enquire as to the amount and

   a likelihood – which did happen in August 1837. Robert Stewart of Ardvorlich was much involved on behalf of the Whig party in Fox Maule's Perthshire constituency. Graham made reference to this in his letter to Stewart of 22 Feb. 1837 (p. 5).

30   Rutherfurd has replaced Cunninghame as solicitor-general for Scotland on the latter's becoming a judge of the court of session.

31   Robert Steuart (or Stewart) was the Liberal MP for Haddington Burghs from May 1831 to Aug. 1831 and from 1832 to 1841. He was the Scottish treasury lord from 1835 to 1840 and was 'a good deal consulted as to Scotland' by Lord Melbourne (cf. Fry, *Patronage and Principle*, 32, where Fry says Steuart had 'little influence') but was rebuked by Fox Maule for installing injudicious ideas into 'our Premier's ears' on Church matters (NLS, Rutherfurd papers, MS 9697, fos. 294–7, Fox Maule to Rutherfurd (undated)).

32   This is taken from NLS, Rutherfurd papers, MS 9710, fos. 104–5.

33   Not with the NLS, Rutherfurd papers MSS.

34   This is taken from NLS, Rutherfurd papers, MS 9697, fo. 5.

nature of the destitution and to report from time to time as to the mode of relief.

Say if you approve and urge Graham's instant departure. If he objects try if Sir T. Lauder[35] will go but don't say anything to him otherwise. Yours sincerely.

London 7 March 1837 Fox Maule to Graham[36]

My dear Graham, You seem to have misunderstood my letter and to have overlooked the 'Private' at its head. The enquiry you are to make is confidential for the information of Government and not as [. . .] agent in conjunction with the committees either of Glasgow or Edinburgh. You are to report to me your observations and your knowledge gathered on the spot and what local proprietors have done and that, with any other information you can afford in to decide Government in forming a judgment as to its future course. Should any difficulties occur, you will consult the solicitor-general.

Under these views no correspondence except with this department will be necessary and of course no arrangements as to franking[37] will be necessary. If you have involved yourself with either of the committees, pray get rid of them as quickly as possible. Yours in haste.[38]

8 March 1837 Fox Maule to Rutherfurd[39]

My dear Sir, I am glad to hear Graham is off and I hope he will give us every information with as little delay as is possible. He put himself in communication with the committees of Edinburgh and Glasgow which I think was more than in prudence he should have done, and I wrote him to say the inquiry was to be quite confidential and his returns sent to me here for the information of Government. . . ..[40] Yours very faithfully.

[35] This may be Sir Thomas Dick-Lauder, seventh baronet of Fountainhall, a close friend of Henry Cockburn and an active Liberal who was later appointed secretary to the Board of Manufactures and Fisheries in Scotland and to the Board of British White Herring Fishery.
[36] This is taken from NLS, Rutherfurd papers, MS 9697, fos. 7–8.
[37] To frank a letter was to ensure its being sent without charge under the Franking Act of 1764 (4 Geo. III c. 24) as amended by the 1784 Act (24 Geo. III [Sess. 2] c. 8).
[38] There is a note in Graham's hand on the letter as follows: 'answered 12th stating my views – that I was not involved with either of the committees – that secrecy was impossible – calling for franks as essential to the correspondence required about the matter'.
[39] This is taken from NLS, Rutherfurd papers, MS 9697, fos. 9–10.
[40] The remainder of the letter is omitted as it refers to other matters.

Edinburgh 14 March 1837 Rutherfurd to Fox Maule[41]

My dear Sir, Graham, as you may recollect, suggested[42] that he should be relieved of the Shetlands, as Orkney and Caithness made no demands for his assistance, and those islands were thus entirely removed from the districts which would mainly occupy his attention. This appeared to me so reasonable that I have since done what I could here to acquire information that might be of use to Government. It is difficult to get any <u>recent</u> or relative to the existing distress, on which one can securely rely; and the enquiries of the voluntary association[43] have been much more directed to bring out a case of destitution than to show the mode or measure of relief. Their leading object has been to make good a demand on the public purse, leaving to you the care and responsibility of the expenditure.

I have been at some pains to ascertain the circumstances of the Shetland proprietors and their character as landlords. In the last respect they do not rank high. With some very few exceptions, I understand them to be greedy and rapacious and to hold their tenantry in a state of [. . .] subjection. But as to fortune, they are tolerably well off. Two only, Gifford of Busta[44] and Scott of Scalloway,[45] were said to be in great pecuniary difficulty; others were very rich and others not ill at ease. The better class of farmers even, though the supplies of seed and food are difficult, are not unable to pay a fair price if they were brought within their reach.

I have seen a communication from Hay & Ogilvie, the great Lerwick merchants and themselves considerable proprietors.[46] I know generally the result of the information got by the gentlemen who with their usual activity and charity have expended [. . .] hundred pounds already there, and I have read hurriedly most of the reports received by the voluntary association from the clergy. Judging from all this I would say that the necessary supply of seed, in corn and potatoes, should be sent <u>instantly</u>, that it should be sold at the price it may cost Government without any charge for transport or at a somewhat lower price – but with indulgence as to the terms of payment and that in the case of the small tenants, when the minister of the parish or the minister of the congregation in the case of disputes certified the party to be in such indigent circumstances as to be unable to pay it should be given at a much lower rate, or if necessary without time. It is plain, however, that great care should be taken about the last as it would lead to great

41   This taken from NLI, Monteagle papers, MS 13384/8.
42   In his letter to Fox Maule of 6 Mar. 1837 (p. 6).
43   The Edinburgh committee.
44   Arthur Gifford.
45   John Scott.
46   The leading light of the firm was William Hay who entered partnership with his wife's family in 1822. The firm invested in the herring fishery, and vessels landed the catches at their Freefield base next to the dock. As trade grew the site boomed with great stores, docks and harbours, ships and quays. By 1839 the firm was prosperous, owning or managing 100 fishing vessels; but by 1842 the firm was bankrupt.

abuse; and it must always be in view that in furnishing seed the landlords are especially interested and they must reasonably and justly be required to come forward – because that seed gives them security, which they would otherwise want, for their rent of next year. It is very necessary to furnish a supply of seed, but there is no necessity and no reason to give charity to the <u>landlords</u>. They should pay for, or guarantee the payment of the seed, by which they will benefit in the end, and the benevolence – the unpaid benevolence of the State – should be directed to the maintenance of the pauper population.

To show how much this is the feeling of those who have previously and separately enquired, I send you an extract from a letter of Hay & Ogilvie to Mr Cruickshank[47] the quaker here[48] and another extract from a letter of Mr Wigham, the quaker, to myself.[49] I consider their suggestions of great importance, otherwise the aid of government will find its way into the pockets of the proprietors – who certainly have no peculiar claim.[50] Still a supply of seed must in any view be sent, because from other information the landlords are so supine, and so discordant, that if left to themselves it would not be had in time. In fact, not an hour should be lost.

As to food, the case is very different – for there the dispensation must be in great part one of pure charity – without any return. The seed recommended is the early Angus oats. What they [. . .] here in Shetland is the black or [. . .] oats to be had in Caithness, but I understand the improving farmers prefer the first and are all anxious for its introduction. The other corn seed is bear. The best seed potatoes they seem to say may be had still from Orkney. They are afraid of failing potatoes. But I see some speak of the [. . .]Scotch [. . .] potato as the best. About the quantity required, I have however no information and I suspect you must apply to Mr Balfour[51] who is bound to give you the proper information on the subject.

[47]   Alexander Cruickshank.
[48]   NLI, Monteagle papers, MS 13384/8, Extract of Hay and Ogilvie to Cruickshank, 23 Feb. 1837. There is also an extract of a letter from Alexander Cruickshank to Rutherfurd dated 11 Mar. 1837 in which Cruickshank tells Rutherfurd that the landlords hardly ever act as a body cordially, and that he believes most of them are, to some extent at least, financially able to supply the necessary seed.
[49]   NLI, Monteagle papers, MS 13384/8, Wigham to Rutherfurd, 11 Mar. 1837.
[50]   Wigham had suggested in his letter to Rutherfurd that, to avoid putting money into the hands of the proprietors, the seed should be provided to the Lerwick committee with directions given to the committee to sell the seed at prime cost for cash to farmers known to possess some substance, making a gift of limited portions to very small farmers who were certified to be unable to pay for it by the minister and two elders of the respective parishes. Wigham had also suggested that for a farm paying £5 annual rent (which comprised the greatest number of farms in Shetland), four to five pounds of seed would be sufficient quantity. Wigham had based these recommendations on a long conversation with William Merrilees of Gremista, one of the largest sheep farmers in the island, and he had told Rutherfurd not to disclose Merrilee's name 'as he might be blamed by some of his neighbours who magnify the distress more than he does'.
[51]   This is probably Thomas Balfour, the MP for Orkney and Shetland.

As for the means of distribution, I do not believe anything can be done or known unless some intelligent person be put in charge and actually goes to the spot. The quakers speak with great confidence of the local committee to whom they entrusted their charity at Lerwick with Mr [Charles] Ogilvie of Hay & Ogilvie at the head of it.

I beg your pardon for having detained you so long when I am sensible that I say little that is quite satisfactory. But I am quite sure that nothing very satisfactory can be had at this distance, beyond this, that there is a case for interposition, that aid should be given really to the poor, and so as not to relieve a sufficiently rich and not very deserving set of proprietors, and that it can only be well and judiciously applied by sending it under the direction of some honest, firm and intelligent agent.

I have so often to beg your forgiveness for the hurry in which I write, that I shall do so for the last time. Parting as [. . ..] Ever always with great haste.

PS. A supply of meal and potatoes for food should certainly accompany the seed. And there is one wretched place, Fair Island – half way between Shetland and Orkney – containing about 300 souls, visited only once a year by the minister, probably this year starving – that should positively not be overlooked [. . ..] With respect to Shetland, I think they have made out generally a case for aid, in consequence of the failure of the crops and greater failure of the fisheries, in 1835 and 1836. That is to say, feeling the greatest danger from the interference of Government on such occasions and holding that nothing short of urgent necessity can justify it, I do not believe that the local resources tasked to the utmost, and joined to all that can be hoped for from private benevolence would be sufficient to avert grievous and appalling calamity.

Food, I fear, will ere long be required and in considerable quantity – at least until the fishing season begins to tell. But in the meanwhile, the pressing demand, and it is of infinite importance and strongest urgency – is for seed in corn and potatoes. Even where they have the means to pay for it, they will be unable to procure it without the immediate help of Government, and an adequate supply for the coming spring gives the only chance of preventing the continuance of scarcity.

I shall send tomorrow morning the extracts of the letters I refer to. AR

Edinburgh 15 March 1837 Fox Maule to Spring Rice[52]

Private.

My dear Rice, As I think you will be more connected with the administration of the relief of the Highlands than Lord John, I trouble you with the enclosed

---

[52]   Taken from NLI, Monteagle papers, MS 13384/8.

documents[53] that I have received since I arrived here. I have also had a long conversation with the solicitor-general and he perfectly concurs in all the representations made as to the necessity of immediately attending to the island of Shetland, in fact his note No. 1 shows his opinion so distinctly that I entreat your attention to it. I also enclose 2 letters from Robert Graham and I think he should be the openly accredited agent of Government and his request for official franks[54] should be attended to as soon as possible for he says truly that unless the letter be free highlanders will lift it from the office [. . .] the [. . ..] He will furnish you with a valuable report and I do not think it will be long in completing as I have urged him to use the utmost dispatch in so doing. He has been disappointed of his cutter, but I hope in this the matter is arranged.[55] You will hardly have time to attend to all these documents, but I would suggest your consigning their perusal to Robert Stewart[56] and talking to him on the subject.

I perfectly agree in all the [. . .] says as to Shetland, but where you require certificates of ministers, they should not be confined merely to the ministers of kirk sessions of the establishment, but where the sufferer belongs to a dissenting congregation, his own pastor should be called on to certify as to the extent of his necessities. I send you a public and a private despatch from Graham, both of which will explain his future course of proceeding and if there is anything you wish to change in it you should write to me without loss of time. Your own plan of sending Sir John Hill will be most satisfactory to all parties I am quite sure, as they all talk of the necessity of some Government officer to superintend the administration of relief. But pray consider Shetland as a separate case and deal with it direct from London. The local committee seem to be a very respectable body[57] and may be trusted especially where no time is to be lost. The kind of corn is pointed out in Mr Wigham's letter[58] and the mode of giving it appears to be fair to all interests.

Excuse my troubling you on this so long, but I would not do so unless it were absolutely necessary. Believe me, yours very sincerely.

---

[53] Not with the letter in the manuscript, but they will have included Rutherfurd's letter to Fox Maule of 14 Mar. 1837 and the documents sent with that letter, especially Wigham's letter to Rutherfurd of 11 Mar. 1837.

[54] See Graham's note to Fox Maule's letter to him of 7 Mar. 1837 (p. 259); Spring Rice's action as to the request for franking is set out in his letter of 18 Mar. 1837 to Rutherfurd at p. 264 below.

[55] The promised coastguard cutter for Graham's and Stewart's use had not arrived, as arranged, at Fort William (See Graham's letter of 18 Mar. 1837 to his mother (p. 24).

[56] Robert Steuart, MP for Haddington Burghs and a treasury lord.

[57] According to the information Rutherfurd had provided to Fox Maule with his letter of 14 Mar. 1837, the Lerwick committee comprised: Charles Ogilvy, chairman; Robert Bannatyne, secretary; Robert Hicks; David Nicolson; Gilbert Tait; John Smith, cordwainer; David Leisk; Laurence Tait; James Hunter; and James Mowatt, jr.

[58] To Rutherfurd, dated 11 Mar. 1837.

Downing Street 18 March 1837 Spring Rice to Rutherfurd[59]

Sir, Not being quite certain when a letter is likely to reach either Mr Fox Maule or Mr R. Graham, I take the liberty of addressing you on the steps taken by His Majesty's Government for the relief of distress in the Highlands being aware of the attention you have already given to that subject.

Sir John Hill was despatched by me on Thursday last with specific instructions and with a credit and funds enabling him to act at once for the promotion of the object of his commission. The first point in importance seemed to me to be the provision of seed required for the year's cultivation. To this his attention was more immediately directed and he was ordered to communicate with the committees in Edinburgh and Glasgow as well as with Mr Robert Graham in order to ascertain where the supplies could best be procured, to what parts they should be sent and on what principles disposed of. The object necessarily, was 1st to do as much good as a given sum could effect; 2nd to avoid the evils which over-excited expectations of relief could not fail to occasion; and 3rd to create, in place of discouraging, the charitable efforts of those who from benevolent feelings or local duty were disposed to assist in relieving or mitigating the distress.

In order to accomplish these objects and to steer clear of dangers, we have instructed Sir John Hill to put himself in immediate communication with Mr Graham and the several committees and to make his interposition and assistance distinctly in combination with them and with the charitable subscriptions received or which may be collected.

If the inhabitants of the suffering districts consider that the Treasury will do all that is required there will be at once loss of economy in husbanding the supplies on hand and which may be sent and there will also be an exaggerated expectation of the relief which may be obtained. I also feel convinced that there will be a higher moral feeling in administering relief if it is distinctly understood that it is to a certain extent relief provided by the alms of the benevolent.

Sir John Hill has a credit of £10,000 to assist in the supply of seed oats, barley and potatoes. If he can add to this a portion of the subscription he may set immediately to work and make contracts to ensure the safe delivery and distribution of the seed purchased and if, as under the Edinburgh resolutions[60] is proposed, this can be sold at a price of ½, 2/3 and prime cost, £10,000, £15,000 and £20,000 may represent relief to the extent of double that sum. The deputation

---

[59] Taken from NLS, Rutherfurd papers, MS 9710, fos. 108–9. Spring Rice also wrote to Hill on 19 Mar. 1837 to tell him, inter alia, that he had written this long letter to Rutherfurd and that it was 'equally intended for [Hill] as for [Rutherfurd]' (p. 265). There is also a copy of the letter at NLS, Sir John Hill, 1837: diary and papers, Acc 12738, and according to a note on this copy in Hill's hand, Hill received from the solicitor-general a copy of the letter on 26 Mar. 1837.

[60] Dated 2 Mar. 1837 (p. 245).

to London[61] considered that an actual loss of from £10,000 to £15,000 would enable the Government and the Committee to extend relief as far as was essential under this head. This responsibility the Treasury will incur and if more is required for seed do not hesitate in going further, but always connect some of the charity funds with those of the Government. I have considered the papers respecting Shetland. If the case of the northern islands is similar to those of the western islands and coast similar steps should be taken, more especially in the supply of seed. Of this I presume you, Mr Graham, Sir John Hill and the committees in Edinburgh and Glasgow will be enabled to judge. But the landed proprietors and the public must be asked to contribute, as such efforts will be, though not the precise measure, at least the best foundation of the Government assistance.

Mr Graham is desirous that his letters should be enabled to pass free through the Post Office. The best mode of attaining this object is that the postage of all such correspondence should be paid and the amount so advanced by Mr Graham or Sir John Hill should be made up by the Treasury. At Edinburgh I shall write to the Secretary of the Post Office directing him to frank and to receive under his cover all letters which the committee may wish to dispatch.

Pray make the contents of this letter known to Mr Graham and Sir John Hill as well as to Mr Fox Maule should he continue in Edinburgh. I fear the case of Orkney requires attention as well as that of Shetland. I have the honour to be, Sir, your very faithful servant.

Downing Street 19 March 1837 Spring Rice to Hill[62]

My dear Sir, I have written a long letter to the solicitor-general of Scotland on the subject of the existing distress which is equally intended for you as for him.[63] I have addressed it to the solicitor-general because I am more certain of his address than I can be either of you or Mr Graham. Do not have any fear or reluctance in acting boldly as far as the supply of seed is concerned. In this part of the subject this is everything.

Look to the case of Orkney and Shetland if the circumstances seem to require it in the judgment of Mr Graham,[64] the committee and yourself. Endeavour to include them in your operations.

But in all cases the impression of some of the money raised by subscription is essential to the careful administration of the fund provided by Government. I am, dear Sir, your faithful servant.

---

61   Comprising the Rev. Dr Norman Macleod, John Bowie and Charles Baird from Edinburgh and Glasgow.
62   This is taken from NLI, Monteagle papers, MS 545.
63   Spring Rice's letter of 18 Mar. 1837 (p. 264).
64   But by time Spring Rice was writing, Graham had been told not to visit Orkney and Shetland.

Downing Street 11 August 1837 Spring Rice to Hill[65]

Sir, As your functions in Scotland are now terminated, I have felt it to be my duty to lay before Her Majesty the Queen an account of your proceedings.

The representations that were made to the Government in the month of March were of the most formidable description and proved the existence to an alarming extent of distress in the Highlands and the Islands of Scotland. This distress was attributed generally to the failure of the crops of grain and of potatoes in former years, to the unproductiveness of the Fisheries in certain districts, and to an excess of population as compared with the means of employment. Two calamities were either felt or considered as imminent: the one a want of seed oats and potatoes to provide for the spring tillage: the other a deficiency of supplies of food for the people.

The Government whilst they felt the deepest sympathy for the existing distress felt also that they had a great and paramount duty to fulfil towards the community at large. They felt that if any large portion of the subjects of Her Majesty were to be impressed with a belief that they had a right to rely upon the interposition of the state in order to supply them with food, the strongest motives to foresight, industry and frugality would be withdrawn and a principle would be laid down inconsistent with the well being of Society.

But the calamity as stated to exist was so overwhelming that it appeared certain that without assistance from other sources, suffering and loss of life must have ensued among the inhabitants of the distressed districts. It was also manifest that unless the means of spring cultivation were afforded without delay, this dearth would be continued and extended in future years.

It appeared to the Government that the case was one which could not be overlooked or disregarded, and that whilst the general principles on which it behoves states to act should not be forgotten, the application of these general principles should be subject to certain modifications.

The parties on whom the primary obligation of relieving this distress appeared to the Government to fall were the landed proprietors within the several districts. If they were proved to have already contributed as much as might be reasonably have been expected, the next claim appeared to be on the charity of private individuals, or Committees for raising subscriptions, and it would only be when these two sources of relief had been proved to be inadequate, that the funds of the State could have been with justice and propriety applied for such a purpose. It was evident that if public money

---

[65] This is taken from NLS, Sir John Hill, 1837: diary and papers, Acc 12783. When Hill's appointment at Deptford was under threat, Spring Rice suggested a copy of this letter should be sent to the Admiralty as a testament of Hill's service in Scotland (see the Biographical Notes).

were inconsiderately granted an appeal would be made in vain either to the sympathy of landlords, or to the benevolence of charitable persons.

The Government therefore determined to adhere to the principle of aiding the efforts of Committees, and of individuals only, and not of substituting the relief given by the State for that which might be derived from these sources. This appeared important, not so much on economical grounds, as because it was manifest that a stricter application of the funds, a more attentive discrimination – between the applications for relief, and a higher moral principle of administration, would be the result of an expenditure of this combined nature, than if the supplies were exclusively provided by the Treasury.

The expectations of relief would also be much less in the one case than in the other; and the interposition of the public would have the effect of stimulating charity in place of repressing it. But to act on these principles required great caution, prudence and well directed benevolence.

The experience which you had acquired in the execution of similar duties in Ireland, and that satisfactory mode in which those duties had been performed pointed you out as a proper person to be employed on such an occasion.

By the permission of The Lords Commissioners of the Admiralty you obtained leave of absence, and means were placed at your command which would readily have been augmented had circumstances rendered it necessary to do so. You were directed to communicate with the Charitable Committees, and to make your interposition dependent on and connected with theirs. Your attention was first to be directed to the supply of seed so as to prevent the recurrence of the existing calamity in a future year, and you were ordered to act in conjunction with Mr Graham employed under the direction of the Secretary of State in a survey of the distressed districts. The event has fully justified the principles laid down in your instructions, and the reliance which the Government placed in your ability. The large subscriptions raised at Edinburgh, Glasgow, Aberdeen, as well as in the Metropolis, and in other parts of South Britain, gave you the fullest means of appropriating the funds at your command according to the orders you had received, and it is with infinite gratification that Her Majesty learns that the relief given has been adequate and effectual. The question of emigration to which so many allusions have been made has been referred to the Colonial Department whose attention has been for some time directed to this most important subject.

Her Majesty is aware that for your services in Ireland, I was authorised by our late Sovereign to convey to you His Majesty's satisfaction for your zeal and activity, and more especially, for the caution, prudence and conciliatory spirit in which you acted.[66] Her Majesty is pleased to command me to express

---

[66] This was for his services in Ireland in 1836; Hill had been knighted for similar work in 1831 (see the Biographical Notes above).

to you her gracious approval on this present occasion. No part of Her Majesty's functions can be more gratifying to Her Majesty's feelings, than such as may enable Her Majesty to avert or mitigate distress among any portion of her faithful subjects – and on the present occasion Her Majesty rejoices that this has been done by combining the interposition of the State with the generous charity of individuals, and through the agency of one who has on former occasions shewn his ability by important public services.

I have the honour to be, Sir, Your very faithful servant.

Section 2

Colonial Office 29 July 1837 Elliot to Stephen[67]

Sir, In pursuance of your directions, I have perused and attentively considered Mr Spearman's letter of the 21st ultimo, accompanied by a report from Mr Graham on the distress in the Western Isles and Highlands of Scotland, and I have now the honour to submit my report for Lord Glenelg's information, on the suggestion that recourse should be had to an extensive emigration to New South Wales and Van Diemen's Land. It must be admitted that few cases could arise to which the remedy of emigration on a great scale would appear more appropriate than to this of the distress in the Hebrides. Owing to a change in the processes of the manufacture in which kelp used to be employed and to the decline of the fisheries, a majority of the population is represented to have become a clear superfluity in the country which it inhabits. What is described is not a mere diminution of employment, which might be of longer or shorter duration and the people be afterwards restored to as good a condition as before, but an absolute cessation of the only occupations by which the bulk of the population lived, without a prospect of their revival. And the reduced profitableness of the fisheries is partly owing to natural causes which cannot be controlled, and partly to an abolition of bounties of which the renewal cannot be expected consistently with the policy of the times. Seventy thousand people are reported to be brought to a condition in which, long before the commencement of the next crop, they will be without supply of food at home; and unprovided as they are with the means of paying for importations, will yet have to look to foreign sources to avoid

---

[67] James Stephen, permanent under-secretary at the Colonial Office. Under direction of the Treasury minute of 20 June 1837 (p. 283) Spearman wrote on 21 June 1837 to Stephen at the Colonial Office with a copy of Robert Graham's letter of 6 May 1837 asking for Lord Glenelg's opinion on Graham's recommendation that extensive emigration should be sought, 'with reference more especially to the fact that considerable sums are at the disposal of the Crown for defraying the expense of such emigration to the Australian colonies'. Glenelg asked T. F. Elliot, the agent-general for emigration for a report so that Glenelg could respond to the Treasury and this letter is Elliot's report to Glenelg.

starvation. And though this effect may have been enhanced by the character of the seasons of the last two years, the more remote causes of it are said to be permanent.

Certainly no resource could suggest itself more naturally under these circumstances, than a removal of the people, bodily, from a land which is no longer adequate to support them. It is necessary, however, frankly to contemplate the difficulties which stand in the way of this expedient; not with a view of describing them as insurmountable (that being a question involving general principles of policy, upon which I have not been called to report on this occasion, and which are too important to render it fitting to attempt to dispose of them incidentally), but in order at least to show what it is that must be provided for before this remedy will be applicable.

In the first place, in order to be effectual, the removal of the people must really be in a body. Whether or not a partial and selected emigration, such as I shall presently have occasion to describe as in progress to Australia, may be serviceable as a palliative, it cannot be denied that as several of the proprietors have already urged in reference to that undertaking, it can afford no radical cure. To make a deep impression on the case, not merely the active and the enterprising, but the weak, the aged and the sickly must accompany the general migration. And in throwing a body of people so composed upon the shores of the colonies, it would be indispensable to guard against the unfair burden which it might otherwise produce there, in its transit to the place fixed upon for its ultimate settlement. Provision must be made at the chief towns through which they pass, for the support of persons disabled by accident or by sickness; for their accommodation in hospitals; and for the care of the widows and orphans who, in the journey of such large numbers, would become so during the course of the expedition.

It would be an error to suppose that, as the colonies must benefit, on the whole, by the addition of fresh settlers to their population, it is equitable that the cities on their coasts should bear any inconvenience inherent in their introduction. This can only be true when the community is so new and so limited in extent that the benefit of one district must be felt sensibly by the rest. But in America, to which continent alone, I apprehend, can emigration on any very grand scale be conducted, the people often have to be pushed vast distances into the interior before they reach the spot where their presence is an advantage. The towns where they land or through which they first pass, reap no benefit from them and generally do not even belong to the territories where they finally settle; the useful and the capable pass on and it is only those who are detained by misfortune (or what is worse by intemperate habits) who remain behind to be a burden to the cities near the places of disembarkation.

These cases have as yet been provided for in Lower Canada by a small capitation tax on all passengers, which goes to support hospitals and other useful institutions for their accommodation, and in fact constitutes a sort of benefit fund for the whole body. It is doubtful, however, whether in the present state of political affairs in Lower Canada there will be an opportunity to renew this tax which is about to expire, and at any rate it is probable that if the number of emigrants were very largely increased by Government funds and, moreover, with a much larger admixture of persons likely to fall into distress than in spontaneous emigrations composed of those only who had vigour to effect their own removal, a demand would loudly arise for some security from the British Government against the misery with which the places of transit would become liable to be charged.

It is not, however, only in a provision for casualties that more would be required than the mere conveyance of the people, if Government undertook to conduct a great emigration by its own means and on its own responsibility. The nature of a voluntary emigration, as I have just hinted, is to be composed principally of persons who can shift themselves. That very circumstance brings them there. They have therefore been left hitherto and successfully to the general resources of the country and demand for labour in the places whither they have gone, and have been merely aided by Government with the best information as to the abundance of lands or of employment in different directions. But where persons should be enabled to emigrate not so much from their aptitude to better their fortunes elsewhere, as from their being burdens where they actually were and when likewise they should be assisted in great masses taken from the same parts of this country and likely to remain congregated in the same districts in the colony, instead of scattering in search of employment, it would become quite indispensable, I should apprehend, to take some more decided precautions against their falling into want. In short, it would be necessary to provide not merely for their conveyance but for their settlement. This is precisely the plan which was always contemplated in the proceedings before the Emigration committee in 1826 and 1827 and of which the gigantic expensiveness and responsibility may probably have constituted one of the principal reasons that no practical measure was founded on those elaborate enquiries.[68] £14 for each family was the very lowest estimate at that time for the cost of settlement, and I have seen none lower since.[69]

I would by no means wish, as I have already said, to represent the preceding difficulties as conclusive objections to emigration on a great scale and by aid of public resources. Many more topics must be reviewed than could be conveniently brought within the compass of this report, or than perhaps it would be becoming in me to offer my humble views upon without their being specially required,

[68] A figure of £1,140,000 to remove 95,000 persons was given in [PP] 1826–7 V (550), 19.
[69] This sentence in the copy letter as reproduced in [PP] 1837–8 XL (388) and [PP] 1841 XXVII (60) is different: it is 'The estimate which the last Committee adopted of the charge for settlement amounted to no less than £60 for each family'. The figure of £60 per family appears in [PP] 1826–7 V (550), 19.

before that large question could be considered to have been adequately treated of. But I fear it follows from what has been said that very comprehensive arrangements must be decided on and parliamentary funds be voted and the determination of the Government be taken on the general principle it would be willing to act upon in similar cases before an extensive emigration to America by public aid could be resorted to as a remedy for the present distress in the Highlands.

The next question is the applicability to the same purpose of the funds yielded by the Australian Colonies. You are aware that the sums derived from sales of Crown lands in New South Wales and Van Diemen's Land are at present expended in giving free passages to young married people and their relatives, belonging to the class of agricultural labourers or mechanics, and found to be of a description for which there is some demand in the colony. This course of proceeding is recommended by the Colonial authorities at New South Wales and appears to be cordially assented to by the community there. It has received the sanction of Her Majesty's Government, and it is in accordance with the views of the committee of the House of Commons which sat on wild lands last year.[70] It certainly has the merit of at once providing for the advantage of the colony in the kind of emigrants taken out, and also affording the best security for the welfare of the people themselves. But if, instead of adhering to this plan, it were attempted to apply the funds directly to the discharge of extensive and over-peopled districts in this country from their surplus population, I fear that disappointment would be the result. The distance of the Australian Colonies and consequent cost of conveyance, present one obvious obstacle to any such project; and even if they did not, the limited numbers, as yet, of their inhabitants, would present another still more formidable. However adequate to receive a gradual and regulated emigration carefully suited to their wants, it could not be expected that such comparatively new communities should be able to sustain the simultaneous influx of large bodies of people without discrimination of age or occupation. They would soon be glutted, and the old settlers find themselves burdened and the new reduced to want. It was on such considerations as these that I hazarded the observation that North America seemed the only field at present available for a very large and comprehensive emigration; and on the same grounds I apprehend that the Australian funds cannot be rendered conducive to relief of the distress in the Highlands further than in the mode which has already been adopted for that purpose.[71]

---

[70] [PP] 1836 XI (512), *Select Committee on Disposal of Lands in British Colonies*, iv–v; the committee referred to a judicious selection of emigrants which would give preference to young recently married couples and that it would be perfectly practicable to raise, on the security of future land sales, 'the Funds necessary to set on foot a plan of systematic emigration upon a scale sufficiently large to meet the exigencies of the Colonies and of the Mother Country'.

[71] This is Elliot's answer to the statement in the Treasury minute of 20 June 1837 that 'considerable sums are at the disposal of the Crown for defraying the expense of such emigration to the Australian colonies'.

Dr Boyter has already been employed for some time in the distressed districts, with authority to send out as many ships containing persons of the description required by the colonies as he might find wished for on the spot, and likely to be beneficial there; and he has power, within moderate limits, not to object to the reception of aged relatives of such emigrants, provided the cost of passage of these individuals beyond the prescribed years, be paid for by their friends or landlords.[72] The second ship sent under this arrangement is about to sail;[73] and a third will go in August.[74] Dr Boyter is then to report how much further there seems an opportunity of carrying the plan with advantage.

If this measure professed to be aimed directly at the relief of the Highlands, there can be no question that it would be very inefficient; but I think proprietors are beginning to understand that the primary object being a benefit to the colony, and to the individuals removed, the wish is to render it subservient, as far as it will go, to the convenience of the distressed district here; and that if this order were reversed and the preference given to the last-mentioned purpose, it is probable that all the ends in view would be frustrated; that the Australian funds would, after all, be unequal to carry out any very great numbers to that distance; while, from being taken indiscriminately, the individuals removed would miss their advantage, and the colonies incur a heavy burden.

Accordingly, it is gratifying to receive the accounts which now arrive from the Highlands, of satisfaction with the details of the arrangements for the emigration to New South Wales and Van Diemen's Land; while those who desire a more comprehensive mode of removing the people, turn their attention principally to the American colonies. On that subject I have already submitted what views I have to offer in the first part of this Report. I have the honour to be.

Downing Street 19 August 1837 Stephen to Spearman

Sir, I am directed by Lord Glenelg to acknowledge the receipt of your letter of 21st of June last transmitting a report of Mr Robert Graham on the state of the destitute poor in the Highlands of Scotland, in which he suggests that recourse should be had to an extensive emigration to the colonies.

This report having been referred by Lord Glenelg's desire to Mr Elliot, the agent-general for emigration, a copy of this officer's report is herewith

[72] TNA:PRO, War and Colonial Department and Colonial Office: Emigration original correspondence, CO 384/42, Grey to Boyter, 11 Apr. 1837.
[73] This was the first ship to sail from the Hebrides and was the *William Nicholl*, which sailed on 6 July 1837 with 321 emigrants and which is referred to in Hill's journal (p. 165).
[74] The *Brilliant*, which sailed on 16 Sept. 1837 with 320 emigrants. The emigrants were described as 'the most valuable that have ever left the shores of Great Britain; they are all of excellent moral character, and from their knowledge of agriculture, the management of sheep and cattle must prove as a most valuable addition to the colony of New South Wales' (*Inverness Courier*, 11 Oct. 1837).

transmitted for the information of the Lords Commissioners of the Treasury. Lord Glenelg concurs generally in the opinions expressed by Mr Elliot, although his Lordship must qualify his assent to those opinions by two remarks. First, it appears to him that although it may be impracticable to remove so large a population as 70,000 persons from the north of Scotland to British North America,[75] there is no insuperable difficulty in affecting the removal of many families, or even the inhabitants of some part of the district in question; and secondly, although it may be impracticable to settle any large number of these persons in the interior of the Canadas, yet as their business is that of fishing, it appears to Lord Glenelg not improbable that a considerable number of these might find profitable employment in the same line of life on the coasts of New Brunswick, Nova Scotia and Lower Canada. It is however clear that the funds at the disposal of Her Majesty's Government for the purpose of emigration are not applicable to this service, and the removal, if effected at all at the public expense, can be accomplished only at the charge of the public revenue of this Kingdom. I am, Sir, your most obedient humble servant.

[75] Graham's report said that the population of the destitute districts amounted to at least 105,000 and that two-thirds of this number would be without a supply of food until the next crop and would have to rely on others to prevent starvation (p. 95). Elliot referred in his report to this number of 70,000 people. Graham's estimate did not, however, include Sutherland, Caithness, Orkney and Shetland which had not been visited by him.

PART 5

TREASURY MINUTES

This Part contains the minutes of the Treasury that related to the decisions and actions of the Treasury in connection with Government aid provided to the distressed districts of the Highlands and Islands in 1837.

Minute 6001 dated 14 March 1837

Viscount Melbourne and the chancellor of the exchequer inform the Board that they have received communications from various noblemen and gentlemen connected with parts of the Highlands and Western Islands of Scotland stating that much urgent and pressing distress prevailed in certain districts by reason of the failure of the crops during the last harvest and that a great proportion of the population were in a state of absolute destitution for want of food and seed for the present year.[1] Lord Melbourne and the chancellor of the exchequer are informed that subscriptions have been collected in Scotland to the amount of about £10,000 and that a similar sum may be relied on from the contributions of benevolent persons in other parts of the Empire.

While Lord Melbourne and the chancellor of the exchequer are well aware that much risk attends all interference of the Government in matters relating to the supply of food and affecting the general price of provisions and while they are also aware that unless under very peculiar circumstances a disturbance of the ordinary markets by forced sales of food at prices unnaturally depressed may interfere with the ordinary transactions of commerce and of private enterprise, and may prevent the abundance of one district being brought in aid of the deficiency of another, the present appears to them to be a case in which, in reference more particularly to the supply of seed oats, barley and potatoes, some assistance is required from the public in aid of the private contributions already received or which may be collected hereafter.

Lord Melbourne and the chancellor of the exchequer inform the Board further that committees have been established at Edinburgh and Glasgow for the administration of the charitable funds already collected and they lay before their Lordships the resolutions passed by the Edinburgh committee.[2] They state at the same time that the secretary of state for the Home department has commissioned Robert Graham Esq. to make an enquiry into the present state of the poor in these districts, to communicate with the committees at Edinburgh and Glasgow[3] upon the subject and to report upon the facts for the more full information of His Majesty's Government.

---

[1] This is a reference to the petition and memorials to the Treasury set out in Part 3 (pp. 201 to 209) and the deputation of MPs and others that had an interview with the Chancellor of the Exchequer on 13 Mar. 1837.

[2] Resolutions passed by the Edinburgh committee on 25 Jan. 1837 (p. 211) and 2 Mar. 1837 (p. 245).

[3] Rather confusingly, Fox Maule had already written to Graham and told him the enquiry he was to make was confidential for the information of the government and that if Graham had already involved himself with the committees he should 'pray get rid of them as quickly as possible' (p. 259).

But as the necessity of procuring the supplies of seed is urgent and as it would be inexpedient to allow any delay to occur, Lord Melbourne and the chancellor of the exchequer recommend that Captain Sir John Hill, superintendent of the Victualling Department at Deptford should at once be directed to proceed to Scotland to put himself into communication with Mr Graham and the committees at Edinburgh and Glasgow and to take such steps in conjunction with them as may appear necessary in the urgency of the case for the immediate supply of seed corn and potatoes.

My Lords entirely concur in opinion with Lord Melbourne and the chancellor of the exchequer and desire that directions may be forthwith given to Sir John Hill accordingly.

In order to give effect to the recommendation of Lord Melbourne and the chancellor of the exchequer and to the intention of their Lordships it will be proper that Sir John Hill should be authorised to enter into contracts on the most favourable terms for the supply of seed oats, barley and potatoes at such of the ports and places in the distressed districts as may seem most advisable to the extent of such sum as may be necessary not exceeding £10,000 which My Lords will place at his disposal for this object, a proportionate contribution being furnished by the charitable committees and that he should report his proceedings in this matter from time to time to this Board taking care that no time is lost making the purchases and dispatching the supplies so as to ensure their reaching the distressed districts before the proper period for the due cultivation of the soil shall have passed away.

My Lords are also of opinion that in making the arrangements for the delivery of the seed he should be governed by the principles laid down in the resolutions of the Edinburgh committee of which my Lords entirely approve.[4]

It will likewise be necessary that he should keep the accounts of his expenditure and of the application of seed purchased in such manner as to enable him to render a clear and satisfactory account of his proceedings in this matter for the information of my Lords and that he should be authorised to draw upon the paymaster of civil services for such sums as may be required within the limits fixed by this minute.

Transmit copy of this minute to Sir John Hill for his information and government in this matter and authorise him to draw from time to time upon Mr Sargent[5] in bills at 3 days sight on account of the service for which he is dispatched to Scotland.

State to him at the same time that my Lords will instruct the commissioner of the Customs to direct their officers and the commanders of all revenue cruisers and of the coast guard to afford him every aid and assistance in their power.

---

[4]　Resolutions passed by the Edinburgh committee on 2 Mar. 1837 (p. 245).
[5]　Frederick Sargent, an assistant clerk in the Treasury.

Let directions be accordingly given to the commissioners of Customs and let Mr Sargent be instructed to accept and pay for from civil contingencies any bills drawn by Sir John Hill at 3 days sight for this service not exceeding £10,000.

My Lords reserve the question of the supply of food for consideration when by the reports expected from Mr Graham they shall be made acquainted with the actual state of the population in the districts in question in that respect.

Let a copy of this minute be transmitted to his grace the duke of Argyll for the information of those noblemen and gentlemen by whom the representation upon this subject was addressed to Lord Melbourne and the chancellor of the exchequer.

Minute 5483 dated 17 March 1837

Read letter from the secretary to the directors of the Highland & Agricultural Society of Scotland dated 7th instant on the subject of the distress and destitution which the inhabitants of the Islands and Highlands suffer, and suggesting that speedy relief be afforded them.[6]

Write memorialists that the subject is under the consideration of the Government.

Minute 6664 dated 31 March 1837

Read memorial of the Glasgow committee for the relief of the inhabitants in the Highlands and Islands of Scotland dated 27th ultimo for pecuniary assistance.[7]

Write parties that the subject has already been under the consideration of Government and that they have already commanded such measures under the circumstances have appeared to be most advisable.[8]

---

[6] The Society had authorised its directors to use the name and influence of the Society to support relief measures to be set on foot by the landed proprietors – the constitution preluded it giving direct relief – and it is noteworthy that its first action had been this letter to the Treasury to ask for 'such grant as will avert the dreadful consequences of famine which, if the means of supplying seed are not afforded immediately, may be extended over two years' (TNA:PRO, Treasury, T 1/4201 Society to Treasury, 7 Mar. 1837; *The Scotsman*, 14 Jan. 1837).

[7] The memorial from the Glasgow committee dated 27 Feb. 1837 (which was sent to the Treasury on 25 Mar. 1837) (p. 207).

[8] The committee was sent a copy of the Treasury minute of 14 Mar. 1837 and was also told, orally, that Robert Graham had been sent to the Hebrides to investigate the reality and extent of the destitution (TNA:PRO, Treasury, T 1/4201, Interim report by the committee in Glasgow for the relief of the destitute inhabitants of the Highlands and Islands of Scotland, 29 Apr. 1837) (p. 230).

Minute dated 31 March 1837[9]

Write to Sir John Hill to acquaint him in reply to these letters sent,[10] my Lords entirely approve of the steps taken by him in fulfilment of their Lordship's instructions.

Transmit to him a copy of the application made by the Glasgow committee[11] and acquaint him that there is nothing stated therein of a nature to incline this Board to change or vary the instructions already communicated to him, that my Lords will make a reply to that effect to the committee and that they desire he will apprise the committee that unless they shall concur with him in the arrangement for giving effect to the calculations of this Board, he is directed to take all his future measures in communication with the committee in Edinburgh only.[12]

Write to the Glasgow committee that my Lords however fully considered the representations addressed by them to this Board but that my Lords are by no means prepared to authorise any departure from the instructions given by them to Sir John Hill.

Minute 7326 dated 6 April 1837

Read letter from Sir John Hill dated 31st ultimo reporting his proceedings since the 25th ultimo with reference to the service on which he is engaged in Scotland.

Write to Sir John Hill approving of the proceedings reported by him in this letter.

Minute 7695 dated 11 April 1837

Read letter from Sir John Hill dated 4th instant stating his proceedings in connection with the committee at Aberdeen for the relief of the distress in the Highlands etc.

Write to Sir John Hill approving of his proceedings as reported in this letter.

---

9   This minute is taken from NRS, Commissary General and Treasury, HD 7/9.
10 Hill's letters to Spearman of 21 Mar. 1837 (p. 116) and 25 Mar. 1837 (p. 118).
11 In its memorial to the Treasury of 25 Mar. 1837 (p. 210) the Glasgow committee had asked that it should not be obliged to spend, on a pound for pound basis, any of its funds on seed to be entitled to share in the government aid because the committee could not justify applying any of their funds in the purchase of seed, given the overwhelming need for all their funds to be spent on food.
12 On receiving this negative response from the Treasury, the Glasgow committee determined, in effect, to go it alone and leave the government and the Edinburgh committee to concentrate on the supply of seed (TNA:PRO, Treasury, T 1/4201, Glasgow interim report, 29 Apr. 1837; p. 227).

Minute 8646 dated 21 April 1837

Read letter from Sir John Hill dated 16th instant respecting supply of seed potatoes for the Highlands and Islands of Scotland.

Write to Sir John Hill approving the proceedings taken by him as reported by this letter.

Minutes 8965 and 8966 dated 25 April 1837

Read letter from Sir John Hill dated 19th instant advising of a bill for £300.[13] As this bill will be accepted and paid under the general directions relating to this service issued to Mr Sargent, no order upon the subject is necessary.

Read letter from the same of the same date with copy of a letter from the Collector of Customs at Kirkwall in Orkney relative to the supply of seed corn for the Orkneys. It does not appear to my Lords that any directions from this Board are required upon this letter.

Minute dated 28 April 1837[14]

My Lords read again the letter of Mr Fox Maule communicating to the Board the decision of Lord John Russell the intention of His Majesty's Government to dispatch Mr Robert Graham to the Western Coast of Scotland to make enquiry into the present state of the poor in the Highlands who are reported to be in a destitute situation in consequence of the failure of the late harvest.

Write to Mr Maule and request he will move Lord John Russell to furnish my Lords with copies of any reports he may have received from Mr Robert Graham on this subject and that he will also give directions that copies of any further reports that may be made by Mr Graham may be transmitted to this Board from time to time as they are received.

---

13 The archive sources do not contain this letter.
14 This minute is taken from TNA:PRO, Treasury, T 1/4201. It refers to Fox Maule's letter of 2 Mar. 1837 to the Admiralty for the information of the Treasury as to the appointment by the Home Office of Graham (TNA:PRO, Treasury, T 1/4201, Fox Maule to Wood, 2 Mar. 1837). Although a note on the letter of 2 Mar. confirms the Treasury read the letter on 3 Mar., it does not appear the Treasury took any further action on it until this minute of 28 Apr. By this stage, Graham had, of course, completed his visit to the Highlands and Islands and so, quite remarkably, it appears that the Treasury had not received any of Graham's letters written to Fox Maule as his visit progressed and was, therefore, unaware of what Graham had said or recommended in those letters. This is the more remarkable given the Treasury minute of 14 Mar. 1837 had quite explicitly acknowledged the importance of these letters in relation to the consideration of any further aid from the government.

Minute dated 16 May 1837[15]

My Lords have before them the several letters of Sir John Hill dated 22nd and 29th April and 6th May reporting his proceedings in procuring, in conjunction with the local committees of Edinburgh and Aberdeen, supplies of seed corn and potatoes for those districts in the Highlands and Islands of Scotland to which his attention was directed by the order of this Board in consequence of the severe pressure of distress existing therein.

The amount drawn for by Sir John Hill to the latest date to which any of his bills have been presented is £3,037–1–4 but my Lords have reason to believe from his communications that the whole expense incurred in providing seed corn and potatoes will amount to about £6,500.

Sir John Hill having performed to the entire satisfaction of my Lords the more immediate and pressing duty for which he was despatched to Scotland, My Lords advert to that part of their minute of 14 March last, in which they stated that they reserved the question of the supply of food for consideration when by the reports expected from Mr Graham they should be acquainted with the actual state of the population of the districts in question in that respect; and their Lordships have before them the reports which have been made from time to time by Mr Graham to the Secretary of State to the 26th April last.[16]

It appears to my Lords upon a careful consideration of these reports and of the facts stated therein that the attention of Sir John Hill should now be turned to the measures which should be taken for affording relief in food to those districts in which the distress is of such a character and description as to require the interposition of Government in aid of the exertions of individual benevolence. My Lords cannot doubt that every exertion will be made by subscriptions and otherwise, not only in the distressed districts, but throughout the Empire, to afford that relief which appears from these papers (copies of which have been

---

[15]   This minute is taken from NRS, Commissary General and Treasury, HD 7/9.

[16]   In response to the Treasury request from its minute of 28 Apr. for copies of Graham's reports, Fox Maule responded by letter on 3 May that the reports would be sent as soon as possible but, as they were 'very voluminous, some delay will necessarily occur in the transmission of them' (NRS, Commissary General and Treasury, HD 7/9, Fox Maule to Spearman, 3 May 1837). The copies of the letters from Graham by then received at the Home Office were forwarded to the Treasury by Fox Maule on 6 May 1837 (NRS, Commissary General and Treasury, HD 7/9, Fox Maule to Spearman, 6 May 1837) but by then, of course, the Home Office had not received Graham's final report dated 6 May which was finally forwarded to the Treasury on 23 May 1837 (TNA:PRO, Treasury, T 1/4201, Fox Maule to Spearman, 23 May 1837). Indeed, it may be that the Treasury did not, by 6 May, receive *all* of Graham's letters because it appears the Home Office had lost five of Graham's letters written before 22 Mar. 1837 (see Graham's letter to Stewart of 18 May 1837, p. 110). In any event, it was only on 10 July 1837 that Graham's final letter of 6 May was presented by Francis Baring, the financial secretary to the Treasury, to the House of Commons when it was ordered to lie on the table and be printed (*House of Commons Journals* 92 (1837), 615–17).

furnished by the Secretary of State to Sir John Hill) to be so much needed, but they are at the same time of opinion that he should be authorised immediately to proceed, in conjunction with the local committees, in making such purchases of food to be despatched to the distressed districts as may appear in his judgement to be necessary, taking care as far as possible to act upon the same principle as that laid down for his government with respect to the supply of seed – that is to make his purchases contingent, to as great an extent as may be, upon an equal contribution from private funds, adopting for the distribution of the food the principles laid down in the resolutions of the Edinburgh Committee as may appear to him to be the best calculated to effect the object of my Lords in sanctioning this expenditure with such variations where necessary.

My Lords are of opinion that he should in the meantime and until he receives further directions, apply to this object the balance of the £10,000 already placed at his disposal beyond the sum already expended in the purchase of seed.

Transmit copy of this minute to Sir John Hill for his information and request him to communicate his proceedings from time to time to my Lords.

Transmit copy also to Mr Fox Maule for the information of the Secretary of State.[17]

Minute dated 20 June 1837[18]

My Lords read the report of Mr Graham of the 6th May on the state of the poor in the Highlands of Scotland which has been transmitted to this Board by the secretary of state for the Home Department;[19] and in which Mr Graham suggests among modes of alleviating the distress and preventing as far as possible the recurrences of it that recourse should be had to an extensive emigration to His (sic) Majesty's Colonies abroad,[20] and that assistance should be given in work by opening new roads which might, he states, be undertaken with great public advantage, one half of the expense being defrayed by the Government, the other half by the proprietors.

My Lords are aware that the attention of the secretary of state for the Colonies[21] has already been called to the state of these districts and that arrangements are already and have been for some time in course of progress with a view to the emigration of portions of the surplus population to the colonies

[17] TNA:PRO, Home Office: Treasury and Customs correspondence, HO 35/31, Spearman to Fox Maule, 18 May 1837.
[18] This minute is taken from NRS, Commissary General and Treasury, HD 7/9.
[19] It had been transmitted to the Treasury on 23 May 1837.
[20] The minute does not indicate that emigration was the principal course of action suggested by Graham, rather than just one of a number of possible courses.
[21] Lord Glenelg.

of New South Wales and Van Diemen's Land;[22] but my Lords are nevertheless of opinion that a copy of the report of Mr Graham which enters fully into the whole subject should be transmitted to Lord Glenelg and that his Lordship should be requested to favour my Lords with his opinion on the recommendation of Mr Graham with reference more especially to the fact that considerable sums are at the disposal of the Crown for defraying the expense of such emigration to the Australian colonies. Write to Mr Stephen accordingly.[23]

My Lords are further of opinion that it will be proper to transmit to the Commissioners of Highland Roads and Bridges an extract from that part of this report which relates to the formation of new lines of communication and that they may be required to apprise my Lords whether they could undertake the superintendence of such works as they may deem of general advantage to the public provided Her Majesty's Government should consider it advisable to ask sanction of Parliament to such works being undertaken on condition that one half of the expense was borne by the proprietors locally interested, in which case my Lords request they will consider and report what lines of communication would be in their judgment expedient to undertake and what would be the probable expense incurred.[24]

Transmit copy of this minute to Mr Fox Maule for the information of Lord John Russell.

Minute 13989 dated 27 June 1837

Read letter from Sir John Hill dated 23rd instant advising of a bill for £5,910–2–6. As this bill will be accepted under the general authority given to Mr Sargent, no directions are necessary upon this letter.

---

[22] See the Introduction.
[23] TNA:PRO, War and Colonial Department and Colonial Office: Emigration original correspondence, CO 384/43/300, Spearman to Stephen, 21 June 1837. On receipt of the letter, Lord Glenelg asked T. F. Elliot, the agent-general for emigration, to report on Graham's suggestion for an extensive emigration to the colonies, which Elliot did on 29 July 1837; whereupon Stephen wrote to the Treasury on 19 Aug. 1837 giving Lord Glenelg's formal response to the Treasury on Graham's suggestion (Elliot's report and Glenelg's response are set out on pp. 268–73).
[24] The Commissioners of Highland Roads and Bridges responded to this by recommending the Dingwall to Ullapool and Poolewe to Achnasheen lines, as well as a road from Barvas to Ness in Lewis, and roads in Mull. But the dissolution of the government had weakened the political impetus to act and the half-hearted response of proprietors had not been encouraging (Smith, 'From Isolation to Integration', 161).

Minute 15189 dated 14 July 1837

Read letter from Sir John Hill dated 11th instant advising of his having drawn a bill for £500. As this bill will be accepted under the general authority given to Mr Sargent, no directions are necessary upon this matter.

Minute dated 28 July 1837[25]

Read letters.[26] Write to Sir John Hill conveying to him my Lords' approval of the several steps taken by him as reported in his letters and expressing to him the satisfaction with which their Lordships have received the information communicated in his letter of the 2nd instant, from which and from his previous reports my Lords have no doubt that the arrangements made by him and by the local authorities have produced all those results the expectations of which induced this Board to dispatch him to Scotland to give the assistance of the Government in aid of local exertions in relief of the distress in those districts to which the attention of their Lordships was so urgently called; and he is now, therefore, at liberty to return to London to report fully upon his proceedings.

Minute 17014 dated 11 August 1837

Read letter from Sir John Hill dated the 4th instant transmitting an account of the proceedings of the Edinburgh committee for the relief of destitution in the Highlands in which, after bearing the highest testimony to the zeal and energy displayed by Sir John Hill in the irksome and laborious duties in which he has been engaged, a very strong representation is made in favour of emigration to Canada and Australia, and Sir John Hill is requested to urge upon the attention of Her Majesty's Government the beneficial results which may arise to the highlanders of Scotland from an encouragement to emigrate in the ensuing spring.

My Lords receive this testimony to the manner in which, in the opinion of the Edinburgh committee, Sir John Hill has discharged the important duty confided in him, with much satisfaction.

My Lords at the same time are pleased to desire that an extract from that part of the resolution of the committee which relate to emigration from the districts in question may be transmitted to Mr Stephen, with their Lordships' request that he will lay it before Lord Glenelg and state that he is desired by

---

[25]   This minute is taken from TNA:PRO, Treasury, T 1/4201.
[26]   Hill's letters to Spearman of 7 June, 16 June, 23 June and 2 July 1837 (pp. 157, 168, 174 and 179).

their Lordships to call the attention of his Lordship to the opinion expressed by the committee on this subject, with reference to the former papers which my Lords have already forwarded to him relating thereto.[27] Write to Mr Stephen accordingly.[28]

Write at the same time to the secretary of the Admiralty and request he will acquaint the Lords of the Admiralty that Sir John Hill having now fulfilled the important duty in Scotland committed to his charge, and for which he received their Lordships' permission to be absent from Deptford, my Lords consider it will be due to that officer to make known to the Lords of the Admiralty that in the discharge of that duty Sir John Hill has given entire satisfaction to this Board. Transmit to Sir John Hill copy of the letter addressed to the secretary of the Admiralty.[29]

Minute 20127 dated 29 September 1837

Read letter from Mr Fox Maule dated 22nd instant requesting that directions may be given for payment of the expenses incurred by Mr R. Graham and Mr R. Stewart in their inquiry into the destitution in the Highlands and Islands of Scotland, amounting to the sum of £127–2–10.[30]

Direct Mr Sargent to pay the amount of this account to Mr Robert Graham charging such payment to civil contingencies.

Acquaint Mr Fox Maule with the directions given and request he will move Lord John Russell to give instructions to Mr Graham to draw upon Mr Sargent for the amount of this account.

---

[27] This is a reference to Graham's letter of 6 May 1837.

[28] TNA:PRO, War and Colonial Department and Colonial Office: Emigration original correspondence, CO 384/43/337, Spearman to Stephen, 18 Aug. 1837. A copy of Spearman's letter and the extract were sent to T. F. Elliot on 29 Aug. 1837.

[29] See NLS, Sir John Hill, 1837: diary and papers, Acc 12738, Spearman to Hill, 18 Aug. 1837, and Spearman to Admiralty, 18 Aug. 1837.

[30] TNA:PRO, Treasury, T 1/4201, Fox Maule to Baring, 22 Sept. 1837.

BIBLIOGRAPHY

Manuscript Sources

British Library
  Add. MS 34614, Macvey Napier papers
  Add. MS 37299, Wellesley papers (Series II) vol. XXVI
  Add. MS 40294, Peel papers vol. CXIV
  Add. MS 40328, Peel papers vol. CXLVIII
  Add. MS 40576, Peel papers vol. CCCXCVI
  Add. MS 79659, Graham papers

Clan Donald Centre, Isle of Skye
  GD 221, Macdonald papers

National Records of Scotland, General Register House, Edinburgh
  CH 1, Register of general assembly at Edinburgh
  GD 40, Lothian muniments
  GD 45, Papers of the Maule family, earls of Dalhousie
  GD 46, Papers of the Mackenzie family, earls of Seaforth
  GD 155, Papers of the Maxtone Graham family of Cultoquhey, Perthshire
  GD 174, Maclaine of Lochbuie papers
  GD 201, Papers of the MacDonald family of Clanranald
  GD 224, Papers of the Montague-Douglas-Scott family, dukes of Buccleuch
  GD 268, Papers of the Loch family of Drylaw

National Records of Scotland, West Register House, Edinburgh
  AD 58, Lord Advocate's Department, Miscellaneous papers
  CS 96, Court of Session: productions in process
  HD 7, Commissary General and Treasury

National Register of Archives for Scotland, Edinburgh
  MS 2177, Douglas-Hamilton family
  MS 2654, Stewart family of Ardvorlich papers

National Library of Scotland, Edinburgh
  Acc 12738, Sir John Hill 1837: diary and papers
  MS 3621, Lynedoch papers
  MS 16005, Lynedoch Papers

MS 16009, Lynedoch papers
MS 16011, Lynedoch papers
MS 16023, Lynedoch papers
MS 16025, Lynedoch papers
MS 16028, Lynedoch papers
MS 16035, Lynedoch papers
MS 16037, Lynedoch papers
MS 16049, Lynedoch papers
MS 16057, Lynedoch papers
MS 16107, Lynedoch papers
MS 16142, Lynedoch papers
MS 16144, Lynedoch papers
MS 16147, Lynedoch papers
MS 12048E, Minto papers
MS 12058, Minto papers
MS 9654, James Ivory letters
MS 9697, Rutherfurd papers
MS 9710, Rutherfurd papers
Highland Destitution Reports (1846–1851)

National Archives, London
ADM 9, Admiralty
ADM 101, Records of the Admiralty
CO 384 and CO 385, War and Colonial Department and Colonial Office:
Emigration Original Correspondence
HO 35, Home Office: Treasury and Customs Correspondence
HO 102, Home Office: Scotland: letters and papers
T 1, Treasury
T 29, Treasury Board: Minute Books

National Register of Archives, London
44729, Hill papers and correspondence

National Library of Ireland, Dublin
MS 542, Monteagle papers
MS 545, Monteagle papers
MS 551, Monteagle papers
MS 13383, Monteagle papers
MS 13384, Monteagle papers
MS 41705, Hill papers
MS 45004, Documents and letters relating to Sir John Hill's involvement
in famine relief in Ireland

New College Library, Edinburgh
CHA4.188.64, Special collections
CHA4.147.2.819, Special collections

Private Archives
Private papers of Robert Maxtone Graham
Private papers of Robert Oliphant Maxtone Graham
University Library, Cambridge
MS 26, Graham papers
MS 40, Graham papers

Parliamentary Papers

Hansard Parliamentary Debates

1817 VI (462), *Report from the Select Committee on the Poor Laws with the Minutes of Evidence Taken before the Committee and an Appendix*

1818 V (358), *Third Report from the Select Committee on the Poor Laws (1818) with an Appendix Containing Returns from the General Assembly of the Church of Scotland*

1820 XX (195), *Supplementary Report of the Committee of the General Assembly on the Management of the Poor in Scotland*

1826–7 V (550), *Third Report from the Select Committee on Emigration from the United Kingdom*

1831 IX (330), *Sixth Report of the Commissioners for Building Churches in the Highlands and Islands of Scotland*

1835 XXIX (30), *General Report of the Commissioners Appointed to Inquire into the State of Municipal Corporations in Scotland*

1836 XI (512), *Select Committee on Disposal of Lands in British Colonies*

1836 XVIII (430), *Select Committee on Statute Labour on Roads in Scotland*

1837–8 VIII (488), *First Report from the Select Committee on Combinations of Workmen*

1837 LI (69), *Report of Geo. Nicholls, Esq., to His Majesty's Principal Secretary of State for the Home Department, on Poor Laws, Ireland*

1837 LI (501), *Distress in the Highlands (Scotland)*

1837–8 XL (388), *Copy of a Report to the Secretary of State for the Colonies from the Agent-General for Emigration from the United Kingdom*

1839 XX (177), *Report by a Committee of the General Assembly on the Management of the Poor in Scotland*

1841 VI (182) and (333), *First and Second Reports from the Select Committee on Emigration, Scotland*

1841 XXVII (60), *Report from the Agent-General for Emigration on the Applicability of Emigration to Relieve Distress in the Highlands*

1844 XX (557), *Report from Her Majesty's Commissioners for Inquiring into the Administration and Practical Operation of the Poor Laws in Scotland*

1844 XXI (564), *Poor Law Inquiry (Scotland), Appendix, Part II*

1846 XXXVII (281), *Distress (Scotland): Documents Relative to the Distress and Famine in Scotland in the Year 1783, in Consequence of the Late Harvest and Loss of the Potato Crop*

1846 XXXVII (734), *Correspondence and Accounts Relating to the Different Occasions on which Measures were Taken for the Relief of the People Suffering from Scarcity in Ireland between the Years 1822 and 1839*

1847 LIII (788), *Correspondence Relating to the Measures Adopted for the Relief of Distress in Scotland*

1851 XXVI (1397), *Report to the Board of Supervision by Sir John McNeill, GCB on the Western Highlands and Islands*

1884 XXXVI [c.3980 IV], *Napier Commission Evidence*

1914 XXXII. 43 [Cd.7564], *Report to the Board of Agriculture for Scotland on Home Industries in the Highlands and Islands*

Printed Primary Sources

Anonymous, *Observations on the Causes and Remedies of Destitution in the Highlands and Islands of Scotland* (Glasgow, 1837)

Alison, W. P., *Letter to Sir John McNeill, GCB on Highland Destitution and the Adequacy or Inadequacy of Emigration as a Remedy* (Edinburgh, 1851)

Barron, J., *The Northern Highlands in the Nineteenth Century*, 3 vols. (Inverness, 1907)

Bowie, J., *Notes on Australia for the Information of Intending Emigrants* (Edinburgh, 1837)

Burke, E., *Thoughts and Details on Scarcity Originally Presented to the Right Hon. William Pitt, in the Month of November, 1795* (London, 1800)

Chalmers, Rev. T., 'Report from the Select Committee on the Poor-Laws – Causes and Cures of Pauperism', *Edinburgh Review* 29.58 (Feb. 1818), 263–302

Cockburn, H., 'Statement in Regard to the Pauperism of Glasgow from the Experience of the Last Eight Years – Poor Laws of Scotland', *Edinburgh Review* 41.81 (Oct. 1824), 228–58

Cockburn, H., *Letters Chiefly Connected with the Affairs of Scotland from Henry Cockburn to Thomas Francis Kennedy, MP* (London, 1874)

Cockburn, H., *Journal of Henry Cockburn 1831–1854*, 2 vols. (Edinburgh, 1874)

Dunlop, A., *A Treatise on the Law of Scotland Relative to the Poor* (Edinburgh, 1825)

Dunlop, A., *The Law of Scotland Regarding the Poor* (Edinburgh, 1854)

Dunlop, A., *Parochial Law* (Edinburgh, 1835)

Fullarton, A. and C. R. Baird, *Remarks on the Evils at Present Affecting the Highlands and Islands of Scotland; with Some Suggestions as to their Remedies* (Glasgow, 1838)

Johnson, S., *A Journey to the Western Islands of Scotland* (London, 1775)

Kay, J., *A Series of Original Portraits and Caricature Etchings*, 2 vols. (Edinburgh, 1838)

Knox, J., *View of the British Empire, More Especially Scotland* (Edinburgh, 1784)

Lang, J. D., *Transportation and Colonization* (London and Edinburgh, 1837)

Lang, J. D., *Historical and Statistical Account of New South Wales* (London, 1875)

Macculloch, J., *The Highlands and Western Isles of Scotland*, 4 vols. (London, 1824)

Macdonald, The Revs. A., *The Macdonald Collection of Gaelic Poetry* (Inverness, 1911)

Macgregor, the Rev. A., 'On the causes of the destitution of food in the Highlands and Islands of Scotland in the years 1836 and 1837', *Quarterly Journal of Agriculture* 9, xlii (1839), 159–99

Macgregor, the Rev. A., 'On the advantages of a Government grant for emigration from the Highlands and Islands of Scotland', *Quarterly Journal of Agriculture* 11, li (1840–1), 277–97

Macinnes, V. D. Lieut. -Col. J., *The Brave Sons of Skye* (London, 1899)

Mackenzie, Dr J., *Letter to Lord John Russell on Sir John McNeill's Report of the State of the Highlands and Islands of Scotland* (Edinburgh, 1851)

Macleod, J. N., *Memorials of the Rev. Norman Macleod D.D.* (Edinburgh, 1898)

Mitchell, J., *Reminiscences of My Life in the Highlands*, 2 vols. (Newton Abbot, 1971)

Mercer, General A. C., *Journal of the Waterloo Campaign* (London, 1870), 2012 edition, ed. A. Uffindell

Monypenny, D., *Remarks on the Poor Laws and on the Method of Providing for the Poor in Scotland* (Edinburgh, 1834)

Mulock, T., *The Western Highlands and Islands of Scotland Socially Considered* (Edinburgh, 1850)

Peel, Sir R., *Memoirs by the Rt. Hon. Sir Robert Peel*, 2 vols. (London, 1856–7)

Pennant, T., *A Tour in Scotland and Voyage to the Hebrides 1772* (Chester, 1774)

Selkirk, the earl of, *Observations on the Present State of the Highlands of Scotland with a View of the Possible Causes and Probable Consequences of Emigration* (London, 1805)

Sinclair, Sir J., *Analysis of the Statistical Account of Scotland*, 2 vols. (London, 1826)

Smith, A., *An Inquiry into the Nature and Causes of the Wealth of Nations*, 2 vols. (Oxford, 1979)

Reference Works

Anderson, G. and P., *Guide to the Highlands and Islands of Scotland* (London, 1834)

Bamford, A., *The British Army in the Low Countries, 1813–1814* (http://www.napoleon-series.org/military/battles/)

Cameron, N. M. de S., *et al.* (eds.), *Dictionary of Scottish Church History and Theology* (Edinburgh, 1993)

Dictionary of the Scots Language (http://www.dsl.ac.uk/)

Findlay, J., *Directory to Gentlemen's Seats, Villages etc. in Scotland* (Edinburgh, 1843)

Grant, W. (ed.), *Scottish National Dictionary* (Edinburgh, 1931–76)

Groome, F. H., *Ordnance Gazetteer of Scotland, A Survey of Scottish Topography, Statistical, Bibliographical and Historical*, 6 vols. (London, 1893–5)

Lumsden & Sons Steam-Boat Companion or Stranger's Guide to the Western Isles and Highlands of Scotland (Glasgow, 1839)

Lynch, M. (ed.), *The Oxford Companion to Scottish History* (Oxford, 2001),

Officer, L. H., and S. H. Williamson, 'Purchasing Power of British Pounds from 1245 to Present', *MeasuringWorth* 2011 (http://www.measuringworth.com/ppoweruk/)

Ordnance Survey Gazetteer of Great Britain (London, 1999)

Oxford Dictionary of National Biography (Oxford University Press online edition, http://www.oxforddnb.com)

Pigot & Co.'s National Commercial Directory of the whole of Scotland (London, 1837)

Scott, H. (ed.), *Fasti Ecclesiae Scoticanae: The Succession of Ministers in the Parish Churches of Scotland, from the Reformation, 1560, to the Present Time*, 7 vols. (Edinburgh, 1915–28)

The Edinburgh Almanac or Universal Scots and Imperial Register for 1837 (Edinburgh, 1837)

The New Statistical Account of Scotland, 15 vols. (Edinburgh, 1845)

The Traveller's Guide Through Scotland, and its Islands, 2 vols. (Edinburgh, 1814)

Walker, D. M., *The Oxford Companion to Law* (Oxford, 1980)

Walker, D. M., *A Legal History of Scotland: The Nineteenth Century*, vol. vi (Edinburgh, 2001)

Secondary Sources

Adam, M. I., 'Eighteenth century Highland landlords and the poverty problem', *SHR* 19.75 (April 1922), 161–79

Bourke, A., *'The Visitation of God'? The Potato and the Great Irish Famine* (Dublin, 1993)

Cage, R. A., 'Debate – the making of the old Scottish poor law', *Past and Present* 69 (Nov. 1975), 113–18

Cage, R. A., *The Scottish Poor Law 1745–1845* (Edinburgh, 1981)

Campbell, J. L., *Canna – The Story of a Hebridean Island* (Edinburgh, 1994)

Canavan, F., *The Political Economy of Edmund Burke – The Role of Property in his Thought* (New York, 1995)

Checkland, O., 'Chalmers and William Pulteney Alison: A conflict of views on Scottish social policy', in A. C. Cheyne (ed.), *The Practical and the Pious: Essays on Thomas Chalmers (1780–1847)* (Edinburgh, 1985)

Clarkson, L. A., and E. M. Crawford, *Feast and Famine – Food and Nutrition in Ireland 1500–1920* (Oxford, 2001)

Clow, A. and N. L., 'The Natural and Economic History of Kelp', *Annals of Science* 5.4 (15 July 1947), 297–316

Cockburn, H. A., *A History of the New Club, Edinburgh 1787–1937* (Edinburgh, 1938)

Collison Black, R. D., *Economic Thought and the Irish Question 1817–1870* (Cambridge 1960)

Cullen, K. J., *Famine in Scotland: The 'Ill Years of the 1690s'* (Edinburgh, 2010)

Currie, J., *Mull – the Island and its People* (Edinburgh, 2000)

Day, J. P., *Public Administration in the Highlands and Islands of Scotland* (London, 1918)

Devine, T. M., *The Great Highland Famine – Hunger, Emigration and the Scottish Highlands in the Nineteenth Century* (Edinburgh, 1988)

Devine, T. M., 'Highland landowners and the Highland potato famine', in L. Leneman (ed.), *Perspectives in Scottish Social History. Essays in Honour of Rosalind Mitchison* (Aberdeen, 1988)

Devine, T. M., 'The emergence of the new elite in the Western Highlands and Islands, 1800–60', in T. Devine (ed.), *Improvement and Enlightenment* (Edinburgh, 1989), 108–42

Devine, T. M., *Clanship to Crofters' War – The Social Transformation of the Scottish Highlands* (Manchester, 1994)

Dodgshon, R. A., 'Coping with risk: subsistence crises in the Scottish Highlands and Islands, 1600–1800', *Rural History* 15 (2004), 1–25

Dodgshon, R. A., 'The Little Ice Age in the Scottish Highlands and Islands: Documenting its human impact', *Scottish Geographical Journal* 121.4 (2008), 321–37

Donnelly, J. S., Jr, '"Irish property must pay for Irish poverty" – British public opinion and the Great Irish Famine', in C. Morash and R. Hayes (eds.), *'Fearful Realities' – New Perspectives on the Famine* (Dublin, 1996), 60–76

Dunlop, J., *The British Fisheries Society 1786–1893* (Edinburgh, 1978)

Dunn, C. L., *Highland Settler: A Portrait of the Scottish Gael in Nova Scotia* (Toronto, 1953)

Edwards, R. D., and T. D. Williams (eds.), *The Great Famine – Studies in Irish History 1845–52* (Dublin, 1994)

Flinn, M. W., 'Malthus, emigration and potatoes in the Scottish north-west, 1770–1870', in L. M. Cullen and T. C. Smout (eds.), *Comparative Aspects of Scottish and Irish Economic and Social History 1600–1900* (Edinburgh, 1977)

Flinn, M. W., et al. (eds.), *Scottish Population History from the 17th century to the 1930s* (Cambridge, 1977)

Fry, M., *Patronage and Principal – A Political History of Modern Scotland* (Aberdeen, 1987)

Fry, M., *The Dundas Despotism* (Edinburgh, 1992)

Gaskell, P., *Morvern Transformed – a Highland Parish in the Nineteenth Century* (Cambridge, 1968)

Gillies, W. (ed.), *Ris a' Bhruthaich – The Criticism and Prose Writings of Sorley Maclean* (Stornoway, 1985)

Gittins, L., 'The manufacture of alkali in Britain, 1779–1789', *Annals of Science* 22 (1966), 175–89

Gray, P., '"Potatoes and providence": British government responses to the Great Famine', *Bullan – An Irish Studies Journal* 1.1 (Spring 1994), 75–90

Gray, P., 'Ideology and the Famine', in C. Poirteir, *The Great Irish Famine* (Dublin, 1995)

Gray, P., *Famine, Land and Politics – British Government and Irish Society 1843–50* (Dublin, 1999)

Gray, P., 'National humiliation and the Great Hunger: fast and famine in 1847', *Irish Historical Studies* 32.126 (Nov. 2000), 193–216

Guy, J., *'My Heart is My Own' – The Life of Mary Queen of Scots* (London, 2004)

Haines, R., 'Indigent misfits or shrewd operators? Government-assisted emigrants from the United Kingdom to Australia, 1831–1860', *Population Studies* 48.2 (July 1994), 223–47

Haldane, A. R. B., *The Drove Roads of Scotland* (Argyll, 1951)

Haldane, A. R. B., *New Ways through the Glen* (Argyll, 1995)

Hanham, H. J., 'The creation of the Scottish Office', *Juridical Review* (1965), 205–44

Harper, M., *Emigration from North-East Scotland*, vol. i, *Willing Exiles* (Aberdeen, 1988)

Harper, M., *Adventurers and Exiles – The Great Scottish Exodus* (London, 2003)

Harrison, B., 'Philanthropy and the Victorians', *Victorian Studies* 19 (June 1966), 353–74

Hart, J., 'Sir Charles Trevelyan at the Treasury', *English Historical Review* 75.295 (Jan. 1960), 92–110

Heaney, H., *A Scottish Whig in Ireland, 1835–1838 – The Irish Journals of Robert Graham of Redgorton* (Dublin 1999)

Hilton, B., *The Age of Atonement – The Influence of Evangelicalism on Social and Economic Thought 1785–1865* (Oxford 1986)

Hornsby, S. J., 'Patterns of Scottish emigration to Canada, 1750–1870', *Journal of Historical Geography* 18. 4 (1992), 397–416

Howe, P., and S. Devereux, 'Famine intensity and magnitude scales: a proposal for an instrumental definition of famine', *Disasters* 28.4 (2008), 353–72

Hume, J. R., and M. S. Moss, *The Making of the Scotch Whisky Distillery Industry* (Edinburgh, 2000)

Hunter, J., *The Making of the Crofting Community* (Edinburgh, 1976)

Hunter, J., *The Islanders and the Orb – The History of the Harris Tweed Industry 1835–1995* (Stornoway, 2001)

Hutchison, I. G. C., *A Political History of Scotland, 1832–1924* (Edinburgh, 1986)

Innes, J., 'Legislating for three kingdoms: how the Westminster parliament legislated for England, Scotland and Ireland, 1707–1830', in J. Hoppit (ed.), *Parliaments, Nations and Identities in Britain and Ireland, 1660–1850* (Manchester, 2003)

Jackson, A., *Ireland 1798–1998 – War, Peace and Beyond* (Oxford, 2010)

Jackson, A., *The Two Unions – Ireland, Scotland, and the Survival of the United Kingdom* (Oxford, 2012)

Johnson, C., 'Scottish secular clergy, 1830–1878: the western district', *The Innes Review* 40.1 (Spring 1989), 106–52

Jones, N., 'Life on the Ocean Wave', *Literary Review* (Oct. 2008), 42

Jupp, P. J., 'The landed elite and political authority in Britain, ca. 1760–1850', *The Journal of British Studies* 29.1 (Jan. 1990), 53–79

Jupp, P. J, *The Governing of Britain 1688–1848* (London, 2006)

Kidd, S. M., 'The Writer behind the Pen-Names: the Rev. Alexander Macgregor', in *Transactions of the Gaelic Society of Inverness* 61 (1998–2000), 1–24

Kidd, S. M., '"Caraid nan Gaidheal" and friend of emigration', *SHR* 80.1, no. 21 (April 2002), 52–69

Kinealy, C., 'The role of the poor law during the Famine', in C. Poirteir, *The Great Irish Famine* (Dublin, 1995)

Kinealy, C., *This Great Calamity – The Irish Famine 1845–52* (Dublin, 1994, 2006)

Levitt, I., and C. Smout, 'Some weights and measures in Scotland, 1843', *SHR* 56.2, no. 162 (Oct. 1977), 146–52

Lawson, B., *Harris in History and Legend* (Edinburgh, 2002)

Lawson, B., *Lewis in History and Legend – The West Coast* (Edinburgh, 2008)

MacArthur, E. M., *Iona: The Living Memory of a Crofting Community 1751–1914* (Edinburgh, 1990)

MacAskill, J., '"The most arbitrary, scandalous act of tyranny': The crown, private proprietors and the ownership of the Scottish foreshore in the nineteenth century', *SHR* 85.2, no. 220 (Oct. 2006), 277–304

MacAskill, J., 'The Highland kelp proprietors and their struggle over the salt and barilla duties, 1817–1831', *Journal of Scottish Historical Studies* 26.1+2 (2006), 60–82

MacAskill, J., ' "It is truly, in the expressive language of Burke, a nation crying for bread": the public response to the highland famine of 1836–1837', *The Innes Review* 61.2 (Autumn 2010), 169–206

MacAskill, J., 'Foreshore' in M. Mulhern (ed.), *Scottish Life and Society – A Compendium of Scottish Ethnology*, 14 vols., xiii, The Law (Edinburgh, 2012)

MacColl, A. W., *Land, Faith and the Crofting Community – Christianity and Social Criticism in the Highlands and Islands of Scotland, 1843–1893* (Edinburgh, 2006)

Macdonnell, M., *The Emigrant Experience: Songs of Highland Emigrants in North America* (Toronto, 1982)

MacGillivray, N., 'Medical practice in the Highlands and Islands at the time of the potato famine: 1845–1855', *Transactions of the Gaelic Society of Inverness* 64 (2004–6), 273–98

MacGillivray, N., 'Dr John Mackenzie (1803–1886): proponent of scientific agriculture and opponent of Highland emigration', *Journal of Scottish Historical Studies* 33.1 (2013), 81–100

Mackillop, A., *'More Fruitful than the Soil' – Army, Empire and the Scottish Highlands, 1715–1815* (East Linton, 2000)

Maclean, A., *Telford's Highland Churches* (Coll, 1989)

Macleod, J., *Banner in the West – A Spiritual History of Lewis and Harris* (Edinburgh, 2010)

Macleod, M. D., 'An Dotair Ban', *The Caledonian Medical Journal*, new series 4 (1901), 4–17

Macleod, Canon R. C., *The Book of Dunvegan*, Third Spalding Club, 2 vols. (Aberdeen, 1938–9)

Macmillan, D. S., *Scotland and Australia 1788–1850* (Oxford, 1967)

Madgwick, R. B., *Immigration into Eastern Australia 1788–1851* (Sydney, 1969)

Mandler, P., *Aristocratic Government in the Age of Reform – Whigs and Liberals 1830–1852* (Oxford, 1990)

Maxtone Graham, E., *The Maxtones of Cultoquhey* (Edinburgh, 1935)

McCaffery, J. F., 'A Scottish Whig in Ireland, 1835–1838: The Irish Journals of Robert Graham of Redgorton', *SHR* 80.1, no. 209 (April 2001), 144–5

McCrae, M. (ed.), *The New Club – A History* (Edinburgh, 2004)

Meek, D. E. (ed.), *Tuath is Tighearna – Tenants and Landlords* (Edinburgh, 1995)

Mitchison, R., 'The making of the old Scottish poor law', *Past and Present* 63 (May 1974), 58–93

Mitchison, R., 'The making of the old Scottish poor law: a rejoinder', *Past and Present* 69 (Nov. 1975), 119–21

Mitchison, R., 'The creation of the disablement rule in the Scottish poor law', in T. C. Smout (ed.), *The Search for Wealth and Security* (London, 1979), 199–217

Mitchison, R., 'The poor law', in T. M. Devine and R. Mitchison (eds.), *People and Society in Scotland*, vol. i, *1769–1830* (Edinburgh, 1988)

Mitchison, R., *Coping with Destitution – Poverty and Relief in Western Europe* (Toronto, 1991)

Mitchison, R., *The Old Poor Law in Scotland – The Experience of Poverty, 1574–1845* (Edinburgh, 2000)

Murdoch, A., *'The People Above' – Politics and Administration in Mid-Eighteenth Century Scotland* (Edinburgh, 1980)

Newman, L. F., et al. (eds.), *Hunger in History – Food Shortage, Poverty, and Deprivation* (Oxford, 1990)

Nicolson, A., *History of Skye – A Record of the Families, the Social Conditions and Literature of the Island* (Skye, 1995)

O'Grada, C., *Black '47 and Beyond – The Great Irish Famine* (Princeton, 1999)

O'Grada, C., *Famine – A Short History* (Oxford, 2012)

O'Neill, T. P., 'Fever and public health in Pre-Famine Ireland', *The Journal of the Royal Society of Antiquaries of Ireland* 103 (1973), 1–34

Paton, D., *The Clergy and the Clearances – The Church and the Highland Crises 1790–1850* (Edinburgh, 2006)

Prebble, J., *The King's Jaunt* (Edinburgh, 2000)

Prentis, M. D., *The Scots in Australia* (Sydney, 1983)

Rossner, P. R., 'The 1738–1741 Harvest Crisis in Scotland', *SHR* 90.1, no. 229 (Apr. 2011), 27–63

Richards, E., *The Leviathan of Wealth* (London, 1973)

Richards, E., *A History of the Highland Clearances – Agrarian Transformation and the Evictions 1746–1886* (London, 1982)

Richards, E., *A History of the Highland Clearances*, vol. ii, *Emigration, Protest, Reasons* (London, 1985)

Richards, E., 'How did poor people emigrate from the British Isles to Australia in the nineteenth century?', *The Journal of British Studies* 32.3 (July 1993), 250–79

Richards, E., *The Highland Clearances – People, Landlords and Rural Turmoil* (Edinburgh, 2008)

Richards, E., 'Highland emigration in the age of Malthus: Scourie, 1841–55', *Northern Scotland*, new series 2 (2011), 60–82

Richards, E., and M. Clough, *Cromartie: Highland Life 1650–1914* (Aberdeen, 1989)

Richards, E., and A. M. Tindley, 'After the clearances: Evander McIver and the "Highland Question", 1835–73', *Rural History* 23.1 (2012), 41–57

Richards, E., 'Malthus and the uses of British emigration', in K. Fedorowich and A. S. Thompson (eds.), *Empire, Identity and Migration in the British World* (Manchester, 2013)

Ritchie, L. A., 'The floating church of Loch Sunart', *Records of the Scottish Church History Society* 22 (1985), 159–73

Sellar, W. D. H., 'William Forbes Skene (1809–92): historian of Celtic Scotland', *Proceedings of the Society of Antiquaries of Scotland* 131 (2001), 3–21

Smith, D. C., *Passive Obedience and Prophetic Protest – Social Criticism in the Scottish Church 1830–1945* (New York, 1988)

Smout, T. C., *A History of the Scottish People 1560–1830* (London, 1969)

Smout, T. C., 'Famine and famine-relief in Scotland', in L. M. Cullen and T. C. Smout (eds.), *Comparative Aspects of Scottish and Irish Economic and Social History 1600–1900* (Edinburgh, 1977)

Sugden, J., *Nelson – The Sword of Albion* (London, 2012)

Taylor, A. J., *Laissez-faire and State Intervention in Nineteenth-century Britain* (London 1972)

Tindley, A. M., *The Sutherland Estate, 1850–1920* (Edinburgh, 2010)

Tindley, A. M., ' "Actual pinching and suffering": estate responses to poverty in Sutherland, c. 1845–56', *SHR* 90.2, no. 230 (Oct. 2011), 236–56

Tindley, A. M., ' "They sow the wind, they reap the whirlwind': estate management in the post-clearance Highlands, c. 1815 – c. 1900', *Northern Scotland* 3 (2012), 66–85

Vernon, J., *Hunger – A Modern History* (London, 2007)

Walker, S. P., 'Agents of dispossession and acculturation. Edinburgh accountants and the Highland clearances', *Critical Perspectives on Accounting* 14 (2003), 815–53

Western, J., 'The formation of the Scottish militia in 1797', *SHR* 34, no. 117 (Apr. 1955), 1–18

Whatley, C. A., *Scottish Society 1707–1830 – Beyond Jacobitism, towards Industrialisation* (Manchester, 2000)

Wiebe, M. G., *et al.* (eds), *Benjamin Disraeli Letters: 1838–1841*, 8 vols. (Toronto, 1982–)

William, E. T., 'The Colonial Office in the thirties', *Historical Studies – Australia and New Zealand* 2.7 (May 1943), 141–60

Withers, C. W. J., 'Highland migration to Dundee, Perth and Stirling, 1753–1891', *Journal of Historical Geography* 11.4 (1985), 395–418

Withers, C. W. J., *Gaelic Scotland – The Transformation of a Culture Region* (London, 1988)

Withers, C. W. J., 'Destitution and migration: labour mobility and relief from famine in Highland Scotland, 1836–1850', *Journal of Historical Geography* 14.2 (1988), 128–50

Withers, C. W. J., *Urban Highlanders – Highland-Lowland Migration and Urban Gaelic Culture 1799–1900* (East Linton, 1998)

Withers, C. W. J., 'Landscape, memory, history: *Gloomy Memories* and the nineteenth century Scottish Highlands', *Scottish Geographical Journal* 121.1 (2008), 29–44.

Williams, W. H. A., *Tourism, Landscape and the Irish Character – British Travel Writers in Pre-Famine Ireland* (Madison, 2008)

Young, L., 'Paupers, property and place: a geographical analysis of the English, Irish, and Scottish Poor Laws in the mid-19th century', *Environment and Planning D: Society and Space* 12 (1994), 325–40

Young, L., 'Spaces for famine: a comparative geographical analysis of famine in Ireland and the Highlands in the 1840s', *Transactions of the Institute of British Geographers*, new series 21.4 (1996), 666–80

Newspapers

Aberdeen Journal

Caledonian Mercury

Edinburgh Evening Courant

Glasgow Herald

Inverness Courier

Morning Chronicle

Press and Journal

Tait's Edinburgh Magazine

The Belfast News-Letter

The Manchester Times and Gazette

The Scotsman

The Times

Unpublished Sources

Cameron, J. M., 'A Study of the Factors that Assisted and Directed Scottish Emigration to Upper Canada, 1815–1855' (University of Glasgow, Ph.D. thesis, 1970)

Campey, L. H., 'The Regional Characteristics of Scottish Emigration to British North America 1784 to 1854', 2 vols. (University of Aberdeen, Ph.D. thesis, 1997)

Kidd, S. M., 'The Prose Writings of Rev. Alexander MacGregor, 1806–1881' (University of Edinburgh, Ph.D. thesis 1999)

Murphy, C. M., 'The Life and Politics of Thomas Spring Rice, 1st Baron Monteagle of Brandon, 1790–1866' (University College Cork, MA thesis, 1991)

O'Neill, T. P., 'State, Poverty and Distress in Ireland, 1815–1845' (National University of Ireland, Dublin, Ph.D. thesis, 1971–2)

Paton, D., 'The Church in the Northern Highlands 1790–1850: Spiritual Witness and Social Crisis' (Open University, Ph.D. thesis, 2000)

Smith, J. A. R., 'From Isolation to Integration: The Development of Roads in the Northern Highlands of Scotland 1800–1850' (University of Aberdeen, Ph.D. thesis, 2001)

Trant, M. A., 'Government Policy and Irish Distress 1816–19' (University College, Dublin, MA thesis, 1965)

INDEX

Note: page references in *italics* refer to illustrations, those in **bold** to the entries in the biographical notes. RG refers to Robert Graham and JH to Sir John Hill.

Aberdeen committee xxx, liii, 125, 193, 216–18, 221
  supplies to Orkney and Shetland 116, 129, 136, 229–30, 234–5
accounts
  Aberdeen committee 226
  Edinburgh committee 224–6
  Glasgow committee 226–7, 239
  of JH lii–liii, 142–3, 194, 195–7
  London committee 241–3, 244
Acharacal 29, 30, 38
Adam, Sir C. 113, 141
Ailort, Loch 28
Alison, Archibald 176, 177
Alison, Mrs 177
Alms, James xvii
Alsh, Loch 53, 66
Angus, John 124, 135
Angus, Mr (of Ewing & May) 122
Appin 10, 18
Applecross 68, 69, 76
Arbuckle, Alexander 66–7
Ardchattan 15
Ardfenaig 42
Ardgour estate 19
Ardnamurchan 12, 24–5, 29, 31, 32, 38
Argyll, duke of 42–3
Argyllshire 8, 9–10, 12, 19, 151
Arisaig 23, 25, 28, 76, 152, 159
Armadale Castle 165
Arrow, John J. 126, 127, 129
assessments xxxviii–xli, 16–17, 64, 69, 92, 102–3
  lack of 31, 33, 35, 57, 85
  views on 14, 15, 40, 59
Auckland, Lord xix

Baillie, Henry xlvii–xlix
Baillie, Hugh lviii
Baird, Charles
  deputation to London xxvii, 221
  dines with JH 177
  on emigration xlv
  Glasgow committee xxx, 128, 148, 176, 187
  sustainability of the Highlands lxvii
Balfour, Thomas 8, 142, 179, 261
Ballachulish 21, 172
Bannatyne Club xiv
Bannerman, Alexander 124, 125, 126
Barclay, Capt. R. A. 9, 135
Barclay, Rev. 136, 137
Baring, Francis xlix, lviii
Barra 12, 86, 89–90, 91, 92, 155
Barrow, Sir J. 113
Barvas 76, 78, 79, 237–8
Beatson, Captain H. D. 41, 42, 51
Beith, Alexander 57, 74
Belhaven, Lord 144, 145
Bell, G. J. xiv
Bell, Mr 164
Benbecula 46, 86, 88, 91, 160
Bentinck, Lord W. 186, 187
Bernisdale 63
Bervie, Janet xix
Bethune, Mr 64
Binstead, Mr 177, 179
Black, Mr 74
Blair, Alexander 133
Boisdale 86, 88, 89, 90, 92
Borrodale 23
Bowie, John
  Edinburgh committee 126

amendments to the resolutions
    of 2 March 133, 246–9
deputation to London
    xxvii, 221, 253
funds and emigration xlvii
General Assembly breakfast 147
and JH
    application regarding Islay 134
    to Glasgow with 128
    meets in Edinburgh 127,
        129, 130, 139, 141, 146
    meets on tour 165–6, 170
and landed proprietors xxviii
Mr Waller dines with 145
Boyle, David 145
Boyle, Mrs 145
Boyter, Dr David
    arrangements for emigration 152,
        153, 165, 166, 170, 272
    Hugh Maclean to meet 171
    selection of candidates for emigration
        xliii–xliv, 164, 231–2, 272
Bracadale 75, 83, 85
Bracadale, Loch 170
Breadalbane, marquis of (formerly
    earl of Ormelie) xv, 14, 257
British Fishery Society 40
Broadford 57, 66, 165, 170
Brooman, Mr 193
Brown, John 124
Brown, Robert xxxii, xxxiii,
    xxxv, 10, 117, 118–19
Bruce, Cumming lxv
Bruce, Lady lii, 125
Bruce, Sir Michael 125–6
Buchanan, Mr 180
Bunessan 42
Burke, Edmund lix, lx
Burke, Sir Richard xliii
Burnett, Miss 137
Burnett, Mrs 138
Burnett, Thomas 124, 126,
    135, 137, 138, 145

Cairinish 86, 87
Cairndow 185
Caithness 8, 260, 261
Caledonian Canal xxxvii, 20–1, 23
Caledonian Mercury lvii

Cameron, John 80
Campbell, General, of Lochnell 15
Campbell, Mr, of Jura 140, 141
Campbell, Mr, of Otter 229,
    233–4, 237–8
Campbell, Mr (session clerk) 16
Campbell, Archibald James 150
Campbell, Sir Donald 10,
    134, 184, 185, 254, 256
Campbell, Donald, of Breachacha 39, 50
Campbell, Col. Donald, of Knock
    causes of destitution and need
        for emigration 48–9
    on kelp manufacture 35
    level of destitution in Tobermory 40
    local committees 38, 39
    meets Dr Boyter 171
    reports local needs to JH
        151, 167–8, 174
Campbell, Sir H. 114, 115
Campbell, James 127
Campbell, John, of Cornaig 151–2
Campbell, John, of Glenmore 14–15
Campbell, Sir John and Lady 141
Campbell, Mungo 118
Campbell, Paterson 173, 175
Campbell, Mrs R. 179
Campbell, Richard 10, 130, 146, 147, 179
Campbell, W. F. of Islay 146,
    184, 185, 236, 257
Campbell, Walter Frederick xxxiii
Canna xxxviii, 12, 38, 108–9
Cape Breton 60, 79
cattle
    fair 153
    JH's observations of stock
        158, 164, 166, 170
    loss of 48, 202, 204, 219
    low prices 33, 35, 48, 63, 94, 102, 247
    poor quality 238
Caustey, Mr 150
Central Board xxx, xxxvi–xxxvii
Chalmers, Thomas lix–lx
charitable giving liv, lvi–lvii,
    lx, 257, 266, 267
    collections 32, 33–4, 36, 40,
        41, 54, 59, 64, 69
    local charity 14, 19, 27, 35–6, 89
    work and charity 45, 46

Cheyne, Henry 116, 122, 139
Chisholm, Alexander 30
Chisholm, James 88
Church of Scotland xxxviii–xxxix
Clanranald, Ranald Macdonald, of 257
Clark, Dr 81, 155, 156, 160
Clark, Duncan 35, 171, 175
Clark, Francis W. 47
clearances xxxvii
Clephane, Mary Ann D. Maclean 52
Clerk, Lord Justice 146
clothing 236
Clyde, river 13
Cockburn, Henry xiv, xv,
    xix–xx, lxiii, 121, 145
Coll 12, 38, 47, 50, 70, 96
Colonsay 10, 11
committees
    local (district) xxxvi, 234
        JH's tour 150–1, 154, 156,
            158, 163, 164, 172, 174
        recommended by RG 38–9,
            46, 56, 73–6, 80
        see also Aberdeen committee;
            Edinburgh committee; Glasgow
            committee; Inverness committee
Conal 10
Corpach 21
Craigie, Mr 127, 141, 146
Craignish 14
Cranstoun, Lord 25, 26–7
Crichton Club xiv
Crinan Canal 13
crofting system 17, 21, 101, 223
Croker, John Wilson xviii
Cromarty fishery trial 121, 122
Crombie, John 241
crops
    failure of xxiv, 94–6, 204,
        208, 212, 219, 238
    Orkney and Sheltand 9, 131–2,
        201–3
    RG's inquiry 11, 15, 21, 30, 33,
        36, 58, 64, 67, 78, 81, 84, 89
    good harvests 19, 88
    JH's observations of present
        cultivation 155, 163, 165,
        166, 169, 171, 172, 174–5
Cross 76

Cruickshank, Alexander 261
Cuillin mountains 164
Cumberland, Capt. 148
Cumming, Mr 126
Cummings, Mr 178
Cunninghame, John, Lord xiii
    and the commisioning of a
        tour and report xxx, xxxi,
        xxxiv, lxi, lxiii, lxv
    letters 253–8
    meets with JH 115–17,
        121, 122, 130, 146
Cuthbertson, Barbara Harriet 152

Dalelia 24, 30
Davidson, Thomas 21
Day, J. P. lxiv
Dennistoun, Mr 186, 187
depots
    JH to visit li, 146
    RG's proposal for 37–8, 46
destitution, levels of xxvii
    belief distress overstated 133, 176
    communications to government
        203–9, 232–3, 277–9
    Cunninghame on 256–7
    reports of McPhail and
        Campbell 237–8
    RG on 37, 43–4, 94–6, 109
Devine, T. M. xlii
Dickson, Dr 75
Dirk-Cleland, Mr 118
distress see destitution, levels of
district (local) committees xxxvi, 234
    JH's tour 120–1, 154, 156,
        158, 163, 164, 172, 174
    recommended by RG 38–9,
        46, 56, 73–6, 80
Dornie 58
Douglas, Mr and Mrs 127
Douglas, Mr (Mrs Campbell's father) 130
Downie, Robert 18
Drevor, Mr 141, 146
Duff, Mr 135, 137
Duich, Loch 59
Duirinish 75, 83, 85
Dumbarton 186
Dunbar, Mr 182
Dundas, Capt. 133

Dundas, James, of Dundas
  Castle 127, 130, 133, 144
Dundas, James, of Ochtertyre xxi
Dunlop, Alexander xl

Easdale 13–14
Edinburgh committee
  emigration xliv, xlvii, 191
  establishment and responsibilities
    xxvi–xxviii, 211–14, 277
    memorial to the Treasury 203–6
  expenditure and accounts
    xxx, 179, 224–6
  and JH
    appointment and commission
      264–5, 267
    appreciation of liii, 285
    meetings and communications
      121, 122–3, 126, 129,
      130, 132, 188, 190–1
  not received subscriptions
    raised in London 123
  report of 21 December 1837 220–4
  resolutions of 2 March lvi, 245–6
    amendments of Macleod and
      Bowie 133, 246–9
    Glasgow committee
      response 118, 119–20
    Macleod complains about 128
  and RG xxxii, 6
Edinburgh Review lix
education 91–2, 104, 166
Eigg 12, 38, 152
Eilt, Loch 24
Elder, Colin 165
Elliot, Thomas F. xliii–xliv, xlvi–xlvii
  report on emigration 268–72
emigration
  Archibald MacNiven
    (emigrant agent) 60–1
  from the districts 25, 28, 39–40, 82
  Dr Alexander Macleod 155
  Dr Boyter
    arrangements for emigration
      152, 153, 165, 166, 170, 272
    selection of candidates for
      emigration xliii–xliv,
      164, 231–2, 272
  Dr Roderick Millar 181–2

Edinburgh committee 191, 222–3
Glasgow committee 192, 234
JH requested to urge assistance for 285
John Wigham 132
report of T. F. Elliot 268–72
RG's views and recommendations
  xlii–l, 62, 107–9, 283–4
views on
  compared to public works 19–20
  government assistance 15, 48–9
  necessity of 33, 42, 84–5
  and selection 59–60, 64–5,
    68, 79, 91, 166
  willingness to emigrate 23,
    30, 41, 52–3, 66–7, 156
Engledene, S. Lt. 148
Ewe, Loch 169
Ewing & May 122

factors xxxv
Fair Island 123, 261
Fairbairn, William 80
famine xxiii–xxiv, xlii, 94
  Great Irish Famine lviii–lix, lx–lxi,
    lxii
Farquhar, Sir Arthur 124
Ferguson, Miss 130
Ferguson, Mr (reported on Islay) 236
Ferguson, Mr (writer of the signet) 127
Ferguson, Robert xxi
Finlayson, Mr 88, 92, 140, 154, 159–60
Finlayson, Rev. Robert 80
fishing
  Boisdale estate 92
  British Fishery Society 40
  Capt. Knight on 133
  failure of fisheries 100, 204, 208, 237–8
    Orkney Islands 131
    RG on xxxvii
    RG's tour 15, 42, 63, 64, 67–8, 84
    Shetland Islands 9, 132, 201–3
  JH's tour 151, 154, 155,
    158, 160, 168, 169
  curing 156–7
  Loch Duich 59
  potential improvement 20, 35,
    44, 59, 79, 90, 106–7
  RG observes 29
  Shetland Islands 137

Fle[e]ming, Admiral Charles Elphinstone 127, 148, 177, 183, 186, 187
Fle[e]ming, Mrs 148, 176, 178, 183, 186
Fletcher, Angus 254, 256, 257
Flyter, Robert 19, 20
Forbes, Mr 137, 138
Forbes, Sir J. 135
Fort William 12, 19, 21, 71, 172, 175
Fraser, Mr 68
Fullarton, Allan
  Glasgow committee 130, 174, 176, 187
  is ill 186
  meets with JH 118, 177
  sustainability of the Highlands lxvii

Gairloch 67, 68, 69, 76
General Assembly breakfast 147
Gibbon, Edward 74, 84, 85, 166–7, 170
Gibbs, Moyes 115, 148
Gifford, Arthur 260
Glamis castle 138
Glasgow committee
  and the Edinburgh resolutions of 2
    March xxix–xxx, 118, 119–20, 128
  amendments to the resolutions 133
  establishment and responsibilities
    xxvii, 207–9, 214–16, 277
  memorial to the Treasury 279
  memorials on destitution 207–11
  expenditure and accounts
    xxx, 179, 226–7, 239
  and JH
    appointment and commission
      264–5, 267
    appreciation of liii, 192
    meetings and communications 119,
      129, 130, 136, 176, 177, 187, 188
    treasury minute 280
  mystery about 128
  reports 227–37
  and RG xxxii, 6–7, 9
  subscriptions raised in London 123
Glass, Rev. S. 73
Glenelg 27, 57–8, 76
Glenelg, Lord xliii–xliv, xlvi–
  xlvii, 57, 272–3, 285
Glengarry estate 23
Glenshiel 57–9, 76
Gometra 42

Gordon, Mr 138
Gordon, Sir Charles 145, 146, 178, 190
Gordon, Sir J. 137
government xxx–xxxi, lxiii, lxv–lxvi
  emigration 108–9, 270–1, 273
  policies and principles liii–lviii
  and RG's reporting l, 110, 143
  salt and barilla taxes xxxvii
Graeme, John, of Eskbank xiv
Graham, Dr Robert xxvi, 180
Graham, Eliza xvi
Graham, Mary (mother of RG)
  correspondence from RG xvi,
    12–13, 23, 50, 66, 80, 83, 93
  meets with JH 115, 126, 128, 130,
    134, 140, 178, 179, 180, 182
Graham, Robert, of Fintry xiv
Graham, Robert, of
  Redgorton **xiv–xvi**, 3
inquiry
  appointment xxxi–xxxii, xxxiv,
    5–6, 257–60, 263, 277, 279
  approach to xxxii–xxxiii, xxxiv, 6–12
  expenses 286
  meeting on Highland distress 256
  returns to London 147
  tour route xxxiii–xxxiv, 4
  views on his tour 184, 185
and JH
  correspondence 61
  information from RG 151
  JH and RG's reports 126,
    139, 140, 143, 144, 150
  JH to liaise with RG 264–5, 267
  meets 141, 142, 145, 178
  recommended by RG 5
reports and findings lxvi–lxvii
  final report 93–110
  noted in Treasury minutes 282, 283–4
  poor government response xlix–l
views and recommendations
  allowance of meal required xxxvi
  assessments 17
  character of local population 57
  education 104
  emigration xliii–xlvi, 62, 107–9
  employment and works
    20–1, 45–6, 104–5
  fisheries 106–7

landlords 101–2
local (district) committees
  38–9, 46, 56, 73–6, 80
measurement of the degree
  of destitution 37
overpopulation xxxvii–
  xxxviii, xlii, 96
poor laws xxxix–xli, 102–3
proposed depots 37–8, 46
road building lxiv, 45, 105–6
seed distribution xxviii, 22–3
Graham, Sir James xviii, lviii–lix
Graham, Sir Thomas, Lord Lynedoch
  xiv, xv, xviii, 47, 134
  correspondence from JH 114
Graham family xvi, 127, 145, 189
Grant, Mr (Aberdeen) 135
Grant, Mr and Mrs (Edinburgh) 127
Gray, Peter lxii
Green, Miss 187
Greenfield, William xix
Greenock 120, 148, 183
Gregorson, John 35, 38, 39, 168, 174
Grey, Earl xx
Grey, Lord Justice 146
Grey, Sir George lix, 231

Hall, Capt. and Mrs Basil 176–7
Hallin-in-Waternish 83
Hamilton, duke of xxxiii, 10
Hamilton, Mr (Edinburgh) 147
Hamilton, Mr (Glasgow) 118
Hamilton, Mrs 147
Hamilton, William 241
Harris 80–3, 155, 160
harvests see crops
Hay & Ogilvie 9, 260, 261, 262
Heatherfield 63
Henderson, Captain 126
Henderson, Mr 19, 31, 39
Herring Fishery Board 140
Heytesbury, Lord lix
Highland and Agricultural Society
  of Scotland xv, 279
Hill, Captain Sir John xvii–xix
  and the Aberdeen committee
    124, 125, 136
  records appreciation of JH 193
  accounts lii–liii, 142–3, 194, 195–7

appointment l–liii, 113–14, 139–40,
  263
arrangements for role 146, 147,
  264–8, 278–9, 280–3, 284–5
conclusion of duties 189, 286
and the Edinburgh committee 117, 126,
  128, 129, 130, 133–4, 146, 179, 188
  records appreciation of JH 190–1
and the Glasgow committee
  xxix–xxx, 118, 119–20, 128,
  129, 133, 176–7, 179, 188
  letter to Fullarton 187
  records appreciation of JH 192
holiday with family 183–6
Ireland l, lviii–lix, 267–8
purchasing and supply
  process 120–3, 139, 141
and RG
  correspondence 61
  JH recommended by RG 5
  meets 141, 142, 145, 178
  RG's reports 126, 139,
    140, 143, 144, 150
  tour of Highlands and
    Islands li, 112, 147–76
  travels to Scotland 114–15
  view of Highlanders lii, 155, 158,
    160, 161, 163, 166, 168, 175
Hill, Emma 178
Hill, Lucy 115
Hilton, Boyd lix, lxii
Holyrood House 144–5
Home Office xxxi, lxiii–lxiv, lxiv, 143
Hume, Joseph xlix, lxv–lxvi
Huntly, marquess of 23

Inchmurrin 185
Ingram, James 9
Inveraray 149, 173, 175, 184–5
Inverness committee 230
Invernessshire 8, 70, 96
Iona 34, 38, 41, 44, 46, 51
Ireland
  emigration xliii, xliv
  famine lviii–lix, lx–lxi, lxii
  government policies and principles lviii
  JH's services l, 267–8
  RG's Irish journeys xxxiv
Islay 10–11, 134, 146, 236–7

Jackson, Alvin lxii
Jamieson, John 153, 163
Jeffrey, Miss 145
Jeffrey, Mrs 145
Jeffrey, Francis, Lord xiv, 145
Jura 10, 11

Keal, Loch na 42
Kelly, Alexander 15
kelp manufacture
    collapse of xlviii, lviii, 204–5,
        208, 219, 231, 238, 268
        Orkney Islands 131
        RG's report 97–100
    diversification 104–5
    removal of fiscal support xxxvii, xlv
    RG's tour 32, 34, 35, 42, 49, 54,
        58, 84
    and the removal of duty
        from salt 47–8
Kendrick, Mr 178
Kennedy, Mr 66, 85
Kerrera 150
Kilburlford 14
Kilchrenan and Inishail 15
Kilenan 14
Kilfinichen and Kilvicheoan 34, 38, 41
Kilmallie 21, 22
Kilmonivaig 21, 22
Kilmore and Kilbride 15–16
Kilmuir xl–xli, 75, 83, 85
Kilninian and Kilmore 34, 36, 38, 52–3
Kilninver 14
Kinlochmoidart 23, 30
    family 24, 29
Kinlochspelvie 34, 35, 38
Kintail 57–8, 59, 76
Kintyre 10
Kirkwall 131
Kishorn, Loch 66
Knight, Capt. G. W. H.
    believes distress overstated 133
    and JH 116, 127, 180
    travel arrangements 126, 147, 159
Knock 76, 78–9
Knox, Thomas xxxvi–xxxvii,
    77–8, 80, 156, 161–2
Kyle 55
Kyleakin 55

laissez-faire principle liv, lx–lxi, lxii
    see also self-reliance
Lamont, Alexander 10, 141
landed proprietors
    domination of committees xxvii
    and emigration xlv, 59–60, 108
    estate management, failure of xxxviii
    problems of change of landlord 51–2
    role and responsibilities xxviii–xxix,
        liv, lvi–lvii, lxi, 255, 256, 257
    and the supply of seed 261
    want of regulations 101–2
Landowne, Mr 135
Lathaich, Loch na 41
Lauder, Sir Thomas Dick 127, 259
Lees, Sir Edward S. 116, 133
Lerwick 137–8
Leven, Loch 123, 138
Lewis lvi, 76–9, 155, 156, 161–2, 237–8
Lismore 15, 18
Loch, James xxxii, 40
Lochaber estate 23
Lochailort 24
Lochalsh 57–8, 59, 76
Lochboisdale 142, 154
Lochbroom 67, 68, 76
Lochcarron 67, 68, 69, 76
Lochmaddy 86–7, 154, 160
Lochs 76, 78, 79, 80
Lomond, Loch 185
London committee 218–20,
    240, 241–3, 244
Long Island 70, 71, 86, 96, 102
Lord Provost, Glasgow 176, 177, 183
Lorn 10
Louis, Sir Thomas xvii
Lovat, Lord 254
Lumsden, Mr 177
Lynedale 63
Lynedoch, Sir Thomas Graham,
    Lord xiv, xv, xviii, 47, 134
    correspondence from JH 114

Macalister, Dr Norman 57
McAlister, James 80
McArthur, Mr 150
McAskill, Hugh 74
Macbeth 138
McCallum, Duncan 65

McCallum, M. 25, 74
McClellan, Mr 88
McCrae, Mr 154
Macdonald, Lord 55, 57, 64, 92
Macdonald, Mr (from Barra) 89
Macdonald, Mr, of Kingsburgh 84
Macdonald, Mr (of Portree
    committee) 164
Macdonald, Alexander (Catholic
    clergyman, Knoydart) 39
Macdonald, Alexander (minister
    of Plockton) 74
Macdonald, Alexander, of Glenaladale
    xxxiii, 24, 25, 28, 29
Macdonald, Angus 74
Macdonald, Coll (Lochshiel) 39
Macdonald, Coll (minister
    at Portree) 64, 73
Macdonald, Donald, of
    Drumnatorran 31, 39
Macdonald, Donald, of
    Kingsborough 63, 64
Macdonald, Henry 74
Macdonald, Hugh P. 74
Macdonald, James Thomas 88
Macdonald, John 42
Macdonald, Ranald, of Clanranald 257
Macdonald, Robert 39, 42
Macdonald, W. 73
McDougall, Dugald 16, 19
Macdougall, Hugh 19
McDougall, Capt. John 150, 158, 172
McEachan, Dr 74
Mcfee, Mr 81
MacGeorge, Mr and Mrs 183
Macgregor, Alexander Murray lxvii, 30
Macgregor, Alexander (son of the
    minister of Kilmuir) 73
McGregor, James 23, 172, 175
McGregor, Dr John Peter 151, 158
Macgregor, Robert 73
McInnes, Mr (inn keeper) 165
McInnes, John 55
MacIntosh, Mr 89
Macintyre, John 21
Maciver, John 81, 155–6, 160, 161
McIver, Rev. Alexander 73
MacKay, Rev. Donald 39
Mackenzie, Alexander 16–17

Mackenzie, Colin 75
Mackenzie, Hector 75
Mackenzie, Lady Hood lvi
McKenzie, Hugh 55
Mackenzie, John 75
Mackenzie, Kenneth 75
Mackinnon, Alexander 73
McKinnon, Duncan 55
Mackinnon, John 54, 57, 60, 73
Mackinnon, Lachlan 54, 57
MacLachlan, Col. 133
MacLachlan, D. 87, 154
Maclachlan, James 150
McLaine, Rev. Angus 32–3
McLauchlan, Mr 160
McLauchlan, Mrs 164
McLauchlan, Rev. S. F. 73, 164
Maclean, Alexander of Ardgour 13
Maclean, Duncan 13–14
Maclean, Hector 74
Maclean, Hugh, of Coll 39,
    40, 50, 168, 171
Maclean, Mr, of Ardgour 20
Maclean, Mr (tacksman) 42
Maclean, Murdo 45
Maclean, Neil 52
McLeay, Alexander 156
Maclennan, John 64
Macleod, Miss 164
Macleod, Mr, of Macleod 85
Macleod, Dr Alexander 143, 155, 160
Macleod, Rev. Alexander 80
Macleod, John 33–4, 39, 64
Macleod, Martin 166–7, 170
Macleod, Dr Norman
    amendments to the Edinburgh
       committee's resolutions 133, 246–9
    application to JH regarding Islay 134
    deputation to London xxvii,
       221, 253, 256
    General Assembly breakfast 147
    Glasgow committee 128, 174, 176, 187
    sermon 145
Macleod, Rev. R. 73
McLeod, Roderick 55
Macleod, Roderick 74, 164
Macnab, Peter 39
McNeil, Mr 168
McNeill, Mr John 11

McNeill, Sir John 1
MacNiven, Archibald 60–1
McPhail, Mr 68, 227, 233–4
  extracts from reports 237–8
Macpherson, Mr (agent for Islay) 134
Macpherson, Mr (member
  Glasgow committee) 186
Macpherson-Grant, George, of
  Ballindalloch 253, 254, 256
Macrae, Donald 68, 75, 163
Macrae, John (minister of Cross) 80
Macrae, John (minister of Glenshiel) 75
Macrae, Mr (Auchertyre) 74
Macrae, Mr (missionary of Boisdale) 88
Macrae, Roderick 75
Macrae, William 80
Maitland, Sir F. 182
Malthus, Robert xlii–xliii
manufactures 104–5
Martin, Dr 30
Martin, Duncan 55
Mary, Queen of Scots 123, 138
Mather, Mr 143
Matheson, Duncan 80
Maule, Fox **xiii–xiv**
  correspondence relating to the
    appointment of RG and JH 253–63
  election to county seat xxi
  and government reluctance to
    be open about aid lxv
  meets with JH 116
  and the payment of expenses
    to RG and Stewart 286
  and RG's mission xxxii, 5, 6, 110, 281
  and the role of the Home
    Office lxiii–lxiv
Maule, William Ramsay xiii
Maxtone, Alexina (née
  Graham) xvi, xxi, 47
Maxtone, Anthony xvi, xxi
Maxtone, Helen xxi
Maxtone, James, of Cultoquhey xxi
Maxwell, Miss 164
Maxwell, Mr 118
Maxwell, John A.
  JH's tour 153, 164, 165–6, 170
  Portree committee 73
  RG's tour 63, 65
Melbourne, Viscount xx, xxi, 277–9

Melfort, estate of 15
Melville, Lady 133
Melville, Lord 121, 130, 133
Mercer, Alexander xvii
Middleton, Mr 39
Miginish 83
Millar, Dr Roderick 157, 162, 180, 181–2
Milne, James (Lord Provost) 124,
  126, 135, 137, 138, 193
Milne, Mrs 124, 126
ministers xxxv–xxxvi, xxxviii
Minto, Lord xviii, 113, 141
Mitchison, Rosalind xxxix
Moidart 28, 29, 30
Moncrieff, James xiv
Monteagle, Lord lviii
Monypenny, David xxxviii
Morrice, Mrs 138
Morrison, Rev. James 74
Morvern 33–5, 38
Mowbray, Mr 116
Muck 38, 50, 152
Muckairn 15
Mull
  JH's tour 151, 175–6
  RG's tour 12, 13, 34–5,
    45, 47, 50, 70, 96
  sheep farming 102
Mulock, Thomas xix, xxxvii
Munro, Mr 178
Murray, Alexander 127
Murray, John A. xiv, lxiii
Murray, Sir George xv

Nairne, James 147, 180
Nelson, Horatio xvii
New Brunswick [Land]
  Company 25, 28, 52
New Club, Edinburgh 13
New South Wales xliii–xliv,
  xlvii, 268, 271
Nicholl[s], George xli–xlii, 257
Nicolson, Alexander 89
Nisbet, Henry 39, 40, 50,
  151–2, 167–8, 174
Nisbet, James 241
Noble, James 75
North, Mr and Mrs 124, 126
North Uist 86–8, 90, 91, 154, 160

Nott, Lieutenant 193
Nutter, Mr 193

Oban
    JH's holiday 184
    JH's tour 149–50, 171–2, 175
    RG's tour 12, 13, 15–16, 17–18, 71
O'Brien, William Smith xlvii
Ogilvie, Charles 262
O'Grada, Cormac xliv
Oliver, Capt.
    on the factor of the Boisdale estate 154
    JH's tour 156–7, 164, 167
        JH pays and takes leave of 171–2
        JH praises 175
        travel arrangements 153,
            159, 160, 165, 166
Orkney Islands
    and the Aberdeen committee
        xxx, 116, 234–5
    claims made to JH 134
    letter from Collector of
        Customs 131–2, 281
    local committee 142
    RG not to visit 8, 260, 265
    supplies 136, 138, 139, 143
        seed 121, 123, 129, 221, 261
Ormelie, earl of (later marquis of
    Breadalbane) xv, 14, 257
Oronsay 152
overpopulation xxxvii–xxxviii,
    xlii, 96, 101–2, 204

Paterson, Campbell 150
Paterson, Rev. 142, 143
peace, consequences of the 97
Peel, Sir Robert xx, xlix, lviii–lix
Pennyfillar 63
Perth 138
Pirie, Alderman 213, 241
Pirrie, Mr 75
Pitcairn, James 80
Plockton 57–8, 59
Pollexfen, Thomas (Collector of
    Customs, Kirkwall) 131–2
Pollock v. Darling xl
Poolewe 67, 68–9
Poor Law Report, 1839 xl–xli
poor laws xxxviii–xli, 102–3, 205, 208

population
    of all destitute districts 95
    overpopulation xxxvii–xxxviii,
        xlii, 96, 101–2, 204
Porter, Henry John 236
Portree
    JH's tour 152–3, 159, 163–5, 169–70
    reports of McPhail and Campbell 238
    RG's tour 46, 62–3, 64, 66, 75
Priestman, David 9
proprietors see landed proprietors
public works
    Caledonian Canal 20–1
    cessation of 63, 84, 101–2
    Macleod and Bowie 248
    preferable to emigration 19, 20
    RG's views and recommendations
        xxxvii, 45, 104–5
    see also road building

Raasay 65, 152
Ramsay, Mrs 182
Reid, Captain 57, 74
Reid, Mr 75
Reid, Rev. R. 73
Richards, Eric xlii, lxvii, 116
Riddell, Lady 134
Riddell, Sir James 19, 31, 32, 134, 179, 254
road building
    RG's views and recommendations
        lxiv, 45, 105–6
        Treasury response 283–4
    suggested 35, 42, 47, 59, 68, 90–1
        compared to emigration 64–5
Robertson, David 30
Robertson, George 63, 74
Robertson, James 14
Rodel 155–6, 160
Rose, Mr 177
Ross, Alexander xxviii, 75, 157, 162
Ross, Captain 74
Ross, Thomas 75
Rossshire 8, 70, 96
Rothery, Lieutenant 193
Rum 12, 38
Russell, James 68
Russell, Lord John 253, 257, 281, 286
    on emigration xlviii–xlix
    views on intervention lvii

Russell, Mr 127
Russell, Rev. James 75
Rutherfurd, Andrew, Lord (solicitor-
    general) xiv, **xix–xx**
    1846 failure of potato crop lix
    correspondence 256–9, 259–62, 264–5
    critical of landed proprietors lxi
    displeased with Glasgow
        committee 121
    maintains interest in destitution lxiii
    meets with JH 115–16, 117, 122,
        126, 141, 145, 146, 178
Rutherfurd, Mrs 145

Salen 24, 31, 34, 36, 38, 151
Sanday 132
Sargent, Frederick 114,
    278–9, 281, 284, 286
Saunders, Thomas 120, 148
Scallastle 171
Scalpay 152
schools 91–2, 104, 166
Sconser 170
Scott, Mr 75
Scott, Mr and Mrs 180
Scott, John 260
Scott, Sir Walter xxi
Scottish Guardian 184
Seaforth Estate 77
seed, supply of xxvii–xxix, l–li
    Edinburgh committee 220–1, 231
    Edinburgh committee resolutions
        of 2 March 245
        Glasgow committee's views 210–11
        note of Macleod and Bowie 246–9
    RG on 22–3
    Rutherfurd on 260–1
select committee, 1841 xlix, lxvii
self-reliance lvi–lviii, lx
    see also laissez-faire principle
Shaw, Charles 87, 91, 93, 154, 160
Shaw, Duncan 88, 91, 93, 154
Sheen, Mr 141
sheep xxxvii, 58, 102, 171, 233
    JH's observations of stock 151,
        158, 164, 166, 167, 170
    loss of 202, 204, 219
    poor quality 238
    wool 90, 95

Shepherd, Capt. John and Mrs 137
Sheriff, Dr 130, 134
Sheriff, Mrs 130
Shetland Islands
    and the Aberdeen committee
        xxx, 234–5
    depot surplus 142
    fishermen 132–3
    JH views on distress 137
    levels of destitution 9, 201–3
    Rutherfurd on 262
    special case 7–8, 260, 263, 265
    supplies 123, 136, 138, 139
        seed 121, 125, 129, 221, 261
Shieldaig 67, 68, 69
Shiels, Alexander 52, 53
Shona 29
Sinclair, Mr John 39
Sinclair, Sir John 206
Skeabost 63
Skirving, William 241
Skye
    JH's tour 152, 163–5, 169
    RG's tour 28, 53, 55, 62,
        70, 71, 83–4, 96
    sheep farming 102
Slater, Commander M. A. 123
Sleat 53, 54, 56, 75, 165, 170
Smith, Mr and Mrs 145
Smith, Adam lx
Snizort 62, 64, 66, 76
Society of Friends 7, 9
Somerset, Lord FitzRoy xix
South Uist 86, 88, 90, 91
Spearman, Sir Alexander Young **xx**
    appointment of JH l, 113–14
    correspondence xxvi, li, liii, 268, 272–3
    recalls JH to London 188–9
Speculative Society xiv
Spence, Mr 134
Spittal, Dr 178
Spittal, Lord Provost 144, 178, 189
Spittal, Mrs 178, 189
Spring Rice, Thomas **xx–xxi**
    correspondence
        from Fox Maule 262–8
        RG receives copy of letter 61
    and government reluctance to be
        open about aid lxv–lxvi

and JH xviii, 113, 141
principles of self-reliance lv,
    lvi–lviii, lix, lxii
representation from Islay 134
Staffa 47, 51
Stanley, Edward lxv
Stenscholl 83
Stephen, Mrs 183, 186
Stephen, James 268, 272–3, 285
Steuart, Robert 258
Stevenson, John 150, 158, 173
Stevenson, Robert 116, 121,
    123, 130, 140, 141, 180
Stevenson, Thomas 16–17
Stevenson, William 201–3
Stewart, Alexander 30, 39
Stewart, Archibald 74
Stewart, Charles Edward 23, 24
Stewart, Donald (Harris) 155, 156, 160
Stewart, Donald (minister of
    Kinlochspelvie) 35–6
Stewart, Donald, of Luskintyre 80–1, 82
Stewart, H., of Ballachulish 19
Stewart, John, of Achadashenaig 35, 39
Stewart, John, of Fasnacloich 18–19
Stewart, Marjory xxi, xxv
Stewart, Robert, of Ardvorlich xxi
    RG's tour xxxiii–xxxiv, 12, 31
    appointment 257
    expenses 286
    letter from RG 110
    letters to his sister xxv
    plans for 5–6, 8
Stewart (Steuart), Robert (MP for
    Haddington Burghs) 263
Stewart, William xxi
Stewart Mackenzie, James xxix, lvi
Stormont, Lord 114
Stornoway
    JH's tour 131, 142, 155, 156–7
    RG's tour 46, 78, 79, 80
Strang, John 183
Strath 53–4, 55, 57, 76
Strathmore, Lady lii
Stromness 131
Stronsay 132
Strontian 31, 38
subdivision of possessions 33,
    40, 54, 65, 78, 101

regulation against 85, 192
supplies
    Aberdeen committee xxx, 116
    distribution 129, 136,
        137–8, 139, 141, 147
    JH's tour 150, 154, 158, 160–1
    RG on xxxvi, 77–8, 85
    future requirements 107
    Glasgow committee xxix–xxx
        reports 228–30, 232–6
    JH's role li–lii
    purchase and tenders 117, 120–3, 125
    quantities required for individuals
        and families xxxvi, 37, 69, 77
    seed xxvii–xxviii, xxxi
    terms of government
        supplies grain lv–lvi
    see also accounts; seed, supply of
Sutherland xxxii–xxxiii, 8
Swanson, John 19, 172, 175

Tail, Laurence 9
Tait, Capt. J. H. 127
Tarbert 80
Taylor, Major 135, 138, 145, 146, 179
Taylor, Lady Jane 135, 138, 179
The Times xxxi, xxxvi–xxxvii
Tiree 12, 38, 47–8, 70, 96, 238
Tobermory
    JH's tour 141, 151, 167–8, 174
    RG's tour 12, 31, 34, 36, 38, 39–41, 49
Tolmie, John 84, 85
Tories liii, lxi
    suspicions of Tory jobbery xxxi,
        xxxiv, lxi, lxv, 253
Torosay 34, 35, 38
Trail, Mr 182
Traill, George 254
Treasury xxx–xxxi, liii–liv, lv, lvi
    minutes 277–86
Trevelyan, Sir Charles xx, lxii
Trotter, Capt. 176–7, 178
Trotter, Mrs 176–7
Trumisgarry 86
Tuath, Loch 47, 53
Turnbull, John 9

Uamh, Loch nan 23, 28
Uig 78, 79, 80

Ullapool 68, 69, 162, 163, 168–9
Ulva 34, 38, 47, 51–2

Van Diemen's Land xliii–
 xliv, xlvii, 268, 271
Vansittart, Nicholas lv
Victoria, Queen, proclaimed 176

Walker, Mr 149, 184
Waller, George
 Aberdeen committee acknowledges 193
 to accompany JH l–li, 116
 in Edinburgh 130, 134, 145, 147
 Glasgow committee and the
  resolutions of the Edinburgh
  committee 118, 119
 JH's tour 153, 161, 170
  end of assignment 180, 182
Warden, Dr Adam
 meets with JH 115, 116, 121,
  123, 130, 142, 180
 shows JH parts of Edinburgh 134
 Stevenson shows lighthouse
  drawings 140–1

weather, and the Destitution xxiv, 94–5
Webster, Alexander 193
Wellington, duke of xvii–xviii, xix
Wentworth, Mr [Lt.] 126, 127
Westphal, Sir G. 178
Westray 132
Whigs xiv, xv, xxi, liii, lxi
 and the poor laws xxxix, xli
whisky 108, 126, 153, 159
 distilleries 158, 162
Wigham, John 132, 178, 261, 263
William IV, death of 174
Wood, C. 113
works, public
 Caledonian Canal 20–1
 cessation of 63, 84, 100–1
 Macleod and Bowie 248
 preferable to emigration 19, 20
 RG's views and recommendations
  xxxvii, 45, 104–5
 see also road building

Young, Mr 142, 147, 180
Young, Mrs 147